The
Glenn Miller
Burial File

Wilbur Wright

The UC-64A Noorduyn Norseman

The Glenn Miller Burial File

Wilbur Wright

Author of

**MILLERGATE-
THE REAL GLENN MILLER STORY**

Limited Print First Edition

First published in Great Britain by
Wright Books Allington Lane Southampton
SO3 3HP

Printed by Hobbs the Printers Southampton

ISBN Number 0 9512547 5 8

For Joyce

CONTENTS

BY THE SAME AUTHOR

As David Graham :

GRAVE OF SAND
OPERATION CLEANSWEEP
DOWN TO A SUNLESS SEA
SIDEWALL
SEVEN YEARS TO SUNSET

As Donald Carter :

HARD CASE

As Wilbur Wright :

CARTERS CASTLE
THREE PROUD DANCERS
KELLY'S RUN
NOW CENTURION
MILLERGATE
TIME - GATEWAY TO IMMORTALITY

ABBREVIATIONS

AA	Anti-Aircraft	MSS	Manuscript
ADC	Aide de Camp	NCO	Non-Commissioned Officer
ADRS	Air Depot Repair Squadron	MN,nm	Nautical Miles
AEF	Allied Expeditionery Force	NOTAM	Notice to Airmen
AFB	Air Force Base	NPRC	National Personnel Records Center
AFU	Advanced Flying Unit	OQMG	Office of Quartermaster General
APO	Army Post Ofice	PD	Presumed Dead
ARC	American Red Cross	PDD	Presumed Dead by Drowning
ASR	Air Sea Rescue	PR	Public Relations
ATC	Air Traffic Control	PCA	Pasadena Cemetery Association
BAF	British Armed Forces	POW	Prisoner of War
BAT	Beam Approach Training	PRO	Public Records Office
BBC	British Broadcasting Corporation	PX	Post Exchange
CID	Criminal Investigation Division	QM	Quartermaster
CINFO	Central Office of Information	RCAF	Royal Canadian Air Force
CO	Commanding Officer	ROC	Royal Observer Corps
DC	District of Columbia	ROD	Report of Death Document
DF	Direction-Finding	SAD	Strategic Air Depot
ETA	Estimated Time of Arrival	SE	South-East
ETD	Estimated Time of Departure	SGT	Sergeant
EFTS	Elementary Flying Training School	SOP	Standard Operating Practice
ETO	European Theatre of Operations	SFTS	Service Flying Training School
FBI	Federal Bureau of Investigation	SN	Serial Number
FOD	Finding of Death Document	TV	Television
FOIA	Freedom of Information Act	TVS	Television South Limited
GAC	General Artistes Corporation	UK	United Kingdom
HF	High Frequency	USA	United States of America
HP,Hp	Horsepower	USAAF	United States Army Air Force
Hz	Herz	USAF	United States Air Force
HQ	Headquarters	USAFE	United States Air Forces Europe
Hr	Hour	USFET	US Forces, European Theatre
IFF	Identification Friend or Foe	USO	United Services Organisation
IQ	Intelligence Quotient	VFR	Visual Flight Rules
IFR	Instrument Flight Rules	VHF	Very High Frequency
LA	Los Angeles	VIP	Very Important Person
LACW	Leading Aircraftwoman	WAAF	Womens Auxiliary Air Force
LOC	Library of Congress	WAC	Womens Army Corps
MIA	Missing in Action	WD	War Department
MOD	Ministry of Defence		

LIST OF ILLUSTRATIONS

Frontispiece - UC-64A Noorduyn Norseman.

FOREWORD

IT is not in the nature of any researcher worthy of the name to admit defeat. I began my probe into the Glenn Miller mystery in 1986, published MILLERGATE - THE REAL GLENN MILLER STORY in 1990, and never for one moment doubted that I would crack the mystery one day. My confidence increased as one barrier after another collapsed and more documents, many unseen by the public for 45 years, were released.

Of course I was painfully aware that there was something in the background of the mystery, something concerning Glenn Miller himself, that certain parties wished to remain confidential, and there were times when I suffered agonies of doubt : was my deliberate attempts to invade the privacy of the Miller family really justified ? Or were my motives purely mercenary : I just wanted another best seller ?

I had no difficulty in finding justification for probing as deeply as necessary, regardless of territory : all this had happened almost 50 years ago, most of the main characters were dead, the Miller Mystery had become a historical legend - and in any case, the generals at SHAEF were as guilty as hell, conspiring to conceal the truth. Many people close to me thought it had become an obsession, and they could be right. People on the other side thought it was a damned shame. As Tex Beneke said in a letter : "Poor old Glenn ! Why don't they let him rest in peace ?"

But there were the letters, letters by the score and hundred, from all over the world - people who had read MILLERGATE and wanted me to know they supported my researches fully. And I sensed a real feeling of anger and bitterness - who had given those old soldiers at Versailles and the new soldiers in the Washington AG Department the right to keep Glenn's fate secret ? The millions of Miller fans all over the world wanted to know, deserved to know, had to know - and if it meant uncovering something quite uncharacteristic of the man, as Dale Titler suggested was the case, then that was okay too - whatever had happened, it didn't matter a damn, because this man Glenn Miller had brought happiness and pleasure to billions of people for the last 55 years, and that would go on, year after year decade after decade. His music and his image were big enough to take the knocks - his fans could and would forgive him anything.

And it would be so nice to find out where he finished up, so that maybe people could go along and put a bunch of flowers or maybe a string of pearls where he rested.

So for seven years I kept going until the end was in sight : all I needed was one lousy document, one miserable sheet of paper to unlock the puzzle. The paper was an Army Air Force AG Form 66-2, Section 38, which would tell me precisely how and where Glenn Miller spent his last days on earth. It had been in his 201 File at St. Louis for years - I had letters from the National Personnel Records Center telling me so, but they couldn't release it because the Miller family had denied access.

I progressed appeals against that decision way up through the Army layers of command, from St Louis to Alexandria to Washington, the Pentagon and the White House itself, and at the end of the day they released Miller's 201 File almost complete - but that vital Form 66-2 was missing. The Army Counsel General, the highest legal authority in the US Army, told me it had never been in the File - that I had been given everything *except items protected under the Privacy and Freedom of Information Acts.*

Those items, he said, were simply `third party addresses' of people who had written to the Records Center over the years about Glenn Miller. But there was a built-in fallacy here : the only reason for the intense reactions of the Miller family, and the opposition of the US archival authorities to my research was that there was something to hide. There *must* be. And since I had seen nothing which would qualify under that description, it must still be there in the Files.

What was it ? What did happen to Glenn Miller ? I don't know. I have suspicions - and whatever it was, it was *big* - big enough to warrant intervention by a future President of the United States. And quite frankly I may never find out, because the Army General Counsel said if I wanted to keep the fight going, I would have to do it through the American courts - another broad clue that something does exist somewhere to fight about. But I have no money for American attorneys who appear to be almost as avaricious as American doctors - and that means greedy in eighteen different languages.

I am sending the Miller family a copy of this book, in the hope that they may relent at the last moment and come clean with Glenn's millions of fans - but I am not confident. At the same I think I have not done a bad job here. I know more about the Miller mystery than any previous researcher, and now you know too. Together we stand on the deck of the new *Marie Celeste*, with all the clues in sight and trying to figure out what happened to the crew and captain.

It doesn't end here - any more than it ended when that magic researcher Henry Whiston, and his friend John Flowers died. Others took up the torch - Dale Titler, Ken Perfect, John Edwards and the rest. One day soon, the Pentagon is going to take a phone call from some new Maigret, saying *"Now, what the hell is all this about a missing Form ?"*

The mystery won't go away - they never do, until they're solved.

As for me, I'm a relay runner stumbling up to the change-over box carrying the baton of curiosity and looking in vain for someone to grab it. Someone will - and whoever you are, you have my blessings. Sock it to 'em, brother - after fifty years they have it coming. Good luck.

WILBUR WRIGHT
Southampton
1986-1993

ACKNOWLEDGEMENTS

This book could not have been completed without the invaluable assistance of many organisations including, in America, the Veterans Administration, New York; NPRC St.Louis Mo.; Office of the Surgeon-General, Falls Church Va; Office of the Army Counsel General, the Pentagon, Washington; Department of Military History in Washington DC; US Army Military Institute Carlisle Barracks, Pennsylvania; U.S. Total Army Personnel Command Alexandria Va.; U.S Army Information Systems Command, the Pentagon, Washington DC; AF Historical Research Agency, Maxwell AFB Al.; Command Historian, USAF Europe; Textual Reference Division, National Archives, Washington DC; Archival Program Branch, National Archives, Washington DC; Military Operations Branch, National Archives, Washington DC; Center of Military History, Washington Naval Yard, Washington DC; U.S Army Intelligence and Security Command, Fort George Meade, MD; USAF Inspection and Safety Center, Norton AFB, Cal.; Military Reference Branch, National Archives, Washington DC; Office of AF History, Bolling AFB, Washington DC; U.S Department of Justice, Washington DC; Historical Reference Branch, National Archives, Washington DC; Memorial Affairs and Casualty Support Division, Alexandria Va.; Ramstein AFB, Germany; Randolph AFB NM.

I am also deeply indebted to Dr. David V.Pecora MD PA, Newark Del, Miss J. Houghton, Mr.Harvey Pugh; Mr.K. Hollins, John Edwards, Derek Kilburn, Dale Titler, the late Royal Frey, George Ferguson and Jean Pace USAF Ret., Samuel Kerr Lockhart, Vic Porter, Joan Heath, Denis Cottam, Frank Wappatt, Bruce Halpenny, Presidents Ronald Reagan and George Bush, Sir John Mills, Gp.Capt Tony Bartley, Jonathon Bailey, the late Herb Miller, Mr.Bowyer (ATC Officer Twinwood Farm), Eddie Edmonds, Piers Brendon, Geoffrey Butcher, Desmond Carrington, George Chalou, Lt.Col.Tom Corrigan USAF Ret., Lt.Cwynar and Mr. Pellegrini of Maxwell AFB, Al., Jack Donnelly, Edward Pecora, David Gellman, Russell Harty, Sheridan Morley, Col D.Hignett, Bill McAllister, Mr. Metcalfe, Roy Nesbitt, Mrs.Jean Nichol and Nan, Mrs.Connie Richards, Ken Perfect, George Simon, Alex Sleap, Clive Ward, Ray Shields, the late Henry Whiston, John Flowers, Mr.Woods Jr, Keith Jones, Richard H.Lieve, George E.Buckley, Frank P. Hladky, Allen Petersen, Barry J.Collis, Mrs. J.R. Standen, Mrs. Black of Southampton, Mr. Hoare, Michael M. White, Mr. Weaver, Tony Eaton, Alan Ross, Chris Way, Dennis W. Thorpe, Miss D. Houghton, Michael Heighton, Neville Read, Doug le Vicki, Nat Peck, Tex Benecki and the many others who called briefly on the telephone with sometimes valuable snippets of information.

To those I may have inadvertently omitted, or from whom I may have quoted and forgotten to ask permission, I offer apologies and three viable reasons : age, illhealth and pressure of work. As my 74th birthday approaches, I will heed my wife's warning and `slow down to a gallop'.

Wilbur Wright
Southampton
1993

INTRODUCTION

WHEN MILLERGATE was published in August 1990, I believed that we had accumulated all the available evidence concerning the mysterious disappearance of Major Alton Glenn Miller in December 1944. Whilst some additional input of information might be forthcoming, we accepted reluctantly that despite all efforts, no positive solution had been discovered, and in the end we could only suggest a number of scenarios based on the available evidence, presenting the available proofs and evidence, and thereafter left the reader to make up his or her own mind.

But the Miller Mystery is unique. Thousands of researchers, professional and private, skilled and amateur, still pursue the quest for no other reason that it remains one of the great enigmas of the 20th century. Many, indeed, have little or no interest in the man or his music, but remain obsessed with the puzzle itself. In recent years it has achieved something of the status of traditional riddles like the *Marie Celeste*, Bigfoot and the Loch Ness Monster. It has been said that MILLERGATE reads too much like an official report - too much of the interesting background correspondence was omitted. This view is understandable : one can read a lengthy letter or document several times and miss some vital point which might be picked up by others on first reading. Miller researchers are Walter Mitty characters who dream of finding the ultimate key to the puzzle - and I am no exception. Few if any believed the account of Lt.Don Haynes, the AEF Band Executive Officer, who claimed he drove Miller and an Air Force staff officer, Lt.Col.Norman F.Baessell, from Bedford to nearby R.A.F. Twinwood Farm and put them aboard a Paris-bound C-64 Norseman aircraft flown by Flight Officer Johnny Morgan. The plane and occupants were never seen again.

Yet almost six years passed before the final breakthrough came : early in 1992 we located Joan Heath, a surviving witness who was Air Marshal Tedder's WAAF driver in December 1944, at the time of Miller's disappearance, who provided the ultimate evidence.

Prior to that, our main thrust had been towards penetrating US government bureaucracy in a search for documentary evidence, and from the outset we encountered stiff, almost fanatical resistance. We knew that each airman or officer had a personal 201 File detailing his movements, promotions, medical history, decorations etc. In 1973 researcher John Edwards wrote to the custodians of such Files, the National Personnel Records Center in St.Louis, Missouri, asking for copies of the files for Glenn Miller, and also for Lt.Col. Baessell and Flight Officer John R.S. Morgan who were lost in the Norseman aircraft in which Miller was allegedly a passenger. The reply was startling : `The Files were destroyed in the (1973) fire -'. This effectively sealed off research in that area for almost two decades, but from the start we suspected that Miller's file, at least, had survived. In 1987 we wrote to NPRC St.Louis : they responded, saying that the File *did* exist, but that access was barred by the Miller family in California.

This led to protracted legal arguments centred around the viability of our letter of authorisation from Herb, Glenn Miller's late blood brother. NPRC insisted that because Herb was deceased, that mandate had expired, allowing the adopted Miller children full control of the File, and this was not satisfactorily resolved until spring 1992. At that time, the whole investigation took an extraordinary turn. To date we had concentrated upon exposing the original cover-up at SHAEF in 1944. We had always assumed that the Miller family were aware in some measure of the true circumstances of Glenn's disappearance, and had decided as early as 1953 to publicly accept and support the Haynes story. Indeed, Don Haynes passed on to the Millers the early (Library of Congress) version of his diary, and Helen gave it to the script department at Universal-International for the film `The Glenn Miller Story', featuring James Stewart and June Allyson.

There was also an identifiable chain of witnesses propagating the discredited Haynes account : Royal Frey was a long-standing friend of the Miller family, and for some time was curator at the USAAF Museum at Wright-Paterson AFB, Ohio. In 1983, Frey interviewed George Ferguson, a surviving pilot of the ill-fated Norseman in 1944, and the tape recording (which started with a listing of the people to whom it should be sent, including Steve Miller and the British Glenn Miller Society) was ill-concealed propaganda for the fictitious Haynes story. Indeed, Ferguson relates a garbled version of events, confusing two flights on November 8 and December 15. Frey goes on at great length about the possible fate of the Norseman. Neither debated the possibility that Miller was not on the plane at all. Further, Frey wrote to us saying that he had looked at the Miller 201 File some years previously and had seen nothing in there which might explain Glenn's disappearance ! And incredibly he describes travelling to interview Don Haynes - *and forgetting to take a tape recorder !*

We concluded that there was some evidence in the File which the Millers did not want publicised - a supposition supported by American writer Dale Titler in a letter to us. Another friend of the Miller family, he said that Steve Miller admitted there was something in the File totally uncharacteristic of Glenn, which he would not like to be made public.

We had noticed several disturbing coincidences about the 1973 fire at St.Louis. Further, after Don Haynes died in 1971, he left behind diaries which confirmed beyond doubt that his account of Miller's disappearance was totally fictitious, as proven by documents in Miller's Burial File. But in June 1972, Haynes' widow Polly gave writer George Simon (another long-standing friend of the family) a copy of what she said was Don's genuine diary. This in fact, was the `MINUS ONE', a patently fictionalised account of events in 1944. Simon used the Haynes account in his book `GLENN MILLER AND HIS ORCHES-TRA' written in 1973. Simon, of course, was a member of the AEF Band himself.

Thus we obtain a remarkable timetable of events between 1971 and 1973 which, we submit, amount to much more than sheer coincidence :

June 1971 Don Haynes dies.

June 1972 Polly Haynes presents the `genuine' MINUS ONE diary to George Simon.

June 1973 Simon meets the Miller children for the first time and discusses the case.

June 1973 Simon writes his book, published 1974.

July 1973 A mysterious fire in the St.Louis Records Center destroys the 201 Files of Col. Baessell and John Morgan - but not that of Glenn Miller. And the Monthly History Sheets for 35th Air Depot Repair Squadron Abbotts Ripton for November/December 1944 `go missing'.

In `Glenn Miller and his Orchestra' (Bigbee Promotions 1974) Simon wrote that at that first meeting with the Millers, Steve asked Simon what he knew of Glenn's fate, but reason suggests that Helen must have passed on all she knew to the children; Steve was only 9 in 1953 when Helen and Don Haynes together donated Don's diary to Universal-International script department - ensuring that the Haynes story was enshrined permanently on movie film. He was 23 when Helen died in 1966, and at age 30, Steve Miller knew as much and probably more than George Simon. Yet remarkably, Simon delayed writing his book until after Don Haynes died - from which it is reasonable to assume that this ensured that Don would never be interviewed publicly on the case. Simon, we suggest, may have known the true facts at the time he wrote his book, but this is speculative.

His book quoted the MINUS ONE fiction-diary almost verbatim and propagated the Haynes story, which was believed as long as no contradictory evidence emerged. There were four possible sources of such evidence :

First, assuming it escaped the 1973 fire, John Morgan's 201 File, which contained details of his final days, flights made, air experience, orders for his fatal flight, and his flight log book showing flight departures and destinations.

Second, Colonel Baessell's 201 File containing his orders for the final flight, and why he was going to Bordeaux, France.

Third, the Monthly History Sheets for 35th Air Depot Repair Squadron, Abbotts Ripton, for November and December 1944, which would reveal the true fate of the Norseman.

Fourth, Morgan's flight log book listing his Service flying career.

Yet all four vanished. Coincidence ? And what was Royal Frey doing at St. Louis Records Center anyway ?

In 1973, NPRC St.Louis informed researcher John Edwards that *all three* 201 Files including that of Glenn Miller were `destroyed by fire' in 1973. The Monthly History sheets were reported simply as `missing' when we inquired in 1987. Further, NPRC St.Louis distributed in 1990 a two-page `History of Major Glenn Miller' which stated that Morgan left Twinwood Farm, England, for Bordeaux, France - with no mention of a stop at Paris - and that Morgan and Glenn Miller were the only occupants !

We obtained from St.Louis full details of the fire, which began on July 12 1973 in the Overland complex. VIP Files, including those for Miller, Baessell and Morgan, were kept in a locked vault on the 6th Floor. The fire spread rapidly next day and at 4.49 in the afternoon of July 14 a secondary fire was discovered in the vault, which was rapidly extinguished. Some, but not all 6th Floor records were recovered intact; the Army records 1912-1959 suffered worst, whilst Air Force records 1947-1963 for persons with surnames beginning letter `I' through `Z' were less seriously affected.

Shortly after the fire began FBI agents were on site investigating but failed to discover the cause. Subsequent investigation revealed no evidence of mechanical failure, and the origin of the disaster remains a mystery.

In late 1991, the British Press ran a story that the Miller Family were negotiating to purchase the wrecked Control Tower at R.A.F.Twinwood Farm for re-erection in America - a blatant effort to perpetuate the legend of Miller's departure in the Norseman. Finally, in April 1992 we learned that Vide-Film Producers International of New York were making a documentary of Miller's life and music - supported by Mr.Steve Miller and others. Mr.Sam Lockhart, the producer, told us that the small sequence describing Miller's disappearance featured the Haynes story `in the absence of any proof to refute that story'. We asked him if he had heard of MILLERGATE and he confirmed that he had been told about the book. But, we said, it proved beyond doubt the Haynes story was flawed : Mr.Lockhart simply said `Well, we're still using it - we have to think of the backers.'

+   +   +

In addition to the dogged resistance and ploys of the Miller family to suppress the truth, and the flat refusal of John Morgan's surviving relative Mr.William Gretsinger to help in any way (he said he was helping exclusively another writer, Dale Titler) there is a clear pattern of concealment, suppression and obstruction in all the correspondence we had with the US Archives. To obtain access to the three Burial Files (which were variously described to us as non-existent, missing, misplaced and mis-filed) we had to appeal to President Ronald Reagan to intervene - and when we realised finally that the solution to the whole mystery lay in the Miller 201 File Service record, we were denied access.

If there is nothing untoward in the File, what possible objection could there be to general access ? Why have the Miller family resisted publication so long, even resorting to threats of legal action in our case ? Eventually, St. Louis agreed to release part of Glenn Miller's Service history - but only from his induction in 1942 to his arrival in UK in June 1944, omitting the most sensitive part of his record - the period from June until December 15, when he was supposedly lost in a missing C-64 Norseman. The inference is unmistakable. On August 25 1991, we received a letter from the Military Operations Branch of the U.S. National Archives in Washington :

`Dear Mr. Wright -
This is in response to your letter of May 22 1991, requesting copies of Major Alton G. Miller's official Military Personnel 201 File, under the Freedom of Information Act (FOIA). Only certain information contained in an individual's military record may be released under the Department of Defense Privacy Program. See the attached list based upon Department of Defense Directive 5400.11 for further information. Since Major Miller's brother Herb is now deceased, the prior release you have is no longer valid. Therefore we can only release the information that is enclosed. The National Personnel Records Center follows the guidelines put forth by the Department of Defense since we are only the physical custodian of the records, and do not maintain legal custody. Only the creating agency of the records, in this case the Department of the Army, may release more than the guidelines allow.
If you wish to discuss the authenticity of or correction of any document in Major Miller's record, you should contact the following activity : Department of the Army,*

Center of Military History, 3rd and M Streets SE, Washington Navy Yard, Washington DC 20002, and to obtain the release of further documents or information you will need to contact : USA ISC-P (ASQNS-OP-F)   Room 1146, Hoffman Bldg I, Alexandria VA 22331-0301.'

It was signed by John L. Carver, Chief, Military Operations Branch, in US National Archives, Washington D.C.

On January 2 1992, after obtaining a copy of the Missing Report (Fig.40) which refers to a covering letter and enclosures, I wrote to NPRC St.Louis asking for a copy of the all-important Form 66-2 which normally accompanies such reports. Further letters were sent to the Department of the Army Military Personnel Center, 2461 Eisenhower Avenue, Alexandria Va., Mortuary Affairs and Casualty Support Division, the Archives Military Reference Branch, Maxwell AFB, the Department of the Army Center of Military History and the Adjutant General himself : the letters set out our case as a simple issue.

On the one hand, we had the Miller family and certain upper echelons in the Department of the Army who were using the Freedom of Information and Privacy Acts to restrict access to Miller's 201 Personal File at St. Louis. That File contains the final answer to the mystery. On the other hand, we had the indisputable fact that a group of senior generals at SHAEF in 1944 (including General Eisenhower himself) conspired to conceal the true facts about the death of a VIP and serving officer, Major Glenn Miller - and that was a serious offence under US military law.

On February 6 we received an intriguing response from St.Louis :

`This is in response to your letter dated January 2 1992. We have completely reviewed all of Major Miller's records and have located the Missing Report which is already in your possession as well as those documents which were attached to it. Copies are enclosed and released to you under the Freedom of Information Act as part of the record of official functions and public life of Major Miller. The enclosed documents include :

1. A copy of a transmittal letter dated December 28 1944, forwarding the Report and a WD AGO Form 66-2, AAF Officers Qualification Record, to the Central Records Branch, AG Casualty Division, APO 887.
2. A copy of the Missing Report dated December 28 1944.
3. A copy of a letter attached to the Missing Report dated December 22 1944 and entitled `Report of Missing Personnel'.
The WD AGO Form 66-2. . . was used for Army Air Force personnel and includes sections relating to flying status and restrictions, civilian flying experience and pilot qualifications.'

This was all very well - but the vital AGO Form 66-2 was not enclosed : Miller was not a pilot, nor did he have any of the other qualifications mentioned. He was always a passenger, never a crew man. What John L.Carver omitted to mention was that Item 38 on the AGO Form 66-2 was Miller's `Chronological Record of Military Experience' which would record all his movements up to the time of death - and this was vital information ! Why did Mr. Carver conceal the essential content of the Form 66-2 - and advise us that it included a Chronological Record of Military Experience, showing Miller's last movements ?

Needless to say, we did not consider it an important line of research, and did not follow it up at that time.

The transmittal letter (Fig.41) states that full details of the incident were in an attached letter - which turned out to be a copy of the General Davis letter to General Eisenhower (Fig.20) dated 22 December 1944. There was no eyewitness statement by Don Haynes, and Davis's letter omits his name - referring instead to the Casualty Report which was released the same day which states `Major Miller was taken to the airfield by an officer of the Army Air Force Band who witnessed the take-off. Now, Davis quotes the names of Lieutenant Colonel Baessell, Major Alton Glenn Miller and the latter's next of kin Helen Miller in full - so why omit Haynes ? Even the opening sentence is suspect : `It is reported that. . .' - why not start `It is reported by Lt.D.Haynes, Executive officer of the Army Air Force Band, that . . .' We are not even sure that this was the true text of the letter - it is a `True Copy' certified by a Lt. Nicholas S.Garigliano.

On 6 February 1992 we were advised that none of the six C-47 aircraft lost in France and England during November-December 1944 took off from R.A.F. Bovingdon. Also, no ATC C-64s (DC-4s) were lost in December 1944. This effectively destroys the Woods story, and we requested information on any C-47 lost out of Bordeaux in December 1944, which might be relevant to the Bordeaux Crash letter in the Burial files.

But I was concerned by the missing Form 66-2 and wrote to John L.Carver at St.Louis on 12 February :

`I have written to your department frequently and each time I manage to extract a little more information. On July 25 1991 you advised me that "After a document-by-document review of Major Miller's Official Military Personnel File there is no indica-tion of any official information relevant to his fate other than what has been previously released." But in your letter dated February 6 you say "We have completely reviewed all of Major Miller's records and have located the original of the Missing Report and the documents attached to it." In fact, it was a `Certified True Copy' - and the Form 66-2 was missing. One feels entitled to ask how many more bits and pieces are going to surface in future ?' Would you have sent the Missing Report if I had not already obtained a copy ?

There was no reply. But I identified the Army Departments to which I should appeal to have the 201 File released in full - USA ISC-P(ASQNS-OP-F) Room 1146 Hoffman Bldg I, 2461 Eisenhower Avenue, Alexandria Va. and the Department of the Army, Adjutant General, The Pentagon, Washington DC. My letter was very much to the point :

Burial and Deceased Files - Major Alton Glenn Miller

`I refer to my letter dated 31 August 1991 to which I have had no response. In it, I provided considerable factual evidence of a criminal conspiracy involving senior generals at SHAEF Versailles in December 1944. These officers conspired to conceal the true facts behind the disappearance and presumed death of Major Glenn Miller, and that was a criminal offence in US military law.
I call upon your department either to release the 201 File in toto or to convene a Congressional Committee Inquiry into the matter. I have written to President George Bush asking him to intervene in this matter.'

There was no response to these letters and in March 1992, following the Joan Heath revelations, I wrote to the Military Archives Department asking for information on the loss of a UC-78 or C-47 from Buc Field on December 17 1944, bound for the United States. But finally, on March 20 1992 came the letter from Mary Anne Quintard at U.S Total Army Personnel Command in Alexandria, in response to the George Bush letter. She had sent to St.Louis for a copy of the 201 File and would be in contact.

In desperation, once again we appealed personally to the President of the United States of America, this time George Bush - and on April 18 we received this reply from Alexandria Va. :

Dear Mr. Wright
This is in reply to your letter of November 18 1991 to President George Bush requesting a copy of the 201 files of Major Miller, Lt.Col.Baessell and F/O Morgan.
A National Personnel Records Center official has provided me with a copy of the 201 file for Major Miller. However, I have been advised by the same official that records pertaining to Col.Baessell and Flight Officer Morgan were not located. It appears these records were destroyed in the NPRC fire in July 1973.
Your request is being processed under the Freedom of Information Act based on your letter of May 22 to NPRC. Due to the number of documents to be reviewed, a brief delay is expected - you may expect a final reply on or about May 4 1992.

Yours sincerely   *Mary Anne Quintard*
                                     Freedom of Information and Privacy Act Officer.

This was an extraordinary development, because in the booklet *The National Personnel Records Center Fire'* by Walter W.Stender and Evans Walker dated 4 October 1974, the fire in the 6th Floor vault containing VIP files was extinguished, and the general files for Air Force personnel with names beginning I through Z were not seriously affected. But at this time, I succeeded in establishing contact with the family of John Morgan in Scotland, and they applied for a full copy of his 201 File. A letter dated April 7 1992 from the Department of the Army, US Information Systems Command in the Pentagon laid out the lines of battle :

This is in response to your March 9 1992 Freedom of Information Act request for a complete copy of Major Alton Glenn Miller's 201 File. Per response from National Personnel Records Center St.Louis, all information deemed releasable without the consent of Major Miller's relatives has been released to you. Release of any pertinent information from the 201 File is the responsibility of the Initial Denial Authority (IDA), National Personnel Records Center.

So I was on the old roundabout again, back at St.Louis ! But we were getting into the range of the Big Guns in Washington ; on May 10 1992 came the following from Personnel and Logistics Division, US Army Total Personnel Command, Alexandria Va.,in a huge parcel of 382 photocopied documents weighing more than 5 pounds and costing $27 to post airmail. A covering letter said :

`This is in reply to your letter of November 18 to President Bush requesting a copy of the 201 Files of Major Glenn Miller. Attached is the requested copy of the File. Some of the home addresses pertaining to third parties have been delet- ed. Although your request is for records of a deceased individual, the privacy interests of others must be considered. In applying the FOIA balancing test we conclude that the privacy interests of others weigh against public release of their home addresses.*

The withholding of information pertaining to your request constitutes a partial denial of your request on behalf of Major General Gerald H.Putman, Command- er, U.S Total Army Command. If you desire, you may appeal this denial with 60 days, to the Secretary of the Army.'

This, of course, was so much waffle. I was totally uninterested in letters written to St.Louis by scores of curious people over the years for information - individuals who had received the same standard reply repeating the Haynes story. The entire package was quite worthless, irrelevant and contained no new information. My appeal to the Secretary of the Army dated May 12 1992 was carefully considered and compiled :

`I submit this Appeal through the channels indicated and the following circum- stances are relevant :*

I received yesterday what purported to be extracts from the Miller 201 File, in a package which constitutes a gross and unwarranted insult to a professional writer and researcher with 14 published books including a best seller. The package weighed 5 pounds and contained some 382 photocopied pages as fol- lows :

127 pages of Miller's service career between 1942 and his departure for England in June 1944 in which I expressed no interest.
60 miscellaneous pages of correspondence with persons writing for information on Major Miller.
101 blurred and unreadable copies.
61 duplicated pages - including 15 copies of one document alone.
23 pages of post-war correspondence on Miller's insurances.
10 pages of hitherto unreleased but unimportant information.

This package cost the US tax-payer £27 to mail : some pages were copies of envelopes received, others were printed in reverse, mirror-fashion, and 18 sheets feature only a copy of General Arnold's signature. There was no pertinent infor- mation of any kind relating to Miller's disappearance.

I followed with a resume of the evidence to date and continued :

`The action of Generals Barker, Davis and Eisenhower, and Barker's ADC Major May, in deliberately concealing the true facts of the death of a serving USAAF officer was a criminal offence under the US Military Code. Whilst ack-*

nowledging the anxiety of the Miller family, it can no longer be denied that the case must be resolved finally, either by a Congressional Committee of Inquiry or by releasing every available or relevant document.

Since access to part of the Miller 201 File has been denied, we must now also request release of the 201 Files for Morgan and Baessell - because when we received the Miller Burial File, important documents had been transferred to the Morgan and Baessell Burial Files.

Our basic request to President Bush was for full and unrestricted access to the Miller 201 File, period June 1944 - December 1944, and that request has been denied. But in view of the extreme gravity of the offence committed by senior officers at SHAEF including General (later President) Eisenhower, we contend that by continuing to restrict access to the Miller 201 File, the Secretary of the Army, the Department of the Army and National Archives are compounding the felony.

We appeal to the Secretary of the Army and once more to President Bush, to override the provisions of the Acts above mentioned and release in full all Files and documents related to the case including those of Baessell and Morgan, and investigative Files held by the Adjutant General and Provost Marshal Department hitherto unreleased.

If the Department of the Army persists in continuing this miscarriage of justice, I propose to take the matter to the World Court in The Hague on July 1 1992.

And for good measure, I addressed similar letters to the Congressional Office of Scientific Inquiries in Washington D.C. and to the Army Surgeon-General in Falls Church, Va. To the latter, I stressed that I was not interested in the whole of Miller's medical history - only information which might throw light on his disappearance. I pointed out that if there was nothing in the 201 File to support my evidence, there was no reason for the Miller family to deny access. Indeed, one might expect them to be only too anxious to see the matter resolved one way or the other.

And finally, I wrote directly to Secretary for Defense Dick Cheyney in Washington :

`*The real issue is whether those who know the facts shall be permitted to go on concealing them under the umbrella of the Freedom of Information and Privacy Acts, when this concealment further compounds the felony committed and initiated at SHAEF in December 1944 by a group of senior generals.*

On May 20 1992, I was officially denied access to Miller's medical files by Lieutenant General Frank L.Ledford, Surgeon-General - but again, I was advised of my right to appeal - this repeated referral of my requests to higher authority was encountered many times. So there was nothing to lose - and I wrote at once appealing to the Surgeon General, stressing that I did not want the whole medical file - only copies of documents related to his disappearance. And as of the time of writing - June 8 1992 - that was the current state of battle.

+   +   +

This sequel to MILLERGATE includes extracts from documents, letters and diaries. In addition, I have incorporated much new material from audio tapes, including those I recorded with the late Herb Miller, who reveals some unexpected insights on the character of Glenn himself. Perhaps most important, this book features a number of unusual and new scenarios with eye-witness evidence, a number of hitherto unpublished documents from the Burial Files of the three central characters, and the final items of evidence released after the intervention of President George Bush. What emerges is a battle fought on three fronts : the ongoing efforts to pry loose Miller's 201 File from NPRC St.Louis; the constant and at times vindictive reluctance of US Archives to release information, and the final conflict with the U.S military authorities to ensure exposure of the Great Cover-Up at SHAEF.

The major difficulty in investigating events which occurred almost half a century ago is that most of the individuals involved are long since deceased. (We started this investigation 30 years too late : if only we could have interviewed Don Haynes, Col.Early from 8th AFSC, General Ray Barker and Major May from SHAEF, the Abbotts Ripton Adjutant Ralph S.Cramer and surviving personnel from 8th AF HQ at Milton Ernest Hall, and from Abbotts Ripton itself. . .)

Further, the period involved coincided with the final convulsions of a World War involving millions of soldiers. All armies, it is said, travel on their bellies - but the essential lubricant is paperwork, in such volume as to defy the imagination. So when such a conflict ends, there is a vast burning of files, documents, lists and photographs, of which only a tiny proportion can be preserved for posterity.

Historic files relating to deceased VIPs and people lost with them would include the 201 File and the Burial File of Major Alton Glenn Miller, arguably the most popular orchestra leader of modern times. Because of public interest, they would be permanently under review. (All USAAF personnel had a 201 File, part of a general group of `293' Files, in which was listed personal details such as date of induction, promotions, moves and postings, medical examinations, course of instruction, leaves and furloughs, marital status and periodic assessments. A Burial File, however, was opened for every deceased soldier or airman, even if he was posted missing and his body was never recovered).

Personal 201 Files are held by the National Personnel Records Center in St. Louis Mo., whilst Burial Files are in the custody of Memorial Affairs Division in Alexandria, accessed via the Washington National Personnel Records Center. No 201 or Burial File is open to general access, and this was the primary obstacle to our research.

Since 1945, American Government departments have received a constant flow of inquiries on the Miller mystery - so many that the Burial files of the three central characters involved (Major Glenn Miller, Lt.Col. Norman F. Baessell and Flight Officer John Morgan) are annotated `KEEP ON TOP OF CABINET AT ALL TIMES'. . .

Predictably, a vast number of speculative theories and rumours about the fate of Glenn Miller have emerged like autumn mushrooms to cloud and distort the true facts. Every reputable investigator walks a fine line drawn between logical justifiable conclusions based on proven evidence, and totally unjustified speculation lacking any viable evidence at all.

In MILLERGATE we concentrated on identifying, analysing and assessing the half-dozen or so populist theories in a process of elimination, based on the documentary evidence and testimonies of surviving witnesses. We asked the reader to make up his or her own mind on that evidence, and in the course of time we were able to arrive at a number of fundamental conclusions :

1)   Miller was not aboard the Norseman.
2)   It did not land at R.A.F. Twinwood Farm on December 15 1944. The base was closed.

3) Morgan and Baessell, the sole passenger, departed Abbotts Ripton, Huntingdon at 13.25 hours bound for Bordeaux via base B-42, Beauvais-Tille in France.

4) The Norseman ditched about an hour later 6 miles west of Le Touquet, France, after mechanical failure.

5) Glenn Miller boarded a Paris flight at R.A.F. Bovingdon on Thursday December 1944.

6) The Band, under Lt.Haynes, arrived at Paris Orly at 1.45 hours Monday December 18.

7) The events between December 13 and 24th described by Lt.Haynes were untrue.

8) For reasons to be disclosed, there was a massive official cover-up of the truth by a group of senior generals at SHAEF, including Dwight D.Eisenhower.

All we had to do was prove it. . .

+   +   +

From the outset we were determined to avoid direct contact with the Miller family in California, to whom the re-emergence of the controversy might be disturbing and a threat to their privacy. After meeting Herb Miller, Glenn's blood brother, we had to accept that we might have to modify our tactics : as part of the general pattern of research we traced Mrs.Helen Miller's movements after the War until her death in June 1966, and some disturbing facts emerged. First, she had not returned immediately to California and her parents in 1945, but stayed in her apartment in Tenafly, New Jersey, until 1948, shunning publicity and living quietly. She visited the West Coast briefly in 1945, living in Lower Canyon Drive, Beverly Hills, but returned to New Jersey. There, she had emerged briefly in February 1945 to receive from Col. F.R.Kerr Glenn's posthumous Bronze Star. Correspondence in the Burial Files shows that she was at Tenafly in November 1948 when a number of important documents were released. They included :

Glenn Miller's Paris orders with incorrect Serial Number.
Report of Death (March 1948).
Amended Casualty Report (March 1948).
Missing Aircrew Report #10770.
An AG Department memorandum confirming that Morgan departed Abbotts Ripton at 13.25 hours on December 15 1944 - quoting the forged MACR #10770.
A Signal from HQ 8th AF Service Command Bedford to SHAEF confirming that Major Miller was on board the missing Norseman (also forged).

These releases may have had no connection with Helen's departure for California - the fact remains that she came west in December 1948 and sold Glenn's big 55-acre ranch, Tuxedo Junction, moving to San Marino. Here the story takes on a strange profile : in January 1949 Helen and her mother Anna May Burger purchased a 6-grave burial lot, No.2584, in Mountain View Cemetery, Altadena, California - but there were only 5 members of the family : Helen, her two children and her parents.

For whom was the 6th grave intended ? We had found evidence, admittedly second-hand and at times circumstantial, that Miller may have been fatally injured in Europe and flown home, unidentified, to die. There was a John Edwards letter from a World War 2 veteran who claimed he was in the same hospital ward in Columbus Ohio as Glenn Miller at the time the bandleader died. There was a letter from the New Jersey State Registrar at

Trenton, stating that Miller died in Columbus Ohio in December 1944. (It was later rescinded as a `typing error' !). And we received a letter from a Mr.Metcalfe in Britain, to the effect that he was attached to a USAAF base at Foggia, Italy, in late 1945, and read in the `Stars and Stripes' or some official document that `A Major Glenn Miller had been court-martialled in New York in December 1944 on charges of black market dealings in the ETO. He had been sentenced to 10 years in military prison.'

Our researches found no proof of such a trial, but the US Court Martial Archives in Falls Church, Virginia, pointed out that if an accused man proved to be `unfit to plead' on medical grounds there would be no record of a court-martial, but there *would* be an entry in the accused's 201 File, Medical Section. American writer Dale Titler wrote to us :

> `Looking back at my own Miller research, a court-martial does not sound inconceivable, considering the strange team of Miller and Baessell, and Miller's drive for money. In 1982-83 I made many inquiries relative to a Miller-Baessell court-martial, even enlisting the aid of my Senator in the search. But it all came to naught : I was informed that if a court-martial had indeed occurred, it would be recorded in Miller's 201 File at St. Louis Record Center. But that's a dead end - permission of the next of kin is required for access to it.'

Was there any basis in fact for this court-martial scenario ? Only this - Miller was a known associate of Lt.Col. Baessell - a noted big spender, party man and fast mover, strongly rumoured to be involved in the black market. Glenn's bags, as per regulations, had been deposited at the London Air Terminal in Old Quebec Street on Wednesday December 13, 24 hours before his booked flight to Paris. They would be taken out to Bovingdon airfield - and possibly searched by Customs. If anything was found, Miller would be detained and interviewed on his arrival next day. He could have been flown out to America that same day for interrogation. The ultimate solution lay in the jealously-guarded Miller 201 File.

We would succeed only by direct frontal assault on the US Government at very highest level, just as we had approached President Ronald Reagan to intervene on our behalf to obtain the release of the Burial Files, and the results of that approach are detailed above. In our first letter to President George Bush, we enclosed a detailed dossier of the Miller affair and the ongoing cover-up : we asked him and the supreme legal authorities of the US State and Defense Departments to rule upon two vital points : first, whether or not the prior release given to us by the late Herb Miller, Glenn's *blood* brother, is still valid and operative, over and above the wishes of the *adopted* Miller children, Steve and Jonnie. Second, whether the criminal nature of the cover-up offence by senior generals at SHAEF warranted over-ruling the Freedom of Information and Privacy Acts.

The first contention was rejected by NPRC at St.Louis, setting us inexorably on the path to the top levels of the U.S Government and the Department of the Army. The results of that odyssey are described in the following pages.

+   +   +

1

OVERTURE AND BEGINNERS

1. Glenn Miller comes to Britain

ALTON Glenn Miller was born on March 1 1904 at 601 South 16th Street in Clarinda, Iowa, one of three sons of Lewis Elmer and Mattie Lou Miller (*nèe* Cavender). His sister Irene married University of Colorado Professor Welby Wolfe. The eldest son was Deane and the youngest, Herb, died in Dulwich, London in 1987. They were a musical family; Mattie Lou played the organ and young Glenn sang in the church choir. His parents gave him a mandolin, which the boy promptly traded for a trumpet, emulating Deane, who played in the Town Band. Then a bandleader friend Jack Mossberger gave Glenn a trombone and from that moment no other instrument existed for the young musician.

Graduating on May 20 1921, Glenn played in small nomadic jazz combinations all over the Mid-West, including Holly Mayer, Max Fisher, Tom Watkins and finally Ben Pollack and his band in the Venice Ballroom, Los Angeles. In October 1928, Glenn married his childhood sweetheart Helen Dorothy Burger from Boulder, Colorado and they settled down in New York where Glenn was working. By 1935, Glenn had his own band but things went badly from the start; they closed down after playing their final date in York, Pennsylvania. Glenn went back to New York tired and disillusioned, to earn a living playing in Broadway theatre orchestras, studying music and composition in his spare time. In spring 1938 Glenn began to put together the orchestra with which he became famous for the next four years.

His income rocketed and they lived in a spacious apartment in Byrne Lane, Tenafly, New Jersey until he volunteered and was inducted into the US Army on November 23 1942 with the rank of captain. The original and rightly famous Miller Orchestra was broken up but Glenn kept in contact with his musicians, having no intention of remaining buried indefinitely in the arid field of marching music. Having miscarried badly, Helen Miller was unable to bear children, but they adopted two; Steve was a year old in 1944 and a girl Jonnie came along soon afterwards. Captain Glenn Miller escaped eventually from military band music, forming the American Air Force Band, known as the 2001st Base Unit (Radio) based in New Haven, Conn., comprising 62 musicians, many from his old outfit. Glenn arranged to have Band Manager Don Haynes appointed as Executive Officer with the rank of Lieutenant. Don was a one-time band booking agent who joined Glenn and his orchestra as manager during their residency at the Cafe Rouge in the Hotel Pennsylvania in New York City.

NPRC St.Louis grudgingly released in 1991 some details of his movements from his 201 File, from 1942 to the time Miller came to England on June 18 1944. Details of the subsequent period up to Glenn's death in December 1944 were suppressed by St. Louis on the instructions of the adopted Miller children in California, under the provisions of the Privacy Act of 1974. At 40 years of age, after being rejected by the US Navy, the Army experience was initially traumatic for him, in seeking adjustment after his demotion from VIP to just another rookie officer. By winter of 1944, he had gone through a long period of hard work, with insufficient sleep and business complexities, and George Simon relates that he was physically and emotionally exhausted. At the time he disappeared, he had gone through the most strenuous six months of his life performing for the troops all over Britain, and in radio broadcasts.

His movements between 1942 and June 13 1944 were as follows :

Date	Organisation/Location	Position/Occupation
7 Dec 42 - 24 Dec 42	Hq, ES Flying Trng Command Maxwell Field, Al.	Asst. Special Service Officer
Jan 43 - 14 Jul 43	Hg AAFTTC Knollwood Field Southern Pines, N.C.	Asst. Special Services Officer and Asst. Public Relations Officer and Director of Band Training.
14 Jul 43 - 28 Jan 44	Hq, TS AAFTTC, Yale University New Haven, Conn. (Attached) Permanent Station Ft. Worth, Texas.	Assistant to Asst. Chief of Staff (G-3) Director of Bands, Hq AAF TTC Ft.Worth Texas, with assign- ment at Yale University, New Ha- ven, Conn.
28 Jan 44 - June 44	TS-AAFTTC Yale Univ. New Haven Conn. Redesignated 3510BU (TS) Yale	Appt as CO 2nd AAF Training 13 Command Radio Unit 18 Feb 44, as Bandleader

Miller's ambition was to entertain the troops overseas, and he sought out a Washington friend, Colonel Ed. Kirby in the Special Services Division. Kirby pulled strings to good effect; Glenn flew to England on June 18 1944 (presumably after only 5 days embarkation leave). The AEF Band moved from New Haven to New Jersey for protective 'shots' and indoctrination and sailed a week later on June 22, in the converted troopship Queen Elizabeth I, eventually rejoining Glenn at their new billets in Sloane Court, London.

This location, as Miller ruefully commented, was right in the middle of `Bomb Alley' with V1 `doodlebugs' coming in frequently. On their second morning Miller, Don Haynes and Sgt. Paul Dudley (Fig.1) went to SHAEF MAIN at Bushey Park, London (which became SHAEF REAR after Paris was liberated), to talk to Colonel Kirby (the Director of Troop Broadcasting) about finding safer billets. The Associate Director of Troop Broadcasting in Special Services, movie star Lt.Col. David Niven (Fig.14), immediately took over administration of the Band and became, *per se*, Glenn Miller's Commanding Officer. Lt.Col. Niven drove the three musicians out to Bedford, a quiet town 50 miles north of London to which most of the BBC had been evacuated during the Blitz. David Niven would play an important but mysterious role in the mystery, as Glenn Miller's immediate superior.

2. Lt.Don Haynes Serial No. 0583260. (Fig.1)

Available details of Haynes' early life are scarce. We know he graduated from Ohio State University and worked as a full-time band booking agent, travelled widely and worked as an agent for GAC (General Artistes). He became liaison man, handling the Glenn Miller Orchestra bookings, and in due course came to know most of the orchestra. Glenn's secretary at that time was Polly Davis, whom Don married, and soon afterwards Glenn offered Haynes a position as personal manager, at the time the orchestra was playing their first stint in the Cafe Rouge, Hotel Pennsylvania in New York City.

Haynes was a tall, dark-haired swarthily-handsome man who later developed something of a reputation as a martinet among the Band musicians - he was never really popular with them, but developed a close and lasting relationship with Glenn Miller - both men shared a passion for golf. When Miller formed his American Band of the AEF in Newhaven before going overseas in 1944, he recruited Haynes with the rank of 1st. lieutenant as Band Executive Officer.

After Miller vanished, Haynes was promoted Captain and remained in charge of the Band until they returned home in August 1945. Post-war, Haynes worked for a while in the various Miller enterprises, but after a misunderstanding with Helen Miller and the family attorney David Mackay, Haynes left and for a while sold insurance. But he craved security and joined the US Mail Service, eventually rising to executive rank before retiring. Haynes died after a massive heart attack on June 4 1971.

Post war, he made sporadic attempts to record his experiences with the Miller Band in Europe, no doubt in order to reinforce and perpetuate his account of Glenn's last days - he produced two diaries (known as the `Library of Congress' <LOC> version and `MINUS ONE'). We obtained copies and from a literary standpoint they are quite unmistakably expanded fictionalised daily records, probably based on rough notes, memories and photographs. They record not only events but Haynes' thoughts, emotions and reactions to events. There is no doubt that, had he so wished, he could have earned a huge fee for ghost-writing an account of those tragic days - and Haynes was never a rich man. So why did he not capitalise on the story ? Why were the diaries not circulated until after his death ?

Reason suggests that he knew they would not stand up to close scrutiny - and right to the end, he was never interrogated officially and no authorised US Government report on the Miller disappearance was ever issued, other than brief summaries incorporating the fictitious story he related. In 1953, however, there were few genuine researchers, because of the dearth of physical evidence : some official documents were released in 1948, but all supported his account : he had no reason, therefore, to refuse Helen Miller's request for a written account of Glenn's days in Europe which she could offer to the script department at Universal-International studios. Indeed, there are strong grounds for believing that the earlier 'LOC' version was written solely for that reason in order to perpetuate the Norseman legend, and it was faithfully incorporated into 'The Glenn Miller Story' movie starring James Stewart and June Allyson.

The original (LOC) document typed by Haynes on 'onion-skin' paper is now in the Library of Congress in Washington. However, when George Simon was presented with a 'genuine' diary by Haynes' widow Polly in June 1972 (a year after Haynes died) it was the MINUS ONE version, which was manifestly written with a view to publication as semi-fiction based on Haynes' experiences.

In retrospect, no matter how serious the historical after-effects of Haynes' deception, there can be no doubt that he was motivated by his loyalty and devotion to his friend and boss, Glenn Miller : it is true that he may have been subjected to some pressure by General Barker and others at SHAEF to keep the secret, and we will never know if Haynes or Barker first conceived the Norseman story as a cover-up. For the rest of his life Haynes kept the faith, refused to capitalise on what he knew, and tried to ensure that the legend lived on after his death through his diaries. For that, Don Haynes deserves all credit.

3. Bedford and Milton Ernest (Figs.15,16)

After the meeting at Bushey Park, Col.Niven arranged adequate Band accommodation for the enlisted men in houses forming an annexe to the ARC Club in Ashburnham Road, Bedford. Band officers Miller, Haynes and Lt.Paul Morden used the ARC Officers Club at the intersection of Kimbolton and Goldington Roads; Glenn also had a small apartment in Bedford but worked mainly from his office in the Langham Hotel, London, and lived in rooms at the Mount Royal Hotel, Marble Arch (Fig.12).

But the ARC Officers Club in Bedford was invariably crowded - the area was jammed with US Air Force bomber and fighter bases (Fig.3). Three miles out of town in the village of Milton Ernest, 8th Air Force Service Command HQ occupied Milton Ernest Hall (Fig. 16). The Band parent organisation was Special Services Division, HQ Command, SHAEF at Bushey Park, London, but for administrative purposes they came under 8th AFSC. (For that reason Glenn Miller never appeared on an 8th AF Casualty List). At 'The Castle', as the Hall was known, Glenn and Don Haynes met several staff officers including the Commanding Officer Brigadier-General Donald F.Goodrich (Fig.17) and his Special Assistant Lt.Col. Norman F.Baessell (Fig.2) who was a central character in the mystery.

The Army career of Goodrich, a gentle and mild-mannered old man affectionately known as 'Poopsie' to his subordinates, had begun in the trenches of WW1, but in December 1944 he was terminally ill with cardiac trouble, and spent all his time in his house 'The Bury' across the river from The Castle. (Army engineers had thrown up a Bailey bridge for access). His Executive Officer Colonel Early effectively ran the Command, and soon after Miller vanished, Goodrich was evacuated back to Maxwell AFB, Alabama, where he died a few days later. In mid-December, in fact, Goodrich was in no condition to take any part in the events which followed. He was never interrogated about the Miller affair.

Eighth AF Service Command was responsible for the supply, repair, servicing and modification of all 8th Air Force aircraft in the UK, and later, on the Continent. Fig.3 shows the airfields featured in the Miller mystery, of which R.A.F.Twinwood Farm assumes great importance. It was a night fighter training airfield eminently suitable for the uplift of the AEF Band when they flew to other US bases for concerts, and for picking up 8th AFSC staff officers flying on duty elsewhere. A typical wartime station with dispersed domestic accommodation against enemy air attack, the main technical site and Control Tower lay south of the triangle of concrete runways, and the main access gate was on the south side. A second gate provided a short cut down to Oakley village, and thence to Milton Ernest. The Station Flight based near the Tower was responsible for receiving and dispatching visiting aircraft, the pilots of which were required to report to Air Traffic Control on landing and before departure. In the context of the Miller enigma, the organisation and function of Air Traffic Control, including procedures, is very relevant to the events in December 1944.

All R.A.F. airfields positioned an Air Traffic Controller in the Tower, and a Runway Controller in a caravan at the runway threshold, to monitor air and ground traffic and initiate emergency signals. When no flying was in progress the caravan and Tower were unmanned save for a skeleton radio watch to monitor emergency channels. A signal square outside the Tower indicated when the airfield was closed to flying, at which time there would be no fire-fighting or ambulance vehicles on standby : no sensible pilot would risk a landing under such circumstances, and it was a serious offence to land without permission. This was usually given over the radio, or by a green light from the ground.

The standard WW2 method of making a controlled approach through cloud involved flying courses and altitudes passed to the aircraft by radio, in response to radio calls from the aircraft which produced a directional indication on a DF screen. This enabled aircraft to be brought safely down through cloud, but not necessarily lined up with the runway in a landing position. Thus, in conditions of low cloud and poor visibility, no pilot could descend and land without radio assistance from the ground - that is to say, from a fully-manned Control Tower.

On Friday 15 December 1944, Don Haynes claimed that Lt.Col.Baessell had offered Glenn Miller a lift to Paris in a Norseman plane flown by Flight Officer Morgan, because all other flights in the UK had been grounded. Haynes described driving Miller and Baessell from Milton Ernest Hall to Twinwood Farm in dreadful weather conditions - 200 foot cloud base, heavy rain and fog. They waited until Morgan came down through cloud, took on board the two men and took off again at 13.45 hours. Haynes watched the plane take-off - remarkably he was the only person to do so - and it was never seen again.

But all R.A.F. stations maintain a Form 540 `Daily History', many of which are preserved in the Public Records Office at Kew, London. The Twinwood Farm entry for Friday December 15 1944 - the date on which Haynes claimed to see the ill-fated Norseman #44-70285 depart - states :

`No flying today. Airfield Closed.

+   +   +

2

SEARCH FOR A LEGEND

1. Aftermath

AT 19.00 hours Paris Time on December 24 1944, the following announcement was broadcast from the Olympia Theatre to a listening world, and was repeated 1 minute later by the BBC in London :

> `Major Alton Glenn Miller, Director of the famous United States Army Air Force Band which has been playing in Paris is reported missing while on a flight from England to Paris. The plane in which he was a passenger left England on December 15 and no trace of it has been found since its take-off. Major Miller, one of the outstanding orchestra leaders in the United States, lived at Tenafly, New Jersey, where his wife presently resides. No members of Major Miller's Band were with him on the missing plane.'

The inexplicable disappearance of Major Glenn Miller generated countless rumours, theories and scenarios which attracted hundreds of researchers over the years. Following this Press Release on Christmas Eve 1944, a few hours before a scheduled Band broadcast to America, a consensus view emerged : this was no ordinary routine loss of a small passenger aircraft in icy foggy weather over the English Channel. Even allowing for wartime censorship, the communique contained virtually no information of value to investigators and was cursory to the point of brevity, compared to the huge Press comment when actor Leslie Howard was lost on a flight home from Gibraltar.

Miller, after all, was a VIP, a serving US Army Air Force officer and arguably the most famous orchestra leader of modern times. As time passed post-war, millions of his fans became totally dissatisfied and suspicious : apparently, there had been no search, no investigation, no official confirmation or publication of the Haynes story, no references to other passengers in the aircraft - and particularly, no explanation of the 9-day delay between the loss of the Norseman and the Press Release.

In fact, four years after the event, very few official documents relating to the affair had been released, and those only on application by dedicated researchers : the public in general were not informed and the US Government applied an almost-total black-out, hoping no doubt that the incident would be forgotten. When the late Sqn.Ldr Jack Taylor suggested that an in-depth investigation might bear fruit, our only evidence was a Missing Aircrew Report (MACR) #10770 (Figs.8,9), Miller's Casualty Report dated December 22 (Fig.6) a week after he vanished, and a Signal from 8th AFSC Milton Ernest to General Ray Barker, G-1 at SHAEF Versailles (Fig.10) confirming that Miller was aboard the lost Norseman. And in time, all three of these documents were proven suspect and unviable.

Slowly, the pieces began falling together : the SHAEF PR Division in a Press Release Memo (Fig.19) had timed the announcement significantly for December 24, just a few hours before a scheduled broadcast to America on Christmas Day. The Memo (found in the Glenn Miller Burial File) had some unusual features : it stressed the embargo on prior release, ensured that the Band musicians' families were reassured - and stated that the Commander, PR Division, Col. Dupuy, 'Did not need to see the release before it went out'. Further, the Memo had to be returned to originator - a very unusual practice, since most memos were destroyed. Why had this one been preserved for 44 years ?

Information in the Press Release was skimpy - but could it have been expanded without jeopardising official secrecy ? The type of aircraft could have been revealed - news broadcasts each day mentioned B-17 Fortresses, B-24 Liberators, Douglas Dakotas, Avro Lancasters and Handley Page Halifaxes. The airfield name, predictably, was censored, but there was no mention whatsoever of other passengers - other than the fact that none of the Band were aboard. Similarly the information on the Casualty Report (which was for official use, not general release) was evasive : `Was taken to airfield by off. of AAF Band who witnessed take-off. No trace of airplane can be found.' This Report, remember, involved a VIP : it would be sent to the War Department in Washington, which would certainly demand more information. The name of the `off.' could have been included - but the Report could hardly say `No trace of airplane can be found because nobody looked'. Yet the Missing Aircrew Report stated specifically `no search', whilst Miller's Report of Death dated March 1948 certifies that no investigation took place ! It seemed extremely probable, in fact, that this Report was composed specifically for post-war publication as an exercise in disinformation.

In a letter dated December 22 1944 to General Dwight D.Eisenhower, the Paris AG General Davis suggested it was time to send a radio casualty signal to the War Department `in view of the planned broadcast to America on Christmas Day' - but not before 18.00 hours Christmas Eve. Obviously, this was intended to give Glenn Miller as much time as possible to turn up : had he done so even an hour before the Press Release, he could have been rushed across Paris to the Olympia Theatre and all would be well.

This delay meant one of two things : either SHAEF and Don Haynes had no idea what had happened to Miller (which seems improbable) or they knew - and were waiting developments. The latter alternative covers a number of possible scenarios - foul play, severe accident, arrest and interrogation, or simply out of touch in France. At that time, we could only speculate on the true course of events.

But at the outset, the problem for most researchers was this : if Miller had not been lost in the Norseman, *what really did happen to him ?* On the available evidence we were able to speculate on his movements from the time he was last seen alive in England - outside the Milroy Club in London's Mayfair at 02.30am on Thursday December 14 1944. Some of these theories (but not all) are supported by evidence.

* Haynes had booked Glenn on a Thursday flight to Paris from Bovingdon.
* His orders authorised him to travel by air transport `on or about December 14'.
* He may have been mugged or killed by a bomb in London.
* If not, he caught the Bovingdon bus next morning, arriving about 10.30am.
* He may have been arrested or detained at the air base.
* If not, he caught his flight, arriving at Paris Orly about 13.30pm.
* He became the victim of foul play and died, SHAEF covering up the truth.
* He was involved in an accident and was flown home to America unidentified.
* He died, unidentified, possibly in Columbus Ohio, in December 1944 and was buried under an incorrect serial number.
* He was found subsequently by Helen Miller and reinterred in California.
* SHAEF may never have learned his fate : rather than admit that they were totally baffled, they fabricated a false explanation around the loss of a Norseman plane.
* His disappearance in France involved circumstances, as yet uncorroborated, later described by WAAF LACW Joan Heath, personal driver to Air Marshal Tedder.

Our investigation centred on examining the available evidence, in order to disprove as many theories as possible, and the first to go were those outlandish stories about Lt.Col. Baessell shooting Miller because of the latter's objection to black market activities; Miller's murder by Parisian black market operators; Miller being shot dead in a Paris hotel, the Georg Cinq; being fatally involved in a street brawl in the Pigalle; being shot down by enemy aircraft and also being bombed by friendly Lancasters.

The last scenario achieved some notoriety in the late Eighties but we were able to disprove it conclusively using documentary evidence in the Miller Burial File. This confirmed that Morgan flew east of London, many miles away from the Channel bomb jettison area south of Eastbourne. (See Pp.55,183,221).

Gradually, more evidence accumulated, especially in regard to the Missing Aircrew Report (MACR #10770) which had been circulated as `genuine' by US National Archives for 44 years. It was quoted and cited *ad infinitum* in official reports, signals and messages - but without mentioning or identifying Lt.Don Haynes as `the Band off. who witnessed the take-off'. The official procedure following the unexplained loss of a USAAF aircraft was explicit and routine : within 48 hours of occupants being officially listed as `missing', a MACR was to be compiled by the aircraft parent unit and copies distributed widely, including one to the War Department and the Adjutant General's department in Washington. `Missing' included aircraft lost on operational missions, but the procedure applied to all US military aircraft, combat or otherwise.

The MACR, in peacetime, would trigger a search and investigation : in wartime, neither were feasible, for as many as 200 combat planes were lost in a single day. But other non-operational types lost unusually on ferrying or transport missions might well be investigated and a search initiated - especially if one or more of the occupants was a VIP of the calibre of Major Glenn Miller. Air Traffic and Air Sea Rescue procedures ensured that a plane was listed as `overdue' after 1 hour without contact, and `missing' after 2 hours. The destination airfield (A-42 Villacoublay south of Paris according to the MACR, B-42 Beauvais-Tille north of Paris according to Morgan's orders and Paris Orly, according to Don Haynes) would contact the departure airfield (Twinwood Farm, Honington, Hendon or Abbotts Ripton ?) and advise the parent unit. By midnight Friday December 15, therefore, 35th Air Depot Repair Squadron at Abbotts Ripton, 2nd Strategic Air Depot HQ at the same base and HQ 8th AF Service Command at Milton Ernest Hall would all know that Morgan had passed zero fuel time and must be considered as lost.

Was a search at that time possible ? Or worthwhile ? Seemingly, no radio distress call was received from Morgan - and since he had the option to choose his own route between England and France, where would a search begin ? Further, Baessell and Ferguson had flown this route several times, and had a habit of disappearing into the French hinterland, flitting from one base to another. The reaction at 8th AFSC would be to wait and see - maybe the Norseman had landed some place out of contact.

But all this assumed that Miller was not aboard the aircraft ! Had he been, there would have been an explosion of activity at 8th AFSC and Abbotts Ripton : a search would have been ordered, covering all possible routes, a local investigation initiated - and above all, Don Haynes (asleep in the Bedford ARC Club and ready to fly out with the Band next morning) would have been roused and told the news.

But none of this happened. Haynes stated that the first intimation of trouble was when he arrived at Paris Orly the following Monday - and found Miller absent.

+   +   +

Let us be perfectly clear about this. SHAEF and 8th AFSC did not order a search because they knew initially that Miller was not at aboard the plane, and further, they did not want a Norseman with only two bodies aboard located, once the Haynes story was officially released. What is more, Haynes knew that Glenn had caught his booked flight on Thursday and was now in Paris. Proof ? When Haynes arrived in Paris, he made no inquiries as to a `missing' Norseman. Instead, he spent two days searching Paris hotels and restaurants for Miller - before reporting to SHAEF at the end of the second day.

Thus from the very beginning Haynes' story is exposed as fraudulent. There was only one explanation. Something terrible had happened to Miller after he reached France - and from Monday December 18, people at very high level at SHAEF were conspiring to conceal the truth.

+   +   +

Fig. 1

L to R : W/O Paul Dudley, Major Glenn Miller, Lt. Don Haynes

Fig. 2

Lt.Col. Norman F. Baessell USAAF

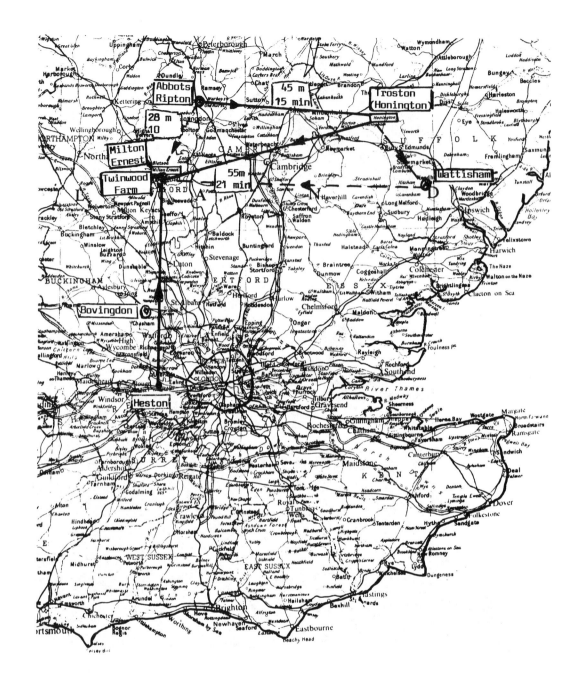

Fig. 3

Airfields in the Miller Mystery

CONFIDENTIAL

SUPREME HEADQUARTERS
ALLIED EXPEDITIONARY FORCE
REAR HEADQUARTERS
APO 413

AG 300-AGP-Miller, Alton G. (Off) 12 December 1944

SUBJECT: Orders.

TO : Major ALTON G. MILLER, 0505273, AC, G-1 Division, SUPREME HQ AEF.

1. You will proceed by military aircraft (ATC) on or about 16 December 1944 from present station to SUPREME HQ AEF [illegible] on the Continent to carry out the instructions of the A.C. of S., G-1, SUPREME HQ AEF, and upon completion thereof return to present station.

2. Travel by military aircraft is directed. Baggage allowance be limited to sixty five (65) pounds.

By command of General EISENHOWER:

[illegible]
[illegible], Col., AGD,
Asst. Adjutant General.

DISTRIBUTION:
Maj Miller........ 4
G-1 Div Rear.... 1
ATC.............. 1
Trans Off, Hq
Comd Rear... 1
CWD Rear........ 1
AGP.............. 1
XXX.............. 1

Fig. 4

Glenn Miller's Orders for Paris (with incorrect serial number)

REPORT OF DEATH

DATE **24 MARCH 1948** ekm

FULL NAME	ARMY SERIAL NUMBER	GRADE
MILLER, ALTON G.	0 505 273	MAJOR

HOME ADDRESS	ARM OR SERVICE	DATE OF BIRTH
Tenafly, New Jersey	AC	1 Mar 1904

PLACE OF DEATH	CAUSE OF DEATH	DATE OF DEATH
European Area	Airplane crash	15 Dec 1944

STATION OF DECEASED	DATE OF ENTRY ON CURRENT ACTIVE SERVICE	LENGTH OF SERVICE FOR PAY PURPOSES
		YEARS	MONTHS	DAYS
European Area	8 Dec 1942			

EMERGENCY ADDRESSEE (Name, relationship, and address)

Mrs. Helen D. Miller, Wife, Byrne Lane, Tenafly, New Jersey

BENEFICIARY (Name, relationship, and address)

Mrs. Helen Dorothy Miller, Wife, Bryne Lane, Tenafly, New Jersey
Steven Davis Miller, Child, Bryne Lane, Tenafly, New Jersey
Mrs. Mattie Lou Miller, Mother, 1740 Sherman Street, Denver, Colorado

INVESTIGATION MADE	IN LINE OF DUTY	OWN MISCONDUCT	WAS DECEASED ON DUTY STATUS	AUTHORIZED ABSENCE	IN FLYING PAY STATUS	OTHER PAY STATUS (Specify below)
YES · NO X	YES X · NO	YES · NO X	YES X · NO	YES · NO	YES · NO X	YES · NO

ADDITIONAL DATA AND/OR STATEMENT

☐ BATTLE   ☒ NON-BATTLE

Finding of death has been issued previously under Sec 5 Public Law 490, 7 Mar 42, as amended, showing presumed date of death as 16 December 1945. This report of death, based on information received since that date is issued in accordance with Sec 9 of said act, and its effect on prior payment and settlements is as prescribed in Sec 9.

In accordance with the provisions of Section 2 and 7 of the Act of 7 March 1942 (56 Stat. 145) as amended the records show that this officer completed 2 years, and 8 days of active service at the time of his death.

BY ORDER OF THE SECRETARY OF THE ARMY
~~XXXXXXXXXXXXXXXXXXXX~~

[signature]

ADJUTANT GENERAL

Fig. 5

Report of Death - Major Glenn Miller

WAR DEPARTMENT
THE ADJUTANT GENERAL'S OFFICE
WASHINGTON 25, D. C.

NON —BATTLE CASUALTY REPORT

NAME	SERIAL NUMBER	GRADE	ARM OR SERVICE	REPORTING THEATRE
MILLER ALTON GLENN	0505273	MAJ	AC	ETO

PLACE OF CASUALTY	DATE OF CASUALTY			FLYING OR JUMPING STAT	TYPE OF CASUALTY	SHIPMENT NUMBER
	DAY	MONTH	YEAR			
ENROUTE ENGLAND TO PARIS, FRANCE	15	DEC	44		MNG	358007-CC-1X

NAME AND ADDRESS OF EMERGENCY ADDRESSEE

THE INDIVIDUAL NAMED ABOVE DESIGNATED THE FOLLOWING PERSON AS THE ONE TO BE NOTIFIED IN CASE OF EMERGENCY, AND THE OFFICIAL TELEGRAPHIC AND LETTER NOTIFICATIONS WILL BE SENT TO THIS PERSON. THE RELATIONSHIP, IF ANY, IS SHOWN BELOW. IT SHOULD BE NOTED THAT THIS PERSON IS NOT NECESSARILY THE NEXT-OF-KIN OR RELATIVE DESIGNATED TO BE PAID SIX MONTHS' PAY GRATUITY IN CASE OF DEATH

MR.-MRS.-MISS—FIRST NAME—MIDDLE INITIAL—LAST NAME	RELATIONSHIP	DATE NOTIFIED
MRS. HELEN D. MILLER	WIFE	23 DEC 44 1mb

NO. AND NAME OF STREET—CITY—STATE

REMARKS: AG 201 (22 Dec 44) ☐ CORRECTED COPY

Paris, B-77699 cas msg 3028. Was taken to airfield by off. of AAF Band who witnessed takeoff. No trace of airplane can be found.

ACTION BY PROCESSING AND VERIFICATION SECTION: REPORT VERIFIED_____ FORM 48_____ AG 201 REQ_____

CASUALTY BRANCH FILE ATTACHED _____ OR CHARGED TO _____ DATE _____

PREVIOUSLY REPORTED NO ✓ YES _____ (AS INDICATED BELOW):

FILE NO.	MESSAGE NO.	TYPE.	DATE AND AREA	E. A. NOTIFIED

FORWARDED TO ▶	SPEC. IDEN.	TELEGRAM	WOUNDED	LETTER	CORRES.	S. R. & D.	CERTIF.	M. & M.	NO. DET.
		✓							

REPORT NOT VERIFIED_____ NO FORM 48_____ NO CAS. BR. FILE _____ CHECKED BY _____ REVIEWED BY _____

THIS SPACE FOR USE OF MACHINE RECORDS BRANCH, A.G.O.

ACCT. AREA	CASUALTY STATUS	ORIGINAL CAS. DATE			MESSAGE NO.	LATEST CAS. DATE			REFERENCE AREA	CAS. POS.	RESIDENCE		COMP	RACE
		DAY	MO.	YR.		DAY	MO.	YR.			STATE	COUNTY		
34	35	36	37	38	39 40 41 42 43 44 45	46	47	48	49 50 51 52		53 54 55 56 57		58	59

DISTRIBUTION "A" ☐ 37 COPIES

(ALL TYPES OF CASUALTIES PERTAINING TO MILITARY PERSONNEL, EXCEPT WOUNDED.)
COPIES FURNISHED: SEE CASUALTY BRANCH MEMORANDUM NO. 48, 1944.

DISTRIBUTION "B" ☐ _____ COPIES

(ALL WOUNDED MILITARY PERSONNEL AND ALL TYPES OF CASUALTIES PERTAINING TO CIVILIANS WHO ARE W. D. EMPLOYEES, EMPLOYEES OF W. D. CONTRACTORS AND OTHERS SUBJECT TO MILITARY LAW.)
COPIES FURNISHED: SEE CASUALTY BRANCH MEMORANDUM NO. 48, 1944.

W.D., A.G.O. FORM NO. 898
18 JUNE 1944

Fig. 6

Casualty Report - Major Glenn Miller

NON —BATTLE CASUALTY REPORT

NAME	GRADE		DATE CAS. REPORT RECEIVED
MILLER ALTON G	MAJ		
ASN 0505273	HUS		

NAME AND AD. DRESS OF E. A.	MRS HELEN D MILLER BYRNE LANE TENAFLY NEW JERSEY		DATE TELEGRAM SENT 19 MAR 48

THE INDIVIDUAL NAMED BELOW DESIGNATED THE ABOVE PERSON AS THE ONE TO BE NOTIFIED IN CASE OF EMERGENCY, AND THE OFFICIAL TELE-GRAPHIC AND LETTER NOTIFICATIONS WILL BE SENT TO THIS PERSON. THE RELATIONSHIP, IF ANY, IS SHOWN BELOW. IT SHOULD BE NOTED THAT THIS PERSON IS NOT NECESSARILY THE NEXT-OF-KIN OR RELATIVE DESIGNATED TO BE PAID SIX MONTHS' PAY GRATUITY IN CASE OF DEATH.

THE SECRETARY OF ~~WAR~~ HAS ASKED ME TO EXPRESS HIS DEEP REGRET THAT YOUR **HUSBAND**

GRADE	NAME	SERIAL NUMBER	ARM OR SERVICE	REPORTING THEATRE	F OR J STATUS	SHIPMENT NUMBER
MAJ.	MILLER, ALTON GLENN	0505273	AC			07201 U-2

TYPE OF CASUALTY	PLACE OF CASUALTY	DATE OF CASUALTY			CASUALTY CODE
		DAY	MONTH	YEAR	
DIED	IN ENGLISH CHANNEL	15	DEC	44	

REMARKS: AG 704 /11 MAR 48/   ☐ CORRECTED COPY REPORT OF DEATH ISSUED 23 MAR 48

MEMO S.R. AND D. UNIT. APPROVED BY OIC. CAS. SEC. PA. BR.   DIED WHEN PLANE CRASHED SOMEWHERE IN THE ENGLISH CHANNEL WHILE ON MISSION FROM TWINWOOD FLD, ENGLAND TO PARIS, FRANCE.   IN PAY AND DUTY STATUS AT TIME OF DEATH, NOT RESULT OF OWN MISC.   FINDING DEATH ISSUED PREVIOUSLY UNDER SEC.5, PUBLIC LAW 490, 7 MAR. 42, AS AMENDED, SHOWING PRESUMED DATE DEATH 16 DEC. 45. RPT DEATH BASED ON INFO REC'D SINCE THAT DATE, IS ISSUED IN ACCORDANCE WITH SEC.9 OF SAID ACT, AND ITS EFFECT ON PRIOR PAYMENTS AND SETTLEMENTS IS AS PROVIDED IN SEC.9.   VIVID.   Home Add: Tenafly, Bergen Co., New Jersey.

PROCESS IN ACCORDANCE WITH PAR. 2B, OPER. BUL. 35, 1945.

ACTION BY COMPOSITE SECTION: REPORT VERIFIED ✓ FORM 43 AG 201 REQ

CASUALTY BRANCH FILE ATTACHED ___ OR CHARGED TO ___ DATE ___

PREVIOUSLY REPORTED ___ NO. ___ YES ___ (AS INDICATED BELOW):

FILE NO.	MESSAGE NO.	TYPE	DATE AND AREA	A. NOTIFIED
Public Law-490		DED	16 Dec 45, ETO	

FORWARDED TO →	SPEC. IDEN.	C. & P.	TELEGRAM	LETTER ✓	CERTIF.	F. REL.	CORRES.	RLPAT.	S. R & D.	NON-DEL

REPORT NOT VERIFIED ___ NO FORM 43 ___ NO CAS. BR. FILE ___ CHECKED BY ___ REVIEWED BY ___

DISTRIBUTION "A" ☐ 29 COPIES   DISTRIBUTION "B" ☐ 831 COPIES

WD AGO FORM 0365   1 MAY 1948   EDITION OF : JAN. 1948 MAY BE USED.

Fig. 7

Amended Casualty Report - Major Glenn Miller

WAR DEPARTMENT
HEADQUARTERS ARMY AIR FORCES
WASHINGTON

Classification changed
~~to RESTRICTED~~
by K. A. BRADUNAS, Lt. Col., AC
by P. M. WUENCH, Capt., AC
Date: Mar 15 1946

MISSING AIR CREW REPORT

IMPORTANT: This Report will be compiled in triplicate by each Army Air
Forces organization within 48 hours of the time an air crew
member is officially reported missing.

1. ORGANIZATION: Location, by Name Abbotts Ripton ; Command or Air Force VIII Air Force Svc
   Group 35th ADG ; Squadron Repair ; Detachment 2d Strategic Air Depot

2. SPECIFY: Place of Departure Abbotts Ripton Course Bordeaux Via A-42
   Target or Intended Destination Bordeaux; A-42 Type of Mission A

3. WEATHER CONDITIONS AND VISIBILITY AT THE OF CRASH OR WHEN LAST REPORTED:
   Unknown

4. GIVE: (a) Day 15 Month Dec Year 44 ; Time 355 ; and Location Twinwood
   of last known whereabouts of missing aircraft.
   (b) Specify whether aircraft was last sighted ( ); XXXXXXXXXXXXXXX
   XXXXXXXXXXXXXXXXXXXXXXXXXXXXXXXXXXXXXXXXXX Information not Available ( )

5. AIRCRAFT WAS LOST, OR IS BELIEVED TO HAVE BEEN LOST, AS A RESULT OF: (Check
   only one) Enemy Aircraft ( ); Enemy Anti-Aircraft ( ); Other Circumstances
   as Follows: Unknown

6. AIRCRAFT: Type, Model and Series UC-64A ; AAF Serial Number 44-70285

7. NICKNAME OF AIRCRAFT, If Any Norseman

8. ENGINES: Type, Model and Series Radial - 1340 P&W ; AAF Serial
   Number (a) Unknown ; (b) ; (c) ; (d)

9. INSTALLED WEAPONS (Furnish below Make, Type and Serial Number); None
   (a) ____ ; (b) ____ ; (c) ____ ; (d) ____ ;
   (e) ____ ; (f) ____ ; (g) ____ ; (h) ____ ;
   (i) ____ ; (j) ____ ; (k) ____ ; (l) ____ ;
   (m) ____ ; (n) ____ ; (o) ____ ; (p) ____ ;

10. THE PERSONS LISTED BELOW WERE REPORTED AS: XXXXXXXXXXXXXXXX
    XXXXXXX Non Battle Casualty

11. NUMBER OF PERSONS ABOARD AIRCRAFT: Crew 1 ; Passengers 2 ; Total 3
    (Starting with Pilot, furnish the following particulars: If more than 11
    persons were aboard aircraft, list similar particulars on separate sheet
    and attach original to this form.)

Crew Position	Name in Full (Last Name First)	Rank	Serial Number	Current Status
1. Pilot	Morgan, John R.S.	F/O	T-190776	Missing ,AC
2. Passenger	Baessell, Norman F.	Lt Col	O-905387	Missing ,AC
3. Passenger	Miller, Alton G.	Major	O-505273	Missing ,AC
4.				
5.				
6.				
7.				
8.				
9.				
10.				
11.				

12. IDENTIFY BELOW THOSE PERSONS WHO ARE BELIEVED TO HAVE LAST KNOWLEDGE OF AIR-
    CRAFT, AND CHECK APPROPRIATE COLUMN TO INDICATE BASIS FOR SAME:

				Check Only One Column			
Name in Full (Last Name First)	Rank	Serial Number	Contacted by Radio	Last Sighted	Saw Crash	Saw Forced Landing	
1. Unknown							
2.							
3.							

Fig.8

The Forged Missing Aircrew Report #10770 - Page 1

13. IF PERSONNEL ARE BELIEVED TO HAVE SURVIVED, ANSWER YES TO ONE OF THE FOLLOWING STATEMENTS: (a) Parachutes were used ___; (b) Persons were seen walking away from scene of crash ___; or (c) Any other reason (Specify) ___Unknown___

14. ATTACH AERIAL PHOTOGRAPH, MAP, CHART, OR SKETCH, SHOWING APPROXIMATE LOCATION WHERE AIRCRAFT WAS LAST SEEN OR HEARD FROM.

15. ATTACH EYEWITNESS DESCRIPTION OF CRASH, FORCED LANDING, OR OTHER CIRCUM-STANCES PERTAINING TO MISSING AIRCRAFT.

16. GIVE NAME, RANK AND SERIAL NUMBER OF OFFICER IN CHARGE OF SEARCH, IF ANY, INCLUDING DESCRIPTION AND EXTENT ___None___

Date of Report ___23 December 1944___

For the Commanding Officer:

(Signature of Preparing Officer)

17. REMARKS OR EYEWITNESS STATEMENTS: None

JAN 22 1945

RECEIVED

Fig. 9

The Forged Missing Aircrew Report #10770 - Page 2

C O P Y

SUBJ: MISSING AIRPLANE

HQ VIII AFSC

AAF Sta 506, APO 636

G-1 SECTION, SHAEF (MAIN)
  Attn GEN BARKER

thru: Eighth AF, AAF Sta 101, APO 634

20 Dec 44

Info copy: SHAEF (REAR)
          CG, US Strategic AF in Europe

VIII AFSC-D-832-G-27-A

CONFIRMING VERBAL INFORMATION TO G-1 SHAEF REAR C-64 AIRPLANE

NUMBER 44-70285 MISSING AND UNREPORTED SINCE DEPARTURE

TWINWOOD FIELD 1355 HOURS 15 DECEMBER FOR FRANCE PILOT FLIGHT

OFFICER MORGAN TWO PASSENGERS INCLUDING MAJOR GLENN MILLER.

                                                EARLY

OFFICIAL:

ALBERT G. BUELOW
Major, AGD
Adjutant General

                        C O P Y

Fig. 10

Falsified Confirmatory Signal to SHAEF dated 20 December 1944

State of New Jersey
DEPARTMENT OF HEALTH

CN 360, TRENTON, N.J. 08625-0360

MOLLY JOEL COYE, M.D., M.P.H.
COMMISSIONER

April 10, 1987

Name: Alton G. Miller
Dod: 12/44
Pod: Ohio

Wilbur Wright
The Shrubs Allington Lane
Southampton SO3 3HP
England

Dear Mr. Wright:

The death of Alton G. Miller occurred in the State
of Ohio. You should write to:

Division of Vital Statistics
Ohio Department of Health
G-20 Ohio Departments Building
65 South Front St.
Columbus, OH 43215

Enclosed is a refund statement for $4.00.

Very truly yours,

Charles A. Karkut
State Registrar

Fig. 11

Letter from New Jersey State Registrar

Fig. 12

The Mount Royal Hotel, London

Fig. 13

Lt.Col. George W. Ferguson USAF (Retd)

Fig. 14

Lt.Col. David G.D. Niven LM

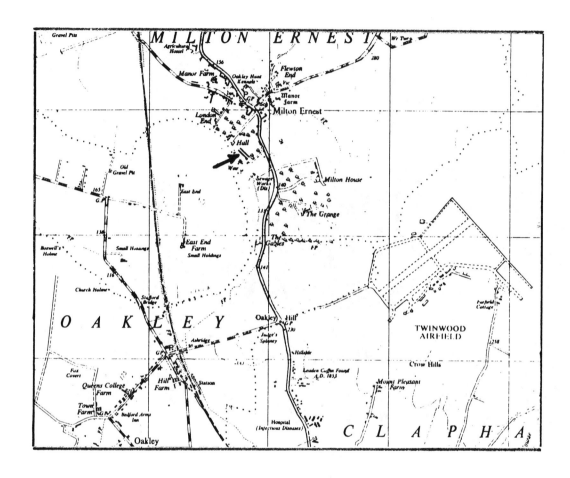

Fig. 15

Milton Ernest and Twinwood Farm

Fig. 16

Milton Ernest Hall, 1944

Flight Officer John R.S. Morgan

Brig.Gen. Donald R. Goodrich

Fig. 17

FOR RELEASE AT
1800 HOURS

24 December 1944

Major Alton Glenn Miller, director of the famous
United States Army Air Force band which has been playing in Paris
is reported missing while on a flight from England to Paris. The
plane in which he was a passenger left England on December 15
and no trace of it has been found since its take-off.

Major Miller, one of the outstanding orchestra
leaders in the United States, lived at Tenafly, New Jersey, where
his wife presently resides.

No members of Major Miller's band were with him on
the missing plane.

* * * * * * * * * *

8   1158

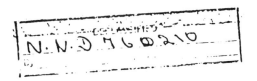

N.N.D 760210

Fig. 18

SHAEF Press Release December 24 1944

PUBLIC RELATIONS DIVISION

S H A E F

_____

24 Dec. _____ 1944

Memo to: __Capt Wade_____
              Information Room

Here is the release on Glenn Miller, with the
embargo of 1800 hours tonight.

Colonel Dupuy merely wants a factual announcement
that he is missing. However, he also wants a statment
added to the effect that"no members of his band
were with him." Or something very much like that.

Capt. Cosgrove.

THIS CORRESPONDENCE MUST BE RETURNED. COLONEL DUPUY
DOES NOT HAVE TO SEE THE RELEASE BEFORE IT GOES OUT.

Done.
Signature __1150___
        24 Dec 44
           P.V.W.

8   1159

Fig.19

Press Release Memo

SUBJECT: Report of Missing Personnel.

TO : Commanding General, European Theater of Operations, U. S. Army, APO 887.

1. It is reported that on 15 December 1944 Major Alton Glenn Miller, O-505273, AC, Army Air Force Band (Special), Headquarters Command, Supreme Headquarters AEF, departed from an airport in England enroute to Paris, France, in an Eighth Air Force Service Command airplane (C-64) piloted by a Flight Officer Morgan. There was one (1) additional passenger on this plane - a Lieutenant Colonel Baessel of the Eighth Air Force. Major Miller was taken to the air field by an officer of the Army Air Force Band who witnessed the take-off. No trace of this plane can be found and this headquarters has been advised by the Eighth Air Force Service Command that this airplane is considered missing. Likewise, Major Miller is considered to be missing.

2. It is requested that an immediate radio casualty report be rendered to the War Department on Major Miller, and the War Department be advised that in view of the circumstances set forth in paragraph 4 below, it is considered highly desirable that this information be released to the press here at 1800A hours, 24 December, and that the War Department should confirm to your headquarters the next of kin has been notified prior to that time.

3. The next of kin of Major Miller is Mrs. Helen D. Miller (wife), Cotswold Apartments, Byrne Lane, Tenafly, New Jersey, telephone, Englewood 3-7311.

4. A Christmas Day broadcast has been scheduled which will be released to the United States. Major Miller was to have participated in this program. It is thought considerable publicity has been given to this broadcast in the United States.

For the Supreme Commander:

T. J. DAVIS,
Brigadier General,
Adjutant General.

8 - 1163

CONFIDENTIAL

DECLASSIFIED
DOD Dir. 5200.9 Sept. 27, 1958
NMW by. date 8/29/10

DECLASSIFIED
NND760210
By

Fig. 20 - Letter - General Davis to General Eisenhower December 22 1944

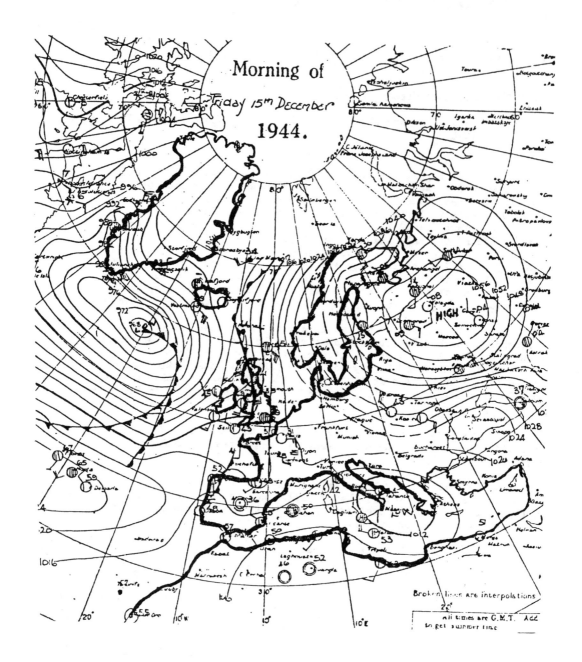

Fig. 21

Synoptic Weather Situation - Friday December 15 1944

METEOROLOGICAL OFFICE Met O 7a
London Road Bracknell Berkshire RG12 2SZ

Telex 84160   Telephone 0344 (Bracknell) 20242 ext 2349

Our reference
AF/M1074/69/Met O 7a

Date
2 October 1972

Dear Mr Edwards

As promised in my letter dated 22 September, I am now able to supply an appraisal of the likely weather conditions over the route from Twinwoods, Bedford to Orly, Paris during the late afternoon of 15 December 1944.

Considering each of the main elements in turn, to the best of our knowledge the position was as follows. Please note that all heights quoted are above mean sea level.

Cloud amounts and types. For take-off there was probably only small amounts of thin layered cloud base between 2000 and 4000 feet but cloud would have soon increased to become ½ to ¾ cover over Essex, and probably remained so over the Thames Estuary and Kent. Along the south coast and over the English Channel, cloud probably was full cover of stratus base 1500 feet top 2000 feet, possibly with further broken layers of stratocumulus above, with tops up to 3500 feet. Over France itself ¾ to full cover of layered cloud would be expected, base 800 to 1500 feet tops 2000 to 3000 feet. In addition, over the Channel and France ¾ to full cover of medium layered cloud base 8000 feet top 11000 to 14000 feet was reported.

Visibility. To the north of the North Downs, a good deal of fog and mist were reported on the day in question, with visibilities varying between 500 and 2000 yards. Over Kent and the English Channel visibility was of the order 1½ to 2½ nautical miles. However, over France visibility was probably curtailed to 1500-2500 yards, and perhaps with some fog patches in the vicinity of Paris itself with visibility around 500 -1000 yards.

Winds and temperatures.

	Bedford – south coast	South coast – Paris
At 3000 feet	180 degrees 12 knots – 1°C	160 degrees 15 knots – 1°C
At 5000 feet	190 degrees 10 knots – 1°C	190 degrees 15 knots – 1°C
At 10000 feet	230 degrees 10 knots – 9°C	240 degrees 15 knots – 7°C

Icing. The height of the zero Celsius isotherm over the route was generally 2000 feet except over France where it was probably somewhat lower at 1500 feet. Temperatures were close to zero Celsius between 2000 feet and 6000 feet over much of the route. No reports of aircraft icing during the period in question can be traced. However, medium opaque icing had been reported over Kent at about 0800 am, in the layer of medium cloud which had moved to France by the late afternoon.

Yours sincerely

C F NEAVE

Fig. 22

Actual Weather Report - Friday December 15 1944

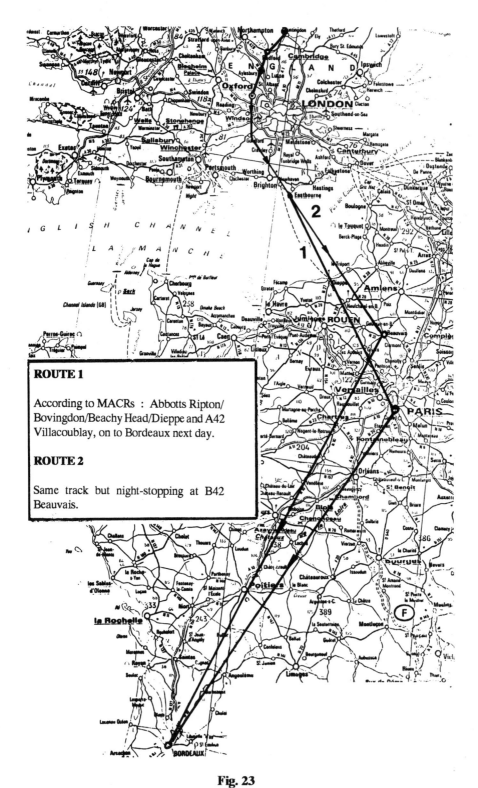

ROUTE 1

According to MACRs : Abbotts Ripton/
Bovingdon/Beachy Head/Dieppe and A42
Villacoublay, on to Bordeaux next day.

ROUTE 2

Same track but night-stopping at B42
Beauvais.

Fig. 23

Map of Cross-Channel Routes

IN REPLY CITE : 8AFSC-D-832-G-27 A   DEC 20   INTERNAL ADDRESS :
FROM : HQ EIGHTH AFSC   TO : G-1 SECTION, SHAEF
                                              (MAIN) ATTN : GEN.
                                              BARKER

TO :   SHAEF (MAIN)

INFO : SHAEF (REAR)   SGD : EARLY
       HQ, USSTAFF

Confirming verbal information to G-1 SHAEF Rear C-64 airplane
number 44-70285 missing and unreported since departure Twinwood
Field 1355 hours 15 December for France pilot Flight Officer Morgan
2 passengers including Major Glenn Miller

USSTAFF MAIN DISTRIBUTION

   : M/OPS
     AG RECORDS

USSTAF MAIN IN 7055

THE MAKING OF AN EXACT COPY OF THIS MESSAGE, OR ANY PART THEREOF, IS FORBIDDEN. IF ADDITIONAL COPIES
ARE NECESSARY, THEY WILL BE PARAPHRASED VERSIONS AND WILL BE MARKED WITH THE SECURITY CLASSI-
FICATION INDICATED HEREON. THE COPY WILL BE SAFEGUARDED WITH THE GREATEST OF CARE.

Fig. 24

Genuine Confirmatory Signal to SHAEF – December 22 1944

WAR DEPARTMENT

THE ADJUTANT GENERAL'S OFFICE

WASHINGTON 25, D. C.

FINDING OF DEATH OF MISSING PERSON

Pursuant to the provisions of Section 5 of the Act of 7 March 1942 (Public Law 490 77th Cong.) as amended, upon direction and delegation by The Secretary of War, The Chief, Casualty Branch, The Adjutant General's Office, finds Major Alton G. Miller, Army Serial Number 0505273, Air Corps,

to be dead. He was officially reported as missing ~~in action~~ *as of the* 15th *day of* December 194 4. *For the purposes stated in said Act, death is presumed to have occurred on the* 16th *day of* December, 194 5.

BY ORDER OF THE SECRETARY OF WAR

George F. Herbert

ADJUTANT GENERAL
CHIEF, CASUALTY BRANCH

SUMMARY OF INFORMATION

AREA		FLYING STATUS	JUMP STATUS	LINE OF DUTY	OWN MIS- CONDUCT	ON DUTY STATUS	ABSENCE AUTH'D
European		No	No	Yes	No	Yes	

PREVIOUS REVIEWS							
None							

DATE OF BIRTH	HOME ADDRESS		DATE OF ENTRY ON CURRENT ACTIVE SERVICE	LENGTH OF SERVICE (AS OF PRESUMED DATE OF DEATH)		
				YEARS	MONTH	DAYS
1 Mar 1904	Tenafly, New Jersey		8 Dec 1942			

EMERGENCY ADDRESSEE

NAME	RELATIONSHIP	ADDRESS
Mrs. Helen D. Miller	Wife	Byrne Lane Tenafly, New Jersey

BENEFICIARIES

NAME	RELATIONSHIP	ADDRESS
Helen Dorothy Miller Steven Davis Miller	Wife Child	Byrne Lane Tenafly, New Jersey
Mattie Lou Miller	Mother	1740 Sherman Street Denver, Colorado

REMARKS

Distribution 56

Circumstances of Disappearance: The aircraft in which he was a passenger failed to arrive at its destination, Bordeaux, France, on a transport mission from England.

No record of service as an enlisted man.

WD AGO FORM 0353
1 FEB 1945

THIS FORM SUPERSEDES WD AGO FORM 0353, 1 NOVEMBER 1944, WHICH MAY BE USED UNTIL EXISTING STOCKS ARE EXHAUSTED.

Fig. 25

Finding of Death (Original) Major Glenn Miller

WAR DEPARTMENT   4902

THE ADJUTANT GENERAL'S OFFICE
WASHINGTON 25, D. C.

FINDING OF DEATH OF MISSING PERSON

Pursuant to the provisions of Section 5 of the Act of 7 March 1942 (Public Law 490 77th Cong.) as amended, upon direction and delegation by The Secretary of War, The Chief, Casualty Branch, The Adjutant General's Office, finds Flight Officer John R. S. Morgan,

Army Serial Number T190776, Air Corps,

to be dead. He was officially reported as missing ~~in action~~ *as of the* 15th *day of* December 1944 *. For the purposes stated in said Act, death is presumed to have occurred on the* 16th *day of* December *,* 1945 *.*

BY ORDER OF THE SECRETARY OF WAR

George F. Herbert

ADJUTANT GENERAL
CHIEF, CASUALTY BRANCH

SUMMARY OF INFORMATION

AREA		FLYING STATUS	JUMP STATUS	LINE OF DUTY	OWN MIS-CONDUCT	ON DUTY STATUS	ABSENCE AUTH'D
European		Yes	No	Yes	No	Yes	

PREVIOUS REVIEWS			
None			

DATE OF BIRTH	HOME ADDRESS		DATE OF ENTRY ON CURRENT ACTIVE SERVICE	LENGTH OF SERVICE (AS OF PRESCHLD DATE OF DEATH)		
				YEARS	MONTH	DAYS
14 Jun 1922	Detroit, Michigan		25 May 1943			

EMERGENCY ADDRESSEE

NAME	RELATIONSHIP	ADDRESS
Mrs. W. Morgan	Mother	11716 Memorial Avenue Detroit, Michigan

BENEFICIARIES

NAME	RELATIONSHIP	ADDRESS
Beneficiaries not of record		
NAME	RELATIONSHIP	ADDRESS

REMARKS

Distribution _56_

Circumstances of Disappearance: The aircraft which he was piloting failed to arrive at its destination, Bordeaux, France, on a transport mission from England.

Appointed from Royal Canadian Air Force.

WD AGO FORM 0353
1 FEB 1945

THIS FORM SUPERSEDES WD AGO FORM 0353, 1 NOVEMBER 1944,
WHICH MAY BE USED UNTIL EXISTING STOCKS ARE EXHAUSTED.

Fig. 26

Finding of Death - Flight Officer John R.S. Morgan

WAR DEPARTMENT

THE ADJUTANT GENERAL'S OFFICE

WASHINGTON 25, D. C.

4902

FINDING OF DEATH OF MISSING PERSON

Pursuant to the provisions of Section 5 of the Act of 7 March 1942 (Public Law 490 77th Cong.) as amended, upon direction and delegation by The Secretary of War, The Chief, Casualty Branch, The Adjutant General's Office, finds Lieutenant Colonel Norman F. Baessell, Army Serial Number O905387, Air Corps, ~~IN COMBAT~~ to be dead. He was officially reported as missing ~~IN ACTION~~ as of the 15th day of December 1944. For the purposes stated in said Act, death is presumed to have occurred on the 16th day of December , 1945.

BY ORDER OF THE SECRETARY OF WAR

George F. Herbert

ADJUTANT GENERAL
CHIEF, CASUALTY BRANCH

SUMMARY OF INFORMATION

AREA		FLYING STATUS	JUMP STATUS	LINE OF DUTY	OWN MISCONDUCT	ON DUTY STATUS	ABSENCE AUTH'D
European		No	No	Yes	No	Yes	

PREVIOUS REVIEWS	
None	

DATE OF BIRTH	HOME ADDRESS	DATE OF ENTRY ON CURRENT ACTIVE SERVICE	LENGTH OF SERVICE (AS OF PRESUMED DATE OF DEATH)		
			YEARS	MONTHS	DAYS
2 Aug 1900	Washington, D. C.	18 May 1942			

EMERGENCY ADDRESSEE

NAME	RELATIONSHIP	ADDRESS
Mrs. Amanda L. Baessell	Wife	

BENEFICIARIES

NAME	RELATIONSHIP	ADDRESS
Amanda L. Baessell	Wife	
Karl B. Baessell	Brother	

REMARKS

Distribution 56

Circumstances of Disappearance: The aircraft in which he was a passenger failed to arrive at its destination, Bordeaux, France, on a transport mission from England.

Comp, No rec,

N-2530358 No record of service as an enlisted man.

no = K-H-T-U-J-P,

12-27-45

55.

WD AGO FORM 0353
1 FEB 1945

THIS FORM SUPERSEDES WD AGO FORM 0353, 1 NOVEMBER 1944,
WHICH MAY BE USED UNTIL EXISTING STOCKS ARE EXHAUSTED.

Fig. 27

Finding of Death - Lt.Col. Norman F. Baessell

REPORT OF DEATH   DATE 23 MARCH 1948 ekm

FULL NAME	ARMY SERIAL NUMBER	GRADE
MORGAN, JOHN R. S.	T 190 776	F/O

HOME ADDRESS	ARM OR SERVICE	DATE OF BIRTH
Detroit, Michigan	AC	14 Jun 1922

PLACE OF DEATH	CAUSE OF DEATH	DATE OF DEATH
European Area	Airplane crash	15 Dec 1944

STATION OF DECEASED	DATE OF ENTRY ON CURRENT ACTIVE SERVICE	LENGTH OF SERVICE FOR PAY PURPOSES
		YEARS. MONTHS DAYS
European Area	25 May 1943	

EMERGENCY ADDRESSEE (Name, relationship, and address)

Mrs. W. Morgan, Mother, 11716 Memorial Avenue, Detroit, Michigan

BENEFICIARY (Name, relationship, and address)

Beneficiaries not of record

FILE
DEF C E
ADJ. GEN. OFFICE
APR 5 1948

INVESTIGATION MADE	IN LINE OF DUTY	OWN MISCONDUCT	WAS DECEASED ON DUTY STATUS	AUTHORIZED ABSENCE	IN FLYING PAY STATUS	OTHER PAY STATUS (Specify below)
YES	NO x	YES x	NO	YES	NO x	YES x	NO	YES	NO	YES x	NO BY	YES	NO

BATTLE x   NON-BATTLE ☐

ADDITIONAL DATA AND/OR STATEMENT

Appointed from Royal Canadian Air Force.

Finding of death has been issued previously under Sec 5 Public Law 490, 7 Mar 42,
as amended showing presumed date of death as 16 December 1945. This report
of death, based on information received since that date is issued in accordance
with Sec 9 of said act, and its effect on prior payments and settlements is as
prescribed in Sec 9.

In accordance with the provisions of Section 2 and 7 of the Act of 7 March 1942
(56 Stat. 145) as amended the records show that this officer completed 1 year,
6 months and 21 days of active service at the time of his death.

XC-6-036-049

3-25-48

BY ORDER OF THE SECRETARY OF THE ARMY

ADJUTANT GENERAL

WD AGO FORM 52-1
1 JUN 1945   EDITION OF 1 FEBRUARY 1945 MAY BE USED.

Fig. 28

Report of Death - Flight Officer John R.S. Morgan

REPORT OF DEATH	mo 1B 719		DATE 25 March 1948	

FULL NAME		ARMY SERIAL NUMBER	GRADE
Baessell, Norman F.		0905387	Lt. Col.

HOME ADDRESS		ARM OR SERVICE	DATE OF BIRTH
Washington, D. C.		AC	2 Aug 1900

PLACE OF DEATH	CAUSE OF DEATH Incident to disappear-	DATE OF DEATH
European Area	ance of airplane	15 Dec 1944

STATION OF DECEASED		DATE OF ENTRY ON CURRENT ACTIVE SERVICE	LENGTH OF SERVICE FOR PAY PURPOSES		
			YEARS	MONTHS	DAYS
European Area		18 May 1942			

EMERGENCY ADDRESSEE (*Name, relationship, and address*)

Mrs. Amanda L. Baessell, wife,

BENEFICIARY (*Name, relationship, and address*)

Amanda L. Baessell, wife, same as above
Karl B. Baessell, brother,

INVESTIGATION MADE		IN LINE OF DUTY		OWN MISCONDUCT		WAS DECEASED ON DUTY STATUS		AUTHORIZED ABSENCE		IN FLYING PAY STATUS		OTHER PAY STATUS (*Specify below*)	
YES	NO X	YES X	NO	YES	NO X	YES X	NO	YES	NO	YES	NO X	YES	NO

ADDITIONAL DATA AND/OR STATEMENT

☐ BATTLE   ☒ NON-BATTLE

Finding of death has been issued previously under Sec 5, Public Law 490 7 Mar 42, as amended, showing presumed date of death as 16 Dec 45. This Report of death, based on information received since that date is issued in accordance with Sec 9, of said Act, and its effect on prior payments and settlements is as prescribed in Sec 9.

In accordance with the provisions of Section 2 and 7 of the Act of 7 Mar 42 (56 Stat. 145) as amended, the records show that this officer completed 2 years 6 months and 28 days of active service at the time of his death.

BY ORDER OF THE SECRETARY OF THE ARMY

ADJUTANT GENERAL

Fig. 29

Report of Death - Lt.Col. Norman F. Baessell

The Adminstrator   46 Woodwarde Rd
Mountain View Cemetery   Dulwich Village
Altadena   London SE
Cal. U.S.A.   England

15 January 1987

Dear Sir -

This letter will introduce Mr.Wilbur Wright from Southampton in England, who is researching with my permission and approval the resting places of various members of my family.

I refer particularly to my deceased sister-in-law, Mrs. Helen Miller, who is buried in Grave No. 5, Lot 2584, and her family.

I would be deeply grateful if you would afford Mr.Wright your full cooperation during his visit to Mountain View Cemetery.

Yours sincerely

John Herbert Miller

JOHN HERBERT MILLER

Fig. 30

Authorisation Letter - Herb Miller to Wilbur Wright

AEROPLANE

Noorduyn C-64 Norseman. (Contemporary USAAF designation UC-64A).

1 Pratt & Whitney 600hp R-1340-AN-1 Wasp radial engine.

USAAF serial 44-70285[1]. (Engine number unknown).

On charge to 35th Depot Repair Squadron (2nd Strategic Air Depot detachment), 35th Air Depot Group, 8th Air Force.

Based at Abbots Ripton, Cambridgeshire.

PERSONNEL

Crew (1) - Pilot : Flight Officer John R.S. Morgan (personal pilot to General Goodrich), personal serial T-190776.

Passengers (2):   Lieutenant Colonel Normal F. Baessell, personal serial O-905387.
Major Alton G. Miller, personal serial O-505273.

FLIGHT

Type "A" mission (non-operational flight).

RAF Station Twinwood Farm to Bordeaux, via Villacoublay [2].

Take-off 13.55 hours, 15 December 1944.

Cause of loss - unknown; fate of aircraft - unknown; fate of crew/passengers - unknown; whether or not aircraft was sighted en route - unknown; whether or not aircraft was contacted by radio en route - unknown; witness(es) to airborne incident, forced landing or crash - unknown.

No search was carried out following confirmation that aircraft was missing; official acknowledgement of loss not provided until 1947 (retrospective "inventory" entry in Cumulative Loss Listing).

NOTES

(1)   44-70285 has sometimes been confused with Norseman 43-5367.   The latter was on charge to the 314th Transport Squadron, 31st Transport Group, 9th Air Force based at Grove, Berkshire, and was lost on 26 December 1944. Confusion has arisen in part becuase 44-70285 was the subject of a Missing Air Crew Report, but did not appear in the official Cumulative Loss Listing.   43-5367 did, however, appear in the Cumulative Loss Listing but was not quoted in a Missing Air Crew Report.

(2)   Villacoublay, 40 kilometres west-southwest of the Eifel Tower, Paris, was designated AAF Station A-42, being used in December 1944 as an advanced air depot by the 9th Air Force Service Command.

Fig. 31

MOD Air Historical Branch Report (circa 1973)

REPORT OF MICHAEL ANSELL MA
No. 861205
in the matter of
MISSING AIRCREW REPORT
15 January 1987

Introduction

I hold the degrees of B.A. and M.A. at the University of Oxford, and I am experienced in the scientific examination of documents and handwriting, having retired from the post of Deputy Head of Documents Section of the Metropolitan Police Forensic Laboratory in October 1983. During my 14 years exclusive experience I have examined tens of thousands of documents on behalf of the Police, Government Departments, Banks, Building Societies and other companies, as well as for private individuals. During part of my time at the MPFL I was the British representative on the Interpol Committee for identification of typescript.

On 4th December 1986 I received by post from Wilbur Wright of Southampton a number of photocopy items as listed below.

1. Missing Aircrew Report – 2 pages.
2. Fig. 33 (later renumbered 17) Blow-Up of Item 1.
3. Fig. 31 (later renumbered 18) Classification Change.
4. Fig. 12 Record Card of Flight Officer Morgan.
5. App. 13 Non-Battle Casualty Report (Glenn Miller).

I have examined these.

Assumptions

I have taken these items to be true copes of their originals except where they have been reasonably edited or enlarged in order to illustrate certain points in the text of the book.

Instructions

I have been asked to express an opinion as to:-
(a) Whether the route details were typed by a similar model but different machine to that used in the rest of the Report.
(b) Whether, if (a) be correct, the same other machine was used to type the Classification Change Certificate.
(c) Whether either of these machines was used on both first and second pages of the Report, such that a falsified first page could have been attached to a genuine signed second page.

Observations

There are two restrictions to my examination. Firstly, the examination of photocopies is never as good as the examination of originals for a number of reasons, and secondly because the type of machine(s) used here, as is often the case with Government machines, particularly of that period, were of poor quality having a number of loose characters.

The first limitation means, for example, the colour of ink and depth of impression cannot be seen. The second means that, for example, the same machine can easily type a raised 'B' on one occasion and a lowered 'B' on a different occasion. This means that two apparently-different, in regard to defects, entries may in fact be by the same typewriter and vice versa.

However, the impression is given here that the Missing Aircrew Report was printed or duplicated in some way, albeit from a possibly-typed original which incorporated the word 'pilot' as part of the original document. The particulars 'Morgan, John R.S., F/O, T-190776' and 'Missing' appear to have been typed by one machine which I designate 'A'. The particulars 'Passenger' against 2 and 3 appear to have been made by a different machine which I designate 'B'. The remaining particulars for the two passengers and the three entries '.AC' including that against Pilot appear to have been typed by machine B but on a different occasion.

I also notice that the number of passengers '2' and total '3' have a peculiar 'thick' appearance as if they may have been typed more than once. I also note that the 'B' is consistently lowered in 'Bordeaux' in the route details. This also occurs in the words 'Norseman' and 'Morgan' but not 'Norman' or 'Major' against Passenger details.

Conclusions

It is difficult to reach any firm conclusions because of the combination of the photocopying process and variable and poor quality of the typescript. It is not possible to tell, for example, how many of the details at the top right were typed, and how many stamped. However, I am able to comment that the following are likely to have taken place:
A. The Pilot's particulars (Para. 11-1) except '.AC' were typed by machine 'A'.
B. The words 'Passenger' (Paras. 11-2 and 11-3) were typed by machine 'B'.
C. All other passenger details including the three words '.AC' were typed by machine 'B' but on a different occasion.

I am unable to account for the peculiar appearance of the figures '2' and '3' for the number of passengers and total. The words 'unknown' on each sheet all appear to have been typed by the same machine, therefore I think it unlikely that the first sheet was a complete substitution unless it was by a different person with access to the same machine. However, I do think it possible that the whole Report was prepared for Pilot only and the number of passengers and their details added later, for whatever reason.

M. Ansell M.A. 15th January 1987

Fig. 32

The Michael Ansell Report on Missing Aircrew Report # 10770

3

AIRCRAFT, PILOTS AND PERSONALITIES

1. Eighth Air Force - 1944

TO grasp all the implications of the Miller mystery, it is essential to have a working knowledge of the aircraft and occupants involved, in addition to certain aviation procedures in use in World War 2. The United Kingdom airfields which feature in the narrative are shown in Fig.3.

From *The Castle* at Milton Ernest 8th AF Service Command operated Air Depot Groups on several R.A.F. bases including Alconbury, Honington, Wattisham and Burton-wood. The 44th Strategic Air Depot at Wattisham ran subsidiary depots within operational airfields including 35th ADRS at Abbotts Ripton (R.A.F. Alconbury, 25 miles north of Bedford) and the Air Depot at Troston (R.A.F. Honington). Whilst 44 SAD Wattisham specialised in servicing and repairing fighter aircraft such as the P-38 Lightning, P-47 Thunderbolt and P-51 Mustang, 2 SAD at Abbotts Ripton handled heavy bombers - B-17 Fortresses and B-24 Liberators. 35 ADRS ferried spares/personnel, using a Cessna Cub, Percival Proctor and Airspeed Oxford. All US bases were given code numbers used in signal transmission, e.g :

Station :	**101 - Camp Lynn, Air Signals Depot Medmenham Bucks.**
	112 - R.A.F. Bovingdon, USAAF Troop Staging Post.
	470 - 44 Strategic Air Depot R.A.F. Wattisham, Suffolk.
	582 - HQ 8th AFSC Milton Ernest, Bedford.
	525 - R.A.F. Heston, Middlesex (USAAF Transport Base)
	595 - R.A.F. Honington/Troston Air Depot, Suffolk.

In June 1944, four new Noorduyn C-64 Norseman aircraft were delivered to 44 SAD.

Wattisham, including aircraft #44-70285. (The prefix `44' denotes the year of manufacture).

2.   The UC-64A Noorduyn Norseman (Frontispiece)

The UC64A Norseman was a high-wing single-engined monoplane passenger/cargo/ liaison aircraft manufactured by Noorduyn Aviation Company Inc. of Montreal, Canada. Its Pratt & Whitney Wasp R-1340-AN1 radial air-cooled engine drove a 2 or 3-blade Hamilton-Standard electro-hydraulic constant-speed propeller direct from the crankshaft without a reduction, identical to the AT6A Harvard engine installation. This configuration produced propeller-tip speeds close to the velocity of sound, to generate the typical flat engine-roar for which both types were well-known. The constant-speed device automatically changes the angle of attack of the airscrew blades to maintain constant engine RPM regardless of the aircraft attitude, to a figure pre-selected by means of a cockpit control lever.

Power output at 5,000 feet was 550 hp, with 600 hp available for take-off. The gravity-fed wing fuel tanks held 240 US gallons, whilst extra under-floor tanks provided a further 150 gallons, giving the UC64A a still-air range of 1150 miles on full tanks. In practice, for normal usage, only the wing tanks were filled, giving a range of 700 miles, to increase the cargo or passenger capacity. The enclosed cockpit accommodated side-by-side seating for two pilots; behind the seats was a metal bulkhead with an access aperture to the flight deck from the cabin. Along each side of the cabin, facing inwards, were four passenger seats with lap straps, and the main entrance door was just aft of the rear port-side passenger seat. Just aft of the main door was a second bulkhead with access to a storage compartment containing the rubber life-raft, life-jackets and other emergency equipment. It was also used as a baggage compartment.

The basic construction of the aircraft was a tubular steel frame with wooden formers covered with doped fabric; the wing leading edges alone were metal-covered. The standard de-icing equipment included a heated Pitot Head (airspeed sensor) and carburettor heating to prevent ice forming in the air intake, provided by circulation of hot engine oil around the carburettor jacket. It was possible to fit wing de-icers, but USAAF Technical order No.01-155CB-1, the flight manual for the version used by the US Air Forces does not include a de-icer system. Aircraft 44-70285, therefore, was not so equipped, despite the assertations of an ex-USAAF mechanic who claimed to have serviced Morgan's aircraft the day it was lost. Two surviving pilots who flew that aircraft state categorically that it had no wing de-icers, which usually took the form of air-expanded rubber casings attached to the wing leading edges.

As for navigational equipment, UC-64A Norseman #44-70285 was ill-equipped even by standards of the day. In fact, none was carried, other than radio on which bearings and fixes could be obtained if a ground station was within range. Directional beam approach equipment could be carried (and Morgan had trained on such equipment) but again, this aircraft had no such facilities. It carried an SCR-274N radio with 3 receivers and 2 transmitters : the former could be used for voice or Morse Code transmission, either individually or simultaneously, and were equipped with tuning and volume controls. The transmitters were pre-set on different frequencies. The aircraft had no VHF radio which could carry a range of crystallised frequencies and had much improved range. Nor did that aircraft carry an SCR 595 (Identification Friend or Foe) equipment which might ward off attacks by `friendly' aircraft. In fact, the somewhat prehistoric radios had a very poor range with a maximum 25-35 miles at 1,000 feet altitude.

At maximum load, the UC64A cruised quite sedately at about 100/110 mph, but with two or three occupants and minimal load, it could maintain 120mph in still air. It could carry a useful load of 2,692 pounds, and had a slow stall speed of 55 mph. To an experienced pilot, therefore, a forced landing or ditching at sea would present little difficulty, provided he had time to set up a stable descent and prepare for impact.

3.   Norseman #44-70285

This aircraft was used frequently for ferrying personnel, especially staff officers, from *The Castle* at Milton Ernest, including Lt.Col. Norman F.Baessell. As General Goodrich's Special Assistant, he was charged with locating and recovering damaged 8th AF aircraft on the Continent, and with finding and equipping advance repair bases so that they could be repaired without being returned to English bases.

Lt. George Ferguson, based at Wattisham, had the duty of flying Baessell around Europe until September 1944, and would land at R.A.F. Twinwood Farm to pick up the Colonel. Sometimes he would drop in at Bovingdon to file a Continental flight plan, or more often, Baessell would pull rank and obtain a telephone clearance to fly direct from Twinwood Farm to his French destination. This, clearly, would give Baessell considerable scope if, indeed, he was involved in black market activities. George made three Continental trips with the Colonel, usually lasting 2 weeks, but Baessell was a brash reckless individual with scant respect for his own or others' safety - his favourite aphorism was `What d'you wanna do - live forever ?'. The pilot had first met Baessell in New Orleans, where the Colonel was his Commanding Officer, and he became increasingly concerned about the staff officer's reckless behaviour. On one occasion, visiting a rear USAAF base in France, Baessell delayed take-off for Brussels until almost dusk, with the weather worsening perceptibly : George flew the aircraft back at 50 feet, following a railway line until it vanished into a tunnel, before picking up a tram-car heading for the airfield at Everes. He landed safely - but it was a close thing.

On another occasion, they were flying from Brussels to Antwerp and ran into the airborne invasion armada heading for Arnhem. Baessell, excited, told George to follow the stream up into the battle area and they were almost shot down. In the end George asked to be relieved of the duty, and was assigned to Brussels Everes, with one of the other UC64A Norseman aircraft. The Baessell assignment - and 44-70285 - were given to Lt. Jean Pace at Wattisham, and by that time the aircraft had flown no more than 400 hours total. The possibility of mechanical failure seemed to be remote, but Jean Pace relates that 44-70285 had an endemic history of propeller hydraulic trouble. Making his first trip to Paris with Baessell, he aborted the flight after landing at Bovingdon for clearance and returned to Wattisham. The Colonel, predictably, was furious ! Pace wrote :

`Knowing how the aircraft was equipped, and George's experiences, I decided the aircraft would be flown within its proper limitations It was not equipped to fly safely over long stretches of water and had absolutely no radio navigational equipment. I lasted just this one trip with Baessell - picked him up at Twinwood Farm and went down to Bovingdon to file a flight clearance to Paris. The C-64 developed a propeller leak on the way and we returned to Wattisham for repairs. After luncheon my boss Lt.Col.Perry advised me that I had been removed from the assignment and requested me to fly the aircraft to Alconbury, where it was* *assigned to Abbotts Ripton. John Morgan was then assigned to the duty.'*

4.   The George Ferguson Tape

We are indebted to Mrs. Connie Richards of Oakley, near Twinwood Farm, for this tape, which she supplied in 1986. Lt. George Ferguson was one of the three pilots who flew Norseman 44-70285 and ferried Lt.Col. Baessell round Europe. Another was Lt. Jean Pace, who is still with us, and the third was the ill-fated John R.S. Morgan. George was interviewed by Royal Frey, one-time custodian/curator of the Wright-Paterson AFB Museum in Ohio. In this extract from the interview we take the liberty of injecting additional information which will assist in building up a mental image of the people described. Editing has been minimised to provide continuity whilst preserving the context of the interview. The names of George Ferguson and Royal Frey have been suitably abbreviated.

It is also important to bear in mind that in 1983, George was fully convinced that the events he describes occurred on December 15 1944, whereas we know that they occurred on November 8.

FREY   Okay, now I got the date, place and centre. This is 28th March 1983, and this is the Hilton North, Columbus Ohio, and you are George W. Ferguson, Retired ?

GEO.   That is correct, sir. Retired, retarded, whatever.

FREY   Just for the record, you're giving this interview freely, of your own accord, you're not being reimbursed in any way, you're not being threatened, I'm not holding a gun to your head -

GEO.   No - except you're paying for lunch !

FREY   (laughs) Okay. Is it all right if I send copies of this to Glenn Miller's son, and to that `Moonlight Serenader' - *(Glenn Miller Society Magazine - Auth.)* and to some other researchers to spread this information ?

GEO.   Perfectly all right, yes -

FREY   Okay. Let's start with you. Where and when did you graduate from flying school ?

GEO.   Class 43C, Turner Field, Albany, Georgia. Twin-engined.

FREY   And where did you first meet Colonel Baessell ?

GEO.   New Orleans Army Air Base. I graduated in March, reported there for duty in April 1943. Baessell was commander of the 22 Air Base Group.

FREY   When you first met him, how did he impress you ? What kind of a guy was he ?

GEO.   A braggadocio. A very loud individual - you could hear him for blocks. He was a sort of military bigot - if you responded to him in a military manner, you didn't have much trouble. I got along swimmingly with him up to the time of his death - though he accused me on many occasions with his favourite expression `What do you want to do - live forever ?'

FREY   What was his background ? Do you know anything of that ?

GEO.   I know very little of his background, except I think he was either a plantation owner or plantation manager. He loved to push blacks around, didn't speak softly and carried a big stick. He apparently came from a moneyed group. Talking about blacks, I remember he said one time that `they had their place'. Louis Armstrong was appearing in New Orleans and I said didn't consider it was fair that he should have to stay in a black hotel. Baessell said that Armstrong had entertained at his plantation once or twice and he was treated as an equal. But outside the plantation grounds, he was treated like any other black. He was a bigoted individual, very outspoken in many ways.

FREY   What did he look like, physically ?

GEO.   He was a stocky individual, about five ten, five nine, in good physical condition.

FREY   You were with him on the 22 Air Base Group at New Orleans until when ?

GEO.   I was transferred to Mobile, Alabama in July, the 44th Air Depot Group. We went to Europe on the Queen Mary, landed at Gouroch in Scotland on August 25 1943.

FREY   When you got to England, where were you assigned and what was your mission ?

GEO.   The R.A.F. base at Wattisham, about 18 miles north-west of Ipswich, which was a grass field. Later they put in one concrete and one steel plank runway. My mission ? We were one of three Air Depot Groups there, falling over each, until they broke the organisation up into the 8th and 9th Air Forces and the other two groups went. Our Group split into two and I had an option, stayed at Wattisham. The Base Commander was Benny B. Moulder, a World War 1 pilot. He was replaced by Colonel Howard H. Moody. My mission involved fighters - we did modifications to them - P38s, P47s and P51s. I was a Test Pilot/Engineering Officer and test-hopped these aircraft. We also had a Piper Cub, a Proctor and an Oxford. We got four C64s in around invasion time, May 1944. We used them to run spare parts around. Around that time I was put in charge of the Mobile Repair organisations, about 8 crews repairing aircraft in the field in England. It was extended to battle-damaged aircraft which didn't dare chance the sea crossing and landed in France or Belgium.

FREY   Now somewhere along here, you met a guy called John Morgan ?

GEO.   Right. He came into Wattisham some time during the winter - Bob or Nipper Morgan. He came from English origins - John R.S. Morgan. He was a Flight officer, an American who went north and trained under the RCAF, ended up over here in England. I believe he did some operational missions, not many, with the R.A.F.

FREY   Bombers or fighters ?

GEO.   Bombers, I think - I'm guessing now. Wore the RCAF wings on one side, the American wings on the other.

FREY   He was a Flight officer - not commissioned ?

GEO.   Right. He got the `blue pickle' - second lieutenant's bars with blue bands across.

FREY   In your opinion, had he had any physical combat time ? American flight officers were commissioned after 5 or 10 missions -

GEO.   I believe so. I think we can safely assume so. I know that Colonel Baessell was supposed to have related to Major Miller, on the day they were waiting for Morgan to come in, Baessell said `Don't worry about this guy Morgan - he's flown a complete tour in B24s ! But Morgan had never been inside a B24 ! (*NOTE : This is clearly a direct quote from the Don Haynes story, but Ferguson may have read the George Simon book* "GLENN MILLER AND HIS ORCHESTRA" *published in New York originally in 1974. This interview took place in 1983. Auth.*) Morgan came in as a liaison pilot and he was limited to liaison, wasn't permitted to fly any of our fighters. He was a rather frail guy - I don't know if he could have reached the rudder pedals.

FREY   What did he look like ?

GEO.   He was a dapper little guy, well-mannered, about five six or seven. He wore lifts on his heels, if I remember correctly. He weighed around 135, 140 pounds, black hair. Rather quiet - we used to get rather boisterous in the Club at night - we'd finally get him involved but he had to be cajoled into it. I flew with him in the Oxford - he was already checked out. I'd describe him as a good VFR (NOTE : *Good weather. Auth.*) pilot but a lousy instrument pilot - the RCAF gave them very low time. I recall one flight over to Wales - Bob was in the pilot seat and I was cringing in the idiot seat, and the course was due west. We took off on Runway 18 (*South - Auth.*) and we kept drilling along and I assumed he knew what he was doing. We got into cloud and he started losing a lot of altitude, and we got close to some barrage balloons. I said we should turn onto course 270 but he was totally confused. One time he did the proverbial spin, crash and burn thing on internal instruments in heavy weather and started a tight spiral to the left. He didn't seem to know much so we concentrated a lot on instrument flying. Seemingly, the day he went and picked up Baessell and Miller, the weather was stinking and he did a pretty good job. (*NOTE : another mis-quote from the Haynes story. The weather on December 15 1944 was fair, 3000 foot cloud base, no rain. Auth.*)

FREY   In those days we had three kinds of pilot - those with a green card, those with a white card and those with no rating at all.

GEO. Right. Morgan had no rating as far as I know. I went to Brussels in September and he may have acquired a card later. I don't know.

FREY Now around that time you ran into Baessell again ?

GEO. Right. Norman F. Baessell. He walked into the Wattisham Officers Club one day, became Deputy Dog to Col. Howard Moody the Base Commander, just prior to Christmas 1943. He only stayed a month or two - Col. Moody wrote to Dale Titler *(an American Miller researcher/writer - Auth.)* describing Baessell - said he was very fastidious, uniform impeccable, but was "pretty much of a horse's ass" and Moody got rid of him, sent him back to The Castle -

FREY Milton Ernest Hall ?

GEO. Right.

FREY How did you get into the position of being chauffeur for this guy ?

GEO. I had these Mobile Repair crews ready to go into Europe after the invasion to pick all these crashed aircraft and Gen. Goodrich called Col.Moody and I to 8th AFSC. Moody thought I was being court-martialled for sure, but the General asked me `Where are all these aircraft ?' I showed him where they were and he asked how we could get to them. I said I had five crews ready and we should move over, establish a kind of beach-head. Goodrich said we should look for a permanent location - he couldn't go himself and said Baessell should go.

FREY At this time Goodrich was Commanding General. What was Baessell ?

GEO. Special Assistant to the Commander. I remember they brought a WAC outfit in there one time *(To Milton Ernest - Auth.)* and they put him in charge of it. He tried everything to get out of the way - "who the hell wants an outfit that goes on Sick Call every month ?"

FREY He was a crude type - (laughs)

GEO. He was. Extremely crude. As subtle as a loaded .45 pointing right at you. Well, I got a C-64 and Baessell and I took off - that was my first time into Paris, soon after it was liberated. Brussels was not yet liberated until 3rd September. We were up there about the 7th or 8th on this same trip with Baessell, looking for an advanced base - he was detailed by the Commanding General to do that. We did a total of three trips and they were legitimate. In the Metropole Hotel bar in Brussels one night we saw Ernest Hemingway and Walter Cronkite, Ernie Pyle and all the top reporters who surmised something was up. There was - the Arnhem invasion was next day. We were going up to Antwerp in the C-64 and suddenly this armada swooped in from England - C-47s and C-46s, and British aircraft as well. Colonel Baessell said "Follow them !" So we did, up to the point where they started shooting at us and we turned around. Baessell wanted to pursue them all the way - he said "What do you want to do - live forever ?"

FREY   He had no fear of being over enemy territory ?

GEO.   None. I never did figure the guy out - whether he was ultra-smart or super-dumb. He had a relatively good IQ but his rationale could not apply to all things, in the sense of danger. There were occasions when I said the weather was too bad and we could not go and he'd say "What do you want to do, live forever ?" but then say he'd see me tomorrow. He usually sat in the right seat, didn't touch anything or fiddle around. On our third flight, I was usually very touchy about Mae Wests *(Life-jackets - Auth.)* and he hated that - he would usually loosen the parachute straps and he'd just keep the Mae West close to him. We kept them in the locked baggage compartment and this last flight back to England, crossing out to sea, I suddenly remembered the Mae Wests were in back and no one could get to them. Baessell said `What happened to the Mae Wests ?' and I said `Well, I just hope we're gonna live forever Colonel'. He said `Well, we don't need those goddam things anyway'.

FREY   Okay. Now let's get to the December 15 flight - you were in Brussels at the time -

GEO.   Right. 8th Air Force Advance was B-58 at Brussels and we were in bad weather at the time of the Ardennes thing - it was Baessell's bad judgment to go on the 15th. Some time in October, early November, he came over with General Goodrich and said the Miller Band were opening in Paris Christmas Eve, he and Glenn were going over a week ahead of time, so he could show him around Paris. *(NOTE : Incorrect. The first concert was December 21 1944 - Auth.).* "I want you to be the pilot." I said I'd be pleased but I had to get permission from my new Commander - he's a little ticklish on things like this. He said General Goodrich would approve. Baessell called me later in Zaventen and said `Okay, Ferguson - copy this. I want you over here at such and such a time and so on -'. I said I still didn't have my Commander's approval and Baessell said `Goddammit, get down there and talk to him ! I did and when he called back, I said it was doubtful. On the day I called him at The Castle - but he had taken off with Morgan as pilot and as far as I understood he had filed for Paris. In the flight plan it was Paris and then Bordeaux.

FREY   Right. I thought Morgan filed for Bordeaux with a passenger drop-off in Paris.

GEO.   Maybe Morgan wanted to go to Bordeaux. Anyway, I started getting calls about every hour *(NOTE : at Brussels, presumably in Air Traffic or Operations. Auth.)* asking `Where do you think they might be ?' The weather never broke and they alerted Search and Rescue and so forth. *(NOTE : Incorrect. No search was ever ordered. Auth.)* I surmised that if they hadn't been in contact from some beach in France or something like that, they undoubtedly went down in the Channel. And when they hit the water the fabric-covered aircraft probably just broke up and went in 29 directions. So by the end of the second day I felt that the aircraft had been lost. The general evaluation was that Baessell had killed himself and unfortunately killed some other people with him.

FREY   Now you flew the UC64 Norseman, and you heard that broadcast from the engineer who preflighted Morgan's plane and said the de-icing system was okay -

GEO.   It had none. Some models had propeller de-icers but that ship had no wing de-icer. There was carburettor heat, in case you got icing in the carburettor.

FREY   What kind of radio did you have on it ? An organ-grinder or VHF ?

GEO.   A standard type mid-range, mid-frequency radios. *(NOTE : the `organ-grinder was a tunable HF radio using a small handle which was turned to change frequency. Auth.)* We did not have VHF - 3495 was the standard transmission frequency.

FREY   Did you have IFF on board ? *(NOTE : `Identification Friend or Foe' transmitter).*

GEO.   Not to my knowledge. These were excellent cargo aircraft, carried about 2 tons.

FREY   Right. Now, you flew over there, you knew the aircraft and the guy who flew it. In your mind, what do you think happened after they took off from Twinwood Farm ?

GEO.   Two things. One would be that they got into heavy instrument weather. The cloud cover went up to 15, 18,000 feet, so they were in the overcast on instruments. Morgan, as I said, being a poor instrument pilot, he may have got into a steep left spiral and if that happened, there was no real mechanical failure on the aircraft itself. The other thing is that he'd forgotten to put on the carburettor heat, the engine iced up and started back-firing, panic broke out aboard ship and before he could get the thing back on, they'd lost power and altitude and struck the water.

FREY   Whatever happened, it happened in a hell of a hurry. If he'd been icing up on the wings, he would have called.

GEO.   He would have called - and also changed altitude. Many times in heavy wing icing you can climb to get out of it. Those radios didn't have much of a range, intentionally so. He may have been out of range, crossing out over Southampton, for a landfall near Le Havre. *(NOTE : we found this extract amazing. Ferguson had done the trip to Paris a number of times, via Dymchurch to Cap Gris Nez for a short sea crossing - yet he suggests Morgan might attempt the 90-mile Southampton-Le Havre crossing ! And why would Morgan be so far west as Southampton ? Auth.)*

FREY   I always assumed there were certain channels you had to use - when you flew to Paris you crossed out over the South Coast. Most people think Morgan took off from Twinwood Farm, flew directly south on the west side of London to the English Channel, Brest Peninsula and then turned east to Paris. According to you, you didn't do that. As long as you weren't over enemy territory you made a direct flight. *(NOTE : Frey, we believe, had but a rudimentary concept of European geography. The idea that any pilot bound from Bedford to Paris would fly almost*

400 miles to Brest on the west coast of France and another 300 eastwards to Paris is ludicrous. Auth.)

GEO. Depends which way you went. East of London there was the buzz-bombs and there were channels reserved for anti-aircraft firing, barrage balloons and so forth. But the route that *they* had was completely free of operational aircraft and you just drew a straight line on the map.

FREY In other words he was going south-east from Bedford to Paris, east of London. I always assumed they went down in the Channel somewhere off the south coast -

GEO. They probably crossed at the widest part. Southampton to Le Havre is one of the widest parts of the Channel - 98 or 105 miles. *(NOTE : We were at a loss to explain why Ferguson imagined Morgan would deliberately choose the longest and most dangerous sea crossing, or such a long flight when he was pressed for time to get to his destination before darkness fell. Auth.)*

FREY When you flew from Brussels to Wattisham, which way did you go ?

GEO. The only thing we had to avoid was Dunkirk - the Germans were holed up in there right to the end of the war. Three towns you had to avoid -

FREY Zeebrugge, Dieppe and Dunkirk - *(NOTE : Both men were way off line here. Zeebrugge and Dunkirk were much too far east to worry Morgan, whilst Dieppe was liberated by the Canadians on September 1 1944, three months before the Norseman went down. Auth.)* Here's a hypothetical situation. Let's say that before they took off, Miller said he'd like to see some enemy territory, like Dunkirk, St.Nazaire, Cherbourg, one of those occupied towns. If he said that, what would be the reaction of Morgan and Baessell ? *(NOTE : Another extraordinary statement ! St.Nazaire is at the mouth of the Loire Estuary on the distant west coast of France, far from the Channel. Cherbourg is even further west than Southampton and Dunkirk, as we said, was far to the east of the English Channel. Why should Frey suggest these places, when the nearest occupied enclave was Dunkirk ? Auth.)*

GEO. First, I don't think Miller would have said that. I think he was just interested in getting from Point A to Point B. He knew that all enemy territories other than these enclaves were pushed up back to the Rhine. You had a NOTAM - Notice to Airmen - to avoid Dunkirk and Morgan knew that. He could have taken a low pass over St.Nazaire - that's possible. *(NOTE : That was impossible. With a take-off time of 13.25 from Abbotts Ripton, Morgan had barely enough time to make Beauvais (or Paris, as Haynes would say) before dark. Further, St.Nazaire had long since been liberated. Why would Frey, an experienced pilot, suggest such a thing ? Auth.)*

FREY Now, how about all these rumours about Baessell being mixed up in the black market ?

GEO. I can't confirm that now. He could have been -

FREY   You want this on or off the record ?

GEO.   No - for these reasons. Every time we flew to the Continent, our first destination was Paris. Just before take-off, a weapons carrier would pull up with these supplies from the Post Exchange which were put aboard. Mostly cigarettes. I said to Baessell one time `That's a hell of a lot of cigarettes' and he said `Well, the guys over there can't get any and I'm doing them a favour bringing this over !' *(NOTE : Untrue. The US Army gave cigarettes top priority - Auth.).* For me, it was `keep your mouth closed, your bowels open and stay out of the Orderly Room' - I thought that as Goodrich was authorising these flights, maybe it was okay. Dale Titler asked me if I knew the brand and I was almost sure it was Chesterfields, all in white cases, maybe 5 or 6 cases. *(NOTE : in France in 1944 cigarettes were used as currency or to barter. After four years of occupation the French had virtually no luxuries but plenty of money - francs were still interchangeable with other currencies until the BAF money was brought in. Civilians might pay the equivalent of £5.00 for a pack of cigarettes - so 5 cases represented a large sum of money. Auth.)* I did think at one time it was strange all being the same brand - if they had been for a squadron or some unit, it made sense to take different brands. Baessell would always come back with some perfume and a box or two of champagne -

FREY   But you never saw him benefit personally from this ?

GEO.   No. We landed, he was met with military transportation and he would say `Ferguson, I will see you here on Wednesday at 08.00' or something like that.

FREY   Now, you said the day after Miller went down you got a call - but Don Haynes said the first thing they realised Miller was missing was on 18 December ?

GEO.   I do recall that - I could have been wrong on that. But I think it was the day after - we got a call from Flying Control to say `Had Flight Officer Morgan landed there ?' or `Where is Miller ?' and I said `They didn't come in here - the weather was stinking and they turned back !' They said `No, he didn't return here'. It was a Flying Control inquiry, they went on for a couple of days. *(NOTE : This is a very important extract. We know that the Norseman was posted missing late on Friday afternoon, and that ATC at Beauvais and Alconbury would be making telephone inquiries to all bases at which Morgan may have landed. But they would inquire at Air Traffic Control, not Ferguson's office. Unless he was in the Tower on Saturday morning December 16, it is difficult to understand how he could have received such a call, since Morgan would not be anywhere near Brussels, more than 100 miles east of Cap Gris Nez. And why did George Ferguson say they had turned back because of bad weather ? But this item confirms that 8th AFSC knew the Norseman was down by Saturday morning - but did not inform Haynes because there was no need - Miller was not board the plane. Auth.)*

FREY   Now, Morgan - did he, or did he not file a flight plan ?

GEO.   Oh yes - he would have to.

FREY I've never seen or heard of anyone who has seen the flight plan. A lot of people say that he didn't file a flight plan - *(NOTE : Morgan filed no flight plan from Bovingdon. Baessell obtained telephone clearance from Abbotts Ripton direct to Beauvais. Auth.)*

GEO. He may have filed it from the other base -

FREY Wattisham, you mean ?

GEO. I don't think he came out of Wattisham that morning - he was supposed to come from some other point. Flying Control officers always wanted Arrival Reports - they wanted to know where the aircraft got to at night. That was probably the first call I got. And then shortly after that some discreet calls from Staff members asking `Where's Miller ?' *(NOTE : Presumably from Milton Ernest ? But George Ferguson was out of order here - because we know beyond reasonable doubt that Miller was not aboard the Norseman. These calls may well have been inquiries about Morgan and his C-64, but not about Miller. Ferguson, for some reason, embroidered his story but went too far. His memory may have been suspect : certainly he confused the November 8 flight with that on December 15. Auth.)*

FREY Could it have been that these people who were trying to find the airplane actually never officially reported it was down and it never got to top level ?

GEO. They were afraid to, I think, because this was an incident that was earth-shaking in a way - *(NOTE : Of course it had been reported - why else would Ferguson be receiving Air Traffic Control phone calls about Morgan ? Auth.)*

FREY Were you and Morgan still based at Wattisham on the 15th ?

GEO. I'd been permanently transferred to Brussels. Morgan was still based at Wattisham.

FREY But you don't think he took off from there ?

GEO. I'm not sure. I had no idea he was anywhere in the area. When they said that Major Miller and Col. Baessell had left I said `Did they go to the Club ?' and they said "Oh no, sir - they took off !" *(NOTE : There is a peculiar phrase following the word `left' we were unable to decipher. It sounded like `L...S.' or Ellis or `left the list on'. We were never entirely happy about it. It may well have been `Abbotts Ripton'. Auth.)* I was over-whelmed. I said `Who's the pilot ?' and they said Flight Officer Morgan. I remember thinking `Oh, my God.'

FREY But he was in one of the four C-6 3 from Wattisham ?

GEO. Right. One of them was transferred with me to 8th Air Force Advance in Brussels.

FREY The American Graves Registration book has `John R.S. Morgan Flight Officer T-190776, 35 Rep. Squadron, 35th Air Depot Group. Is that where he was assigned ?

GEO. It could be that was at Wattisham.

FREY And on Baessell, Headquarters Squadron 8th Air Force Service Command.

GEO. Right. *(NOTE : This little pantomime is extraordinary. Frey, a staff member at Wright-Paterson AFB, Ohio, had investigated the mystery for years, and had access to most of the documents including MACR #10770, Reports and Findings of Death etc. Ferguson knew very well 35 ADRS was at Abbotts Ripton. He had read George Simon's book (in circulation since 1974) and quoted from it. So too had Frey, who was a close friend of the Miller family. Auth.)* Frey continues : `Now, let's kick this around a little. More questions are going to pop up -

At this point there is a perceptible editing break. The tape continues in mid-sentence :

GEO. - he was a regular officer. - AO was the reservist prefix and he was an `O'. *(NOTE - they are talking again about Baessell. Auth.)* I don't think he was a career officer.

FREY Let me ask you again, that bit about the black market and whether you wanted it on or off the record - is it okay if I pass it on ?

GEO. It's okay - it's only supposition. I do know we loaded on Base Exchange supplies.

FREY. He wasn't exporting diamonds or gold bricks -

GEO. No ! It would have got pretty heavy carrying gold bricks.

FREY Did you ever meet Don Haynes ? He was the one who was supposed to have gone on December 15 - Miller pulled him off and took his place -

GEO. No. But I did meet Miller once at The Castle. He was coming down the hallway with Baessell who stopped and said `Glenn, this is the pilot that's gonna take us over to Paris'. Here are some names - Morgan was assigned to 35th Air Depot Repair Squadron at Abbotts Ripton - we used to call it Rabbit's Rectum - and he filed for Bordeaux via A-42 which was Villacoublay in Paris.

FREY Which was a famous World War One airfield -

GEO. But no longer - it's now real estate -

FREY I went by there ten years ago and it was pretty well closed down - *(NOTE : These remarks were disturbing. We visited Villacoublay for research in the summer of 1987 and the airfield was fully developed and in use. A Guard officer told us the base had been in continuous use since 1917. We could not understand their reasoning - was it an attempt to dissuade researchers from visiting ? Auth.)*

GEO. I did three trips with Baessell, each about two weeks. I had no crew chief along on two flights. I crewed up with a sixpence for releasing Zeüss fasteners.

FREY   Right ! Now, was there any sort of official inquiry or investigation, or even an unofficial investigation that you know of ?

GEO.   I was not involved if there were. I'm sure there was because of the magnitude of the disaster -

FREY   No one can find any records at all.

GEO.   Well, I had the feeling that for a week. . . it was the 15th when he went down and the Band opened on Christmas Eve - so practically a week expired, and in that time they were covering-up. They were hoping that. . .they had their fingers and legs and everything else crossed, hoping that he'd show up and walk in and it would all quieten down, God would be back in his Heaven and the troops would be back in barracks and the Band would be playing, the officers in their club and everything's well with the world again !

FREY   But you don't know of any inquiry at all ?

GEO.   No.

FREY   Back about 1969 I interviewed Don Haynes and I forgot to take a tape recorder. A lot of this stuff I asked him, but I don't remember what he said !

GEO.   Hmm-mm -

FREY   (Quietly) Okay - let's take this off now. *(NOTE : For us, this was the most extraordinary remark on the whole tape. Frey - a professional researcher, a Museum curator, a close friend of the Millers who had researched the mystery almost from the day it happened, goes to interview the one man who had all the answers - and `forgets' his tape recorder ! And never tried to interview Haynes again. Finally, we have this obvious stopping of the recorder, after which there is no further mention of Haynes ! And the final twist is that Frey says he can't recall any of the answers that Haynes gave him. The reader must make up his own mind. Auth.)* Frey continues : `After he went, who took over Baessell's position ?

GEO.   He was just on that Special Assistant job - he didn't have command of anything.

FREY   Can you think of anything else we ought to put down for posterity ?

GEO.   In my own mind - and this is for publication - the man directly responsible for Glenn Miller's death, being lost in this aircraft accident, was Colonel Baessell. The man lacked judgement - he had an overwhelming bravado and this attitude of `What do you want to do, live forever ?' He was that type of person who thought he was possibly like George Patton, or George Washington or Field Marshal Montgomery in that he didn't have to duck - the enemy fire would never hit him, and so he was singled out to be a man of destiny, and whoever was close by him would be unharmed too. It was his lack of judgement and his military influence on

Flight Officer Morgan, as I'm certain that the weather conditions that day were not conducive to VFR flying, and the possible cause was his poorness in instrument flying and ended up in a spiral or lost altitude without knowing it, or carburettor ice, or icing.

FREY   And of course he's up there at 800 feet, he's not going to stay up there long. That's it, then - I sure do thank you, George. *(NOTE : This is the first identifiable mention of Morgan being at 800 feet when disaster struck. How did Frey know that ? Auth.)*

The tape ends with an extraordinary telephone call from Frey, intent on getting it on the record that Glenn Miller would never become involved in Baessell's black market cigarette deals, even if he was advertising Chesterfields at the time. And there is a further `editing' break in the tape towards the end. This ambiguous tape caused us considerable misgivings : there was Ferguson quoting the Haynes story and Simon's book about Morgan's combat missions on B-24s, and the fictitious bad weather on December 15 1944. There was his confusion, deliberate or otherwise, between the two flights (November 8, December 15) and his insistence that no search took place (but that `search and rescue were notified'); we wondered how he managed to take a phone call between two Air Traffic Control Towers about Morgan's aircraft, and especially, his calls from 8th AFSC staff officers - which could have been true if Glenn Miller had really been on the Norseman. But those calls could not have happened unless, perhaps, the inquiry was for Morgan and his C-64, not for Miller.

Worse - George insists the Norseman iced up and ditched in the Channel, that perhaps Morgan crossed from Southampton to Le Havre or even flew to Cherbourg before heading east for Paris. We have Frey talking about a route via the Brest Peninsula or St. Nazaire, and his interview with Haynes at which he `forgot to take along a tape recorder . .'

We must ask why George told someone on the telephone `*No, they didn't land here - the weather was stinking and they turned back. . .'* Did he know something that no one else knew ? There seemed to be no logical reason why both men should suggest (incorrectly) that Villacoublay no longer existed as an airfield, and there were all those disquieting breaks in an obviously edited tape. Moreover, as the introduction indicates, it was targeted not only at the Glenn Miller Society (the membership of which still clings to the Norseman legend despite the evidence) but at Glenn Miller's son Steve and *all other researchers* !

Was it possible the tape had been a specially-prepared exercise in misinformation, just too good to be true ? Surely it should have centred around Frey's meeting with Don Haynes, at which we believe Frey learned much more than he was prepared to put on record, possibly to protect the Miller family, who regarded him as a close friend.

Whilst Royal Frey's letters were helpful to a degree, his tape had seriously undermined my confidence and I could detect an underlying resentment of my researches in America and Altadena, California, when we investigated the matter of the unused graves in the Helen Miller Burial Lot. Sadly, Royal Frey died in Spring 1993 before we could meet. But I had written to him in 1987 asking some pertinent questions, and he replied on 19 January :

`The reason I did not mention the Don Haynes draft (MINUS ONE) to George Ferguson was because I wanted unclouded responses to my questions. I learned years ago that when interviewing in person, never to bring in facts, thoughts,

ideas, conjectures etc. that might have some effect upon the answers the subject being interviewed would give. I knew Don Haynes and never considered his draft fictional. In fact, in 1969 I spent quite some time with him in Los Angeles discussing Miller's last flight and not once did I have reason to suspect he was not completely truthful to the best of his memory. It was at that time he loaned me his copy of MINUS ONE in order to make a copy. Since it had been typed in the late '40s from notes he made during his days in England, possibly he did include some inaccuracies due to limited recall, confusion as to exact facts. etc.'

Frey's remarks are baffling in the context of the Ferguson tape, for he spends much of the tape telling George what *his* ideas are. Whilst MACR #10770 was widely available in 1969, Frey avoids the subject when discussing Morgan's departure and destination airfields. He continues :

`*I also know his widow Polly quite well and I would trust her with my check book. She is a wonderful old lady and 100% honest. If Don Haynes had hood-winked all of us, he did the same to his wife. And that I cannot believe. There were several points in George's responses on that tape that did not jell with me, and I have wanted to get with him in order to explore them further. But to date I have not been able to arrange this because of personal family matters that require my time practically every day.*
`*I wish I could be of some assistance to you in this matter because no one wants more than me to see someone come up with 100% proof of what happened to Miller. His son Steve is almost like one of my family, and I know how deeply all this trash that has floated around thru the years has gotten to him.'*

In March 1987 Royal wrote again :

`*The day I got your letter with your approval to send copies of all the material you sent me to Steve Miller, I went over to the library, copied everything and sent the whole batch to Steve including your personal letters to him and Polly. I have not heard from him regarding his reaction. He has a lot of irons in the fire and maybe he is just too busy to drop me a line or call. Again, maybe he does not want to become involved.*

As the letter confirms, I wrote several times to Steve Miller without response. Royal's third letter was dated May 1989 :

`*I've talked several times to Steve (Miller) this past month but he never commented on your project. He is a quiet unassuming guy and this is not unusual for him. He probably figures it is none of my concern, despite how very close we are, and in reality, it isn't. He is a fine fellow and Glenn Miller would have been most proud of him. I have never met his sister. Looking at the documents you sent me, I realise how much I screwed up during all those (22) years at the USAF Museum. I had an official reason to get access to Miller's files and I never came near to what you have acquired. I even held his official 201 Files in my hand at St.Louis and there wasn't anything of interest in them except for the original* *letter he wrote in 1942 to join the US Army (after the US Navy turned him down). That letter is now on public display at the USAF Museum. Practically everything else in there was physical exams, assignment and transfer orders, and military pay records. There was not a single document relating to his `missing' status.'*

There was much food for thought there. For example - if there was nothing but routine documents in the 201 File, why had the Miller family fought doggedly for 5 years to deny access ? Why had Steve ignored all my letters ? Why had St.Louis finally agreed to provide a copy of Miller's service history from 1942 to June 1944 - but suppressed details of the last six months of his life, on strict instructions from the Miller family ? And why had they used every possible legal ploy and pressure to prevent the publication of MILLERGATE ? Was it possible that Frey, in that close circle of friends, knew the truth but was sworn to silence ? The only alternative is that the 201 File is two-tiered : one section for documents available to the public, and another protected by the Privacy Act of 1974 - in which case even Frey would be denied access to sensitive material.

We had serious reservations about the motivation behind the Ferguson tape, and our earlier suspicions were reinforced. How could such an experienced researcher as Frey be unaware, in 1983, of the existence of the two diaries - both of which were economic with the truth but of which the LOC Version appeared to be the more authentic of the two ? George may well have simply confused the November 8 and December 15 flights - but like Frey he sticks rigidly to the Haynes story. Here is an edited quotation by Frey from George Simon's book *GLENN MILLER AND HIS ORCHESTRA* - which also favoured heavily the Haynes story :

> *`Miller's plane took off at about two in the afternoon in low clouds (800 to 1,000 feet) with a mist or light rain coming down and a a temperature of 34 degrees, which meant that they wouldn't have had to climb more than about 1,200 to 1,500 feet before they would have been in the freezing layer. . . As the plane passed through the air moisture could have collected and frozen onto the wings and propeller - in fact, all over the plane. . . It would have increased the weight of the aircraft and disturbed the aerofoil decreasing wing lift. . . Also, if the propeller blades had collected ice, it would tend to decrease propeller efficiency'.*

This is remarkable. We know from the Burial File that Morgan took off from Abbotts Ripton at 13.25 but Frey quotes the MACR (Haynes) time of 13.55 hours. The cloud base was 3,000 feet - not 800 + as Frey suggests, but he supports the Haynes story of bad weather, quoting the rain situation (but there was no rain in Bedfordshire that day). He quotes Haynes' famous `34 degrees' temperature, which the Band officer variously attributed to the Control Tower thermometer at Twinwood Farm and to the bedridden General Goodrich.

Further, Frey suggests that searches continue even today in the Chiltern Hills near Bovingdon : had a UC-64A crashed, it would not have been buried deeply like high-speed fighter aircraft such as Spitfires and P-38s and may have been easy to find. He says : `*I don't think Miller's plane went down in England, unless it dove into a river or a bank of quicksand. . .'* Quicksand ? In rural England ? Having eliminated the possibility of the Norseman having crashed on land, he goes on : `*Let's assume the plane crossed out over the coastline headed for France - what could have happened ?'* Frey cites a number of possibili-

PROTECTION OF COPYRIGHT CERTIFICATE

I,..............of (Address) ....
(Block Letters Please)

hereby promise and agree not to release to any third person the contents of the Special Supplement to *THE GLENN MILLER BURIAL FILE* by Wilbur Wright, for a period of 12 months following receipt of the Supplement, or the release of the drama-documentary programme (whichever is the earliest). I understand that any breach of confidentiality will constitute an infringement of the Copyright Acts and may lead to a prosecution in Civil Court involving substantial damages. I obtained my copy of *THE GLENN MILLER BURIAL FILE* from :

....

Signed ....Date ....

WRIGHT BOOKS

A SPECIAL COMMUNICATION
TO ALL PURCHASERS OF THE GLENN MILLER BURIAL FILE

When this book went to print in May 1993, it was the culmination of 9 years of research into the mysterious disappearance of Major Glenn Miller in 1944.

You will learn, after reading it, that the three persons at the core of the remarkable events in Paris were Lt. Don Haynes (the AEF Band Manager), General Ray Barker (G-1 at SHAEF) and his ADC Major May. Haynes died in 1971, Barker in 1988, and we had always assumed that May (who was a senior officer in 1944) had also passed away. Together, we believed, the three had 'cooked up' the spurious story of the 'missing' Norseman.

Two weeks after going to press, we learned that Major May is still alive and well, 80 years of age, living in Tennessee. He is possibly the only living person who knows the true story. We have sent him a copy of this book, with a list of questions which - if answered fully and truthfully - may reveal the truth behind Miller's disappearance and the immense subsequent cover-up.

We plan to interview Major (now Colonel, USAF Retd) May. If we achieve the final breakthrough, every purchaser of this book will receive a free Special Supplement giving the new information - but on one condition. We are currently negotiating drama-documentary rights with British producers and we must prevent premature disclosure of the final revelations. The Supplement, therefore, will be sent *only* to book purchasers who sign and return the Copyright Certificate below.

Effectively, this means that by disclosing the information to any third party, you will be infringing the Copyright Acts, and also negate totally the research work of the past 9 years. This restriction will apply only for the 12 months following the issue of the Supplement, or the release of the drama-documentary itself.

ties - which include the aircraft being struck by a meteor, hitting the conning tower of a German submarine, running into a seagull. . . but then harps back to the scenario he has been preparing. `Based on the experience of most people who fly. . .what is most likely to have happened is that the plane headed out over the water in these bad weather conditions and probably iced up. . .'

Morgan, Frey suggests, had little experience and specifically, little instrument flying experience - but the pilot had been flying two years, had completed a Beam Approach Instrument Training Course to enable him to ferry aircraft in all weathers, and had spent almost a year on the 27th Ferry Squadron - he had probably three times as much flight time as the average R.A.F. pilot joining a squadron. But why did not Frey, with his wide USAAF experience, fail to query MACR #10770, and to ask Don Haynes why his name does not appear in the Report as the sole witness, and why he made no eyewitness statement ? Frey did not obtain accurate weather reports from the British Meteorological Archives - why ? And why not query Haynes' statement that Morgan was going to Orly, when the MACR states A-42 Villacoublay ? Why did he ignore the Library of Congress diary version and concentrate on MINUS ONE ? Frey was a long-time friend of the Miller children but failed to ask Helen why she gave Universal-International the Haynes' LOC diary in 1953 - when only 9 years previously she had publicly stated her disbelief in the Haynes account.

There are many unanswered questions like this - all we can do is speculate, and if we are doing Royal Frey an injustice, he has our humble apologies.

5.   Lt.Col. Norman F. Baessell USAAF Serial Number 0905387 (Fig.2)

■ Black Market Activities

Controversy has raged about his affluence and possibly-undeserved reputation. Perhaps Baessell's excuse for shipping cigarettes was altruistic - but cigarette supplies were given high priority everywhere, whilst Baessell's interests in Paris involved night clubs, restaurants and expensive shops. Troston 8th AFSC storage depot at R.A.F. Honington held all aircraft first aid kits, of which each heavy bomber carried eight, each containing 10 morphine ampoules. Colonel Baessell had little or no contact with front-line troops short of cigarettes - what else could be in those crates other than Chesterfields ?

Further, his direct clearances to the Continent avoided Bovingdon Customs, leaving him free to carry whatever cargo he wished. Beauvais-Tille had no Customs facilities - no wonder he pressurised Morgan into flying in deteriorating weather with little safety margin against being trapped by darkness.

John Morgan was at Troston on November 8 1944 when Baessell decided to use him instead of the non-available Ferguson for a trip to Paris. If, as a matter of speculation, one of Baessell's `cigarette' crates was filled with morphine ampoules, it would have a 1944 value of at least $100,000 - big bucks for a Colonel on $85 a week flat pay.

■ Baessell and the Norseman

We learned much about this enigmatic character from the Ferguson tape, but we found some extremely interesting material in his Burial File received in 1987. The first item was a report by the Identification Division of Memorial Affairs and Casualty Support Division in Alexandria, Virginia which was undated, but originated after his death, the details of which are stated as :

> `Aircraft in which he was a passenger failed to arrive at its destination Bordeaux, France, from England.`

Another official document citing Bordeaux as Baessell's only destination ! Others include his Finding of Death document (Fig.27) and an AG entry in his 293 File. Yet remarkably, his Non-Battle Casualty Report dated 19 March 1948 (Fig.69) states :

> `Died when plane crashed somewhere in the English Channel while on mission from Twinwood Field, England, to France.'` Yet his Report of Death document (Fig.29) states : `Incident to disappearance of airplane'!`

We could not explain this apparent contradiction. We will deal with the question of Morgan's route presently, but first, back to basics and an examination of the flight from Day One. According to Morgan's flight orders (Fig.36) which, in the absence of a flight plan, are the best available guide to the true route, the plan was to fly to B-42 Beauvais and then on to Bordeaux, on a personnel ferrying mission. We now know that Morgan did not visit Twinwood Farm (which was closed to all flying on December 15 1944) and he was given telephone clearance, possibly via Baessell, direct to the Continent. This is confirmed in Col. Donnell's letter to Helen Miller (Fig.58) the take-off time from Abbotts Ripton recorded in the NRB memorandum (Figs.49-51) as 13.25 hours, and lastly, the simple fact that Morgan neither landed at Bovingdon, nor crashed en route there.

In effect, this plan did not require Morgan to land at Bovingdon, west of London, and provided the anti-V1 AA Gun Box in the Thames Estuary was inactive, Morgan could fly directly from Abbotts Ripton to Dymchurch on the Kent coast (where he was spotted by a female ROC look-out). The danger area, in fact, was inoperative and, as Royal Frey points out, Morgan took the east of London route heading for the shortest sea crossing to Cap Gris Nez.

Here we come back to Baessell. If he was aboard the Norseman bound for Bordeaux, why was Morgan stopping at B-42 Beauvais, north of Paris ? We can speculate that Baessell was making a black-market contraband delivery - and it is extremely unlikely that he had official business there, because the squadrons based at Beauvais belonged to 9th Air Force. So did Morgan drop a passenger there ? Certainly, it was no one from 35th ADRS at Abbotts Ripton - we obtained the unit history and Morgan was the only casualty reported in December 1944. Nor, similarly, can we trace anyone posted as missing from 8th AFSC at Milton Ernest except Baessell. Yet the Ansell Report suggests significantly that the MACR may have been made out for `pilot alone' and the passenger names inserted later. Well, we know that is not quite correct, because the `ORIGINAL' MACR L-19 had the same names - but did Ralph Cramer refuse to sign the report because he knew that those names were incorrect ?

Now, up to this point we firmly believed that Morgan and Baessell were the only occupants, Baessell coming aboard at Abbotts Ripton. Why ? We know Morgan started from there on December 15 - but as a lowly N.C.O pilot, he would not have the `pull' to persuade Bovingdon to clear him direct to France, especially in view of the weather and his flight experience. Baessell, waiting at Abbotts Ripton for the fog to clear, knew if they delayed further, or had to clear through Bovingdon, they would not make France by dusk -

and finally got short-circuit clearance. Ralph Cramer's major difficulty, of course, was that he had been asked to include Miller on the passenger list of an aircraft which never landed to pick him up.

But why did Baessell, if he was a passenger with Morgan, pull strings to get direct clearance ? We can think of a number of reasons : first, the delayed take-off due to morning fog - Morgan had barely three hours to reach Beauvais before darkness fell. Second, if he was carrying (as he had with George Ferguson) a large load of black market items including cigarettes and possibly drugs, he knew that the aircraft would be checked at Bovingdon and he would have to make a Customs declaration. Third, if the Colonel had an appointment with black market operators at Beauvais, the most direct route was essential. Fourth, a multiplicity of routes was available but the time each version would take varied considerably.

✻ The MACR Enigma and Baessell

Once we established beyond doubt that MACR #10770 was a forgery, we tried to obtain a copy of the relevant page in the MACR Register. We needed to confirm that the ORIGINAL MACR #N-19 was not in the Register, and check the Register details against the information in MACR #10770. Between 1989 and 1992 we wrote to various National Archives in Washington for a copy of the December 15 1944 Register, but all we learned was that, predictably, MACR #N-19 was not on record.

But I discovered that Maxwell AFB Historical Research Center in Alabama also maintained a copy of the MACR Register. In June 1992 I requested one or two sample MACRs relating to aircraft posted missing that same day, December 15 1944 - I wanted to check the Register format, particularly the `Course' entry, which seemed peculiar.

I received not only copy MACRs for two P51 Mustang aircraft lost that day, but a copy of the Register page for December 15 (Fig. 70). And there was the entry for MACR #10770 - listing the Air Force, Group, locale of Loss (France), type and serial number of aircraft, date of loss - and the last column was `Number of Crew'.

This showed the figure `1' - implying that John Morgan was alone in the aircraft when it was lost - until we saw that the document had been photocopied in such a way that an inch or more had been `clipped' from the right-hand margin. We wrote back to Maxwell AFB at once requesting a full page copy - which showed the penultimate column (Number of Crew) as 1 and `Total Occupants' as 3.

In other words, the Register reflected the crew/passenger details in MACR #10770 - which we knew was forged. But the problem we faced was this : was the omission of the most important facts on the Register page accidental - or deliberate ? This was a document requested by an overseas inquirer - an `accident' seems highly improbable.

We were, by this time, convinced that MACR #10770 was forged and the Michael Ansell Report had stated the true position - the MACR was prepared for pilot only and the names of Miller and Baessell added subsequently.

On the strength of the defective photocopy, we had assumed that there were two MACR #10770s - the first was that stored in the Burial Files in Washington and circulated by National Archives for 45 years, showing Miller and Baessell as passengers, and the second the document actually in the MACR File at Maxwell AFB, showing Flight Officer Morgan as the sole occupant. But further evidence came to light to clarify the situation : we already knew that Major Miller was not a passenger, and the Norseman had not landed at

Twinwood Farm on December 15 1944. It followed that Col. Baessell, if he was a passenger, had boarded at Abbotts Ripton - he may even have been driven there by Lt. Haynes ! But we learned that his name is not included in the `missing' category at the USAAF Cemetery at Maddingley, Cambridgeshire, and also that there were Federal records in America suggesting that Baessell survived the war and drew a pension for a number of years in his own name.

Further, there was the curious Information Sheet issued by NPRC St. Louis and routinely given to inquirers, which states that Miller was the sole passenger : `The plane never reached its destination and the two men were reported missing. . .'

One hesitates to speak ill of the dead, but Col. Baessell, as George Ferguson said, was loud, vulgar and coarse, a flashy dresser and big spender, a military bigot of the worst kind in dealing with black people. Worse, he was so brash and foolhardy that two pilots refused to fly with him; a third probably died because Baessell pulled rank and privilege to obtain clearance for a flight that was doomed from the start. Ferguson laid blame for the death of Glenn Miller directly on Colonel Baessell, but he was wrong : Glenn was not aboard the ill-fated Norseman - and quite possibly, nor was Baessell. But if he was, the Colonel beyond doubt was directly responsible for the death of Flight Officer John Robert Stuart Morgan.

Why ? We know Morgan did not land at Bovingdon for clearance, but flew east of London to Dymchurch (Fig.75) a distance of 110 miles or almost exactly a 1 hour flight and an ETA Dymchurch of 14.25 hours (which corresponds very closely to the ROC sighting confirmed by a listener to a Radio Bedford programme in 1990). The sea crossing to Cap Gris Nez was 35 miles, a 20 minute `leg' with ETA 14.45 hours. The final stretch from Cap Gris Nez-Beauvais was 105 miles, a 58 minute flight bringing Morgan to Beauvais at 15.43 hours, with perhaps half an hour of daylight left. This, provided he did not get lost or had to do a ground-controlled approach into Beauvais, which would require a further 15 minutes. Indeed, Paris was an additional 25 minutes flying time, and this, of course, was cutting it very fine.

Looking at the alternative route west of London, the situation becomes complicated. Ferguson and Pace, rather than risk a long (110 mile) sea crossing from Beachy Head to St. Valery in Normandy (Fig.75) after clearing through Bovingdon, flew south to Guildford, following the rail line south of London via Ashford and Maidstone down to Hythe and Dymchurch, intersecting Morgan's direct route. But this flight path was much longer : Abbotts Ripton - Bovingdon - Guildford - Maidstone - Dymchurch was 165 miles, 1 hr. 30m flying time - and they would spend at least an hour on the ground at Bovingdon getting clearance. Morgan would arrive at Dymchurch 2½ hours after leaving Abbotts Ripton, i.e. at 15.55, with another 1 hour 15 minutes flying to Beauvais. He would reach B-42 at 17.10 hours - half an hour after nightfall. And this was no good to Col. Baessell.

Even if Morgan flew via Bovingdon-Guildford-Beachy Head-Beauvais with its 100 mile sea crossing, the distance is 275 miles, a 2 hrs.32m flight bringing him to Beauvais at 16.00 hours, 20 minutes before nightfall. So under extreme pressure from Baessell (`What do you want to do - live forever ?') Morgan departed Abbotts Ripton direct for Beauvais, and probably would have made it before darkness fell. Of one thing we can be sure - after landing safely at Beauvais, they would never contemplate going on to Bordeaux at night. The 320 mile flight would take almost exactly 3 hours : assuming a 10 minute stop to drop a possible second passenger, Morgan would land at Bordeaux at 7.00 pm on a dark foggy December night.

Why was Baessell going there - if indeed he was ? He was responsible for locating, commissioning, equipping and supplying advanced 8th Air Force bases on the Continent - but until the invading armies liberated France in 1944, replacement aircraft for the most part flew the northern route Newfoundland-Greenland-Iceland-Scotland, a hazardous enterprise at the best of times, but dangerous in wintertime. A staging post such as Bordeaux on the west coast of France would enable aircraft to take the southern route through Bermuda and the Azores - particularly the 4-engined bombers, the B-17s and B-24s which were the backbone of the 8th Air Force.

Here, we can quote the evidence of Sqn.Ldr Tony Bartley, DFC and Bar, a Battle of Britain ace who now lives in Southern Ireland. On December 10 1944, he flew a Transport Command C-47 Dakota into Bordeaux-Merignac, Base Y-37, with Lt.Tony Pulitzer USAAF as co-pilot, on a very similar mission to Baessell - to open up the field as an R.A.F. Transport Command Staging Post. They found the base was operated by the Free French and it was operational from 6 December 1944, housing two medium bomber squadrons of 8th Air Force.

Bartley and Pulitzer came to an arrangement with the Free French to purchase ground equipment and a sum of $2,000 changed hands. The pilots got back in their aircraft the next day and returned to Northolt near London. Four days later Baessell left Abbotts Ripton and reason suggests that he intended to open up the base as a staging post for 8th Air Force aircraft crossing the Atlantic by the southern route through the Azores.

The whole question of Baessell's flight to Bordeaux must also be considered in the light of the Bordeaux Search Letter in the Burial File (Fig.39 and Page 98). We have also considered, earlier in this book, the possibility that Morgan may have flown direct from Abbotts Ripton to Bordeaux, but the length of sea crossing and his orders in his Service Record Card appear to rule that out.

The Memorial Affairs Identification Data document (Page 137) contains some hitherto unknown information about Col. Baessell : he was 5 feet eight inches tall, weighed 164 pounds, had never fractured any bones and he had no tattoos or distinguishing marks. We have previously mentioned the dental data requested in October 1950 for identification purposes. His service history up to October 1943 is outlined below (but the Burial File contained no information on his subsequent movements in Britain). We found precisely the same dearth of information in the Glenn Miller file. Col. Baessell was born on August 2 1900, and he was a Catholic.

Lt.Col. Norman F. Baessell

25 June 1942	Miami Beach Florida
14 July 1942	Mobile, Alabama
20 July 1942	Brookley Field Alabama
17 Sept 1942	New Orleans Army Air Base
8 Sept 1943	AAF Station 582 (Milton Ernest)
16 Sept 1943	29 Air Depot Group HQ (Wattisham)
19 Oct. 1943	3 BAT AD Area HQ

The next line reads : `(See other side)' - but no second side covering the remainder of Baessell's life in England was enclosed in the Burial File. His `Memorialisation of Non-Recoverable Remains' document is astonishingly brief : it gives his name, rank and serial number, the date of death (15 December 1944) and place of death `English Channel'. But if his remains were in the sea, non-recoverable, the 1950 USAFE demand for dental charts from the AG in Washington could only have been for the identification of a body.

But interestingly, we note that as George Ferguson related, Colonel Baessell's tour of duty as Deputy Base Commander of 29 Air Depot Group at R.A.F. Wattisham was brief - 16 September to 19 October 1942, when he was moved to 3 BAT AD Area HQ. We were unable to determine where and what role that Headquarters played, but before much time passed, he was back at Milton Ernest working under General Goodrich as Special Assistant.

The File contained a number of documents relating to his effects, addressed to his wife Mrs. Amanda Baessell, 724 South St Asaph St, Alexandria Va. (She had previously resided at 615 K. Street NW Washington DC). We found this address thought-provoking : Baessell, and presumably his wife too, had been of Southern extraction; further we have no record of him serving in the Washington or Alexandria area, i.e. the location of the Memorial Affairs and Casualty Support Division which is the nominal custodian of the Burial Files. The items returned to Mrs. Baessell from the Army Effects Bureau in Kansas City on September 26 1945 were packed in a single carton, and Mrs. Baessell signed for the package on 10 December 1945 (Fig.71) - almost a year to the day since her husband had vanished. The items enclosed included a bath robe, lounging `pajamas', three pairs of shoes, a coat, suitcase and sundry small items.

But there is something very strange about the Army Effects Bureau advice note and Mrs. Baessell's signature. We found a second advice notice (Fig.72), this time for a `package and contents', and Mrs. Baessell, apparently, signed for this one on September 17 1945. What is so strange about these two documents ? They are signed by a Lt. P.L. Koob for the QM Department, and by Mrs. Baessell - yet the signatures on the two documents do not resemble each other in any way ! But in the Morgan Burial File we found another letter signed by Lt. Koob, in which his signature corresponds to that in the December letter to Mrs. Baessell. Clearly, the earlier (17 September 1945) document had been forged - but why ? What was in that `package and contents' ? Was it something extraordinary which could not be released to Baessell's widow ? Or had it been stolen by staff at the Army Effects Bureau in Kansas City and the receipt forged to conceal the loss ? Part of the answer lay in another document, an Inventory of Effects, which listed amongst other items books, miscellaneous articles, personal papers and photographs. We could only speculate - had these items revealed something of Baessell's black market activities ? Or perhaps mention of Glenn Miller ? Did Miller appear in the photographs ? Perhaps we shall never know - but this is yet another instance of an official document being tampered with - and all this cannot be simple coincidence.

There is one further item in Baessell's File we found strange :

WAR DEPARTMENT
OFFICE OF THE QUARTERMASTER GENERAL
WASHINGTON 25 DC

25 November 1946

Baessell, Norman F.
SN 0905387

SUBJECT : Additional information that may lead to the Recovery and Identification of Remains not yet accounted for.

TO : Commanding Officer, American Graves Registration Command European Theater Area APO 887

    1. Reference is made to letter this office QMCQMCYG
314.6, Subject Additional methods of Locating and identifying unknowns and Resolving Cases of Remains Not Yet Recovered, dated 4 October 1946.
    2. Attached hereto in duplicate OQMG Form 371 for
the following individual whose Remains have not yet been
recovered or identified :

Baessell, Norman F.   Lt.Col.   0905387

But there were no duplicate Forms 371 in the Burial File, and this made us still more
uneasy. What was this 'additional information' that had come to light ? Had the USFET
inquiry in February of that year 1946 discovered some vital evidence ? We believed it was
possible that these Forms 371 were still on file - but where ? There were a number of serious discrepancies and inconsistencies in the Baessell File which would require further investigation.

6. Flight Officer John R.S. Morgan SN T 190776 (Fig.4)

■ Origins

We began our research on the Norseman pilot by locating his next of kin with the help
of NPRC St.Louis, and we wrote to his sister Jean Gretsinger, receiving the following reply
from her son Mr. William Gretsinger :

December 3 1986   11122 Windhurst Drive
                                             Union Lake
                                        Michigan 48085

Dear Mr. Wright,

    In answer to your letter of 13 November 1986 to my mother
Mrs. Jean Gretsinger, I am her son William Gretsinger and
will do her correspondence for her on this matter.
    I'm very sorry we cannot help you in any way, as we are
both committed to assisting another researcher and I am not
at liberty to say who. We wish you good luck in your research on your book.

We found this response slightly baffling. The correspondence took place in 1986 and
at the time of writing in 1992, no other researcher as far as we can ascertain has published a
definitive record of the Miller mystery and especially, the part played by John Morgan. The
researcher, in fact, was Dale Titler in America. Initially we failed to extract Morgan's 201
File from NPRC St.Louis, without the permission of the next of kin - which is clearly not
forthcoming, but we located the Scottish branch of the Morgan family which included

Morgan's Aunt Jean who was his oldest surviving relative and next of kin. They submitted a request on our behalf to NPRC St.Louis for Morgan's 201 File. The file, they said, had been destroyed in the 1973 fire.

The story of John Robert Stuart Morgan begins in the small Scottish town of Hamilton, where he was born on June 14 1922, (Fig.62), one of eight children of Jean McGarvie and William Morgan. Soon after his birth the family emigrated to America and settled in Detroit, Michigan - his mother's address in his Report of Death and all other documents was 11716 Memorial Avenue. His sister Nan married a Gavin Brown and had five children, including Jean Nicol, living in Deans, Livingston, W.Lothian. In 1942, in common with many UK-born Americans, Morgan travelled north to Canada to train as a pilot with the RCAF. His eligibility suggests that his father may not have taken out American citizenship. We learned that he visited his Scottish relatives in 1943.

But there is a marked inconsistency in the documents which *were* in his Burial File and those which were not. The common denominator is that every missing document appears to refute the Haynes story in entirety : we were able to trace copies of the abstracted documents which were his Service Record Card from Abbotts Ripton (Fig.22), and his Forms 5 (Record of Flight Times). The former was sent to us anonymously with a Washington DC postmark in 1987, and the Forms 5 by a member of the Glenn Miller Society, who asked us not to publish them. But in July 1991 after the publication of *MILLERGATE* , we were sent two further copies by members of the public in Atlanta, Georgia and Macclesfield, England, Clearly the documents were in general circulation and we felt free to publish. This amends the information we gave in MILLERGATE.

■ **Flying Career**

Morgan's record of service was follows :

1942 - April-July	No. 3 EFTS London, Ontario Canada.
- July-November	No. 16 SFTS Haggersville, Canada.
1943 - February-March	No. 9 EFTS Anstey. Leicestershire, England
- March-May	No. 14 AFU Ossington, Yorkshire, England.
- May-June	Beam Approach Training Course. (Location unknown).
- June-August	87 Ferry Command Sqdn. 27 Group, Heston, Middlesex.
1944 - August-September	44 SAD R.A.F. Wattisham, Suffolk.
- Sept. - December	35 ADRS Abbotts Ripton, R.A.F Alconbury, Huntingdon.

George Ferguson said :

`Morgan came in as a liaison pilot and he was limited to liaison, wasn't permitted to fly any of our fighters. He was a rather frail guy - I don't know if he could have reached the rudder pedals. He was a dapper little guy, well-mannered, about five six or seven. He wore lifts on his heels, if I remember correctly. He weighed around 135, 140 pounds, black hair. Rather quiet - we used to get rather boisterous in the Club at night - we'd finally get him involved but he had to be cajoled into it. He was a good VFR pilot but a poor instrument pilot. He had no rating as far as I know.*

In fact, in the course of the Beam Approach Training Course Morgan attended in May 1943, he would complete some 60 hours of concentrated instrument flying, some in actual bad weather and the rest in mutual training (in which one student monitors another's instrument flying and keeps a look-out for other aircraft). The same applied to the R.A.F. Beam Approach Training Courses in England, some of which were at Hullavington : we can obtain a fairly accurate estimate of Morgan's total flying time as follows :

Initial training in Canada	200 hours.
Refresher course at Anstey	60
Advanced Flying, Ossington	100
Beam Approach Course	60
Ferry Squadron Heston (1 year) appr.	360
44 SAD Wattisham (1 month) appr.	30
35 ADRS Abbotts Ripton, October appr.	20
35 ADRS November + December	19

His total hours, therefore, were about 850 and included no operational missions. We estimated his flying time at Heston as 30 hours a month, but was probably less. But these figures caused us to look again, more closely, at George Ferguson's evidence about Morgan's sub-standard instrument flying capabilities. Remember that George repeated the Haynes story about Morgan having flown 34 bomber missions, but George said he knew Morgan very well at Wattisham, before he went to Brussels and Morgan to Abbotts Ripton in September 1944. Further, George was a rated pilot, responsible for checking out new pilots on the aircraft in use, which would involve looking at Morgan's logbook.

From personal experience we knew that no pilot would be allowed to ferry a large selection of aircraft in all kinds of weather if he wasn't up to standard in instrument flying - which Morgan may have been before he transferred to the USAAF on May 23 1943. So the Americans took the obvious precaution of sending him on a Beam Approach Training Course involving about 60 hours of intensive instrument flying : that this training was beneficial is indicated by the length of his stay on the Ferry Squadron (1 year) which involved delivering aircraft throughout the winter of 1943 - which was exceptionally bitter. (I was snowed in for 6 weeks at a Hurricane Operational Training Unit in Scotland).

We can safely assume, therefore, that John Morgan was at least average in instrument flying ability, and had appreciably more total air time than many pilots sent on operations - which appears to contradict Ferguson's assessment and throws doubt on his whole scenario of Morgan losing control in cloud and spinning in. Further, it explains why Baessell was able to obtain telephone clearance from Bovingdon on December 15 - Morgan had an acceptable instrument rating for the flight. In fact, Haynes himself said during a radio interview in 1954 that Morgan was able to get into Twinwood Farm in bad weather `because of his instrument flying'. He had accompanied Morgan, Miller and Baessell on the November 8 flight to Paris, during which the visibility was poor (evidence of Mr. Woods) and Morgan probably had to execute a ground-assisted cloud penetration to get into Orly.

There may be viable reasons why Ferguson made these errors of assessment, but in view of Morgan's instrument training and ferry duties in all weathers, the story of him getting into a `spin, burn and crash' situation in the Oxford with George seems a little unviable, to say the least. The pilot's experience was comparable to mine : I left Operational Training Unit with 400 hours (100 on Hurricanes) flew 300 hours as a bomber attack instructor and began operations on Hawker Tempests in 1945 with 700 hours total time).

■ At Abbotts Ripton

When Morgan came to Abbotts Ripton three months before his death, his Primary T/O (Table of Organisation) Mission was Assistant Engineer Officer and Assistant Flight Test and Flight Line Officer, but his principal duties were liaison, ferrying senior officers from 8th AFSC 25 miles away at Milton Ernest, and the delivery/collection of spares in any available general duties aircraft. These included the C-64 Norseman, Proctor and Oxford, and during flying training in the UK he also flew the Tiger Moth. He never flew a fighter or bomber, and contrary to the belief of some researchers, he was not Gen. Goodrich's personal pilot. The General had a personal B-17, probably of an early and obsolescent type since the B-17G with dorsal fin, nose and ventral gun turrets was in general use by December 1944.

So Morgan, based at Wattisham in August, probably flew the Proctor and Oxford, sometimes accompanied by George Ferguson until Norseman 44-70285 was transferred to Abbotts Ripton in September 1944 and George flew off to Brussels in his own C-64. Certainly, the Forms 5 confirm that in November 1944 Morgan flew the Norseman only 7 times and twice in December. He was most certainly not in good flying practice on December 15. Two weeks had passed since he last flew in from Paris with Col. Baessell on December 2.

Some one at Abbotts Ripton, in December 1944, made a clean sweep : all the aircraft documents, copies of orders, flight plans, details of missions flown and John Morgan's Flying Log Book had been removed - and when his next of kin were sent his Forms 5 for November and December, on June 12 1945, the log book was not enclosed. But from various records and witness statements, we can identify the flights he did make in the last two months of his life :

Date	Duration	Landings	Route/Duty
Nov. 6	1 hr. 45m.	4	Various UK bases incl. Troston, R.A.F. Honington
8	3 hr. 30m.	3	Twinwood-Bovingdon (drop Miller) Orly.
10	1 hr. 10m.	1	Local flight Paris Area.
18	2 hr. 40m.	2	Twinwood (drop Baessell) Abbotts Ripton.
28	2 hr. 50m.	2	Twinwood (pick up Baessell) Orly.
29	2 hr. 15m.	2	Twinwood (drop Baessell) Abbotts Ripton.
30	2 hr. 10m.	2	Twinwood (pick up Baessell) Orly.
Dec. 2	2 hr. 40m.	2	Twinwood (drop Baessell) Abbotts Ripton.
15	Appr. 90m.	1	Ditched English Channel 6m west of Le Touquet.

■ The November 8 Flight

The average time for the five completed Continental flights out or inbound is 2 hr. 35m. which agrees with the total distance and the C-64 cruising speed of about 110 mph. But why was the November 8 flight an hour longer ? On that flight Morgan had to land at Bovingdon to drop Glenn Miller, but had been cleared all the way to the Continent before leaving Abbotts Ripton, by Col. Baessell - and this applied to the five completed flights and the fateful December 15 flight. In other words, as Ferguson and Pace confirm, it was SOP for Baessell, who wanted to get to Paris fast and wasn't prepared to go through the hassle of landing for clearance at Bovingdon.

George Ferguson confused the November 8 and December 15 flights accidentally : Don Haynes did so deliberately, using events from the earlier flight to add authenticity to his story. From evidence in the Haynes diary and other sources, on Tuesday November 7 Glenn and the Band played at the Granada Theatre Bedford; Miller was booked on a Bovingdon flight next day for the November 15 SHAEF Band tour conference. He planned to drive the 50 miles from Bedford, but Baessell, hopefully poised to fly to Orly next day with Ferguson, offered to drop Glenn at Bovingdon. Haynes was to drive Miller and Baessell to Twinwood and go to Paris with them. The Band could manage without them for a few days.

But Ferguson dropped out and Baessell had to use Morgan, who was at Troston, the 8th AFSC depot at R.A.F. Honington. After waiting for clearance until midday Morgan flew his C-64 to Twinwood Farm, where he was waiting when the three men arrived from Milton Ernest soon after 13.30 hours. They boarded the plane and took off about 13.45 hours, dropping Glenn Miller at Bovingdon, Morgan flew on to Orly with Baessell and Haynes, who used the same take-off time in his fictitious December 15 account.

■ The Dixie Clerke Story

Confirming evidence came from two sources : a WAAF working in Twinwood Control Tower at that time, Dixie Clerke, related that she came on duty at 13.00 hours to find a Norseman parked outside the Control Tower. From the balcony she saw three men arrive in a staff car : the 'tall Entertainments officer' (Lt.Haynes), Glenn Miller and Col. Baessell, who used Twinwood frequently. The pilot was a 'Warrant Officer' (USAAF Flight Officer). They boarded the Norseman and took off. She heard Morgan radio Bovingdon for permission to land and drop a passenger, and later heard Morgan take off and leave the frequency.

But Dixie, like many others, confused dates. She described the weather as sunny (untrue for December 15, correct for November 8); the airfield was open (it was closed on December 15) and most of the Band boarded a large 4-engined aircraft; the rest were to be picked up at Bovingdon. But this actually happened on Monday December 18 ! Confirming evidence : the majority of the Band were picked up at Twinwood on Monday December 18 by two C-47s, whilst a third picked up the remainder at Bovingdon. Four-engined DC4 planes were reserved for long-distance flights - and strangely, in the 1953 film 'The Glenn Miller Story' the Band arrived at Orly in a DC-4. Dixie had obviously seen the movie !

Now, Mr. Alex Sleap, a civilian ground engineer employed at Bovingdon in 1944 to meet visiting aircraft, was a Glenn Miller fan and saw him arrive in a Norseman and later board a C-47 for Paris. Sleap was photographed standing beside Morgan's Norseman; he had checked a possible fuel leak, identified as an overflow from the filler cap, clearly visible in the photograph (Fig.55). In 1992 Mrs.Standen wrote from Chingford to say that she had a print of the photo given to her husband by Mr.Sleap. On the back is written 'Bovingdon, Herts 1944. Norseman - Glenn Miller's.'

Major Miller, beyond doubt, had trans-shipped from a Norseman to a C-47 at Bovingdon - but was it on November 8 or December 15 ? The solution lay in the photograph itself : a light coating of snow lay on the ground, and we checked the weather archives for Bovingdon very carefully. We learned that it had not snowed on December 14 or 15 - but there had been light falls on November 7 and 8 !

The story was now taking shape. After dropping Miller at Bovingdon, Morgan flew on to Orly with Baessell and Haynes. The latter returned to Twinwood Farm a few days later in Gen. Goodrich's B-17, whilst Miller and Baessell sampled the night life of Paris until the conference on November 15. Glenn returned on November 18, with Mr. Wood.

The similarities between these events and Haynes' account of the December 15 flight are numerous - Miller waiting for a Paris flight, Baessell offering a lift, Haynes driving the car to Twinwood Farm. Morgan arriving from *Station 595* Honington, Morgan's destination Paris Orly and his delayed take-off from Honington because of poor visibility - all part of Haynes' story as related in his diary for December 15 1944. Don Haynes even informed General Ray Barker that Morgan got clearance from Honington ! But the final demolition of his account of events on December 15 stems from the Honington connection. If we could show that the *Station 595* scenario was fabricated, then the whole of Haynes' story would be exposed as fraudulent.

■ The Honington Connection

In Haynes' diary for December 15 1944, we read that he brought Glenn up from London the previous day, after Baessell offered the latter a ride to Paris. Next morning, Baessell phoned Haynes in Bedford to say that he had been 'unable to get clearance', that Haynes and Miller should come out to Milton Ernest for lunch. When they arrived, Baessell said he had spoken to Morgan at Station 595 Honington : the pilot said he hoped to get clearance soon and would call back. During lunch, he did so and told Baessell he would be with them 'within the hour'. The three men finished lunch and drove out to Twinwood Farm in very bad weather, to wait for Morgan to arrive from Honington. He came down through low cloud at 13.40, took aboard his passengers and left at 13.45, never to be seen again. That was Haynes' account of the December 15 trip : we obtain this imaginary timetable :

09.00   Baessell calls Haynes in Bedford, advises him to come to Milton Ernest.
11.00   Haynes, Miller arrive at 8th AFSC. Baessell had spoken to Morgan, who said he would know shortly after noon if he had clearance. Lunch at Milton Ernest would begin at noon : we estimate Morgan's return call at :
12.05   He reports clearance OK - would be at Twinwood Farm 'within the hour' - i.e before 13.00 hours. Flight time 30 minutes.
12.10   Morgan departs Honington for Twinwood, *ETA 12.40 hours.*
13.10   Haynes, Baessell, Miller arrive Twinwood Farm. No Norseman !
13.40   Morgan arrives - *one hour overdue !*
13.45   Norseman takes off, never seen again - according to Haynes.

So where *was* John Morgan during the hour he was adrift ? Perhaps, as John Edwards joked, he was 'hanging from the local sky-hook' ! Haynes was no pilot : when a layman writes about technical aviation matters such as airspeed, ground speed, wind drift, ground distances, cruising speeds and flight times, he will come to grief every time. The early morning sequence refers to the November 8 flight : Baessell had called George in Brussels to confirm he was coming over to Twinwood, but he is out of luck. He checks out Morgan, finds he is at Honington (the pilot's records show several local UK flights on November 6/7, ending at Troston, Honington, but there are no positioning flights during December !). Baessell orders Morgan down to Twinwood but the take-off is delayed.

At this point Haynes changes tack. On November 8, Dixie Clerke said the Norseman was parked at the Tower when she came on duty at 13.00 hours - but Haynes needed to stress his `bad weather' on December 15, which grounded Miller in London but did not deter the `experienced' Morgan from landing at Twinwood. So he ignores flight times, relates that he and the others waited outside the Control Tower until Morgan landed.

It all fits in - far beyond the bounds of coincidence. There is more : Haynes quotes a take-off time of 13.45 in his December 15 narrative - the same as November 8. He said Morgan was going to Paris Orly (not Villacoublay cf MACR, or Beauvais cf Morgan's records) and that was true of the November 8 flight. When Gen.Barker asks Haynes where Morgan obtained clearance, he replies : `Station 595, Honington -'. And Haynes accounts for being in France on November 8 by saying that Glenn okayed a 7-day leave and Haynes left Twinwood Farm on November 7 with a courier in a B-17 for Station 595. His leave papers said he was heading for Scotland, but he had a SHAEF pass, was going to Paris. Haynes stayed over-night at Honington, left at 08.45 am for France in a cargo-laden C-47 but had to turn back because of a terrific storm). So he returned to Bedford and flew out next day with Morgan, Miller and Baessell.

In the face of such corroborated evidence there can be no doubt. *Haynes was lying.*

+   +   +

The four short flights Morgan made commencing November 6 1944 included a final stop at the 8th AFSC storage depot at Troston, within the perimeter of R.A.F. Honington. Morgan clearly stayed there until the morning of November 8, comfortably contemplating an easy ride back to Abbotts Ripton. But Baessell, denied the use of the Ferguson Norseman, phoned Morgan and told him to get his butt off the ground and down to Twinwood. All this is not conjecture - it is written in Haynes' diary *but he said that all these events occurred on December 15 1944 !* In regard to that mission, we can state :

1. Baessell was possibly the sole passenger, or Morgan may have been alone.
2. He departed Abbotts Ripton at 13.25 hours.
3. He was cleared direct to Beauvais, final destination Bordeaux.
4. The C-64 flew east of London to Dymchurch en route Cap Gris Nez.
5. They were reported at Dymchurch approximately 14.25 hours.
6. Morgan ditched 6 miles west of Le Touquet at approximately 14.45 hours.
7. No distress call was received.
8. The weather at Abbotts Ripton was 3000 foot cloudbase, light wind, no rain.
9. Cloudbase over the Channel was 800 feet, full cover, visibility 1 mile.
10. No search was initiated.
11. Morgan possibly filed a flight plan as far as Bovingdon, planning to land for Continental clearance, but weather delayed the take-off, forcing Baessell to obtain telephone clearance from Bovingdon direct to Beauvais, to save time.

■ **Personal Effects**

John Morgan's Medical Data Sheet gives his height as 5 ft 3½ inches, weight 114 pounds. We know little of the pilot's last days - he came to London Tuesday December 12 1944 for the Band's last Queensberry Club concert, and was at the Milroy Club on Wednesday night, leaving before midnight to return to Bedford with Lt.Haynes. But we can formulate an accurate timetable of his last day on earth. His Burial File contains an extensive inventory of the personal effects sent home : strangely, most of his Forms 5 were `lost' and the remaining sheets (November/December 1944) were sent to his mother 6 months after the rest of his effects.

When we came to examine the minutæ of Morgan's Effects Inventory, we were astonished to find that in the Accounting Inventory he was shown as `Missing in Action'. And this is very disturbing, because the Inventory was prepared by Adjutant Ralph Cramer's staff at Abbotts Ripton - *and Cramer must have known what had happened to Morgan.* Is there anything in the Inventory of Effects of particular significance ? Here it is :

Foot Locker containing :
1 Jewel Box, empty
2 Pipes
1 Schaeffer pen
3 Towels, Bath
3 Pictures, Plexiglas frames.
8 Neckties
1 Cap, Garrison
1 Cap, Service
1 Overcoat
1 Blouse
2 Pants, Pink
1 Wallet, leather
1 Undersuit, wool
11 Undershirts Cotton
13 Drawers, Cotton
10 Shirts, Khaki
8 Handkerchiefs
Hand Bag, Leather containing ....

1 Undershirt, Wool
3 Towels, Bath
3 Pr Pajamas
2 Pr Slippers
3 Shirts, Pink
1 Sweater, Sleeveless
1 Perfume, Cattleys
1 Handbag, Ladies
1 Scarf Wool
1 Comb. Pocket
1 Box Misc Insignia
24 Pr Socks
1 Undershirt, Wool
1 Box Stationery
1 Dressing Robe
4 Hand Towels
2 Pr Oxfords, Hi-Taps
3 Pr Pajamas
2 Wallets, Leather

Other items included a sum of $11.30 in American money, which was refunded to his mother, and on May 31 1945 the Quartermaster Depot in Kansas City sent her five money orders for a total of $350, in US postal money orders on 4 January 1946. Remarkably this letter too shows Morgan as `Missing in Action' !

We have shown that Baessell's File contained some documentation on disposal of personal effects, whereas none were ever recovered in Miller's case. In the Morgan File we found extensive documentation, the most interesting of which was a letter from 35th ADRS Abbotts Ripton to the Effects Quartermaster, UK, APO 607. It refers to an Inventory (attached) of Morgan's effects and was dated 29 December 1944. Is this date significant ? If we look at other relevant dates for Morgan, we find :

1. Date posted missing 15 December 1944.
2. Missing Aircrew Report compiled 23 December 1944.
3. Press Release 24 December 1944.
4. Casualty Report 2 January 1945 (as was Baessell's but not Miller's !)
5. Finding of Death 16 December 1945.
6. Effects returned to next of kin 2 October 1945. Why the delay ?

7. Life Insurance settlement March 1 1946.

8. Report of Death 23 March 1948.

The letter to the Effects QM was signed by Capt. James F. Love, Commanding 35 ADRS at Abbotts Ripton (his Adjutant was Capt. Ralph S. Cramer) and it lists Morgan as `Missing on 15 December 1944'. But he was not `officially' missing until 23 December when Cramer compiled MACR #N-19. We could find no logical reason why he was posted as a Casualty two weeks after Miller, when they were allegedly on the same missing aircraft - but if we assume that Baessell (also posted missing w.e.f. 2 January 1945) and Morgan were the sole occupants and Miller actually went missing elsewhere *before the Norseman went down* it begins to make sense. It would take but a few hours to collect Morgan's effects and close his account at the National Provincial Bank in Stowmarket, although the latter did not occur until 27 June 1945 and Morgan's closing balance was £1.18.10d, about 95p in modern currency. Few soldiers got rich in wartime, except for the Colonel Baessells of this world. . .

■ Personal Papers

We could find no reference to a Last Will and Testament and Morgan's effects were shipped out of Abbotts Ripton to 2 SAD at Wattisham, Station 636, on 29 December 1944. But of much more interest were the two Forms 5 for November and December 1944, perhaps the most sensitive documents in Morgan's record as we have shown. A covering letter dated 4 January 1945 from Wattisham (Morgan's home base) to the Effects Quartermaster asked for the enclosed Forms 5 to be included in the Inventory - but why had they not been included in that raised on 29 December 1944 ? We believe they had been impounded by Capt. Cramer since Saturday December 16 when he learned that his Norseman was down, but we found it strange that the Forms 5 were sent to the Effects Bureau rather than to the AG Department (Personnel Records) or Memorial Affairs (Burial File). Even more peculiar, there is a Note on the December Form 5 which states : `*When pilot was transferred from 27 ATG (Air Transport Group) to SERVICE COMMAND many of his Forms 5 were lost'*. This meant that, without Morgan's own flying logbook (*which is not included in his effects*) there was no means of determining his total experience, flying hours and flight test assessments. This left Haynes free to assert that Morgan had flown 34 bomber missions and was a very skillful pilot !

We should be quite clear on this point. In concocting the Norseman story, Haynes had to show why Morgan could fly into Twinwood Farm in the extremely bad weather Haynes described, when `*all other flights had been washed out'*, and why he was given clearance. The pilot's flight record had to be concealed - and the best way was to conveniently `lose' his Forms 5. We believe that they were not lost in transit from 27 ATG Hendon to Wattisham - for the simple reason that records existed from which replacement Forms 5 could be prepared. 8th AFSC simply impounded the tell-tale records (and Morgan's Log Book) to support Haynes' story - but they were not destroyed : eventually, those for November and December 1944 were released on June 12 1945, copied and circulated. We believe all Morgan's Forms 5 and his Log Book were stored in his 201 File in St.Louis.

This explained, of course, why they had not been included in the Burial File - and if they reached the next of kin, as seems probable, Mr. William Gretsinger may have made them available to other researchers including Dale Titler. We believe that a copy reached our anonymous correspondent in Atlanta Ga.

Did the same thing happen to his Record Card which was sent anonymously from Washington ? It is impossible to say - but the fact remains that these two documents, and the still-missing Forms 5 originals play a major part in discounting the Haynes story of the December 15 flight.

The Burial File also included a Life Insurance document (Fig.63) for Morgan in the sum of $10,000 taken out on 6 January 1943 at the end of his Canadian training and before he came to England in February 1943. It states briefly that Morgan was carried as : `Missing when aircraft failed to arrive at its destination in France. Officially declared dead. On transport mission. It was dated March 1 1948, about the time when the Reports of Death documents were released. This certificate, with the Finding of Death document, provided the legal authority for the insurance pay-out to Morgan's next of kin, but since it would need to be released publicly, via the insurance company, it was essential to include as little information as possible. It certainly does that !

■ Morgan's Route

Controversy has raged for decades about the route taken by John Morgan that fateful day in December 1944. It was not until we gained access to the Burial Files in 1987 that the riddle was solved at last, but it will be of value to review the situation prior to that time. Up to 1972 or 1973, most people had looked askance at the Missing Aircrew Report #10770, but regarded it as genuine, despite the many discrepancies. It appeared to confirm the story told by Haynes (never officially) and the brief facts in various official documents like the Finding of Death document, the Miller Casualty Report and Confirmatory Signal.

All three MACRs gave the departure airfield as Abbotts Ripton (Alconbury, near Huntingdon) and the route as Bordeaux, with stops at Twinwood Farm and A-42 Villacoublay to pick up and drop Glenn Miller respectively. From this, researchers were able to make some basic assumptions :

* Morgan had not landed at Bovingdon for clearance.
* He had not crashed on land between Twinwood Farm and the coast.
* He may have steered west of London, over-flying Bovingdon south to Beachy Head.
* He may have flown east of London, flying direct to Dymchurch and Cap Gris Nez.

There was one apparently incontrovertible reason for assuming that Morgan took the westerly route : over the Thames Estuary was a `Diver Gun Box', an anti-aircraft artillery concentration to deal with V-1 buzz-bombs coming from the Continent (Fig.75). When the Box was active, even fighter aircraft were prohibited - as were transient aircraft whose course took them through the area. The western route seemed the best bet - but there were other problems. All Norseman pilots, including Morgan, accepted that it was not a safe aircraft for long sea crossings : engine failure over the ocean, particularly in wintertime, would be fatal. Ferguson tells us that whenever they had to stage through Bovingdon for flight clearance to Paris, they proceeded south of London along the railway lines to Ashford, Hythe, Dymchurch and Cap Gris Nez - a 35-mile crossing, compared with 100 miles from Beachy Head to Dieppe.

All scheduled multi-engined aircraft such as Transport Command C-47s flew from Bovingdon-Guildford-Beachy Head-Dieppe-Paris (Dieppe was liberated by the Canadians on September 1 1944). But the Norseman was a different kettle of fish : it cruised much more slowly than the C-47, and the Paris route described would take at least 2½ hours. No problem - on fine summer days with endless daylight. But on Friday December 15 1944, Morgan had little or no time leeway : darkness fell in Paris at about 16.20, and on the day of the flight, the weather was foggy, visibility poor until around 13.00 hours. Facing a minimum 3-hour flight (it would take Morgan 30 minutes to file a flight plan at Bovingdon) and taking off at 13.55 according to Haynes, they could not possibly arrive at Villacoublay before 17.00 hours - well after dusk - in an aircraft with no navigational aids.

Further, we have the press-on reckless Colonel Baessell, determined to reach his Continental destination that day, urging on the shy retiring non-commissioned pilot John Morgan. And two things would influence Baessell's decision to go : if he could obtain telephone clearance from Bovingdon to fly direct to his destination (which meant flying the easterly route to Dymchurch) he would avoid Customs and arrive in daylight - provided the Diver Gun Box was inactive.

Those two things settled the Norseman's fate : George Ferguson tells us that senior staff officers such as Baessell could `pull a few strings' to get clearance, and a search of all available records indicated that there was no V-1 activity on Friday December 15 1944. So Morgan was free to fly the easterly route - in fact, a force of 134 R.A.F. Lancasters from East Anglia en route to bomb the marshalling yards at Siegen, near Cologne, flew through the Diver Gun Box at 2,000 feet only an hour before the Norseman came through. And we have the evidence of a surviving female member of the Royal Observer Corps who put in a sighting report of a Norseman heading out to sea at very low level over Dymchurch about 2.25 pm - which corresponds to Morgan's 13.25 take-off from Abbotts Ripton.

Controversy has always raged concerning the MACR route : it is common to all three versions (#10770, #N-19 and the `Sample') but is markedly unclear. The destination is `Bordeaux A-42' which is, in effect, reversed - it should read `A-42 to Bordeaux' or possibly `Bordeaux *via* A-42'. So why was this particular terminology used ? We must try to avoid paranoia about deliberate `red herrings', but the interpretation of `Bordeaux A-42' by many researchers was that Bordeaux *was* A-42 !

To make matters worse, this reversal of locations opened up the possibility that Morgan's route may, in fact, have been Abbotts Ripton - Bordeaux - Villacoublay (ignoring the Twinwood Farm gambit for the moment). But we have seen that this possibility, governed largely by the delayed take-off time, length of flight and night landing facilities at Bordeaux, was untenable. Once more we encounter the inconsistencies common in the Miller mystery : many official reports including the Finding of Death documents and the Missing Report indicate that Bordeaux was the sole destination of all three men - and this anomaly triggered Helen Miller's campaign against the AG Department in 1946.

Finally, the MACR route clashes totally with John Morgan's Service Record Card (Fig.36) (which has been judged typical and valid by George Ferguson and Jean Pace). It states `*From Duty to Temporary Duty Bordeaux France B-42 for purpose of ferrying personnel per Operations Order #5, Hq 2d SAD, Office of the Operations Officer. 15 December 1944.*' That entry is followed by `*From Temporary Duty to absent missing (non-Battle) on ferrying flight over English Channel en route to B-42, 15 December.*' There was some initial confusion in which we identified B-42 as Dijon, but Ramstein AFB Historical Center in Germany confirmed it as Beauvais-Tille, also known as A-61. We have described elsewhere our reasons for believing that Baessell was bound for Bordeaux, possibly to survey it for staging post duty, and at this time we can discard the propositions that Morgan's route may have been Abbotts Ripton - Bordeaux - B-42 Beauvais, or that he may have landed at Beauvais just before darkness fell and taken off again immediately for Bordeaux.

We must differentiate between an official search for the Norseman, Haynes' search of Paris for Glenn Miller from December 18 to 20 1944, and an official inquiry into the band leader's disappearance. We described the procedures adopted when an aircraft was reported missing - in wartime it was impossible to mount a sea or air search for a missing aircraft lacking certain essential information, i.e. a reasonably accurate and recent position report from the aircraft before ditching. An approximate location might be established by calculating the elapsed time between a distress call and the last known position; for this reason all position reports included vital data on location, heading, airspeed, altitude and type of emergency. This data would be assessed in the light of the flight plan, and any decision to start a search depended on several variables : facilities available (boats and aircraft) weather conditions, proximity to enemy-held territory and so on.

Did Morgan manage to transmit a distress call ? There is no such call on record but we can make certain assumptions : at the approximate time (14.45 hours) he ditched off Le Touquet, the Channel weather conditions were poor on December 15 1944 (Figs.21,22). The cloud base was full cover stratus (layer) at 1500 feet, with tops at 2,000 feet and cloud base down to 800 feet approaching the French coast. The Norseman, therefore, would be flying at around 500 feet at a speed of 100-110 mph. The visibility was also poor - between 1 and 1½ miles. Assuming basic engine failure, the UC-64A would lose height at about 500 feet per minute, and Morgan would have only 60 seconds before they struck the water. In that period he would have to warn Baessell, check the aircraft to see if remedial action was possible (e.g. changing to a full fuel tank, turning on carburettor heat etc.) carry out ditching drill, maintain control of the aircraft and set up a controlled descent. In order to make a distress `Mayday' call on the International Distress Frequency 121.5 Hz, he would have to manually tune a transmitter by turning a handle. Even a very skilled pilot might have difficulty in coping with all these tasks in an extremely limited space of time; panic might severely reduce chances of survival - and Morgan was by no means a skilled pilot.

Additionally, the aircraft radio's range would be very poor below 1,000 feet altitude. Only one `Mayday' call was received on December 15 1944, from an American aircraft far away over the North Sea. So Morgan may have got a call out - but no one heard.

The `No search' MACR entry was controversial. If a unit had some of its own aircraft available to participate in a search, it would be entered in the MACR, but the main search effort would be organised by the Search and Rescue Organisation. The Public Records Office, Kew, London, confirmed that no search for a missing aircraft was carried out on December 15 or the days following until Monday December 18, when a sweep was made near Dunkirk for the pilot of a ditched P-47 shot down when attacking the German enclave. John Edwards received a letter from an R.A.F. F/Sgt Fox, who had served on an Air Sea Rescue Launch unit at Ramsgate, describing a multi-boat search for Miller's plane on Saturday December 16 - but we traced him to a nursing home in Sussex and suggested that he could have been mistaken because no `Mayday' call had been received and no viable search area was known. He agreed with that view.

Whilst Morgan had obtained clearance from Abbotts Ripton to B-42 Beauvais, the route as usual was left to the pilot's discretion, provided he transmitted position reports at regular intervals. Morgan may have done so - no records exist - until he reached Dymchurch, and it was mandatory to report crossing out over the coast. But for the next 20 minutes until he ditched, he sent no position report because he did not know his location accurately and he was too low for radio contact. His next report would be made when crossing the French coast inbound. And if he never reached the coast, no routine position report would be transmitted.

■ The SHAEF Dilemma

To determine SHAEF's attitude to the missing Norseman we must go back to Haynes' arrival in Paris on Monday December 18. The Operations Staff at SHAEF would have received a routine Missing Aircraft Bulletin on the Norseman on Saturday December 16, a fact which did not escape the notice of Haynes and General Barker. Further, we believe Haynes undoubtedly learned during the weekend at Milton Ernest that Morgan was down. SHAEF that week, if we are correct, was delaying all reporting procedures for one of two reasons :

1) Either they knew Miller had landed in France and was simply out of touch - they were waiting for him to make contact, or :

2) They knew what had happened and were awaiting developments.

By Wednesday December 20 they had already taken on board the possibility that Glenn might never turn up; alternatively, they knew of a possible accident or detention and made the same assumption. Barker took the precaution of getting the Norseman story on record by asking 8th AFSC to signal back confirmation, which was done by Col.Early on December 22, but they were haunted by the possibility that the Norseman might be found, with only two bodies, *after* they released the Haynes story ! This, almost certainly, was the reason for delaying the Press Release until the very last moment, and the Christmas Day radio broadcast to America was a secondary consideration.

It was very much to SHAEF's advantage, in the circumstances, to *make sure* that the aircraft would not be found - and the word went out. There was to be no official search for the aircraft - or any official investigation into its disappearance, or that of Major Glenn Miller. No doubt that, as the days passed with no news of the aircraft, confidence at SHAEF increased exponentially. Further, in 1950 when a body was located which might be that of Colonel Baessell, USAFE in Paris lost no time in signalling the AG Department in Washington for dental details - but we do not know with what result.

Lastly, there remains our own search for the Norseman off Le Touquet in 1987, which was described in MILLERGATE.

■ The Passing of John R.S.Morgan

So we can fit together a picture of the pilot's last day on earth : from 11.00 hours onwards, he waits in Alconbury Air Traffic Control for clearance. Outside, it is a still cold and damp winter day, with stratus cloud at around 3,000 feet; Morgan watches the visibility anxiously, knowing that every minute of delay is a minute late in arriving at Beauvais. Soon

Lt.Col Baessell arrives from Milton Ernest, driven by Band Executive Officer Lt. Haynes, who is waiting to fly to Paris next day with the Band. Glenn Miller has flown over the previous day by shuttle from Bovingdon. Baessell, ever impatient, chafes at the bit and watches the clock. By 13.00 the weather is clearing, visibility improving, but he and Morgan argue about the situation : the pilot says it is too late now to make Beauvais if they have to stage through Bovingdon, but Baessell says `Look, leave the clearance to me - if that goddam Gunbox is clear, will you go ?'

Morgan has little choice, and at 13.25 hours they taxi out and take off, adopting a direct course for Dymchurch. All the way south, the cloud base is lowering, and Morgan's altitude decreases : approaching the Channel coast, visibility is down to a mile, the cloud down to 1,000 feet and in a lonely Dymchurch ROC Post a half-frozen female observer notes the aircraft type, heading, altitude and time.

Over water, it comes down to 500 feet and Morgan lurches along just above the waves until he sees the coast ahead - but Cap Gris Nez is shrouded in cloud, the waves breaking sullenly against grey cliffs. Morgan turns south, tracking along the coast a few miles out, trying to find a safe ingress over the French coast. The time is approaching 14.40 - they have been flying almost an hour and a quarter - and suddenly disaster strikes, mechanical failure which is both unexpected and severe. Morgan tries desperately to transmit a Mayday message, but he is too low, too little time, and the radio range is minimal. The little aircraft skims the waves, stalls in and a great gout of foam and water rises to 100 feet or more. For a few brief minutes, the plane floats with the nose and cockpit submerged, preventing the occupants from escaping through the side doors. (Thirty six years later, a diver exploring the wreck will find both doors in position and closed).

In the aircraft, they are fighting for survival. Baessell, as Ferguson tells us, disliked wearing the Mae West life jacket, and because it would be only a 25 minute sea crossing, Morgan may not have worn his own. Their only hope is the rubber life raft - but that is in the aft baggage compartment - covered with life jackets, baggage, Col. Baessell's crates of `cigarettes', the emergency tool kit, survival kits, engine cover and a hundred and one essential items. The plane is sinking : abandoning the raft, the men escape through the rear door just in time, swimming desperately - but the December sea temperature is but a few degrees above freezing and their life expectancy is measured only in minutes.

Soon, the tip of the Norseman's rudder pauses almost regretfully above the waves before sinking out of sight, and all that remains is a few bits of debris - a peaked cap, a map, perhaps a pack of cigarettes. Six miles to the east, the citizens of liberated Le Touquet go quietly about their business.

But this is largely speculation : let us stick to the facts we know :

* Morgan was not the inexperienced rookie pilot Haynes described.

* He and Baessell may have been the only occupants of 44-70285, or Morgan may have been alone (evidence of the Ansell Report (Fig.32), the fabricated MACR £10770 (Figs. 8,9), the unsigned `ORIGINAL' MACR £N-19 (Figs.34,35), and the `Missing Report' (Fig. 40) dated 22 December 1944, which apparently infers that Major Miller was missing, but not as a result of an aircraft accident. Further, we can cite the NPRC `Potted Miller History Sheet,' the 1950 request for Baessell's dental data and the Baessell Pension File suppressed by Federal records in Suitland, Maryland.

* Baessell, if he was a passenger, boarded the aircraft at Abbotts Ripton, not at Twin wood Farm, which was closed for all flying on 15 December 1944 - evidence of the official Form 540 records in the PRO, Kew, London and evidence of 3 surviving witnesses stationed there including an Air Traffic Control Officer.

* John Morgan was cleared direct from Abbotts Ripton to B-42 Beauvais-Tille, France. Evidence : his Record Card (Fig.36) and Col.Donnell's letter in the Burial Files (Fig. 58). He could not have departed from any other base - evidence, his Form 5 flight times records which shows no positioning flight between December 2 and 15 1944.

* The weather, contrary to statements by Haynes and Royal Frey, was fair - 3,000 feet cloudbase, visibility 1.5+ miles and no rain, surface wind 2 mph. Evidence - actual weather observations from British Meteorological Archives. (Figs.21,22).

* Because of the delay waiting for the weather to clear, Morgan and/or Baessell knew they would not make Beauvais before darkness fell, if they had to land at Bovingdon and complete a flight plan. With the Diver Gun Box over the Thames Estuary inactive, Baessell (or Morgan if he was alone) obtained telephone clearance for a direct flight which would bring them to Beauvais 30 minutes before dusk. Morgan flew direct from Abbotts Ripton to Dymchurch, passing east of London, and was reported heading out to sea about an hour after take-off.

* This ends all speculation about the route. Since he did not crash on land, or arrive at the French coast, reason suggests he ditched in the Channel following mechanical failure. No icing conditions were reported that day - evidence actual weather observations, Figs.21,22).

* The Haynes story is flawed in all respects, including departure and destination airfields, take-off time, weather conditions, Morgan's experience and so on. Haynes and others attempted desperately to propagate the `icing-up' scenario, but all available evidence confirms that this was a red herring.

* George Ferguson and Jean Pace confirm that the Norseman was considered unsafe for long sea crossings. Whenever the Diver Gun Box was inactive, they used the direct route from Twinwood Farm or Abbotts Ripton to Dymchurch. By obtaining telephone clearance they avoided the much longer route west of London.

* Learning that a UC-64A Norseman had been located west of Le Touquet in 1980, we checked on all 8 other UC-64A aircraft destroyed in December 1944, and accounted for all except #44-70285, which was the only C-64 cited in an MACR.

7. The Niven Connection

Lt.Col. David G.Niven SN P/449959, Rifle Brigade (Fig.14) is better known for his achievements as a film star than for his wartime exploits, and some excellent biographies have been written, including an unofficial version by Sheridan Morley (*THE OTHER SIDE OF THE MOON, Weidenfeld and Nicolson, London*). David's book *BRING ON THE*

EMPTY HORSES was published in 1975, followed by *THE MOON'S A BALLOON, Hamish Hamilton, London.* He went to Hollywood in 1935, but when war broke out he came home and rejoined the Army. He played a prominent but mysterious part in the drama that was to unfold in the winter of 1944; prior to that he had served in the Commandos under Lt.Col. Derek Hignett, but when Glenn Miller brought his American Band of the AEF to Britain in June 1944, Niven had been seconded to Special Services Division at SHAEF, Bushey Park, London, under General Ray Barker (G-1). His position was Associate Director of Troop Broadcasting (one of several in the BBC and elsewhere); the Director was Colonel Ed. Kirby - who had helped to `fix' the Miller Band's trip to Europe.

In Special Services, Niven was in his element, welcoming showbizz personalities to Britain when they came with the USO shows, and at the end of the war he was decorated with the Legion of Merit by none other than General Barker. The invasion came on June 6, followed by Miller's arrival in Sloane Court, where his Band were disturbed by V-1 flying bombs passing overhead each day. When Glenn made his two films in Hollywood (*ORCHESTRA WIVES* and *SUN VALLEY SERENADE*) in 1940/41, he did not meet David Niven as far as we can ascertain - in fact, Niven may already have returned to the UK.

Their meeting at Bushey Park was cordial enough and Niven agreed at once to move the Band to a safer area : most of the BBC had been evacuated to Bedford and so the AEF Band came to live in the small county town. Niven is mentioned in the Special Services letters (P.83) and at Bushey Park he was involved in arranging Band quarters and rehearsal facilities, amplification equipment, the trips to various air bases and hospitals to entertain the troops and the transport arrangements. Towards the end of October the air trips to bases tapered off, since the liberation of France and Belgium had attracted many troops from the UK : at that time SHAEF REAR moved to Versailles and became SHAEF MAIN, whilst Bushey Park became SHAEF REAR. Further, Col. Ed Kirby went home to America and David Niven was appointed Director of Troop Broadcasting, based at Versailles. His place at SHAEF REAR was filled by Major Johnny Hayes. Whilst there was some professional friction between Miller and Niven, they remained on good terms : the latter had also met Col. Baessell and General Goodrich at Milton Ernest. Niven attended the first broadcast concert of the AEF Band from the Corn Exchange, Bedford and sat in the front row of seats with Colonel Baessell.

So we were in good shape to begin research into the part played by Lt.Col.David Niven and what happened to him during the traumatic days between December 14 and Christmas Eve 1944. Our reasoning was this : he was Major Glenn Miller's boss *per se* and had chaired the November 15 conference to approve the Paris Tour, attended by Miller and Don Haynes. We knew from a reference in Marlene Dietrich's biography (*MARLENE* by Charles Higham) that she was in Paris on December 14 1944, preparing for a USO tour of forward bases (including Diekirch in Luxembourg and Honsfeld, near Spa, Belgium) to entertain the troops. David and Marlene were close friends - during his early and penniless days in Hollywood she brought him parcels of food. On December 14 David Niven had provided for her use a Cadillac staff car and driver (Colonel Robert Armstrong). So Niven too, was in Paris that day.

If our speculations were justified and Glenn Miller flew into Orly about 13.45 hours on Thursday December 14, the plane in all probability was met by Col. Niven. Miller, after all, was a VIP meriting special attention. Niven ran a jeep provided by 21st Army Group and had a flat in Paris (the address of which we were never able to identify), commuting to SHAEF each day as necessary. Conversely, if the Haynes/Norseman story was true, Glenn would land at Orly about 15.30 hours *the following day, December 15,*, and Niven would be there (regardless of what the MACR stated). Of course, the Haynes account is totally fabricated, so it was no surprise to read that on December 15 David was far to the north in Spa, Belgium, at 1st Army HQ. In `THE MOON'S A BALLOON' he wrote :

> `In the middle of December I was passing through Spa in the Ardennes. I spent the night with Bob Low and he showed me the Map Room in Intelligence. "You see the trees on top of those hills ? In the forest now they are forming the Sixth Panzer Army and any day now, it's going to come right through this room. . . across the Meuse. . . go north to Antwerp." The next day I went down to. . . Marche. Within hours the last great German offensive of the war erupted. Ahead of it, Skorzeny's Trojan Horse Brigade : American-speaking, with captured American uniforms and transport, sabotaging as they went'.*

There are some remarkable inconsistencies in that extract. The `middle of December' was the 15th, and sure enough the Ardennes offensive broke out at 02.00 hours next morning, December 16. Contrary to Niven's statement about Bob Low knowing of the impending attack, history shows that von Rundstedt very nearly caught the Allies unawares. One or two alert Intelligence officers were warning SHAEF that something was brewing, and one of them made a hazardous flight in an L-1 observation plane in thick fog over German lines : by switching off the engine and gliding, he and the pilot could hear the armoured vehicles manoeuvring in the forest below. Niven's poetic description, of course, was written with hindsight, for it was not until Christmas, nine days later, that the German objectives and tactical plan of a left hook aimed at Antwerp became clear to the Allies.

■ Rescue Mission

Niven continued : `Next day I went down to Marche. . . within hours the offensive erupted'.* But since the Germans moved forward at 02.00 hours on Saturday morning, Niven must have been in bed at Spa ! General Hodges was awoken at 07.30 hours with the news that the Germans had penetrated to Losheim, 30 miles east of Spa - and we find a curious anomaly. According to witness Denis Cottam, Miller was in Paris on Friday December 15 ! Denis was told by the bartender at Fred Payne's British Bar in 1954 that ten years previously, he was working in that same bar when Glenn Miller and friends were drinking and talking ! Niven, who was also in Paris the day before (December 14), learned that an Ardennes break-out was imminent and hastily drove north overnight to Honsfeld via Spa to find Marlene Dietrich. To arrive Friday morning meant driving for 8 hours over icy roads wrapped in fog, departing Paris no later than midnight. But was he alone ?

At this point we anticipated finding extensive evidence of those stirring times in the books he wrote after the war - but we were soon disillusioned : Niven made no reference to his work as Director of Troop Broadcasting, his time with the AEF Band in England, the November 15 conference, the arrival of the Band in Paris and - most surprising of all, he never refers to the tragic loss of his friend, associate and VIP Glenn Miller. Not a word of regret, sympathy for Glenn's family, or bewilderment at the surprising circumstances of Glenn's disappearance. Remarkably, during the period which followed, on to Christmas and New Year's Eve, Niven should have been in Paris helping to save the concert tour he himself had planned - but inexplicably he stayed away from Paris.

However, we managed to locate Niven's old Commando CO Col.Derek Hignett, who had a remarkable tale to tell. At the time the Ardennes battles erupted at 02.00 Saturday December 16, Hignett was bivouacked with his unit in Richmond Park London, and early that morning Niven called him on the military network from 1st Army HQ in Spa, Belgium. As Hignett recalls, the conversation went something like this :

HIGNETT Hello, David. What's the problem ?

NIVEN We're at First Army Spa, Derek - and we have a big problem. Marlene Dietrich was due to perform at Honsfeld, twenty miles east of here, but she may be taken by the Germans - you know what they'll do to her.

HIGNETT What can I do for you, old boy ?

NIVEN We have to try to get her out. Can you send over half a dozen of your roughnecks to help us out ?

HIGNETT I'm sorry old boy - all hell has broken loose. We're standing by to move out.

Disappointed, Niven hung up and Colonel Hignett heard no more from him. Now, we can speculate on the identity of Niven's companion, but of one thing we can be quite sure : Hignett was adamant that he was not alone. Throughout Niven's conversation it was `we' and `us', not `I' and `me'. We could find no viable explanation for the omission of this episode from Niven's books, nor could Sheridan Morley, his unofficial biographer. And why had Niven been absent from Paris during those critical days after Miller vanished ? On the face of it, there could be only a limited number of explanations : Niven may have been injured or incapacitated, but we were told by the MOD that he was not hospitalised during that 2-week period. Second, there may have been an incident in Paris from which he wished to distance himself. Third, he may have learned something about Glenn Miller which forced him to dissociate himself from the band leader - and indeed, the AEF Band, his own role as Director of Troop Broadcasting and the concert tour he had approved and organised.

Now, we have the circumstantial evidence of Mr.Metcalfe about a Major Glenn Miller being court-martialled in New York for black market activities, presumably after being arrested at R.A.F. Bovingdon on Thursday 14 December 1944. Whilst research revealed no supporting evidence, Falls Church, Virginia advised that if Miller had had a nervous collapse and was found unfit to plead there would be no court-martial record - but there would be an entry in the medical section of his 201 File. If this scenario was true, Niven would naturally wish to distance himself from the scandal and delete Miller from his memoirs, but this is pure speculation.

Turning to the Joan Heath story of Miller's unauthorised flight home for Christmas (which technically was desertion), Eisenhower may have told others as well as Joan that `the affair was being kept secret'. Niven, a central character, may have simply been obeying orders. We know he did not attend Ike's party on December 16 1944, and since the first Band concert of the tour was scheduled for December 22, there was nothing unusual about Niven visiting Spa on December 15 to meet old friends.

But he did not return to Paris, as far as we can ascertain, until January 1945, and does not feature in any signals or messages, nor in Haynes' diaries. Niven, sadly, died before this research began, and his widow Hjordis, who had married him many years after the war, knew nothing of these events. We wrote three letters to Marlene Dietrich in Paris without response, and at the time of her death in spring 1992 she was almost 90 years old. We believe Niven did nothing with which he might reproach himself; rather he made a valiant but needless journey to rescue an old friend - Marlene was evacuated east from Honsfeld to Spa in a jeep, on the orders of General Gavin of the Airborne Division.

■ The Jeep Incident

One further scenario relates to David Niven, of which we have no sound proof but a great deal of corroboratory circumstantial evidence. Since 1973 there had been rumours of a death certificate or medical document of some kind signed by a Captain Pecora, US Army Medical Corps, but no one had succeeded in tracing him. Now, in all Marlene's biographies there is a description of an accident involving an over-turned jeep during her journey back to Paris from Spa in a jeep provided by General Gavin and driven by Col. Robert Armstrong. She had been sent to the rear from Honsfeld in the early hours of Saturday December 16 and arrived at Spa probably in mid-morning - to find David Niven and a companion (possibly Glenn Miller) waiting for her.

We can safely assume that the two jeeps left Spa together and their route back to Paris would pass through Marche and Rheims. Niven wrote of passing through Marche - but not of reaching Paris : reason suggests that the `jeep accident' happened between Marche and Rheims on the foggy ice-bound roads crowded with Army traffic heading north-east for the battle area.

So much for evidence - let us speculate that it was Niven's jeep that crashed, and that Miller received serious head injuries. Unconscious and unable to identify himself, he is taken to the nearest military hospital at Rheims - and when we traced Captain Pecora he confirmed that he was stationed at Rheims Military Hospital at that time. At this point we begin to find other interconnecting threads of evidence. Major Alton G. Miller's orders included an incorrect serial number, and because of an endemic skin infection he never wore dog tags, according to his brother Herb. Further, the medics might think it extremely improbable that this unconscious injured Air Force Major was indeed the famous band-leader - what would he be doing in the front line ? The `document' Pecora signed may have been an Evacuation Order, sending the patient back to America for specialist cranial surgery. Pecora states he treated many casualties - but no one he *identified* as Glenn Miller.

Three other items : first, the letter received by John Edwards in 1973 from a WW2 soldier who said he was in the same hospital ward in Columbus Ohio as the band-leader when he died - from head injuries. Second, the letter from the New Jersey State Registrar (Fig.73) stating that `Alton Glenn Miller died in Ohio in December 1944'. Third, the mysterious `sixth grave' in the Burial Lot purchased in Altadena, California, by Helen Miller and her mother in January 1949. In MILLERGATE we described the strenuous conflict with the Miller family and the Pasadena Cemetery Association when we tried to check out that grave. After 18 months the PCA reluctantly confirmed in writing that the name `Alton Glenn Miller' did not appear in the cemetery records - but we did not find that conclusive : we speculated that if Helen in late 1948 had located Glenn's remains in Ohio following the release of his Paris orders with incorrect serial number, she would instantly contact the

Department of the Army and the Adjutant General's department. The latter could hardly permit an announcement to be made, after promulgating the Norseman story to the world - yet Helen would insist on the remains being re-interred in California.

There was the further problem that if the news was released, Mountain View Cemetery would receive hundreds, possibly thousands of Miller fans come to pay their last respects. And the credibility of the US Army would be totally destroyed. In the circumstances the only viable solution would be a quiet but covert re-interment in Altadena, perhaps without the knowledge and cooperation of the Cemetery authorities.

This, naturally, was strenuously denied by the PCA and the Miller family - but only after 18 months of protracted negotiations in the course of which I supplied a copy of the MILLERGATE manuscript and undertook to make any alterations the family requested. But there was a simple test using an electronic scanner which would have confirmed how many bodies were interred - there should be only one, that of Helen Miller, because her parents had been cremated and the ashes buried *between* the 6 graves in the Lot. That test would not have disturbed or vandalised the Lot in any way, and would have finally eliminated this as a possible scenario - but the PCA flatly refused. Further, a friend of mine in Los Angeles, Bill McAllister with a group of friends visited the cemetery with a view to seeing the Miller Lot - and they were unceremoniously ejected by several very large gentlemen in blue suits. The attitude of the Cemetery authorities, Bill reported, was `bizarre in the extreme'.

In the circumstances, faced with such evidence, and until the Altadena scenario can finally be resolved, we felt within our rights as professional investigators to speculate, as so many others have done with impunity.

8. Denis Cottam

Denis, like many other non-professional investigators into the Miller mystery, wasted no opportunity to probe further, and when he visited Paris in 1954 to collect a motor car, he visited Fred Payne's British Bar, the Scribe Hotel and the Hotel des Olympiades (the AEF Band billet in December 1944), all of which are mentioned in the Haynes diaries. In Fred Payne's bar, Denis raised the perennial question of Glenn Miller's disappearance, and the bar-tender smiled indulgently. "I have worked here since the middle of the war," he said. "Isn't it odd ? You English have always believed that Miller was lost in the Channel on December 15 1944. Yet he was in here drinking, that very same night !"

This was remarkable, and Cottam was astounded. But there was more : "If you walk up the other side of the street towards Sacre Coeur, you will see a house with a blue-painted door with brass studs. Speak to the lady there and she will tell you more."

Cottam took the bar-tender's advice and knocked on the door. A well-dressed mature-looking woman appeared, invited him inside, and Denis perceived at once that the place was a high class bordello. He asked her about Glenn Miller.

"Ah, yes, m'sieu - I remember this well. At that time, you understand, I was working in this house, and my boy friend was an American, a Captain in the Army Provost Marshal Division. He told me that he had been called out to investigate the death of an Air Force officer, and he had seen the body, which had been identified as Major Glenn Miller."

"But why was he killed, madame ?" Cottam asked.

"He knew too much, m'sieu," she said quietly. "Too much about the black market - and they killed him to keep him quiet."

And that was the whole story. We spoke to Mr.Cottam, but he had little to add - no names, dates, times, places to back it up. But why did he not quiz the madame further for the name of her boy friend, where and when he had seen the body, what had been the cause of death and whether a doctor had been present or not ? It was an important, even vital piece of evidence which might have solved the mystery once and for all; in fact, John Edwards used the story twenty years later in the Seventies, as we shall see. But on a research visit to Paris in 1987, when we too made the rounds in Mr.Cottam's foot-prints, we encountered a strange reaction : concealed mirth and giggling, sometimes outright ridicule when we broached the subject of Glenn Miller ! To the French, he is as much a tourist attraction as is the Loch Ness monster to Scotland. Had the clients in Fred Payne's Bar been pulling Dennis Cottam's leg ?

There seemed to be an unbridgable chasm between this scenario and that of Miller accompanying David Niven on his rescue trip to the Ardennes : if Glenn was in Fred Payne's British Bar on Friday December 15, how could he be with Niven in Spa ? The Joan Heath account, however, casts a different light on matters : we can conjecture that Miller arrived in Paris Thursday December 14, visited the bar on Friday, played at Ike's party on Saturday and flew off into oblivion from Buc Field on Sunday December 17 1944.

One disquieting incident involved Cottam. Sitting with friends one afternoon in a cafe near Grosvenor Square, they were discussing the Miller mystery and a well-dressed American at the next table turned round and said : `I could not help overhearing - the Miller case is very puzzling. But if you'll take my advice, you won't probe any further - it is a very sensitive subject' A similar incident occurred when the late Sqn.Ldr.Jack Taylor was telephoned in London by a `Colonel Walbrecht of Third Air Force' - the Colonel said `I know what you're digging into and I have some advice for you - if you value your health, lay off the subject - permanently'.

We rang 3rd Air Force at Mildenhall and of course they had never heard of any Colonel Walbrecht. John Edwards received a strong unambiguous warning to the same effect in 1973.

9.   John Edwards

Perhaps the best-known Miller researcher of the Seventies (in 1972, he was Chairman of the Glenn Miller Society) John Edwards was stationed in 1964 with the R.A.F. in Bahrein in the Persian Gulf, where he ran a local Forces radio programme, and he became an avid Glenn Miller fan. Absorbed by the mystery, he returned home and devoted most of his time to research, corresponding with Canadians Henry Whiston and John Flowers. Inevitably, he attracted the attention of the media and was featured in an article in the now-defunct newspaper *REVEILLE* in 1976. (Fig.76). In it, he repeated the Dennis Cottam story of his 1954 visit to Paris, adding some embellishments of his own. He said that Miller was murdered *three days* after the Norseman was lost in the Channel, i.e. on Monday December 18, but did not explain how he arrived at that assumption. However, it is not altogether impossible if Miller arrived in Paris on Thursday December 14. And Edwards rightly states that the loss of the Norseman provided a convenient cover-up for the band-leader's death.

Edwards also insisted that Miller was not aboard the Norseman, and that he had an eyewitness who saw Miller board a Dakota aircraft at Bovingdon that same day. But Edwards failed to correlate the November 8 and December 15 flights, and we have shown conclusively that Alex Sleap met Morgan's Norseman on the earlier flight. But he does point out the inconsistencies in MACR #10770, and when we interviewed him at his home in

Wimborne, Dorset, John revealed some information, the importance of which apparently he was unaware.

10. The Pecora Connection

We have referred previously to an American Army doctor who had been associated with Miller's death documentation - a Captain Pecora. We encountered his name in a 1971 letter from John Flowers to Edwards, in which Flowers asked for further information, and Edwards also told us that a Col.Corrigan, USAAF Ret., had actually seen this `death certificate'. But we laboriously traced Col.Corrigan, who said that he had probably seen Miller's Report of Death or Finding of Death document. The latter serves as a death certificate in the case of missing personnel. This same Captain Corrigan, as he was in 1944, took off from R.A.F. Fairford, Gloucester, in a C-47 Dakota on 15 December 1944 about the same time as Morgan, en route to Chateaudun, France. The weather was poor but he landed safely.

Edwards told us that when he worked for Plessey Communications in Derby in the late Sixties, his departmental head was an American, Jack Donnelly who had known of John Edwards' interest in the Miller case. He told John that he had gone to college years previously with a fellow-student named Pecora. This student told Donnelly that his father, an Army Medical Officer, had signed a death certificate in Europe for Major Glenn Miller. We began immediately a search for Donnelly, who had long since returned to America.

We began with John Edwards' last clue - that he and Donnelly worked for Plessey Communications in Derby in the late Sixties. We called Derby - and learned that Donnelly had indeed gone home seven or eight years ago, i.e. about 1975 - they thought he came from a place with the bizarre name of Paradise Valley, Arizona. Eight days later we ran him down and made a phone call.

"Donnelly here. Who's this ?"

"My name is Wilbur Wright, from England. I'm researching the disappearance of Major Glenn Miller in 1944 and an old friend of yours, John Edwards, said you may have some information on that -"

"John Edwards ? Sure, I remember John. A great guy. Say, what's all this about Glenn Miller ?"

I explained.

"Oh, yeah - I remember something about that. I went to college with this guy - I think his name was Pecora. He told me his father signed Glenn Miller's death certificate. Which college ? Heck, I gotta think about that - I went to quite a few and it was a long time ago, in the Fifties. It was somewhere in the South, as I recall - I remember the family came from Newark."

Well, it was a start - and surprise, surprise - Newark was in New Jersey, not far from the Miller apartment at Tenafly ! Was there a connection ? Did Helen and Glenn know this Captain Pecora ? It might explain a lot of things. Maybe he had been their family physician before he became an Army medic. But New Jersey was a big state - we contacted the American Medical Association for information on all New Jersey physicians named Pecora - and meantime, we began searching for Donnelly's university. There was a great number of them, almost one for every town, but in the end we got lucky and located Florida Southern College near Baton Rouge. And they still had their old student records ! Yes, they had had a student John Donnelly in 1955 - and also an Edward Pecora. They had a local address of an aged relative in Baton Rouge, and Edward's address in Connecticut. They wished us luck in

66

our quest - and we really needed it. Was he still alive ?

Impatiently we listened to the telephone bell ringing in a house 3,000 miles away.

"Edward Pecora here - "

We explained how we had traced him through Jack Donnelly, and about the Glenn Miller connection.

"Jack ? Yeah, I remember Jack Donnelly, for sure. Glenn Miller ? Now, wait a while. . . I do remember something about that, but I'm not a doctor."

"Was your father in the Army Medical Corps in 1944 ?"

Edward laughed. "Hell, no ! He was in World War One !"

Our spirits sagged, listening intently. *End of story.* . . Then Edward said slowly : "Wait a moment. My cousin David was an Army doctor, and he was in Europe in 1944. Maybe it was David who told me about Glenn Miller -"

That was better ! "Do you have his address ?" we said eagerly.

"Uh - no, sir - I don't. But I could sure dig it out - I'll call you back, okay ?"

He was as good as his word : four days later we had an address for Dr. David Pecora - of Newark, *Delaware* ! So much for New Jersey and all that wasted effort. We wrote the good Doctor a long letter explaining how we had traced him through Jack Donnelly and his cousin Edward, in connection with the story he had told Edward after the war. We asked him for his views on the Miller connection. Dr.Pecora replied on March 10 1987 :

> `In reply to your interesting letter of February 26 I'm afraid that I cannot be of assistance. In December of 1944 I was in transit from England to France. I spent Christmas day at Etretat* (a small town on the northern coast of France - Auth.). Following that I was located at Rheims during the battle of the Ardennes ("Bulge"). We treated many casualties. However, I have no recollection of encountering anyone identified as Glenn Miller. I shall look for your book when it is published.'*

We found this note extremely odd. For one thing, Dr.Pecora was not in the least surprised that we had traced him through a long chain of incidents and other people, and he did not deny that he had spoken to cousin Edward about Glenn Miller almost forty years previously. Further, he says `In December of 1944 I was in transit from England to France' - but what date in December ? He spends Christmas Day at Etretat - and goes on to say `*after that* I was located at Rheims during the Battle of the Bulge' - but that offensive began on December 16, less than 12 hours after Morgan left Abbotts Ripton, and not after Christmas. By December 25 the von Rundstedt attack had ground to a halt half way to Antwerp with heavy casualties. This ambiguous letter could be taken to mean that Dr.Pecora came to France some time after December 1, and was based at Rheims Military Hospital from December 16. And when the offensive petered out, he went to Etretat on a well-earned Christmas furlough.

We were particularly intrigued by the doctor's reference to `not encountering anyone identified as Glenn Miller'. Why did he not simply say he never treated anyone named Glenn Miller ? Why the stress on `identification' ? We recalled that Miller's orders contained an incorrect serial number; that his name was listed as `Alton G. Miller' which might not be associated with Glenn Miller the band leader. Thirdly, we know from Herb Miller that Glenn never wore dog tags around his neck, or a wrist identity bracelet, because of an endemic skin infection. Dr.Pecora may not have treated anyone *identified as Glenn Miller* -

but what if Glenn had been brought into hospital unconscious, unrecognised ? In the heat of battle, over-loaded with casualties, was it not possible that the hospital recorded him simply as Major Alton G.Miller, picked up on the battlefield with severe head injuries ?

We thought it was extremely possible, and wrote again to Dr.Pecora some weeks later asking for clarification. We received no further response. It was an unsatisfactory ending to what had seemed a most promising lead. But in retrospect, we went back to the old persistent rumour that a doctor had signed some form of document for Miller. What could it have been ? We could eliminate a death certificate, Finding or Report of Death documents, and Casualty Reports - they were the responsibility of a soldier's parent unit or command, not the hospital. Leaving aside for the moment the question of how Glenn Miller came to be in the Ardennes battle area on December 16 1944, and the letter John Edwards received from the WW2 veteran hospitalised in Columbus, Ohio with Miller, when the latter died of head injuries, the sole remaining option is that the doctor signed a Casevac order - authorising the evacuation of the wounded man to the United States. And we know that many transAtlantic trooping flights terminated at Wright-Paterson AFB, Ohio.

There can be few such intransigent mysteries, with so many devious skeins of evidence, as the disappearance of Major Glenn Miller - and at the same time, so tantalising. By late 1991 we suspected that the solution might be found in the `Missing Report' and its covering letters, enclosures and documentation, which had lain in some secret file in St.Louis for almost fifty years. But we were getting close - at last we could see light at the end of the tunnel. . .

11. The Edwards Interview

John had a great deal of information on file, some valuable, some mere hearsay. He began to attract publicity and on one occasion flew with TV presenter Angela Rippon `along the course taken by the Norseman'. He was unable to explain exactly how he knew the course, for which researchers had sought in vain until 1987. We referred previously to the letter from a World War Two veteran who claimed that he had been in the same ward in a hospital in Columbus, Ohio, with Glenn Miller when the band leader died, still unconscious from severe head injuries. Unfortunately, John classified the letter as a hoax and disposed of it, an action he came to regret.

There are other strange connotations. John Edwards gave us the names and serial numbers of four US Army Provost Marshal officers whom, he said, had investigated the mystery in 1944 - and remarkably, they all came from Albuquerque, New Mexico ! We spent many months searching for these officers, but US military records hold no trace of any of them. The sole information we obtained was that the US Army School for Provost Marshal Officers was indeed based in Albuquerque in 1944 ! (See Page 187).

We discussed with Edwards the question of searches for the aircraft and for Glenn Miller. In 1973, unaware that Burial Files even existed, he tried persistently to trace the personal 201 Miller File, writing to the National Personnel Records Center at St.Louis. They replied :

`We have probed our computer regarding the 201 Files of Major Glenn Miller, Lt.Col. Norman F.Baessell and Flight Officer John R.S.Morgan and have not located any records. It is possible they were destroyed by the fire . . .'

68

Naturally, we wrote to St.Louis to check on this statement, and to ask for information on a possible SHAEF inquiry. They did not deny they held the Files : on March 10, they wrote to us :

`Attached are copies of death and casualty reports located in Major Miller's folder. We also attach copies of prior reports already sent you on August 5 and November 6,1986. There are no documents in Major Miller's record concerning Adjutant General's Historical Records and the inquiry held at SHAEF REAR at Bushey Park on 20 January 1945'.*

John Edwards passed on to us a mass of documentation when he abandoned his own researches, including a letter to him from a Plymouth trawler owner named Eric C. Long. Mr. Long enclosed a Press cutting from a Western newspaper stating that :

`A search for the aircraft which disappeared carrying American band leader Glenn Miller on December 15 1944, has been narrowed down to a 250-square mile area in the English Channel. Mr.Edwards of the Glenn Miller Society said that details of Miller's last flight had enabled the team to determine the area in which the aircraft probably dropped. . . It was hoped to work out how far the aircraft got before weather and ice forced it down.'*

But when we interviewed John, he could not explain how he had worked out the position of the Norseman within an area north of Dunkirk measuring 15 miles square, in the absence of a flight plan, confirmation of a Bovingdon landing or any departure or destination airfield (of which we had a choice of 3 in each case !). At that time, he was relying on a sighting report of a single-engined aircraft seen to be shot down off the coast 6 miles west of Dunkirk - the witnesses were three officers, including a German.

John Edwards' problem, as he now cheerfully admits, was a total lack of objectivity, analytical shrewdness and native caution. He believed implicitly any and all information which came his way, and wasted no time in informing the media instead of checking the material carefully. He always claimed that a cover-up had occurred, but had no concrete evidence to support that theory. We questioned him gently.

"But the visibility," we said, " was only a mile or so that afternoon in the Channel."

John hesitated. "Yes. We found later that it was less than a mile offshore. It was dusk and distances are difficult to judge. But by using a huge computer in Cleveland, Ohio, feeding in all the relevant data, we came up with the location of a Norseman - precisely where the computer predicted !"

We pointed out the total dearth of information of any kind, and the controversy about Morgan's route, but he was unable to expand further. He did, however, produce what at he said was a sidescan sonar image of the Norseman standing on the sea bed. (Fig.74).

"Did you ever find a sponsor for a dive on the aircraft ? Were any dives made ?"

"Oh, yes. Several - the last in November 1985."

Strange, we thought. *There had been no announcements, Press reports.*

"Were you there, John ?"

"Uh - no. I had commitments elsewhere -"

Commitments ? After researching for 20 years ? We tried again, pointing to a map as reproduced in Fig.73.

"Can you mark the position of the Norseman ?"

"Certainly -" We looked at the map in stunned silence. The position was a long way from Dunkirk, away to the west around Cap Gris Nez and down towards Boulogne. We pointed this out, and John nodded.

"It probably drifted round there on the tide and currents -"

"Um. Yes," we said. "This dive - what was the name of the ship ?"

"I think it was the *Midnight Loon* -" *(This may have been correct but we found no ship of that name in Lloyd's Register).*

"What were the names of the divers you employed ?"

"The sponsors Southern TV would know. They provided the divers." *(We checked - the TV company had no record of a dive or divers).*

"What information did the dive produce ?" we asked John. "Was the aircraft identified as a Norseman ?"

"It was. . . difficult to confirm. We only had the aircraft number."

"But," we pointed out reasonably, "all the fabric and the painted number 44-79285 would be rotted away after 40 years -"

"True," John agreed. "The real confirmation will come from the engine number."

"You mean you didn't get the engine number during the dive ?" we said, astonished. *That number was a vital clue to the whole mystery !*

"No, we didn't," John admitted.

"Okay. Now, in what condition was the plane ? Did the divers say ?"

"A high-wing monoplane in reasonably good condition," Edwards said easily. "It was quite heavily silted up but protected by the silt to some extent. Miller was not aboard."

We blinked. *The Norseman discovered off Le Touquet in 1980 was on a flat sand sea bed. And it was only a tubular steel skeleton.*

"Really ?" we said dazedly.

We already knew this, of course. And John believed this implicitly, because he had heard the Cottam tape describing Miller's presence in Fred Payne's British Bar on December 15 1944. It all seemed too good to be true - and it was. It is difficult to figure out what makes John Edwards tick - he had followed up every lead, every rumour with dogged persistence, but in the end he yielded to the insidious pressure of the media - they demanded sensation after sensation, and when he could not produce on time, John let his imagination take over. Yet he is a hugely-likable man, and we owe him a debt of gratitude in that he provided us with three vital clues.

First, the evidence and photograph of Mr. Alex Sleap, meeting the Morgan Norseman at Bovingdon on November 8 1944. This enabled us to prove that both George Ferguson and the late Dixie Clerke had confused their dates, and that Don Haynes had used liberally material from the November 8 flight to construct his imaginary December 15 flight.

Second, John showed us his transcript of his interview with Mr. Teddy Gower, the BBC engineer who claimed to have travelled in the seat behind Miller on a C-47 shuttle flight to Paris at the time he was supposed to have been on the Norseman. This, together with the Special Services Letters found in the Burial Files enabled us to prove that the flight took place on December 14 1944.

Third, he led us to the mysterious US Army doctor mentioned in the *REVEILLE* article (Fig.76) who was based at Rheims Military Hospital in the Ardennes during the period after Glenn Miller vanished.

12. The Herb Miller Tape

I interviewed Herb at his home in Dulwich, and initially he did not want to be recorded, since I was a total stranger. We talked again over lunch in a local restaurant, which was recorded (albeit in competition with the background noise). Both visits occurred in January 1987. The following extracts are from that tape, and it should be born in mind that our investigations were at a very early stage. I began by telling Herb of my research.

WW   Now, I had a long letter from this guy George Ferguson who claimed he was the first-choice pilot for the flight, and he's given me a lot more information than anyone else has received. He tells a completely different story to Don Haynes -

H.M   Of course ! Don's story was a lie from beginning to end.

WW   Well, at the time Ferguson said he was stationed in Brussels and Baessell back at Milton Ernest wanted him to fly over, pick Baessell and Glenn up and fly them to Paris, and this had been pre-planned for weeks beforehand, the idea being for Ferguson to fly over on the Thursday and take them to Paris on the Friday. But his Commander in Brussels said `No way I'm losing you for two days. You can fly over Friday morning, pick them up and I want that airplane back in the barn by nightfall.

H.M   So that plane had to come over from Brussels to pick him up at Twinwood -

WW   Yes. Everybody thought it was going to be the aeroplane already in England at Alconbury. *(NOTE : Abbotts Ripton. Auth.)* There were four of them issued to Wattisham, the 44th Air Depot Group, and when Ferguson was assigned to Brussels, he took one with him. Baessell wanted him to fly to England, pick them up, drop them in Paris and return to Brussels -

H.M   All in the same day -

WW   All in the same day. But Ferguson's Commander said `no way' and finally Baessell rang Ferguson in Brussels. When George said his Commander wouldn't play, Baessell said a very rude word and hung up. *(NOTE : Not strictly accurate. See Page 29. Auth.)*

H.M.   Not two rude words - just one ! (Laughter).

WW   Right ! Anyway, what happened then was that on the Friday morning, Baessell did a bit of shunting around, got hold of Morgan and his Norseman from Abbotts Ripton and all this according to Ferguson was what happened. *(NOTE : Friday December 15 1944 - Auth.)*. Ferguson sticks firmly to the story that Morgan came down from Abbotts Ripton to Twinwood Farm, picked up Baessell and Glenn Miller and flew off into the blue. We thought we could prove that neither Morgan nor the Norseman were at Twinwood, so at first we thought that Ferguson must have been part of the cover-up. But we know now that Haynes picked up Baessell and drove him to

Abbotts Ripton on Friday morning, put him on the Norseman, and the flight plan was from Abbotts Ripton to a place called B-42 - Dijon. *(NOTE : at that stage we had incorrectly identified B-42 as Dijon. In fact there was a small field there numbered B-42A. For Dijon read `Beauvais'. Auth.).* No intention of going to Paris at all. Now, what may have happened was this - Don Haynes spent that weekend at Milton Ernest, had a phone call from France to give him bad news about Glenn and that some plan would have to be worked out. So he says `Well, we have just lost a Norseman from here -' and the whole thing started from there.

H.M   Uh-uh -

WW   It's possible. But from the letter I received from Ferguson last week, there is no two ways about it - he was as deeply involved in the whole thing as anybody ! *(NOTE : This was a remarkable conclusion at this early stage of the inquiry, based on our belief that George had deliberately confused the November 8 and December 15 flights - we could not believe that he was unaware that the Paris Band concert tour was not approved until November 15 1944, whereas the Ferguson/Baessell incident occurred in late October or early November. Auth.).* I wrote to the National Archives for this enlarged copy of that Missing Aircrew Report -

H.M   I saw that !

WW   This is what I was telling you before. *(NOTE : About the falsification of MACR #10770. Auth.).* You see the misplaced `B' in Baessell and Bradunas. Dated March 1946 - and this guy Bradunas, making out the Classification Certificate, used the same machine to type out the route details in 1946 ! Now, I'm still trying to find the original document - *(NOTE : This was before the Ansell Report was produced - in fact, I visited New Scotland Yard after that luncheon and found a typewriter expert - Michael Ansell. It was also some years before we received the Burial Files containing the `ORIGINAL' MACR. Auth.).* He typed in the `B-42' but he was a fool - he used the same typewriter - in 1946 !

H.M   He didn't expect it to get this far, you know -

WW   I already spoke to a typewriter expert at Scotland Yard about the document - she has a copy. She said `Mr. Wright, your assumptions are perfectly correct. We've found some extraordinary things about this document'. So I'm going along there this afternoon.

H.M   Marvellous ! Go along and talk to them -

WW   Then if Scotland Yard confirms it was a forgery, we've got them -

H.M   You can't beat that ! You've got the whole world ! But I can see now why Helen and Polly didn't like. . .They never did like - of course, in later years I didn't say much about it, or do much about it. And I always wondered why Don Haynes was so involved. I was the only one who could do anything about the music because I was

WW   the only one with any training, and naturally they wanted to hold me down and I'm fighting that battle right now.

WW   I think you were the only member of the family who had any suspicions that something was wrong - when did you start thinking that ?

H.M   About seven years ago *(NOTE : 1972-1974, after Don Haynes died and the George Simon book quoting the Haynes story was published. Auth.).* Of course, Helen has been gone all this time. I called Steven the other day when I was in the United States and he's a real cool guy. I mean, he didn't let anything out.

WW   I feel sure that Helen, before she died, told the kids all she knew. There was no reason why she shouldn't. The odd thing about the whole business is that for 30 years, from 1944 to 1974, the only version available was the Don Haynes story. Nobody questioned it - why should they ? When the George Simon book came out -

H.M   Yes - I've read it. I don't like it.

WW   It came out in 1974 but there were so many discrepancies in the Haynes story that that people started asking questions. It was one of two things - either Simon himself was telling a false story, or he got all his material from Don Haynes' diary, given to him by Polly. He was a friend of the Haynes family for 30 odd years - in fact he played in Glenn's band.

H.M   Oh, yeah. I met him on a couple of occasions. Right after the war he came out to see me at Wiley Post Lodge, New York State, and I didn't know at that time he was a drummer. He asked if he could sit in and he did quite a creditable job. We didn't get a picture of him at the time, a pity because I could stuff it down his throat right now. I'd have a lot of fun doing it too. I met him in New York City one day and he made some very denigrating remarks right to my face. What he doesn't know is that I'd do a creditable job with the London Philharmonic if they gave me a chance - I just want to conduct and I'd take my place with any of them. The big job is getting a break to do it.

WW   Of course. Now, Simon had known Polly Haynes for thirty years, and when she gave him what she said was Don's diary, either Simon knew it was a copy of Haynes' fictional manuscript MINUS ONE, or he didn't. But if he knew it was fictional but printed it as fact, he must have known the truth !

H.M   I'm sure he did.

WW   On the other hand, Simon is quite entitled to say `As far as I knew, it was the original diary'. Is there any way he could have been a family friend and not know that it was largely fiction ? We have to ask him for permission to quote from the book -

H.M   Whatever you do, don't mention my name. If he knows you've had anything to do with me, he won't give you anything.

WW   Well, we're solving that by quoting mostly from the MINUS ONE diary - I have a copy - and not from his book. And I can say `here is the narrative Simon quotes from but it's a fictional narrative from the word go !

H.M   And by proving one item wrong, by association everything is wrong -

WW   So if the Haynes narrative is wrong, he was never there at the time (the aircraft took off) or the aeroplane was never at Twinwood and Glenn went at some other time. We're almost certain now he went on the Thursday from Bovingdon. I found out that there were four shuttle flights out of Bovingdon that day, two to Orly and two to Villacoublay, and he could have gone on any one of those.

H.M   Hm-mm -

WW   And this guy Ferguson still sticks to the idea that the weather was terrible, 200 foot cloudbase and pouring rain. I sent him a copy of the actual weather reports - 3000 foot cloud-base and no rain at all. He said that was the information he got over in Belgium for the English weather, and he still believes they were in thick cloud, Morgan lost control on instruments and went into the drink. Maybe Ferguson was implicated because he is still sticking to a story with this piece in. He has to stick to his original story -

H.M   He has to do something -

WW   Right. Tell me, what was Helen like as a woman ?

H.M   Seemed to be a very nice lady. In all the right places too. In fact, Glenn literally stole her, you know, and the story about him calling her from New York is not true. He called her and he said `Get on the next train and come to New York - I'm going to marry you -' and that's all he said ! But she said `I'm engaged !' and Glenn said `Have him bring you to the train -' that was *all* the conversation. Nobody would have believed it if they said it was like it was - so they had to build it up.

WW   Of course this was typically Glenn -

H.M   Oh, typically Glenn ! `I want you to do this right now and don't ask me why - just do it !'

WW   I think this was the only way he could cope with his environment. If he said `Everybody jump up and down' everybody jumped.

H.M   They didn't even ask how high !

WW   I had a nice letter from Jimmy Stewart who played Glenn (in the film). Universal did a good deal of research on Glenn, but there had to be some parts of the film which were a little bit off the truth, to make it an acceptable story.

H.M   That's right. Who would have believed that incredible conversation -

WW   Herb, was it really true that he knocked up Helen at three o'clock in the morning ? *(NOTE : The American interpretation of the expression `knocked up' is totally different to the English, which means waking up by knocking on the door. Herb and I, listening to the tape replay, fell apart with laughter at that point. Auth.)*

H.M   I think he really did !

WW   One of the best character actors in the film was Harry Morgan playing Chummy McGregor *(NOTE : The pianist in the Glenn Miller pre-1942 orchestra. Auth.)* At times I really thought he was playing the piano -

H.M   You almost thought it was Chummy McGregor ! He was a nice guy. You know that one time Chummy was griping around about something, half-drunk, and Glenn walked over and said `Stand up !' and Glenn socked him half-way across the room -

WW   No !

H.M   Yeah ! But Chummy never took another drink - Glenn hit him in the mouth ! He never took another drink. That's what you call `instant AA'. Glenn knew every-thing that was going on - one afternoon we were sitting on the front porch of my home and I was saying I'd been going through some cancellations of the Casa Loma Orchestra and some others with Bunny Berrigan and all of a sudden Glenn got to his feet and said `Helen, pack your suitcase. We're going back to New York right now'. And was off the front the front porch and gone ! He knew that the time was to go back now so he could get those jobs. He had the feeling for this business so much he just knew every little thing -

WW   He was a very astute business man ?

H.M   He was one awful man to work for ! I mean, one day I came in with a suitcase in this room we called an office I had organised myself -

WW   Where was this ?

H.M   Somewhere along the route at a time I was working for him - I only worked for him about ten weeks - and I said `Well, I just want to tell you what I've done today'. `Don't open it up', he said. `I'll tell you what you *haven't* done !' and he listed the five different things I had not done ! And of course, to get those five things done I'd be at it all day - go to see the unions, check all the cards, go see the promoter, get the advance if there was one, check the contracts, send out a roll of tickets in case someone -

WW   Seems you needed three pairs of hand - !

H.M   Listen, that was the most octopus-tale I ever heard of ! As a matter of fact, I used to condemn myself because I'd folded up under it, but I didn't do it any more, because he got three of the sharpest guys in the business to take that job after I left ! Laurie Biggin, Johnny McAteer, Tommy Shields - three of the greatest in the business. And then he took another department and gave it to a guy in the Band to handle - four guys to try and do the job I'd been doing myself ! I tell you I couldn't do it.

WW   Did he know he was overloading you ?

H.M   I don't know whether he did or not. He thought I'd just follow right along in his foot-steps. You see, he could do all this in his head. He didn't have to go round and do the stuff - he didn't realise at the time what it took physically to accomplish these things.

WW   To get the time element right - you were in your early twenties at the time ?

H.M   No - twenty-seven, twenty-eight. Glenn was nine years older than me - I was born in 1913. Glenn was born in 1904, March 1904.

WW   Did he have pretty set ideas about having the family work for him ?

H.M   He wanted anyone in the family who could do the job -

WW   As cheaply as possible !

H.M   It wasn't that which motivated him. He just wanted his family around him. He didn't care how much it cost - he paid me a very fine salary. In fact, for some of the time I worked for him, I was just taking the money.

WW   Did he have any other girl-friends apart from Helen ?

H.M   I haven't the faintest idea. You see, I was raised in a Puritan family and they were literally pure. The idea of another girl-friend or anything like that didn't enter into our thinking. That was absolutely taboo.

WW   I've trying to establish who Glenn spent his last evening with. There are rumours that he spent that Thursday evening with Dorothy Carless, who sang with Geraldo's band.

H.M   And Anne Shelton - and Vera Lynn. She didn't like him, for some reason or other.

WW   So there was no sort of a relationship with any of them -

H.M   Well, it was an Army situation, away from your wife for maybe six months -

WW   Let me put it this way to you. Although Glenn was a family man, he was like all servicemen overseas - he used to let rip once in a while. If he went over to Paris on the Thursday as we think, and went out on the town Thursday night, which way

H.M   would his mind go ? Would he think about a lot of drinks, or maybe a few girls ?

H.M   When I went to join him, the first night I was there, he and one of the guys in the Band - not Chummy - I wasn't drinking at the time, but he and this other guy just sat there and drank. This went on for quite a while and Glenn said he was happy as hell that I was there. Whether he showed a worse side than that - which is not denigrating him - I mean, when you get through some of those jobs he had, you feel like just getting a drink and -

WW   They had just finished a recording session, something like 90 radio programmes, about 25 hours broadcasting - I think he would have been ready to relax over in Europe -

H.M   I'm sure. So that may have been what he was doing. I mean, I don't know what he was sexually. . . He loved Helen very much.

WW   I think all the men who went overseas during war loved their wives - but it takes a superhuman sort of guy - Here's a funny thing. My wife and I were married in Wales on Wednesday December 13 1944, and we went to Cambridge for our honeymoon for a week. So I was very close when all this was going on, only twenty miles - but I didn't know ! I find that quite amazing.

H.M   Your time machine wasn't working ! Well, maybe you understand now that a person of Glenn's experience, being married for say 10 or 12 years, might make him more vulnerable to something like that.

WW   Well, if they'd gone out on the town and had a few drinks and they got into this Place Pigalle which was the red light district, there were girls everywhere. I think that he and four or five other guys - he knew a lot of people at SHAEF Headquarters. One was a Major May, who was Exec Officer to General Barker, who was G-1, in charge of personnel, and he was the man responsible for what happened - he ran the whole she-bang. Major May was his ADC and Glenn got to know him very well when he went across previously in November to talk about the tour. Quite possibly, Glenn and Major May and one or two other guys from SHAEF went out on the town. I have a scenario in my mind where they are standing a little bit tipsy on the pavement, surrounded by girls, and some of the guys want to go, some don't and possibly a little bit of a fight starts. *(NOTE : This essentially was the happening described by researcher John Edwards in 1973. Auth.)* I think that maybe when Glenn had a couple on -

H.M   He wasn't afraid of anybody. He'd have taken on the whole German Army !

WW   He would have got stuck in and it could have been one of these crazy things where he fell backwards, hit his head on the pavement - something simple like that. I'm very excited because we've traced the name of the doctor attached to the Adjutant General's Department - *(NOTE : This lead was later proven untrue. Pecora was a Captain in the US Medical Corps. Auth.)*. If we can trace him, and he wrote the death certificate, he must know what happened.

H.M   He had to know - listen, if you're making out a death certificate and you don't know what happened, are you obliged to make an autopsy ?

WW   I would say in normal times, yes but not in wartime. If this chap Major May was there - and Glenn only knew a few people at SHAEF, the people in Special Duties Branch who handled all these appointments and tours and so on. If May was there, he would have called General Barker and said `Look, something terrible has happened - what are we going to do about it ?' If a decision was made at that time to conceal the death, this Captain Pecora might be asked to sign the death certificate - and put as little as possible on it. Simply that Glenn died from a fractured skull. It's only a guess but it seems to fit together. So if we can get a copy of the certificate showing he died in Paris, Don Haynes' story collapses completely and the cover-up is proven.'

H.M   I want to see a copy of that. Send it to me air mail -

WW   Herb, ever since we met I've been working along those lines - I've shown you every document - no point in doing otherwise, because once you've begun to trust somebody, you have to get a certain amount of trust in return. Also, I wrote to a dozen different departments in American about that shipment number - *(NOTE : In Glenn's Casualty Report. I believed it might refer to a body being shipped home to America. Auth.).* And nobody wanted to know - I've had no replies.

H.M   Would you say you were knocking on the lid ?

WW   Oh, yes ! It's an uncomfortable idea. *(NOTE : At that point I pulled out a sheaf of my letters.).* Look at this - letters I have written in the last six months.

H.M   I never wrote that many letters in my life.

WW   But you don't get replies ! There will be a great deal about misinformation in the book. The people over there are crafty. They never say `We don't know'. Instead, they say that the information you require is not available - which can be taken in different ways - (a) we've got it but we're not letting you see it, or (b) it's not available to you but could be made available to somebody else. They say things like `That information is not on our records' but they never say `Contact so-and-so - it's on *their* records ! It's not concealing information - it's misinformation. I rang up the National Archives in Washington last week and asked them for the personal files of Baessell and Morgan, and they said `We're having problems with this fire and I said `What fire ?' They said `In our records department about four years ago'. I said `Oh, yes ? Where was this fire ?'. They said `Maxwell Air Force Base' and I said `Now hold on. I have a letter from a John Edwards who was told in 1973 that the fire was in St.Louis - and Maxwell AFB doesn't hold personnel information.' So far, no one has seen the personal files for Baessell and Morgan. They contain details of their movements, courses they did and so on, and the last entries in each case will be the same - they will show where they were sent, and on what authority. I have Morgan's orders from Wattisham telling him to go to B-42 Dijon. *(NOTE : At that time I had incorrectly identified B-42 Beauvais as Dijon. Auth.)*

H.M   That's in France - ?

WW   Yes - way over on the eastern side. You know, Herb, I videoed the GLENN MILLER STORY movie and got to the part where Glenn got aboard the plane. I stopped there and tried to relate what I had seen to George Simon's book. I think only about 10 or 15% of the film was true - but they had to make it that way -

H.M   They wouldn't make any money otherwise - and it never gets into circulation if you don't do it.

WW   I suppose so. Now, if we assume Glenn had this fatal accident in France, the doctor who signed the death certificate may have been this Major Pecora *(NOTE : Later to be identified as Captain Pecora. We knew he came from Newark, and assumed this was the New Jersey city. In fact, Dr. Pecora lives in Newark, Delaware. Auth.)* who came from New Jersey, not far from Tenafly where Glenn and Helen lived before he went overseas. It's not beyond the bounds of possibility that Helen knew this guy - and if so -

H.M   They might have had him turned off -

WW   (Laughs) Yes ! Well, perhaps not that. But possibly he may have agreed to whatever she wanted and General Barker wanted in the way of covering up.

H.M   Right. She would have said I wanted this quiet.

WW   Now, how soon after Glenn's death did she move to California ?

H.M   About one year. She stuck it out in Tenafly and then she thought, why do I have to put up with all this rotten weather and this crowded place. . .I don't know whether Don Haynes was out there at that time or not, but I would guess she was referred to an estate agent by Don Haynes.

WW   Now, it's essential to find out where she's buried, because if I am right, in that burial plot -

H.M   We'll find Glenn buried there -

WW   In that burial plot there'll be her father Fred Burger and his wife, Helen herself -

H.M   And Mattie - *(I failed to understand that reference at the time but it has worried me since - Mattie Lou Miller was Herb's own mother, who with his father Elmer was buried in Boulder, Colorado where Fred Burger had been Town Clerk. Why Herb should suggest that his mother was buried in California with her late daughter-in-*

law instead of with her own family in Colorado remains a mystery. Auth.)

WW   That's four - and I think the other one is an unmarked, unnumbered grave.

H.M   So we'd have to have him exhumed -

WW   I'm not sure. The record should be there. I think it was probably a legal and *bona fide* thing and it should be buried somewhere there in the County Records. Since no one suspects he may be there, no one has ever bothered to look. I have friends in California chasing around trying to find the cemetery but there are seven in Pasadena alone ! We have to pin it down a little more closely. If Glenn didn't go down in the Channel - and we're 99% positive of that - then he must have got to Paris and gone back home on that Shipment Number and he must have been buried somewhere under Helen's directions. The obvious place is in her own burial plot. I'll telephone Boulder tomorrow.

H.M   You could do it this afternoon. There's a line open right now !

WW   Indeed. Okay. I've also written to the Registrar of Deaths in Pasadena and they sent me a form asking for a lot of details I don't have - Helen's initials, date and place of birth and death and so on -

H.M   `D'- her name was Helen D for Dorothy.

WW   Do you suppose any of her friends are still alive ?

HM   I doubt it. The only real friends she had were Mattie and Chummy McGregor.

WW   I see. Now, the whole thing hinges on those two things - the shipment number and the death certificate, and I am having all kinds of trouble - they are the last things they will release. But there must have been a death certificate - David Mackay got probate of the estate.

H.M   Well, I know there was a signature - there was a notice among his papers of his death. *(NOTE : This was prior to our finding Glenn's Finding of Death and Report of Death documents. Auth.)*

WW   In Mackay's papers ?

H.M.   No, in Glenn's papers.

WW   That wasn't a death certificate as such ?

H.M.   No - it was just a certificate for insurance purposes.*(NOTE : This was Glenn's 1945 Finding of Death document (Figs.14,15)*

WW   Well, we're getting very close to the end of the line. I've turned over all but the last two stones - that shipment number should tell us where Glenn -

H.M   I can't see why all this secrecy - why don't they just tell us ?

WW   Well, I think that when whatever happened in Paris happened, they were committed almost before they knew it to concealing his death.

H.M   Yes, I could see that -

WW   The cover-up was not a cover-up of his death, but of the people who were guilty of concealing it. In the Nixon case there was an enormous cover-up of what was on those hidden tapes, but it wasn't to cover-up the information - it was to cover-up Nixon who did the bugging ! I don't think Eisenhower was involved - I think Barker went to him and said `Look, we have a problem with Glenn Miller - he's missing' and Eisenhower said `I don't want to know - !'

H.M   Don't bother me - I'm busy. . . !'

WW   Right ! And I think it was all down to General Barker, the guy at the top. No one ever wrote a biography of him - a shadowy figure in history. He had a very important job, in charge of every man in that invasion. In fact, the cover-up would be very damaging -

H.M   Damaging to everyone who took part in it -

WW   Including the United States Army, and the Government. And I know a lot of people over there know that I've caught onto this forgery of the Missing Aircrew Report - and there's going to a lot of questions asked.

H.M   Helen even asked about that. Whether she did it with her eyes wide open, saying `Ah, you told me about the forgery but now, exploiting it - what's this about going to Bordeaux instead of Paris ?

WW   Did she query that ?

H.M   She queried that. So she did it one of two ways. Either `I know you're lying but what's this, telling me he was going to Bordeaux' - you know, play-acting -

WW   So she knew there was something fishy about it ?

H.M   I think she knew all the time. And the first thing she'd do is pick up the phone and say `What's the idea of all this ?' so that puts her clear out of the picture as knowing what happened.

WW   And as you said before, she knew at an early stage and wasn't looking very happy the day after it happened.

H.M   She may have known almost immediately.

WW   I think she probably did. What would be easier than General Barker or General Arnold picking up the phone - I think they probably asked her if she thought it was okay to carry through this process of covering up, before they started. And she'd probably say fine, it's better for Glenn, better for everyone.

H.M   She always thought like that.

WW   Now, the Missing Aircrew Report wasn't compiled until December 23, eight days after Glenn went missing. I wonder when Helen saw a copy of that ?

H.M   She saw a copy of it. I know she did because she's the one that questioned `Why did they go to Bordeaux ? What was this flight doing going to Bordeaux ? What's this little `A-42' in here ?'

WW   Now, you were home when she got this news ?

H.M   I just happened to be at home - I was there when I wrote that letter to Glenn, and his answer came during the time all this was going on, before I knew he was gone. *(NOTE : Herb was referring to the letter in which Glenn said "Barring a nosedive into the Channel, I'll be in Paris when you receive this -" Auth.)*

WW   That's interesting, because normally, the MACR was a secret military document and there is no way Helen would have been shown that unless she was privy to the real story - someone must have sent her a copy, probably from the War Department.

H.M   Yes - I would probably think so. That's the only way - she had someone inside. Otherwise they wouldn't dare -

WW   When did this happen ? Because the MACR didn't get to Washington until 22nd January - *(NOTE : This was almost two years before we were finally given copies of the Miller Burial File containing the real MACR #L-19)*

H.M   I don't really know. Christmas Eve I was home and stopped her crying when the news came through - I just put the whole matter out of my mind and said `He'll be home'. We all knew he'd be home - Helen said that too. But Helen was an actress -

WW   She could conceal what she was thinking - you got the impression that she knew quite a bit -

H.M.   *Now*, I have the impression that she knew about it all the time, and I think maybe it was sort of a shameful thing for her, you know, to have all this - it wasn't like Joan Collins today - in some ways she was a much better actress.

      The remainder of the tape is largely personal. A week previously I had spent a whole afternoon with Herb in his flat, and he described in detail the call which Helen had received,

Herb believed on Saturday December 16 or Sunday 17 but was not absolutely certain. The news, he said, was a severe shock to her, and she almost broke down : at the same time, she would not talk to anyone about it, including Herb : she said nothing until General Arnold made his call from France, on the 23rd, which contained, we can assume, the gist of the Haynes story.

Herb also told me that he always thought Glenn had never boarded an aircraft, that he had died of cancer but did not want his family to know about it. Certainly, he said, from his photographs Glenn lost a good deal of weight during his stay in the UK. But it seemed to me that the Army medics would not have permitted him to continue active duty if he was seriously ill. Nor could we envisage a scenario in which Glenn refused to have his family notified : rather the reverse. He would have asked for Helen to be flown to Britain, or conversely, be repatriated himself on medical grounds - which might explain why a witness described being in the same ward in Columbus Ohio as Miller when he died.

As for the Haynes story, Herb was most scathing : he did not believe a word of it, and as things turned out, he was perfectly right to do so.

13. Lt. Jean Pace

Jean Pace, the third of the Norseman pilots who were assigned the duty of ferrying Lt.Col. Baessell around Europe, has consistently withheld comment on Glenn Miller's disappearance, preferring to concentrate on the fate of the Norseman and, in particular, the route Morgan flew on December 15 1944. He sent us a series of interesting letters dealing with those matters, but in fairness it should be born in mind that when Jean evolved his theory of the Norseman route, he was unaware of the information in the Burial Files and insisted that Morgan flew west of London, overflying Bovingdon en route to Beachy Head and the Channel.

> `Morgan', Jean wrote, `was a youngster, so to speak. Baessell probably talked him into a number of flying decisions against the best interests of the personnel and the C-64 Norseman, Baessell being gruff, boisterous, domineering - and together with his rank. Morgan was possibly intimidated into action contrary to their best interest. Morgan wore R.A.F. wings in addition to USAF wings - he was an interesting short slender-statured individual'.
>
> `Bordeaux' . . . might have been a personal side trip. When I saw the Dijon destination -(this was the period in which I had incorrectly identified B-42 as Dijon, instead of Beauvais) `I had a feeling Baessell might have wanted to procure wine beverages for 8th AFSC personnel and his own use. George Ferguson and I met at Wattisham, where he ran a number of field crews, and we had two C-64s assigned for transporting small lots of personnel and aircraft field supplies.
>
> `Immediately after the D-Day invasion George flew a C-64 to the Continent and moved crews to handle aircraft in the field. He would get them fixed up and I would fly them back to the UK. After Le Havre and Paris were liberated (August 1944) Baessell began to get into the act, and George experienced some very adverse flying with Baessell. George flew back to Wattisham (via Cap Gris Nez, Dymchurch) in a state of exhaustion and requested to be relieved of the assignment. He related his experiences to me - and next day I was told I had been as-

assigned to fly Baessell.

`*So knowing how the aircraft was equipped, and learning from George's experiences, I decided the aircraft would be flown within its proper limitations. It was not equipped to fly safely over long stretches of water and had absolutely no radio navigational aid equipment. I lasted one trip with Baessell - picked him up at Twinwood Farm and down to Bovingdon to file a flight clearance to Paris. The C-64 developed a propeller hydraulic leak on the way and we returned to Wattisham for repairs. After luncheon, my boss Lt.Col. Perry advised me that I had been removed from the assignment and requested me to fly the C-64 to Alconbury, where it was assigned to 35 ADRS. Morgan was then assigned to the duty.*

`*I don't think Morgan was aware of his authority. Being the pilot of an aircraft, you outrank anyone else while you are at the controls. You make the decisions and are responsible for the safety of the craft and its personnel. It is my feeling that Baessell was calling the shots'.*

In a letter to Clive Ward, who discovered a Norseman some 6½ miles west of Le Touquet in 1980, Jean suggested that Morgan flew south from Twinwood Farm, overflying Bovingdon, to Guildford, thereafter taking the railway line route south of London to Hythe and Dymchurch before making for Cap Gris Nez. He goes on `Not being able to penetrate the French coast at Cap Gris Nez on visual flying conditions *(NOTE : The recorded cloud base in that area was 800 feet Auth.)* the aircraft probably parallelled the French coast line at low altitude on a southerly course looking for a visual opening to the Continent. With these weather conditions, 6 to 8 miles west of Le Touquet would be a potential course destined for Paris or Beauvais, as military records indicate. On the aircraft you located, it is my understanding, you found the propeller missing. This indicates the aircraft must have experienced mechanical problems whilst flying at low altitude'.

Jean Pace also sent us a detailed audit of Roy Nesbitt's article which appeared in *The Aeroplane Monthly* in February 1987, entitled `*What did happen to Glenn Miller ?'.* Like Jean Pace, Mr. Nesbitt was unaware of the information contained in the Burial Files, and his main concern was the recent report by a Lancaster navigator Fred Shaw that he had seen a Norseman destroyed by jettisoned bombs in the Channel.

At this point we activate the Time Machine once more and examine the story told by Lt. Donald Wayne Haynes after Major Glenn Miller vanished. Haynes, of course, was the central character in the mystery. He was born at 12.58 p.m. on May 25 1907 and died on June 4 1971 in Valley Receiving Hospital, Van Nuys, Los Angeles, being buried on July 6 1971 in Forest Lawn Memorial Park. The cause of death was arterio-sclerotic cardiac vascular disease and Don was 64 years old at time of death. His last occupation was Customer Relations, working for the US Post Office. His enlisted serial number was 32908442, and after he was commissioned, 0-583260. He served from May 17 1943 to December 19 1945, and on discharge held the rank of captain. His wife was Pauline D. Haynes (neé Davis) and Don was inducted into the USAAF at Miami Beach, Florida.

+   +   +

Ripton

.on, by Name Abbotts   ; Command or Air Force VIII Air
Squadron Repair   · ; Detachment 2d Strategic Air D
partur Abbotts Ripton, Course Bordeaux Via A-42
Destination Bordeaux ; Type of Mission   A
) VISIBILITY AT TIME OF CRASH OR WHEN LAST REPORTED

arting with Pilot, furnish the following particulars: I
sons were aboard aircraft, list similar particulars on s
attach original to this form.)

Crew Position	Name in Full (Last Name First)	Rank	Serial Number
1. Pilot	Morgan, John R.S.	F/O	T-190776
2. Passenger	Baessell, Norman F.	Lt Col	O-905387
3. Passenger	Miller, Alton G.	Major	O-505273
4.			
5.			
6.			
7.			

HEADQUARTERS ARMY AIR FORCES
WASHINGTON

MISSING AIR CREW REPORT

Classification changed
to
by E. A. BRADUKAS, Lt. Col.,
by F. A. WUENCH, Capt., AC
Date MAR 26 1945

This Report will be compiled in triplicate by each Army Air
Forces organization within 48 hours of the time an air crew
member is officially reported missing.

Ripton

Fig. 33

Typescript Blow-Up - MACR # 10770

MISSING AIR CREW REPORT NO.... N-19

1. ORGANIZATION: Location __Abbotts Ripton__ ; Command or Air Force __8th AF__
   Group __35th ADG__ ; Squadron __Repair__ ; Detachment __2d Strategic Air Depot__
2. SPECIFY: Point of Departure __Abbotts Ripton__ ; Course __Bordeaux Via A-42__
   Intended Destination __Bordeaux A-42__ , Type of Mission __A__
3. WEATHER CONDITIONS AND VISIBILITY AT TIME OF CRASH OR WHEN LAST REPORTED
   __unknown__
4. GIVE: (a) Day __15__ ; Month __Dec__ ; Year __44__ ; Time __1355__ and
   location __Twinwood__ of last known whereabouts of missing aircraft
   (b) Specify weather; ( ) Last Sighted; ( ) Last contacted by Radio; ( )
   Forced Down; ( ) Seen to Crash; or Information not Available. (x)
5. AIRCRAFT WAS LOST, OR IS BELIEVED TO HAVE BEEN LOST, AS A RESULT OF: (Check
   only one ( ) Enemy Aircraft; ( ) Enemy Anti-Aircraft; ( ) Other Circumstances
   as follows __unknown__
6. Aircraft: Type, Model and Series __UC-64A__ ; A.A.F. Serial Number __44-70285__
   Aircraft Nickname __Norseman__
7. ENGINES: Type, Model and Series __Radial 1340 P&W__ ; A.F.Serial Number (a) ____
   (b) __unknown__ ; (c) ____ ; (d) ____
8. INSTALLED WEAPONS (Furnish below Make, Type and Serial Number):
   (a) ____ ; (b) ____ ; (c) ____ ; (d) ____
   (e) ____ ; (f) ____ ; (g) ____ ; (h) ____
9. THE PERSONS LISTED BELOW WHERE REPORTED AS: (a) Battle Casualty ____
   or (b) Non-Battle Casualty ____
10. NUMBER OF PERSONS ABOARD AIRCRAFT: Crew __1__ ; Passengers __2__ ; TOTAL __3__
    (Starting with pilot, furnish the following particulars; If more than 10
    persons were aboard aircraft, list similar particulars on separate sheet
    and attach original to this form).

	CREW POSITION	NAME IN FULL (Last Name First)	RANK	SERIAL NUMBER	PRESENT STATUS
1.	PILOT	Morgan John B	F/O	T-190776	MIA PDD
2.		Baessell, Norman F	Lt Col	O-905387	MIA PDD
3.		Miller, Alton G.	Major	O-505273	MIA PDD
4.					
5.					
6.					
7.					
8.					
9.					
10.					

11. REMARKS: PLOTTED BY:

GEOGRAPHICAL COORDINATES ____   DULAG LUFT ____
GRID COORDINATES ____   ISOLATED BURIALS ____
NEAREST TOWN ____   MACR INFORMATION ____
   OTHER INFORMATION ____

ORIGINAL

Fig. 34

'ORIGINAL' Missing Aircrew Report L-19 - Page 1

WD, Hq AAF, Washington, Missing Air Crew Report

Name in Full (Last name first)	Rank	Serial Number	Contacted by Radio	Last Sighted	Saw Crash	Saw Forced Landing
1. Unknown						
2.						
3.						

13. IF PERSONNEL ARE BELIEVED TO HAVE SURVIVED, ANSWER YES TO ONE OF THE FOLLOWING STATEMENTS: (a) Parachutes were used:___; (b) Persons were seen walking away from scene of crash_____; or (c) Any other reason (Specify)___
        Unknown

14. ATTACH AERIAL PHOTOGRAPH, MAP, CHART, OR SKETCH, SHOWING APPROXIMATE LOCATION WHERE AIRCRAFT WAS LAST SEEN.

15. ATTACH EYEWITNESS DESCRIPTION OF CRASH, FORCED LANDING, OR OTHER CIRCUMSTANCES PERTAINING TO MISSING AIRCRAFT.

16. ATTACH A DESCRIPTION OF THE EXTENT OF SEARCH, IF ANY, AND GIVEN NAME, RANK AND SERIAL NUMBER OF OFFICE IN CHARGE HERE____None

Date of Report____23 December 1944.

For The Commanding Officer:

_____
(Signature of Preparing Officer)

RALPH S. CRAMER
Capt-AC
Adjutant

REMARKS:

NICKNAME OF AIRCRAFT:- "Norseman"

Fig. 35

`ORIGINAL' Missing Aircrew Report #L-19 - Page 2

```
F/O      Morgan   John R.S.                    35th Dep Rep Sq.

AC       T-190776

Asgd & jd with Primary T/O Dy as Asst Engr O and Add M/T
Dy as Asst Flt Test & Flt Line O, per par 8, SO 226, Hq
2nd SAD.
Above Asgd O fr Dy to DS Paris, per par 1, SO 227, Hq
VIII AFSC. 8 Nov 44   approx 15 days.
fr TD Patts to Dy as of 18 Nov 44.
Fr Dy to TD Bordeaux France B42 for purpose of ferrying
personnel per Operations Order #5, Hq 2d SAD, Office of
th Operations Officer. 15 Dec 44
   Fr TD to absent missing XX(Non Battle) on ferrying
flight over English Channel enroute to B42, 15 Dec 44.
   fr Absent missing to dropped from rolls of orgn
```

Fig. 36

Service Record Card - Flight Officer John R.S. Morgan

TELEPHONE OR VERBAL CONVERSATION RECORD

For use of this form, see AR 340-15; the proponent agency is The Adjutant General's Office.

DATE: 27 Sep 73

SUBJECT OF CONVERSATION: Col Glen Miller

INCOMING CALL

PERSON CALLING	ADDRESS	PHONE NUMBER AND EXTENSION
Col Halbert	CINFO	76629

PERSON CALLED

PHONE NUMBER AND EXTENSION

PERSON CALLING

PHONE NUMBER AND EXTENSION

PERSON CALLED

PHONE NUMBER AND EXTENSION

Glenn Miller's Plane Said Found

LILLE, France, Sept. 26 —A plane believed to be the one in which band-leader Glenn Miller disappeared into the English Channel 29 years ago has been found, it was claimed here today.

The claim was made by a retired deep-sea diver who said he had located the C-64 Norseman aircraft in 32½ feet of water between Boulogne and Calais.

He said he confirmed the identification of the aircraft by sending an engine identification plate to the United States, where his correspondent affirmed that the engine came from the plane in which Miller—then head of the Army Air Forces Band — disappeared on Christmas Day, 1944, while on a flight from London to Paris.

SUMMARY OF CONVERSATION

CBS news & wire services are running report of a aircraft just found in the English channel. Engine number compares with one for Col Miller's Plane but USAF at Wright-Patt state engines are inter changeable.

Needs to verify this with tail number soonest.

CB.

AC - UC-64

SN# 44-70285

Alton G. Miller

Maj 0505273

FILE DISPOSITION DR. 25 JUN 1974.

DA FORM 1 APR 66 751 REPLACES EDITION OF 1 FEB 59 WHICH WILL BE USED. ☆ GPO: 1970 431-860/1007

Fig. 37

CINFO Press Cutting - 1973

HQ US FORCES EUROPEAN THEATER

STAFF MESSAGE CONTROL

INCOMING C L A S S I F I E D MESSAGE

-.-.-.-.-.-.-

A TRUE COPY:

Taken from 201 file: MILLER, Alton G.

WALTER B. MORROW
Major, Infantry

DUAA

USFET 110/03

TOO 021625A FEB

TOR 030421A FEB

C O N F I D E N T I A L

P R I O R I T Y

FROM : USAFE SIGNED CO MCENUSAFE

TO FOR ACTION : CG USFET ATTN AG CASUALTY DIVISION

REF NO : UA-60821 2 FEBRUARY 1946

Reference your teletype WB - 1925 dated 30 January 1946, concerning Major ALTON GLEN MILLER, 0-595273.

Extensive search of all records available to this Headquarters fails to reveal information desired. Missing air crew report concerning aircraft on which Major MILLER was a passenger does not give any information as to weather conditions at time of take off or on planned route, type of radio equipment, or whether or not aircraft was equiped with de-icing equipment. Missing air crew report states aircraft was enroute to BORDEAUX via A 42 (VILLACOUBLAY). This Headquarters has made every effort to locate initial investigation of this case without results. Aircraft was assigned to 35th Air Depot Group which has been returned to the Zone of Interior.

WB-1925 is not identified in USFET SMC files

ACTION : AG

INFORMATION : IG
AG RECORDS

SMC IN 1766 3 Feb 46 0700A DLH/wkm REF No: UA-60821

COPY NO: 3

C O N F I D E N T I A L

Fig. 38

USFET Message to AG Department Washington - 1946

(Gironde FF-13)

2nd Ind

HEADQUARTERS, 3046 QM Graves Reg Company, APO 809, US ARMY
21 June 1946

TO : Commanding Officer, 551 QM Group, APO 809, US ARMY
(Attn. Operations)

1. During the investigation of the area of Bordeaux, a search was made for the mentioned deceased, and it was found that there is no trace of them in the area of Bordeaux.

2. In order to locate the bodies, more detailed information as to the area of crash must be had by this organization.

FOR THE COMMANDING OFFICER:

Tel : Limoges 7201

Incls: n/e

DONALD K. BRINKMANN
2nd Lt.   Inf
GRS Officer

Fig. 39

The `Bordeaux Crash Letter' dated 1946

To accompany WD AGO Forms 66-1 or 2 of Missing or Missing in Action Personnel
(other than those covered by Missing Air Crew Report).

NAME   Alton Glenn Miller   ASN 0505273 GRADE Major

Arm or
Service   Air Corps   ORG Hq Comd, Supreme Headquarters AEF
Army Air Force Band (Special)

APO 757   Date Reported MIA 15 December 1944

MISSION England to Paris, France

POINT OF DEPARTURE Airport in England   DATE 15 December 1944

INTENDED DESTINATION Paris, France

LAST KNOWN WHEREABOUTS Enroute to Paris, France

BRIEF RESUME OF CIRCUMSTANCES SURROUNDING DISAPPEARANCE:

See attached Letter, Supreme Headquarters AEF, subject: "Report of Missing
Personnel", file: AG 201-Miller, Alton Glenn (Off) dated 22 December 1944.

STATEMENTS OF WITNESSES, IF ANY:

    See letter referred to above.

REMARKS: (Any information not covered above, including details and results of
search, if any, conducted)

For the Commanding Officer:

Date of Report 28 December 1944

(signature of preparing officer)
W. S. STERNS, JR.,
Major, Infantry,
Adjutant.

Classification removed
per authority IAG.

by_____ Date 1-12

Carroll V. En
1st Lt., A. G

FILE IN C1S. JR. FILE

AGO
5 APR 1945

Fig. 40

The 'Missing' Report - December 22 1944

HEADQUARTERS
2D STRATEGIC AIR DEPOT
APO 636

G-A-4

704

AAF Sta 547.
22 December 1944.

SUBJECT: Missing Air Crew Report.

TO: Commanding Officer, VIII Air Force SvC, AAF Sta 506, APO 636, US Army.

Inclosed herewith ETO CAS Form 2 and Missing Air Crew Report per verbal request Lt Colonel Traustor, 21 December 1944.

For the Commanding Officer:

50848

RALPH S. CRAMER
Capt, Air Corps
Adjutant.

2 Incls:
Incl 1 - ETO Cas Form 2
Incl 2 - Missing Air Crew Report

NOTE : This letter confirms Capt. Ralph S. Cramer's instructions over the telephone from Paris by Lt.Col. Traistor on Thursday December 21 1944, after interviewing Lt. Haynes. Also that Cramer's `original' unsigned Missing Aircrew Report was dated December 22. The forged MACR #10770 was dated December 23 to avoid the MACR pre-dating Miller's Casualty Report (Fig.6) issued on December 22 1944.
`Indorsements' refers to additional documents attached to the original Report.

Fig.40 (a)

Covering Letter - 2nd Strategic Air Depot Abbotts Ripton to 8th AF Service Command Milton Ernest

704   1st Ind.   C-C-2

HQ VIII AFSC AAF STA 506 APO 636 US ARMY.   23 DEC 1944

TO: Commanding General, Eighth Air Force, AAF Station 101, APO 634, US Army.

    1. Forwarded in compliance with Cir 94, Hq European T of Opns US Army,
dated 31 August 1944.

    2. Paragraph 10a(4) cited circular complied with per TWX VIIIAFSC-D-832
this Hq, 20 Dec 44, copy attached.

            For the Commanding Officer:

                                        ALBERT G. BUKLOW,
                                        Major,   AGD,
                                        Adjutant General.

4 Incls:
   Added - 2 Incls.
      Incl. 3-ETO Cas Form 2(Lt Col Baessell)(trip)
      Incl. 4-Cy TWX VIIIAFSC-20 Dec 44   23310

NOTE : Ralph Cramer enclosed 2 items - ETO Cas Form 2 for
John Morgan, and the Missing Aircrew Report.
8th AFSC Milton Ernest added 2 further items : ETO Casualty
Form 2 for Col. Baessell, and the genuine Confirmatory Signal to
SHAEF despatched the previous day, Friday December 22. The
forged version was prepared at SHAEF, substituted for the
genuine signal and sent to Washington. See Figs. 10, 24.

Fig. 40 (b)

Covering Letter from 8th AFSC Milton Ernest to HQ 8th Air Force.

(Ltr Hq 2d Strategic Air Depot, subj: "Missing Air Crew Report." dtd 22 Dec 44)

319.1.   2nd Ind.   SCU-D-17

HEADQUARTERS EIGHTH AIR FORCE, APO 634, U. S. ARMY. -3 JAN 1945

TO: Commanding General, European Theater of Operations, APO 887, U. S. Army.

      Forwarded in accordance with letter, War Department, TAGO, AG 704 (5 Jul 44) OB-S-AAF-M, 7 July 1944, subject: "Missing Air Crew Reports".

      For the Commanding General:

H. S. WILSON, Jr
Major, A.G.D.,
Asst. Adjutant General.

1 Incl:
  Incl 1. Missing Air Crew Report, 2d SAD,
        UC-64A, 44-70285, 15 Dec 44 (in trip)

NOTE : This letter provides further confirmation that Cramer's `original' MACR was compiled at Abbotts Ripton on December 22 1944, not December 23.

Fig.40 (c)

Letter from 8th Air Force HQ to Commanding General, SHAEF
(Gen.Bedell Smith) enclosing Missing Aircrew Report

AG 201-AGP-Miller, Alton Glenn (Off) 1st Ind.   HLA/or
 (28 Dec 44)

SUPREME HEADQUARTERS AEF, MAIN, APO 757, U. S. ARMY, 30 December 1944.

TO: Commanding General, European Theater of Operations, U. S. Army,
  APO 887.

    For the Supreme Commander:

2 Incls:
 n/o

               H. L. ALLEN,
               Lt. Col., AGD,
             Asst. Adjutant General.

NOTE : This letter is important, indicating that Eisenhower saw the `original' unsigned Cramer Missing Aircrew Report dated 22 December 1944. The MACRs were un-numbered until Military Records Department recorded the incident in the MACR Register. The two enclosures were the Missing Aircrew Report and the Confirmatory Signal.

Fig.40 (d)

**Covering Letter from 8th Air Force to General Eisenhower at
SHAEF Versailles**

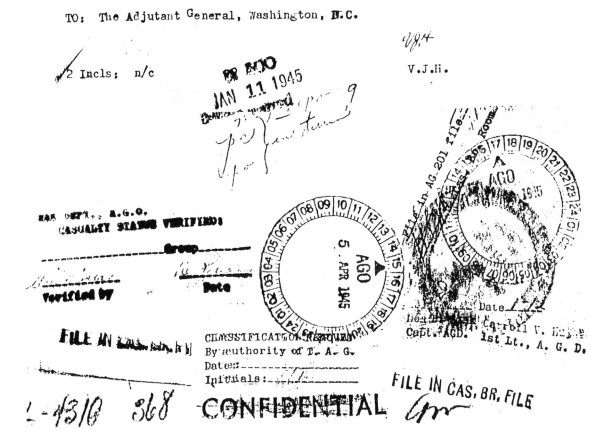

AG 201 Miller, Alton Glenn (Off)   2nd Ind.   VJH/jg
Hq, European T of Opns, APO 887, 2 January 1945.

TO: The Adjutant General, Washington, D.C.

2 Incls: n/c   V.J.H.

WAR DEPT., A.G.O.
CASUALTY STATUS VERIFIED:

Group

Verified by   Date

FILE IN   CLASSIFICATION REMOVED
                       By authority of T. A. G.
                       Date:
                       Initials:

CONFIDENTIAL   FILE IN CAS. BR. FILE

NOTE : This letter was delayed 4 days until January 2 1945. The
'Casualty Status Verification' of Major Miller is signed and
dated - but the 'status' itself has been deleted. Was Miller
'Missing' 'or Missing in Action' ? Or not missing at all ?

Fig.40 (e)

Covering Letter from SHAEF to the AG in Washington DC.

 10770

AG 360.33 Cas   3rd Ind.   JWP/jf
HEADQUARTERS, EUROPEAN THEATER OF OPERATIONS, APO 887, US ARMY, 8 Jan.4

TO: Commanding General, Army Air Forces, Washington, D. C.
     Attention: Statistical Control Division.

        Forwarded in compliance with letter, War Department, AG 704 (5
Jul 44) OB-S-AAF-M, dated 7 July 1944.

                    For the Theater Commander:

                                        H. M. RUND,
                                        Colonel, AGD,
                                  Assistant Adjutant General.

  Incl: n/c (trip w/d)

**NOTE : `Letter 704' refers to Figs.40 (a) and (b), Cramer's letter
to Milton Ernest and 8th AFSC's letter to 8th Air Force HQ.**

Fig.40 (f)

**Covering Letter from SHAEF to USAAF Statistical Control
Division.**

Supreme Headquarters
ALLIED EXPEDITIONARY FORCE
Headquarters Command

WSS/gap/em APO 757
U.S. Army

313.3
x-201-Miller, Alton Glenn (Off)

28 December 1944

Subject: Transmittal of Records.

To : Commanding General, European Theater of Operations, APO 887, U. S. Army, (Attention: Central Records Branch, AG Casualty Division, APO 887, U. S. Army).

Thru : Supreme Commander, Allied Expeditionary Force, APO 757, U. S. Army.

Transmitted herewith Missing Report and WD AGO Form 66-2 as pertains to Major ALTON GLENN MILLER, 0505273, Air Corps, Army Air Force Band (Special), Headquarters Command, Supreme Headquarters Allied Expeditionary Force, reported missing on 15 December 1944 while enroute from an airport in England to Paris, France as outlined in letter attached to Missing Report.

For the Commanding Officer:

W. S. STERNS, JR.,
Major, Infantry,
Adjutant.

2 Incls:
Incl 1 - WD AGO Form 66-2
Incl 2 - Missing Report

AGO 5 APR 1945

Classification removed
per authority Tag.
by ____ Date 1-12
~~Capt. AGD.~~ Carroll V.
1st Lt., A.

FILE IN CAS. AG FILE

Fig. 41

Transmittal Covering Letter 'Missing' Report - December 22 1944

REQUEST FOR INFORMATION

TO: PENTAGON LIAISON SECTION, MEMORIAL DIVISION		DATE 6 October 1950

FROM (Branch and Section) Identification Br., Final Det. Sec.	REQUESTED BY Thomas		TEL. EXT. 73216	ROOM NO. 1521 B

NAME OF DECEDENT (Last, First, Middle Initial) 2 BAESSELL, Norman F.	RANK Lt. Col. AAF	SERIAL NUMBER 0 905 387

INFORMATION REQUIRED

All available dental information on above decedent.

INFORMATION FURNISHED

Attached herewith TWX containing dental data for Norman F. Baessell, 0-905 387.

DENTAL CHART   16 Apr 42

UPPER RIGHT		UPPER LEFT	
X X X			X X
8 7 6 5 4 3 2 1		1 2 3 4 5 6 7 8	

LOWER RIGHT		LOWER LEFT	
X			X X X X
16 15 14 13 12 11 10 9		9 10 11 12 13 14 15 16	

Identification Branch

PENTAGON LIAISON SECTION OFFICER (Signature)

DONALD BENNER
CAPT QMC

OQMG FORM 1933
23 MAR 50

ORIGINAL TO BE FILED IN 293 FILE

A25742

Fig. 42

Letter - Baessell Dental Records

SPECIAL ORDERS   9 May 1947
NUMBER   69

1.   Par 2 SO 21 this hq cs is rescinded.

2.   PAC letter file AGAO-S 293.9 (27 Mar 47) D-M, War Dept, TAGO,
9 Apr 47, Subj: Establishment of Boards of Review for Identification of
Unknown Dead Overseas, the fol ind, this hq, are appointed a Board of
Review for identification of Unknown Dead (European Area):

COL	JOHN H EVANS	015184	INF
LT COL	WILLIAM D MANN	0323364	JAGD
LT COL	JAMES F METCALF	0350280	QMC
MAJ	GEORGE E CILLEY	0336143	FA
MAJ	GEORGE E SPRINGER	0284512	FA
MAJ	GEORGE E WOODS	0252521	CE

James Domenico, WD Civ, CAF-3, Reporter

This Board will comply with instructions of above cited War Dept ltr, and
will take over any unfinished cases referred to Uncoverable Casualty Board
aptd by par 2 SO 21 this hq cs and rescinded by par 1 above.

AUTH: Sec I Cir 157 Hq US Forces European Theater 23 Oct 46.

BY COMMAND OF BRIGADIER GENERAL PECKHAM:

ALFRED B. LEWISTON
Colonel,   QMC
Chief of Staff

OFFICIAL:

/s/ Clara R. Beery
CLARA R. BEERY
Capt,   AGD
Asst Adj Gen

DISTRIBUTION "A" & "B" plus:
Ea Indiv concerned 4
Ea Unit concerned 2
Pers Div 10
Pers Div TAG EUCOM.......2

R E S T R I C T E D

Fig.43

Non-Recoverability Board Members

SUBJECT: Non-recoverable Remains.

TO   : Non-recoverable Board AGRC.

1. It is recommended that the Board take action on the following case:

NAMES: MORGAN,   John R.S.   F/O   T-190776
        BAESSELL, Norman F. Lt. Col. O-905387
        MILLER,   Alton G.   Major   O-505273

ORGANIZATION: 35th ADG Gp.; Repair Sq.; Det.2d Strategic Depot Air;
                                                              8th AF.

PLACE OF DEATH: Unknown (probably English Channel)

DATE OF DEATH : 15. December 1944

SYNOPSIS OF CASE: The three men mentioned above were aboard an Eighth
Air Force Command airplane (C-64) which departed England enroute to Paris,
France. The pilot, F/O Morgan, took off from Abbotts Ripton, England and stopped at Twinwood Farms, where he picked up the other two men as passengers. The
a/c was never seen again and, to this date, no word has ever been received concerning the plane or its passengers. In view of the fact that all territory
crossed in the flight of this a/c was in Allied hands and no information has
been forthcoming from Allied sources, it can only be assumed that the a/c went
down somewhere in the water and that the three men concerned will not be recovered.

Reference is made to 2/nd Indorsement from 2046 QRS Co dated 21 June 1946, to
Classiefied Message from USFET and letter to Mrs. MILLER dated 6 February 1946.

2. Every effort has been made to correlate this case with records in this
Headquarters, pertaining to unknown deceased interred in U.S. Military Cemeteries and reported isolated burials. The results are negative.

3. It is recommended that the remains, based upon the above information
and research, be declared non-recoverable.

WALTER B.MORROW
Major., Infantry
Chief, Isolated Burials

Fig.44 (a)

Major Morrow Letter to Non-Recoverability Board

Proceedings of a Board of Officers appointed in accordance with
letter File AGAO-S 293.9 (27 Mar 47); D-M, War Dept, TAGO, 9 Apr 47.

The Board met pursuant to Par. 2; SO No. 6?, Headquarters, American
Graves Registration Command, 9 May 47, at the Astoria Hotel, Paris,
France, on - 7 OCT 1947   . The purpose of the Board was to determine
recoverabilty/ identity of certain casualties now under consideration
by this command.

The Board reviewed reports of investigation, statements of witnesses
and other papers contained in the files of American Graves Registration
Command, ETA, pertaining to the case of the following named casualty/
casualties, the remains of which have not been recovered. The case files
and other data considered are attached.

CASE No.	NAME		ASN	GRADE
	MORGAN,	John R. S.	T-190776	F/O
	BARKSILL,	Norman P.	0-905387	Lt. Col.
	MILLER,	Alton G.	0-505273	Major

FINDINGS: The Board having carefully considered the evidence before it,
finds the remains of said casualty/casualties may be considered as non-
recoverable and recommends that no further action be taken to recover these
remains.

_____   _____
JOHN H. EVANS, Col., INF.   WILLIAM D. MANN, Lt. Col., JAGD

_____   _____
JAMES F. METCALF, Lt. Col., QMC   GEORGE E. CILLEY, Maj., FA

_____   _____
GEORGE E. SPRINGER, Maj., FA   GEORGE E. WOODS, Maj., CE

Dept. of the Army, OQMG, Washington, D.C.
8 November 1947
                    APPROVED: _____
XXXXXXXXXXXXXXXXXXXXXXXXXXXXXXXX   GEO. A. HORKAN
                                     Brigadier General, QMC
                                     Chief, Memorial Division

Fig.44 (b)

Non-Recoverability Board Findings

(1) SERIAL NO. T-190776 (2) NAME MORGAN JOHN R.S. (3) RANK FLIGHT OFFICER (4) AGE 1920

(5) PERS. CLASS 18 (6) BRANCH AIR CORPS (7) STATION 35th ADG Repair

(8) ORGANIZATION ASSIGNED AFSC

(9) ORGANIZATION ATTACHED 8th

(10) PRESENT RATING & DATE Pilot 25 May 43

(11) ORIGINAL RATING & DATE

(12) TRANSFERRED FROM

(13) FLIGHT RESTRICTIONS

(14) TRANSFERRED TO

(15) TRANSFERRED FROM

(16)

(17) MONTH NOVEMBER 1944

DO NOT WRITE IN THIS SPACE

AIRCRAFT TYPE MODEL & SERIES	NO. LANDINGS 20	FLYING INST. (INCL IN 1ST PL TIME) S 21	COMMD. PILOT C CA 22	CO-PILOT CP 23	QUALIFIED PILOT DUAL QD 24	FIRST PILOT DAY P 25	FIRST PILOT NIGHT P N OR NI 26	RATED (YRS.) IN 27	RATED (YRS.) NON-PILOT 28	NON-RATD OTHER ARMS & SERVICES 30	NON-RATD OTHER CT'W & PA S'GR 31	INSTRUMENT 1 32	NIGHT N 33	INSTRUMENT TRAINER 34	PILOT NON-MIL AIRCRAFT OVER 400 H.P. 35	PILOT NON-MIL AIRCRAFT UNDR 400 H.P. 36
UC-64A	3					3:30										
UC-64A	4					1:45										
UC-64A	1					1:10										
UC-64A	2					2:40										
UC-64A	2					2:50										
UC-64A	2					2:15										
UC-64A	2					2:10										

COLUMN TOTALS ... 16:20

SPECIAL INFORMATION

CERTIFIED CORRECT

Richard H. Watts

RICHARD H. WATTS, JR.
Captain, Air Corps,
Operations Officer.

(42) TOTAL STUDENT PILOT TIME

(43) TOTAL FIRST PILOT TIME
16:20
171:20
187:40

(44) TOTAL PILOT TIME
16:20
216:40
233:00

(37) THIS MONTH

(38) PREVIOUS MONTHS THIS F.Y.

(39) THIS FISCAL YEAR

(40) PREVIOUS FISCAL YEARS

(41) TO DATE

AIRCRAFT	HL 20	21	22	CARD NO. 1 23	24	25	26	27	CARD NO. 2 28	29	30	31	32	CARD NO. 3 33	34	35	36
	19																

Fig.45

Morgan Flight Record (Form 5) November 1944

AAF Form 5 — Individual Flight Record

(5) CLASS ___18___ (6) BRANCH ___AIR CORPS___ (7) STATION ___AAF 547___

ORGANIZATION ASSIGNED ___8th AIR FORCE___ ___AFSC___ COMMAND ___WING___ ___35th ADG___ GROUP ___Repair___ SQUADRON

ORGANIZATION ATTACHED ___ATTACHED FOR FLYING___ ___DETACHMENT___

PRESENT RATING & DATE ___Pilot 25 May 43___   DETACHING FOR FLYING

(11) ORIGINAL RATING & DATE ___Same___

TRANSFERRED FROM   (13) FLIGHT RESTRICTIONS

TRANSFERRED TO   (14) TRANSFER DATE

| | SQUADRON | | GROUP | | WING | | COMMAND | | (15) A.F. | | STATION | | MO. | YR. (17) |
| NO. | TYPE | NO. | TYPE | | | | | | | | | | |

MONTH ___DECEMBER___

AIRCRAFT TYPE, MODEL & SERIES	SON 20	FLYING INST. (INCL IN 1ST PIL) 21	COMMD. PILOT CA 22	CO-PILOT CP 23	QUAL. FIED PILOT DUAL QU 24	FIRST PILOT DAY P 25	NIGHT N OR H 26	NON-PILOT 27	28	29	OTHER ARMS & SERVICES 30	OTHER CREW & PASS'GR 31	INSTRU-MENT I 32	NIGHT N 33	INSTRU-MENT TRAINER 34	PILOT OVER
UC-64A	2				2:40							12	1:33	31	3:2

RATED PERS. — NON-RATED — SPECIAL INFORMATION

NOTE: WHEN PILOT WAS TRANSFERRED FROM 27th ATG TO SERVICE COMMAND MANY OF HIS FORM 5 WERE LOST.

FORM 5 CLOSED: INDIVIDUAL MISSING.

CERTIFIED CORRECT:

Richard H. Watts Jr (signature)

RICHARD H. WATTS, JR.
Captain, Air Corps,
Operations Officer.

Fig. 46   Morgan Flight Record (Form 5) December 1944

CAUTION: Complete all items

CODE: P1

12 *apr* 11

PRIORITY: 0
☐ REQUESTER WAITING
☒ TELEPHONE REPLY NLT _1 5 ap_
☐ LETTER REPLY NLT _____

NAME (Last, first, middle)

MILLER, ALTON GLENN *maj*

SERVICE NUMBER: 0505273 _____

SSAN:

BRANCH OF SERVICE *AF ok* ARMY AIR *Corps*

DATE OF DEATH

DATE OF BIRTH   PLACE OF BIRTH

STATUS AT DEATH

DATES OF SERVICE FOR WHICH INFORMATION IS REQUESTED
WW II

FROM _____ TO _____

FROM _____ TO _____

FROM _____ TO _____

PRESENT MILITARY STATUS:
RETIRED STATUS ☐ YES ☒ NO
MEMBER OF RESERVE OR NATIONAL GUARD ☐ YES ☒ NO
IF SERVED AFTER DATES OF REQUESTED DATA, SHOW DATE OF LAST SEPARATION, AND BRANCH OF SERVICE.

NAME AND ADDRESS OF REQUESTER ☐ Veteran ☐ Other

NAME _____ CKS

FIRM NAME DPMDRO-2

STREET ADDRESS _Randolph_

CITY _AFB_

STATE _Tex_ ZIP _____

TELEPHONE:
BUSINESS/FTS 512 658 5311 c/1S 5 2515
HOME 53 Ro

PURPOSE OF REQUEST:

INFORMATION OR ACTION SOUGHT

are *fingerprints on file*

Congressional Interest

may again
4-14-71

_____
Information clerk

ACTION TAKEN (Classified filed) No fingerprints on file
WW II 10 *may* 54
on 13 *april* 11

Action clerk   Date

Fig.47

Miller Fingerprint Inquiry - Provost Marshal to AG Washington

Name   Miller, Alton Glenn ✓   : Is there a procurement objective ✓ : Yes / XXX

Address   Byrne Lane,   ✓   : To W.D. Personnel Board   ✓ : Yes / XXX

         Tenafly, New Jersey   ✓   : Approved   ✓ Yes

Place &   State : Mo. : Day : Year : If salary exceeds $4500, is case   : Yes
Date of Birth Iowa ✓ :March: 1 ✓: 1904 ✓: approved by Senate   X : No

                        : Yes) :   : Yes
Citizenship. Is proof required ✓ : XXX : Physically qualified   : XXX

                        : Yes : Is applicant's certificate re   : XXX
Is application attached (Form 0850) ✓ : XXX : physical defects attached ✓ : No

                        : XXX :
Is applicant government employee ✓ : No : Briefer's name   Kaplan --1105

                        : XXX :
Is release attached   ✓ : No : Date   September 7, 1942.

Appointment made for duties involving ____moderate____ ✓ physical exertion.

Remarks:
        Age: 38 ✓
        Branch: Special Service, S.O.S. ✓
        S.Q: Orchestra Leader and Owner ✓

Check List
  Inclosures:
    1 - Form for oath
    2 - Fingerprint card
    3 - 2 Penalty envelopes
    4 - Report of Entry on Active Duty
    5 -
    6 -
    7 -
    8 -

Copies of Letter of Appointment to:
   Army Specialist Corps ✓
   Chief of Special Service. ✓

Date appointed _____ September 8, 1942.

A - Civil Service Classification P-4

B - Salary $3300

C - Relative rank Captain

D - Serial Number S-   47

Approved by order of the Secretary of War:

                    Adjutant General.

Fig.48

Document Confirming Miller Fingerprints on Record

AG 704 (11 Mar 48)   WIN/mrh/1B735/9048

11 March 1948

MEMORANDUM TO : Officer in Charge, Casualty Section,
                Personnel Actions Branch, AGO

SUBJECT :   Report of Death

1. The following named officers of the Air Corps were reported missing, non-battle, in flight from England to Paris, France on 15 December
1944, by Casualty Branch Message Numbers 006037 and 358007.

Baessell, Norman F.	Lt.Col.	0905387
Miller, Alton Glenn	Major	0505273
Morgan, John R.S.	F/O	T190776

Flight Officer Morgan, only, was in a flying pay status.

2. Under the provisions of Section 5, Public Law 490, as amended, a
Finding of Death was made in the case of the above named men (Sh&5 No.
4902) showing the presumed date of death as 15 December 1945.

3. Missing Aircrew Report No. 10770, dated 23 December 1944, reveals
that subject persons constituted the crew and passengers aboard a UC-64A
(Noorduyn transport plane), Aircraft Number 44-70285, nicknamed Norseman,
which departed Abbotts Ripton, England, for Bordeaux, France via A42; The
aircraft was last sighted at 13.55 hours on 15 December 1944 at Twinwood
Field, England.

4. The Casualty Section File of Major Miller shows that Flight Officer
Morgan took off from Abbotts Ripton at 13.25 hours on 15 December 1944 for
Twinwood, with operation orders for A-42, Bordeaux. He departed Twinwood
Field at 1355 hours on 15 December 1944, after having picked up two passengers, Lt.Col. Baessell and Major Miller, for Bordeaux, France via A-42
(Villacoublay, France, on the outskirts of Paris, France. General weather
conditions over the English Channel on 15 December 1944, obtained by
telephone from Foreant Weather Division, Assistant Chief of Air Staff, were
intermittent rains, stratus clouds, ceiling 1,000-2,000 feet, southerly
wind of 2 miles per hour, warm front.

5. The Quartermaster General, Washington, D.C., forwarded to this office a copy of a letter to the Commanding General, American Graves Registration Command, European Area, dated 18 December 1947, "Subject : Non-
Recoverability of Remains, reference the Findings of a Board of Officers,
Case No. 8, convened at this Headquarters on 7 October 1947." The Findings
of the Board are as follows :

Fig. 49

Non-Recoverability Board Memorandum - Page 1

AG 704 (11 March 1948).

"Findings : The Board having carefully considered the evidence before it, finds the remains of said casualty/casualties may be considered as non-recoverable and recommends that no further action be taken to recover these remains."

Attached to the Proceedings is a recommendation from the Chief, Isolated Burials, American Graves Registration Command, European Theater Area to the Non-Recoverability Board, AGRC, Subject : Non-Recoverable Remains which is quoted in pertinent part as follows :

1. Place of Death: Unknown. (Probably English Channel)
Date of Death: 15 December 1944.
Synopsis of Case: The three men mentioned above were aboard an Eighth Air Force Command airplane (C-64), which departed England enroute to Paris, France. The pilot, F/O Morgan, took off from Abbotts Ripton, England, and stopped at Twinwood Farms, where he picked up the other two men as passengers. The a/c was never seen again and, to this date, no word has ever been received concerning the plane or its passengers. In view of the fact that all territory crossed in the flight of this a/c was in Allied hands and no information has been forthcoming from Allied sources, it can only be assumed that the a/c went down somewhere in the water and that the three men concerned will not be recovered.

2. Every effort has been made to correlate this case with records in this Headquarters, pertaining to unknown deceased interred in US military cemeteries and reported Isolated Burials. The results are negative.

3. It is recommended that the remains, based upon the above information and research, be declare non-recoverable.

6. The plane was last seen at 1355 hours on 15 December 1944, when it departed Twinwood Field, England, flying on a course to Paris, France. The general weather conditions over the English Channel on 15 December 1944 were "intermittent rains, stratus clouds, ceiling 1,000-2,000 feet, southerly wind of 2 miles per hour, warm front. Exhaustive research in the European Theater of Operations, examination of the AG Files of the subject personnel and records at the Historical office, Army Air Forces, do not reveal any information relative to them or the plane after leaving Twinwood Field. The captured German records were searched with negative results. Considering also the fact that the course of the flight of the plane to Paris, France was in Allied hands, and no information has been received from that source, the only reasonable conclusion is that the plane crashed into the sea and carried the men in it to their deaths.

Fig. 50

Non-Recoverability Board Memorandum - Page 2

7. It is recommended, therefore, that pursuant to the provisions of Section 9, Missing Persons Act, the foregoing information be accepted as an official report of death, and that a casualty report be initiated stating that the men in paragraph 1, above, died, (non-battle, 15 December 1944, when their plane crashed somewhere in the English Channel while on a flight from Twinwood Field, England to Paris, France and that Flight Officer Morgan, only, was in a flying pay status at the time of their death. Subject persons were in pay and duty status at the time of death, which was not the result of their own misconduct. The sytemat will be processed in accordance with Paragraph 2b, Bulletin 36, 1945. The casualty report and official report of death will include the following statement :

Finding of Death has been issued previously under Section 5, Public Law 490, 7 March 1942, as amended, showing the presumed date of death as 15 December 1945
This "Report of Death" based on information received since that date, is issued in accordance with Section 9 of said Act and its effect on prior payments and settlements is as provided in Section 9.

WALTER B. HALLS
Investigator

CONCURRED

SANFORD COFFIN
Captain AGD
OIC Status Review and
Determination Unit

Approved. Recommended action will be taken.

BY ORDER OF THE SECRETARY OF THE ARMY

EARLE E. EWING
Lt.Colonel, AGD
OIC, Casualty Section
Personnel Actions Branch AGO

Fig. 51

Non-Recoverability Board Memorandum - Page 3

AC 201 Miller, Alton G.
(10 Jan 46) *AC-O*

15 January 1946

FINDING OF DEATH OF A MISSING PERSON
Re: 11.190.773

Pursuant to the provisions of Section 5 of the Act of

7 March 1942 (Public Law 490 77th Congress) as amended,

upon direction and delegation by The Secretary of War,

The Chief, Casualty Branch, The Adjutant General's Office,

finds **Major Alton G. Miller, 0505273, Air Corps**

to be dead. He was officially reported as missing in action

as of the **15th**   day of **December 1944**   For the

purpose stated in said Act, death is presumed to have occurred

on the **16th**   day of **December 1945**

Date of birth **1st March 1904**

BY ORDER OF THE SECRETARY OF WAR:

/s/George F. Herbert
Colonel, AGD
Chief, Casualty Branch

Attention:
Mr. J. R. Boldt, Second
Vice President

For The Equitable Life Assurance Society
Department of Policy Claims, 393 Seventh Ave.
New York 1, New York

Fig. 52

Finding of Death - Major Glenn Miller (second issue)

AGPC-S 201 Miller, Alton G.
(16 Dec 45) 0505273

16 December 1945

Mrs. Helen D. Miller
Byrne Lane
Tenafly, New Jersey

Dear Mrs. Miller:

Since your husband, Major Alton G. Miller, 0505273, Air Corps, was reported missing 15 December 1944, the War Department has entertained the hope that he survived and that information would be revealed dispelling the uncertainty surrounding his absence. However, as in many cases, the conditions of warfare deny us such information. The record concerning your husband shows that he was a passenger aboard a C-64 (Noorduyn) transport aircraft which failed to arrive at its destination, Bordeaux, France. The aircraft was last sighted at 1355 hours, 15 December 1944, as it departed Twinwood Field, England. No other facts are known concerning the disappearance of his plane.

Full consideration has recently been given to all available information bearing on the absence of your husband, including all records, reports and circumstances. These have been carefully reviewed and considered. In view of the fact that twelve months have now expired without the receipt of evidence to support a continued presumption of survival, the War Department must terminate such absence by a presumptive finding of death. Accordingly, an official finding of death has been recorded under the provisions of Public Law 490, 77th Congress, approved March 7, 1942, as amended.

The finding does not establish an actual or probable date of death; however, as required by law, it includes a presumptive date of death for the termination of pay and allowances, settlement of accounts and payment of death gratuities. In the case of your husband this date has been set as 16 December 1945, the day following the expiration of twelve months' absence.

I regret the necessity for this message but trust that the ending of a long period of uncertainty may give at least some small measure of consolation. I hope you may find sustaining comfort in the thought that the uncertainty with which war has surrounded the absence of your husband has enhanced the honor of his service to his country and of his sacrifice.

Sincerely yours,

1 Incl.
Copies Furnished:
AG 201
Cas Br File

EDWARD F. WITSELL
Major General
Acting The Adjutant General of the Army

Fig. 53

Letter - Adjutant-General to Helen Miller

WAR DEPARTMENT
HEADQUARTERS ARMY AIR FORCES
WASHINGTON

MACR No. __10770__
COPY

MISSING AIR CREW REPORT

IMPORTANT: This report will be compiled in triplicate by each Army
Air Forces organization within 48 hours of the time an
aircraft is officially reported missing.

1. ORGANIZATION: Location: Abbotts Ripton___ Command or Air Force VIII Air Force SVC
   GROUP 35th ADG____; SQUADRON Repair____; DETACHMENT 2d Strategic-
2. SPECIFY: Point of Departure Abbotts Ripton__; Course Bordeaux Via A-42(Air Dep)
   Intended Destination Bordeaux A-42___; Type of Mission A
3. WEATHER CONDITIONS AND VISIBILITY AT TIME OF CRASH OR WHEN LAST REPORTED:___
   Unknown
4. GIVE: (a) Date 15 Dec 44 Time 1355_____;And Location of Last
   known whereabouts of missing aircraft___ Twinwood
   (b) Specify whether ( ) Last sighted; ( ) XXXXXXXXXXXXXXXXXXXXXXX
   XXXXXXXXXXXXXXXXXXXXXXXXXXXXXXXXXXX) Information not available.
5. AIRCRAFT WAS LOST, OR IS BELIEVED TO HAVE BEEN LOST, AS A RESULT OF (Check
   only one: ( ) Enemy Aircraft; ( ) Enemy Anti-Aircraft; ( ) Other Circumstances as follows___ Unknown
6. AIRCRAFT: Type, Model and Series UC-64A__: AAF Serial No. 44-70285
7. ENGINES: Type, Model and Series R-1340 P&W__; AAF Serial No. (a)_____
   Unknown____(b)_____(c)_____(d)_____
8. INSTALL WEAPONS (Furnish below Make, Type and Serial Number)
   (a)_____(b)_____(c)_____(d)_____
   (e)_____(f)_____(g)_____(h)_____
9. THE PERSONS LISTED BELOW WERE REPORTED AS: XXXXXXXXXXXXXXXXXXX
   XXXXXXXXNon-Battle Casualty
10. NUMBER OF PERSONS ABOARD AIRCRAFT: Crew___1__:Passengers__2___: Total 3
    (Starting with pilot, furnish the following particulars: If more than 11
    persons were aboard aircraft, list similar particulars on separate sheet
    and attach original to this form).

	Crew Position	Name in Full (Last Name First)	Rank	Serial Number	Status
1.	Pilot	Morgan, John R. S.	F/O	T-190776	DED
2.	Passenger	Baessell, Norman F.	Lt. Col	O-905387	DED
3.	Passenger	Miller, Alton G.	Major	O-505273	DED
4.					
5.					
6.					
7.					
8.					
9.					
10.					
11.					

12. IDENTIFY BELOW THESE PERSONS WHO ARE BELIEVED TO HAVE LAST KNOWLEDGE OF
    AIRCRAFT, AND CHECK APPROPRIATE COLUMN TO INDICATE BASIS FOR SAME:

1.

RESTRICTED   C(-80495,AF

Fig. 54

The `Sample' Missing Aircrew Report

Fig. 55

Mr. Alex Sleap at Bovingdon

SPECIAL

From: Headquarters Communications Zone, European Theater of
Operations, US Army, Paris, France

To: War Department

Nr. E 77699   22 December 1944

SPXPC signed Eisenhower E 77699 AG Cas Div casualty
message 3028 Nonbattle.

Miller, Alton Glenn 0505273 Major AC Army Air Force
Band (special) Hq Command, Supreme Hq AEF) is reported
missing since 15 December 44 enroute by Air from
England to Paris, France. Major Miller was taken to
the airfield by an officer of the Army Air Force Band
who witnessed the takeoff. No trace of this airplane
can be found and airplane is considered missing.

Request acknowledgement and that immediate information
be furnished by priority cable when next of kin has
been notified in order that suitable release may be
made to the press here at 1800A hours 24 December
as Major Miller was to have participated in Christmas
Day broadcast concerning which considerable publicity
has been given in the United States

End

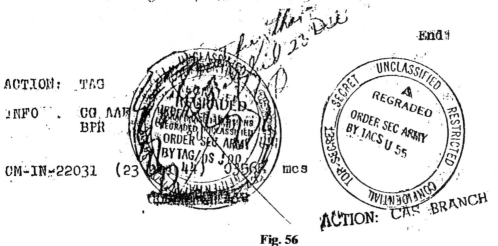

ACTION: TAG

INFO . CG AAF
BPR

CM-IN-22031 (23 Dec 44) 09565 mcs

ACTION: CAS BRANCH

Fig. 56

Radio Signal - SHAEF to War Department December 22 1944

CASUALTY MESSAGE
TELEGRAM

OFFICIAL BUSINESS—GOVERNMENT RATES

FROM WAR DEPARTM.
BUREAU A. G. O.
CHG. APPROPRIATION CJA 3814

201 MILLER, ALTON G 22 DEC SPXPC-N 59007-1 23 DECEMBER 1944
ASN 0505273

DATE

MRS HELEN D MILLER
BYRNE LANE
TENAFLY NEW JERSEY

mng-04.
air Corps
M.L. Craig III

THE SECRETARY OF WAR DESIRES ME TO EXPRESS HIS DEEP REGRET THAT YOUR
HUSBAND MAJOR ALTON G MILLER
(RELATIONSHIP) (GRADE) (NAME)
FLIGHT
XXXXX
HAS BEEN REPORTED MISSING IN ~~ACTION~~ SINCE
FIFTEEN DECEMBER BETWEEN ENGLAND AND PARIS
(DATE) (LOCALITY)
IF FURTHER DETAILS OR OTHER INFORMATION ARE RECEIVED YOU WILL BE PROMPTLY NOTIFIED

XXXXXXXXXX

OFFICIAL: Block ACTING J. A. ULIO
THE ADJUTANT GENERAL
ADJUTANT GENERAL

DISPATCHED 26 DEC 1944

CASUALTY BRANCH FILE COPY

Fig. 57

Telegram - SHAEF to Helen Miller

4

THE DON HAYNES STORY

1. Haynes the Man

When Captain Glenn Miller began forming his Army band in New Haven, Don was inducted into the USAAF with the rank of Lieutenant and become the Band Executive Officer. With orders to move to Britain, Glenn flew over on June 18 1944, and on June 19 Don Haynes took the Band from New Haven to Camp Kilner in preparation for their voyage to Europe. They boarded the Queen Elizabeth at Pier 90, New York City and six days later arrived in Gouroch, in the Firth of Clyde. Haynes, George Simon relates, shared a cabin with 11 other USAF officers, and when they came ashore Glenn Miller was waiting for them.

We have already suggested that Haynes' account of Glenn Miller's disappearance is highly suspect - in fact, it is a fabrication from start to finish, and we began to wonder just what motivated him to initiate, or at least become involved in a huge cover-up of the truth. Perhaps the remarkable thing was that his story was widely believed for almost 25 years, until the publication of his diaries in 1971. Earlier in 1953 the script for the movie *(THE GLENN MILLER STORY)* had been based on the LOC diary supplied to Universal International script department by Helen Miller. The important implication, of course, is that even then the Miller family, for their own reasons, had adopted the Haynes story, despite Helen's immediate reaction of disbelief after the war.

The diaries have been reviewed and assessed extensively in MILLERGATE, but for the benefit of readers new to the mystery, here is the series of events leading up to the disappearance of Glenn Miller, as told by Don Haynes at the time and subsequently, with minor variations. It must be born in mind that the two diaries often contradicted each other as well as most official records : it serves no useful purpose to try to determine truth from falsehoods, because both diaries intermix authentic details of the times with Haynes' totally fabricated story of the flight of the Norseman. Indeed, it is possible to establish precisely when that process began, and this is the story that Don Haynes told.

Initial discussion on a Band tour of Paris took place at a November 15 conference at SHAEF, chaired by Lt.Col.David Niven and attended by both Miller and Haynes. A six-week tour was agreed, starting on December 22, provided that the Band pre-recorded sufficient radio programmes to cover their absence. They set to with a will and the task was completed on December 10 1944; Major Miller's orders were cut and issued on Tuesday December 12 (Fig.4) authorising him to travel `on or about' Thursday December 14. (It is essential to associate days and dates in this narrative, to obtain full understanding of the circumstances). But the Haynes deception began back in November 1944, just before Miller and his Executive Officer flew to Paris for the conference on the 15th.

2.   The Haynes Diaries.

On November 8, Haynes drove Glenn and Baessell out to Twinwood Farm to board Morgan's Norseman, left his staff car there and travelled to Paris with the others. Yet he records in his diary :

> `*Friday 3 November.* Glenn and I got into a poker game at Milton Ernest Officers Club. I won 4½ pounds, Glenn lost twice that amount. On Sunday 5 November Glenn okayed a 7-day leave and I left Twinwood Farm with a courier in a B-17 for Station 595 (Honington) up north. My leave papers said I was heading for Scotland, but I was going to Paris. Had a SHAEF pass. I stayed the night, left 08.45 am for France in cargo-laden C-47. Had to turn back (terrific storm).*

His entries for 6-8 November are most peculiar. Hitherto the MINUS ONE diary had been written in first person singular, apparently by Don Haynes himself, and there are instances of hand-written alterations and amendments. But the following three entries are written by someone else, perhaps the transcriber in the third person, possibly because the entries were too long and tedious. Remarkably, we find Haynes stuck at R.A.F. Honington on 5th November - and he does not tell us how he came to be in Brussels on the 6th and 7th November, arriving at Le Bourget on November 8 ! But these entries, we believe, are significant. We saw that on November 6, John Morgan made a series of local flights culminating in an overnight stop at Station 595 Honington - exactly the time Haynes relates that he arrived in a B-17 hoping for a lift to France. We suggest that Haynes invented this sequence. In the LOC Version he says he arrived at Le Bourget on November 8 (without specifying the aircraft) but it was certainly in Morgan's Norseman. Haynes knew that Morgan came down from Honington that morning - and built his December 15 flight around that fact.

But why invent this imaginary sequence ? The answer is very simple. He knew his account of the December 15 flight was almost wholly based on the November 8 flight - and if that association was to remain undetected, he had to divorce himself from the November 8 flight. But the Fates were against him : he stands convicted in his own words. Remarkably, he relates that Gen. Goodrich's B-17 appears out of the blue in Brussels - just to get him to Paris ! He wrote :

`*November 7 1944* Stayed Brussels overnight waiting for plane to Paris. I was about to give up reaching Paris, when out of the low overcast came a B-17. It circled the field, landed, taxied to Operations. Who gets out but four officers from Milton Ernest (Base to which I was assigned in England). Seemed as glad to see me as I was them. It was now four o'clock, the weather over France not good so we all went into Brussels. We would leave for Paris in the am with two brief stops at 8th AFSC depots. How better to travel than in General Goodrich's green-leather upholstered B-17 ? Listened to a half-hour broadcast by Glenn Miller's American Band of the AEF over the BBC. Sgt Johnny Desmond sang `Day After Forever' followed by the Crew Chiefs in `Got any Gum, Chum ?' On Wednesday November 8 we took off at 9 am in the B-17 for Laon, landed at 10.35. Departed for Paris 1245, unable to land at Villacoublay, tried a landing at Le Bourget. Circled the field for 30 minutes, approaching at 100 feet with wheels and flaps down when our pilot gunned all four motors, overshot and fifteen minutes later came in for landing. We learned that a C-47 hospital plane had just started to take off beneath us. Had we continued we would have landed on top of it and I would not be here writing this account. Had dinner in ARC Club, some sight-seeing.

In his own hand, Lt.Haynes added between the typed lines `Almost a carbon copy of what happened to Glenn and I previously in England !'' This entry is very revealing. The incident Haynes describes really occurred on Wednesday August 16, as Geoffrey Butcher confirms (`NEXT TO A LETTER FROM HOME') : `The Band was to play at a hospital at Bentley Priory, Stanmore, Middlesex. The Band went by road but Haynes and Miller went by air in a C-47. As they were about to land at Hendon, red flares signalled them not to land and the pilot, by then down to 100 feet, managed to go round again. A B-17 had been taking off below them . . .' A classic example of the way Haynes uses past incidents to embroider his account. This time, he actually reverses the aircraft roles !

On Thursday 9 November, Haynes wrote, he went shopping, bought 13,000 francs worth of perfume, dined at the Place de l'Opera and went to bed early, ready to catch the plane back to UK next morning. The take-off was delayed until 09.30 - Haynes embroiders the story in one diary version by describing an engine catching fire on take-off ! And so, Haynes relates, he came back to Twinwood Farm on November 9. In fact, he flew back on November 16 in Goodrich's B-17.

This is a typical instance of the way Haynes manipulates dates and events to suit his purpose - indeed, he goes further, suggesting that Glenn Miller was called to SHAEF Paris and flew on a Bovingdon shuttle on Wednesday 13 November. Yet Band records confirm that Miller did not perform and was not seen in the UK from November 7 to 18th inclusive ! Haynes' intention, obviously, was to distort and conceal every detail of the November 8 flight, because it resembled too closely the December 15 mission he described to the world. Just how closely, we shall see : we begin the crucial part of Haynes' narrative in Bedford on December 10 1944, where the Band are completing the massive pre-recording task which was a prerequisite for the Paris trip.

`*Sunday 10 December 1944.* We recorded all day, finishing the job. Glenn gave every man a four-day pass in London to say goodbye to his friends. On Monday

11 December we had dinner with Jack Harding and Morton Downey, took Morton to the Milroy Club, bed 03.30. Got my orders to leave December 15, one day ahead of Band to arrange the transportation from Orly. A V-2 hit at 04.00, not far away.

Here we learn that Haynes and Miller frequented the Milroy Club, lending authenticity to the evidence of Group Captain Tony Bartley, DFC and Bar, who met Glenn Miller there hours before the band leader vanished. We set out to locate the Visitors Book for the Milroy and contacted joint-owner Sir John Mills. He was very helpful and even went as far as searching his attic, without result. Nor does it seem possible that the late Harry Roy's family have it - not long after Miller was seen at the Milroy, Mills and Harry Roy had a serious argument, after which Roy walked out and never returned.

Further, Haynes also introduces his odd tale of the change in Miller's orders for Paris, and his motives are important. He said that Glenn had insisted on travelling over ahead of the Band `because he had a social engagement', that Miller had been booked on a Thursday December 14 shuttle but since all UK-Continental flights were grounded, Glenn accepted the ride in Morgan's Norseman. But the facts contradict this story : no `early travel' orders for Haynes were ever found, and Miller's orders were quite flexible - `to travel on or about December 14'. Haynes, therefore, had no reason to change orders ! Further, he had no occasion to go over early `to arrange transportation' because he had visited Paris two weeks earlier for precisely that reason ! Interestingly, Miller's `social engagement' could have been Ike's party at SHAEF on Saturday December 16, if Joan Heath's story is true.

This, in effect, marked the start of Haynes' fabrication. He wrote :

`**Tuesday 12 December**. *Band played their last show at the Queensberry Club. Lord Queensberry gave the entire unit a farewell dinner at Kettners Restaurant. Going back to his hotel, Glenn said that he would rather leave for Paris early in my place, to sit down with General Barker and talk about the tour. He said he'd like to stay until the war ended or another six months, whichever came sooner. Asked me to have my orders cancelled, then have orders cut for him to leave on Thursday/Friday, make a list of the things for him to check.*

Wednesday December 13. *I got my orders cancelled and Glenn's orders cut for him to fly to Paris tomorrow and leaving Glenn in London I drove back to Bedford thru the worst pea-soup fog I ever saw ! Conductors walking in front of buses with torches, took four hours to Bedford, 52 miles. The weather has been bad since Sunday. He was unable to go - no planes going out since then.*

Haynes, *per se*, could not have changed those orders on Wednesday December 13. Further, he did not leave London on Wednesday morning after booking Glenn's Thursday flight - he, Glenn Miller and John Morgan spent that Wednesday evening in the Milroy Club. Haynes and Morgan left around midnight, drove back to Bedford; Glenn Miller was last seen outside the Club at 02.30 am by Tony Bartley and Tony Pulitzer. Thus we come to Thursday December 14 - and a sharp division between Haynes' version and what we know to be the truth. Miller probably got to bed about 3 a.m. and rose again early to catch the Air Force bus to R.A.F. Bovingdon to catch his shuttle flight. Haynes' account is quite different - as are the two diary versions of events that day ! In the LOC version he wrote :

`*Thursday 14 December.* A late call from Glenn - there was a big backlog of senior officers waiting for Paris flights. Colonel Baessell heard me talking and asked to speak to Glenn. He said he was flying out to Paris tomorrow with Morgan from Twinwood Farm, for Glenn to bring his bag and go with him - there was plenty of room. I picked up Glenn at the Mount Royal at 16.00 hours, drove him to Bedford and out to Milton Ernest Officers Club to dine with Baessell, who arranged to pick us up at 09.00 next morning (Friday December 15). We went back to the ARC Club in town, sat before fire long after everyone else had retired. Weather horrible, cold, damp. We talked about post-war Band and Glenn wrote it all out on a piece of paper. It was almost 4 am when we finished.*

The MINUS ONE diary entry is strikingly different.

`*Thursday December 14.* Lunch with Colonel Baessell at the Officers Club. He said he was going to France tomorrow, would I like to go ? I said I was taking the Band over on Saturday, Glenn was leaving today if the weather cleared. But Col. Baessell said nothing was flying out of UK today because of weather. He suggested we call Glenn, have him fly over tomorrow with B. and F/Off. Morgan. Glenn welcomed the Colonel's invitation and asked me to drive in and get him. Arrived Mount Royal at 16.00, Glenn was packed ready and we drove back to Bedford where we had dinner with Col.Baessell at Milton Ernest Officers Club. A few hands of poker with Col.B, Major Koch,W/O Earlywine before driving to the ARC Club in Bedford for a good sleep, as Col.B would be calling early, as soon as he got clearance. G. and I sat in front of the fire in Officers Club until 3.30 am, talked, planned about post-war band, taxes etc. Came to the conclusion we'd work 6 months a year, spend the other 6 playing golf, buy a trailer, go up into the NW and do some salmon fishing, raise oranges at "Tuxedo Junction", Glenn's ranch in Monrovia, California. He planned to deed a piece of the ranch to Polly and myself and we'd build a home there. He and I would be partners in the post-war Band, and he said with taxes as they were, he already had a nest-egg socked away and wanted me to be set up the same way financially. We discussed who would be in the post-war Band, first engagement would be Paramount Theater New York, 6 weeks with an option of two more @ $15,000 weekly.*

There are several inconsistencies. Why would they drive back on a wet cold night to ARC Club Bedford, when transient Officers Quarters were available at Milton Ernest ? But remember, these events took place on November 8, not December 14 - and on the earlier occasion the Band had played locally in Bedford on the 7th : Miller stayed in the ARC Club that night and faced a difficult road journey to Bovingdon next day, en route to Paris. The discussion that night would centre on the forthcoming Band tour - and would naturally follow on to post-war plans. Further, Haynes suggested that Baessell was confident that Morgan could make the flight next day (December 15) *regardless of Haynes' assertion that everything else in the UK was grounded - including well-equipped Air Transport Command Dakota crews working out of R.A.F. Bovingdon !* How did Baessell hope to reach France in a small single-engined plane with no radio navigational equipment and a rookie pilot `unsafe' on instruments, in weather as bad as Haynes describes ? And why should Baessell be involved in obtaining `clearance' ? That was Morgan's responsibility - but there is an important item of corroborating evidence here. On November 7, remember, Baessell was anxiously awaiting George Ferguson's call from Brussels to say he could make the pick-up at Twinwood Farm - Baessell, in fact, was trying to arrange `clearance' for the flight through George's local Commander in Brussels.

Lastly, the actual weather reports (Figs.21,22) contradict Haynes' version : there was a 3000 foot cloud base, visibility a mile or more, no rain or fog.

Most surprising is Haynes' addendum about Glenn's post-War proposal deeding him part of "Tuxedo Junction" and fixing Haynes up with a financial nest-egg. It could have formed some kind of post-war claim against the Miller estate - but there is no evidence of this. But in the 9 years between the war ending and the writing of the script for *THE GLENN MILLER STORY* Haynes apparently gave the Miller family the MSS of what became the LOC diary version, and we have to ask ourselves if this was perhaps part of a business transaction. We can speculate that Haynes revealed the truth when he came home, after which the family decided to support the Norseman story whilst suppressing the real story even now contained in Miller's 201 File in St.Louis, Missouri.

And so we come to Don Haynes' version of the fatal flight on Friday December 15 1944. We must bear in mind that no one else but he saw the Norseman land and take off from Twinwood Farm - the airfield, in fact, was closed to all flying that day. Yet it was a busy night fighter training base which should have been a hive of activity - even if flying was suspended because of weather, there would have been many R.A.F. personnel on the airfield, including Station Flight which was responsible for receiving and dispatching visiting aircraft. We succeeded in tracing three surviving witnesses stationed at Twinwood at that time - a ground engineer Mr. Edmonds and his wife, a WAAF at the time, and Mr.Bowyer, the Air Traffic Control officer. None of them recall a Norseman landing during the latter half of December 1944.

Here is Haynes' LOC version :

`*Friday 15 December.* I awakened at 08.20, looked out of the window and the fog and rain could be cut with a knife. Went to desk and called Baessell. He said he'd called Ops. and he and Glenn wouldn't be able to get off this morning, but weather would clear by noon, to bring Glenn's things out to the Club when we came to lunch. We got there about noon, and Col.B. called Ops. - the weather over France clear, if the ceiling here lifted to 200-300 feet, they could get off. After lunch, I drove Glenn and Baessell to General Goodrich's Chateau where Col.Baessell ran in for last-minute instructions. Glenn peered out of car window and said "Even the birds are grounded. We'll never get off today". Col.B. came out and we drove to Twinwood Farm. No one in sight as we came to the Control Tower. Baessell got out and went inside, stayed ten minutes - he had called **Station 525** (R.A.F.Heston) who said Morgan had taken off ten minutes before. (It was about 20 minute flight from Station 525). "Colonel," said Glenn, "Morgan will never find the field in this weather." Col.B. said Morgan had a sixth sense and that he would soon be here.*

`*Fifteen minutes later, we heard a plane's motor approaching from the north. Seemed that he missed the field - the motor got fainter in a southerly direction. But 5 minutes later we heard it again, much lower, the motor louder. All of a sudden a plane broke through the overcast at 200 feet directly over the field, circled and came in for landing. We drove to the end of the strip, Morgan kept the motor running. He opened the door, we shook hands. I hadn't seen him since he, Colonel Baessell and I had dinner in Paris and we went to the Casino de Paris 3 weeks ago. As I threw Glenn's and Baessell's bags aboard, with a case of empty champagne bottles Col. B. was taking back (they were very scarce in Paris) Morgan showed me a Luger pistol he'd picked up in Paris for two cartons of cigarettes. He said he could get me one. I said I'd see him in Paris tomorrow, go ahead and get it, I'd have the cigarettes.*

`As Glenn and Col.B. climbed aboard, I leaned in, shook hands and wished them "Happy Landings". "We'll need it," said Glenn, who closed the door and sat directly behind Col. B., who was sitting in the copilot's seat. It was a C-64 single-engined Norseman, used to fly crews from one base to another, but it carried only 9 or 10 people. Glenn and B. were the only passengers, Morgan at the controls. An able pilot he was, having finished his required missions in B-17s. I drove the car off the runway as Morgan revved up his motor and they took off. In less than half a minute they disappeared.

Note that Haynes is careful to stress that there was no one around as they waited for Morgan - leaving him as the sole surviving witness ! He changed many important items in the MINUS ONE version :

1) Baessell calls Haynes at the ARC Club in Bedford, not the reverse as in LOC.
2) The `Even the birds are grounded' incident happens outside Goodrich's house, again outside the Air Traffic Control tower and once more on the runway !
3) Baessell waits 30 minutes before entering the Tower, not immediately on arrival.
4) Baessell reports that Morgan is coming from Station 595 Honington, Suffolk !
5) Haynes suggests in LOC that Morgan had completed a tour of bomber missions in B-17 Fortresses - but in MINUS ONE, Colonel Baessell specifies B-24 Liberators ! Both untrue.
6) Haynes said he had not seen Morgan for 3 weeks - in fact, they had both been at the Milroy Club two nights previously on Wednesday December 13.
7) Haynes' story about the champagne bottles is a direct crib from November 8 - at that time, there was a shortage in Paris because of damage to roads and railways, but that had been solved by December 1944.
8) From a technical standpoint, Morgan could not have penetrated thick low cloud without radio assistance from the ground - and Twinwood Tower was closed. Further, a radio-guided descent through cloud would bring Morgan into the clear a mile or two from the airfield, to give him space and time to plan his landing. He would not emerge from cloud directly over the field, as Haynes described.
9) The bad weather described by Haynes never occurred. (Fig.21,22). Morgan apologises for being late, saying he had run into some `heavy squalls'. In the synoptic weather situation prevailing, this was impossible.

On Saturday December 16 the Band travelled by bus to R.A.F. Bovingdon - only to find their flight cancelled because of bad weather. The next day's entry reads :

*`**Sunday 17 December**. Up at 06.00, arrived at Bovingdon at 08.30, same deal as*

yesterday. The Flight Control Officer told me there hadn't been a plane take off for the Continent for the past 6 days ! We returned to Bedford but I arranged for 3 C-47s to pick us up at Twinwood Farm if the weather cleared tomorrow.'

This is typical Haynes imagination. He had neither the rank nor the authority to organise three aircraft in this way - arrangements were handled by Air Transport Command, one of the distribution addressees for Miller's orders. The aircraft had to come to Bovingdon from some other base, and it was just as easy for them to land at Twinwood Farm, pick up passengers and fly to Paris. The Transportation Officer at Bovingdon, aware that the Band had travelled 100 miles by bus two days running, took pity and re-scheduled two of the aircraft into Twinwood Farm. Further, Haynes ignores the fact that part of the Band had stayed at Bovingdon overnight, rather than undergo a third bus journey in winter. They were picked up by the third aircraft, and so they came to Paris. Here is how Haynes describes the events of that day in the LOC version :

`***Monday 18 December****. Up at 06.00, called Bovingdon Ops. At 10.00 the Flight Control Officer called, said weather was clear. Three C-47s would pick us up in 45 minutes at Twinwood for the move to Paris. As we drove onto the field, the C-47s were circling for landing. We were delayed 20 minutes by Sgt.Hucko who had left his trumpet in the billet. Loaded up, we took off 11.25, passed the White Cliffs of Dover at 12.15, out across Channel (appr. 90 miles wide in the corridor we used as German-held positions prevented crossing at narrower place). Crossed the French coast 12.50, landed Orly at 13.45. Code message sent from Bovingdon to have transportation ready but none there. Called Major May at SHAEF - he hadn't seen Glenn since his trip in late November. May suggested I call the Billeting Officer, who said Glenn, Baessell and Morgan had not checked in. Now I began to worry and had good reason ! Glenn had left on Friday in a single-motored ship with a cruising speed of 100-125 mph at 13.45. Should have arrived Orly no later than 16.00. Checked with Orly Operations, learned that from 15.00 Friday until late next day they were socked in, no planes had arrived or departed. Made a call to Le Bourget and Villacoublay - same deal.*
`*Came to conclusion they must have landed elsewhere - but why were they not here, now the weather was okay ? Buses arrived 16.10, loaded Band and left for EM's billet in Montmartre. Arrived 17.30, reported in to Billeting Officer. No word yet from Glenn. Dudley and I were billeted at Hotel des Etats-Unis. Checked in, called May at SHAEF - he suggested we wait until tomorrow :*
`*Major Miller will no doubt be here then'. Max, the concierge at the Ritz, said he hadn't seen Baessell, a buddy of his, since late November.*

Haynes' inventiveness is amazing ! He describes *three* C-47s landing at Twinwood, confuses Beachy Head with the White Cliffs of Dover, describes a non-existent 90-mile Channel crossing, insists once more that Morgan was bound for Orly on Friday December 15, says nothing about a Norseman to Major May, fails to check with Orly Air Traffic or Operations about a missing Norseman, fails to report to SHAEF in person and has Major May suggesting that `Major Miller will no doubt be here tomorrow'. No wonder he decided to modify the story extensively in MINUS ONE ! And in LOC he finally reports to Barker on Tuesday evening.

Haynes, of course, was quite out of his depth. MINUS ONE reads :

`**Monday December 18** *Flight Control Bovingdon called at 10 am, said three C-47s would pick us up at Twinwood in 45 minutes. As we drove onto the field they were circling for landing - weather beautiful, sun shining. Took off at 11.25 and passed White Cliffs of Dover at 12.15, landed Orly 1.45. Checked on Friday arrivals, Glenn's plane had not landed at Orly. Checked at Admin. and Operations, no planes had cleared out of there at all last week. Called Transportation Officer at Seine Base who said Glenn had not contacted him. Called Major May at SHAEF. Glenn hadn't checked in, May had not seen or heard from him, said he didn't know that Glenn was coming over a day early. Said he had been expecting me since last Friday. He knew bad weather had grounded all flights out of UK the past week. I said Glenn & Col. B. left Twinwood Farm in a C-64 last Friday at 13.45.*

`*Another voice on the phone said :* `*Where did they get clearance from ? This is General Barker speaking'. Told him they'd gotten clearance at Station 595 Honington. Morgan picked up Glenn and Col. B. at Twinwood Farm. General Barker told me to see the boys were properly billeted, to get a car and get out to SHAEF asap. Meantime he and Major May would do some checking. The General was quite gruff and displeased. Told him I would be at Versailles at about 18.00 (it was not yet 15.00).*

`*Got on the phone, tried to locate Baessell (he was well known in Paris, having made frequent trips here, plus the fact he was a man who left an indelible impression wherever he went, loud & boisterous). First I called concierge Max at the Ritz, said he hadn't seen B. since early November. Maitre D. at the Raphael said the same. Billeting Officer at Seine Base said neither Glenn nor Col. B. had checked in. Last call to Lt. Jerowski. When he said he had not heard from Glenn, I was convinced they had not arrived in Paris. Took the Band to Hotel des Olympiades, secured a staff car at Seine Base and went out to SHAEF at 18.05. Barker and May had been busy calling bases on the Continent and the English coast.*

They found one rather startling fact - a single motor ship had been charted out of a UK southerly point headed over Channel in the general direction of Paris but unreported flying over French coast. Also known that no AA guns had been fired from any coastal point between 14.00 and 18.00. Barker placed a call to Gen. Goodrich at my suggestion, as I felt certain Col. B. would have contacted Goodrich had he encountered any trouble - he was due back Sunday (yesterday). The call came through : Gen. Barker motioned for me to pick up the phone on Major May's desk. Barker and Goodrich knew each other, so after Barker inquired about Gen. Goodrich's condition, he asked if Col. Baessell was there. Goodrich let out a blast, that B. flew to Paris on Friday,was due back yesterday. Barker brought Goodrich up to date on what was going on, said I was on the extension. So I augmented what Gen. Barker had already told him - he was furious when I said they'd flown a C-64, which he said had no icing equipment, and icing conditions were prevalent (34 degrees at Twinwood Farm, and 8-10 *degrees colder over the Channel). Goodrich expressed great disappointment that his personal pilot Morgan was flying a C-64 over the Channel in that kind of weather. Said he would have a search instituted as of daybreak tomorrow, but it appeared to him they had iced up and gone down in the Channel. General Goodrich had quieted down, whereas a few minutes ago, he had been blasting. . . He knew how close Glenn and I were, and would leave no stone unturned. There was a possibility they'd been forced down in some remote spot out of contact. General Barker hung up the phone and said `It looks very bad, Lieutenant. I'm afraid Major Miller has had it !' Called Sgt. Sanderson at the EM's billet, told him what had happened and for him to tell the boys.*

This differs significantly from the LOC version : Haynes relates that he phoned Major May soon after landing at Orly on Monday, omitting all mention of a search of Paris : instead he makes a few phone calls. He introduces gingerly the `missing single-engine plane' but fails to identify it as Morgan's : he then reports to SHAEF about 18.00 hours. The conversation with Goodrich is pure fantasy - Haynes uses it to stress the Norseman had no de-icing equipment, that the ground temperature at Twinwood was only 34F according to Goodrich - and has Barker remark gloomily that Miller and the Norseman had gone down.

So why these drastic changes in MINUS ONE, particularly regarding Haynes' statement that he telephoned Major May as soon as he landed ? Clearly, if the MINUS ONE Norseman story was to be believed, Haynes' 2-day search of Paris for Glenn had to be suppressed : he had to be shown as anxiously checking various airfields for the Norseman, and this is seen in MINUS ONE. Proof ? Well, after talking to Haynes, General Barker is supposed to have contacted 8th AFSC Milton Ernest for news of the aircraft. If MINUS ONE is correct, that should have been on Monday evening. In fact, it was not until Wednesday morning that Barker signalled 8th AFSC - *suggesting strongly that Haynes and the men at SHAEF spent two full days searching for Miller, before deciding that the Norseman cover-up story was necessary.*

The entry for Tuesday December 19 is fascinating. By his very attention to trivial details, Don Haynes totally destroys the viability of his account. One curious inconsistency comes to light : in MINUS ONE, Haynes related that he called the Band billet on Tuesday evening and asked Sgt.Sanderson to inform the men of what had happened. George Simon *(GLENN MILLER AND HIS ORCHESTRA, Da Capo 1974))* said the news only filtered through over a period of days, and the Band slowly became reconciled to his loss. Geoffrey Butcher *(NEXT TO A LETTER FROM HOME, Mainstream 1986)* who like Simon quoted from the fictional MINUS ONE diary, has a new version - that Haynes assembled the Band in the Orderly Room at the Hotel des Olympiades as soon as they arrived on Monday and told them personally that Miller was presumed lost. But this is inconsistent with his account of the loss being confirmed on Wednesday by the signal from 8th Air Force Service Command at Milton Ernest. We believe that some, if not all of the musicians knew more than they were prepared to admit, and this proved to be the case. The `Barker-Goodrich ' telephone conversation is interesting - one must admire Haynes' creative ability ! He continues (LOC version) :

`**Tuesday 19 December**. *Up early, lots to do. Called Billeting Off. first, no news. Got a staff car, went to SHAEF, talked to Barker & May. I suggested that we called General Goodrich - we could barely hear him - he was confined to bed* *with a bad heart. He hadn't heard from Baessell and was displeased, should have returned on Sunday. Goodrich said he would ask Air Ministry to check all fields in UK, we should do the same. May had talked cross-Channel three times that morning, asked me to stay to verify Morgan's take-off time, and not a trace of that plane since it went out over the coast of England. The narrow corridor from the English to the French coast was 90 miles, all over water. The German-held coastal positions prevented going the short route that the Channel swimmers take. Had dinner at Hotel Crillon with Dudley. That night we `made' all of Baessell's old haunts, no word of him anywhere.*

This is a curious mixture of fact and fiction. Don Haynes, on Tuesday evening, is still `looking for Baessell' - four days after the Norseman ditched in the Channel, according to Haynes himself - did he imagine the Colonel had swum ashore and walked to Paris ? Skating gingerly around Goodrich's illness (he had met the General numerous times at Milton Ernest) he suggests that the Commander, on being informed that his Special Assistant who should have returned on Sunday was missing, believed killed, was `displeased' ! Remember - 8th AFSC had been notified as early as Saturday morning that Morgan was missing. But in LOC version, there is no mention here of Goodrich `blasting' as in MINUS ONE ! Haynes still avoids identifying `that plane' as Morgan's Norseman, but suggests (untruthfully) that it took the long sea crossing from Beachy Head to Dieppe because of the German-held positions. We have already rejected this particular point.

But why should Major May wish to clarify Haynes' Norseman take-off time of 13.45 from Twinwood Farm ? This is complex but of vital importance. Documents in the Burial File confirm Morgan departed Abbotts Ripton at 13.25. On landing at Twinwood he would need at least 5 minutes to take on board his passengers, indicating an arrival time at Twinwood of 13.40 at the latest. This allowed Morgan just 15 minutes to take off, fly 25 miles to Twinwood, carry out a radio-controlled descent through Haynes' `200-foot overcast' and land. It wasn't possible - and May knew it, even if Haynes didn't.

At this stage, Tuesday December 19, Capt. Cramer, following orders, had delayed compiling the MACR, pending an official announcement that Morgan and any passengers were missing. Miller's Casualty Report would not be issued until December 22. In his calls from Paris, Major May learned that Morgan had departed at 13.25, had not landed at Twinwood Farm (which was closed to flying on December 15) and that Morgan's orders took him to Bordeaux via Beauvais. He had been cleared direct to Beauvais.

May recognised the problem and modified Haynes' take-off time from Twinwood Farm to 13.55, allowing an additional 10 minutes. In the process he had learned that the Haynes story was totally fictitious - so why did he not advise General Barker ? The implication is staggering : *Barker already knew the story was untrue* - and so, by inference, did the other senior generals at SHAEF - Eisenhower, Bedell Smith and the Paris AG General Davis. They were already deep in plans to implement the false Norseman story. As, indeed, was Haynes. His LOC diary continues :

`**Wednesday 20 December**. *Called May, Barker, too early, not in. Called again, they have heard nothing. May said later that he and General Barker had all but given up hopes of the plane and its occupants. Also, if they didn't get a clue by tomorrow, he'd have to turn in Major Miller on the Casualty Report. Helen Miller will receive a telegram tomorrow afternoon that her husband is `Missing* *in Flight as of December 15 1944'. No way I can get word to Helen or anyone else except by letter - much too slow.*

Compare this with MINUS ONE :

`**Wednesday December 20** Called Major May first thing. He said he and Barker had all but given up hope of finding Glenn, Baessell and Morgan alive. We must prepare ourselves for the worst - if nothing is found today they would have to turn Glenn in on the Casualty report. Helen will receive a telegram - no way I can get word to Polly. May said the newspapers will not be given the story until after Helen gets the wire from War Dept. First concert tonight Palais de Glace, as cold inside as out ! Called May at 18.00, no trace, no findings. Talked him into deferring Casualty Report one more day.*

Haynes, as a mere lieutenant, could bring no pressure to bear on when the Miller Casualty Report was issued. He also omits all reference to the Missing Report (Fig.40) discovered in March 1992 - a document used specifically to report Army personnel who were missing, but not as the result of an aircraft incident. It was accompanied by a Form 66-2, Personal Records, which includes in Section 38 a Chronological Record of Military Experience, embracing the whole of Miller's career from his induction into the USAAF in 1942 to the last day of his life. That document was to assume paramount importance in the mystery.

The Missing Report also refers to an attached letter, which was that written by the Paris AG General Davies to General Eisenhower (Fig.20). But Haynes, writing MINUS ONE specifically to bolster his Norseman story, had to account for the unusual delay in issuing Glenn's Casualty report - and suggests that he manipulated Barker and May. His diary continues :

`**Thursday December 21.** Out to SHAEF first thing, still no word. Got May to hold off one more day on the Casualty Report thinking that something might turn up today, save Helen from getting the wire tomorrow. In conference, Gen. Barker suggested three possibilities :*
1) Flying blind, went over enemy territory, shot down, either killed or captive.
2) Iced up, dove into the Channel, in which case there'd probably be no findings.
3) Crashed in remote spot, not yet found.

Haynes omits totally his interview with the Milton Ernest officers - and any statement he may have made, naturally. And he writes `something may turn up' - meaning Glenn Miller. This suggests strongly that SHAEF still had no clues as to Miller's fate - or that they suspected what had happened and were waiting for confirmation. Meanwhile, Haynes manages to generate three more red herrings all based on Miller being on board the Norseman.

`*I was still clinging to that one chance in a million. First show at the Palais de Glace, 4300 troops. Sgt. Ray McKinley did a good job subbing for the Major. Barker and May were there, very proud we were attached to their HQ. Some rumours were starting to the effect the Band might be disbanded : Barker asked* *me to see him at SHAEF next day. He said `Those are the facts, we must face them. The Casualty Report must be released first thing tomorrow morning'. He asked why I had been so insistent it should be held up another day - I told him that Major Miller may still show up.*

Haynes wrote that he visited SHAEF, where Major May showed him a copy of the 8th Air Force Casualty List including Major Miller - but this is both impossible and untrue. Glenn and the Band were part of Special Services Division, HQ Command, SHAEF REAR at Bushey Park (SHAEF MAIN when they moved to Paris) : nothing to do with the 8th Air Force. Miller never appeared on any 8th AF Casualty List. Baessell and Morgan, of course, were listed - and this is probably what Haynes was shown.

3. Diary Assessment

More than any other item of evidence, the diaries served only to destroy any credibility the Haynes story may have had. It has been suggested that, many years after the war, the writer's memory may have been at fault - but this is not an acceptable defence : we see the similarity between the documents, the obvious manipulations of events, times and dates. We tried to establish Don Haynes' motives in writing the diaries, and after we obtained audio tapes by Haynes, George Ferguson and Royal Frey and others, we perceived an ongoing campaign to propagate the Norseman story - to encapsulate the public image of Major Glenn Miller as an innocent victim of war, caught up in circumstances over which he had no control. Yet significantly, after I published MILLERGATE in 1990, the Miller family made no effort to refute the evidence that Glenn was not aboard the Norseman, that it did not land at Twinwood Farm on December 15 1944, that the Haynes story was a work of fiction and that a major cover-up had occurred. Before publication, their attorneys exerted all their efforts towards preventing publication - but after that, silence.

Don Haynes' motives, predictably, were a function of whatever really happened to Major Glenn Miller, and in that respect we came up with a number of speculative theories on his disappearance :

1. He went AWOL, possibly because of an emotional involvement.
2. He never left England but died and was buried anonymously.
3. Glenn suffered a nervous breakdown and was flown home.
4. He reached Bovingdon but was detained and flown home secretly for trial.
5. He left Bovingdon December 14 but crashed en route.
6. Miller reached Paris and was murdered, his body concealed.
7. He arrived in Paris, was injured and flown home, where he died.
8. When sight-seeing in the Ardennes, he was over-run by the Germans and killed.
9. He was the unidentified victim of an accident, flown home and then died.
10. Miller tried to fly home for Christmas without permission and was lost en route.
11. He flew home to America - and never returned.

We eliminated the more outlandish theories such as being shot down by a German fighter, shot by Col. Baessell, taken POW, being shot in a brawl in the Hotel Georg Cinq in Paris - and in particular, being killed in the Norseman by Lancaster bombs. But we were still faced with the $64,000 question : *if Glenn Miller was not lost with the Norseman, what did happen to him ?* We can draw certain indisputable conclusions from the evidence accumulated to date :

*   Whatever his motives, Don Haynes' account was fictitious from start to finish. We can cite the inconsistencies and anomalies in his diaries, contradictions not only with each other but with all the official documents in the case.

*   Because Glenn Miller's body was never recovered in Britain or Europe, we must assume for the moment that he died in December 1944, or perhaps early 1945. From this, four options deserve consideration : first, he may have been arrested on some charge at Bovingdon on Thursday December 14 and flown home for trial. Second, he may have reached France that day and died accidentally and unidentified in France, because of his incorrect serial number in his orders and lack of dog tags. Third, he may have been the victim of foul play and his body concealed to protect the killer or killers. And fourth he may have flown home to America and failed to return.

*   I am inclined to the theory that he flew out of Bovingdon to Orly on Thursday December 14, attended Ike's party on December 16, flew out of Buc Field on December 17 in a UC-78 operated by 112th Liaison Squadron - and thereafter vanished. We can discount *in toto* the Norseman story - which was adopted simply because a spurious explanation was better than no explanation at all. Don Haynes, Major May and Generals Eisenhower, Barker and Davis felt justified in delaying all reporting procedures until the very last moment. They may have believed that he was in France but simply out of touch, enjoying his first real vacation in years. Alternatively they may have known why he was missing and were forced to await the outcome before deciding on their action. The concept that he was dead, either accidentally or from foul play, simply could not be contemplated at that stage. They were waiting for him to return.

All this provides fascinating grounds for speculation : to assess the relative values involved, we must look at other supporting evidence. For example, whatever occurred, it happened some time between 02.30 hours on Thursday December 14 1944 (when Sqn.Ldr. Tony Bartley said good-night to Glenn outside the Milroy Club in Stratton Street, Mayfair) and Sunday midnight, Paris time (about 7 pm New York time) representing the fuel-out time of any aircraft he may have boarded - three days of uncertainty. Herb Miller told me that he was with Helen in Tenafly that week-end when a call came through from Europe, a call which caused her great distress but the contents of which she would reveal to no one. He was unsure of the precise day. For this period of 72 hours, we had no positive information on events until January 1992 when we located a surviving witness.

In making a final assessment of the Haynes Story, the major anomalies and errors may be tabulated as follows :

1. Don Haynes was totally inaccurate on the Band flight details. Three C-47s were allocated to the task, two flown by standby crews of 315th Troop Carrier Group. One from 34 Squadron was flown by Capt. Wm. M. Perkins and a second from 310 Squadron by Capt. Tappen and copilot 2nd Lt. Richard J. Kucklik from 34 Squadron. Those two aircraft landed at Twinwood as described by Haynes. The third C-47 from Air Transport Command collected a group of Band musicians

from Bovingdon, where they had spent the night rather than make a third 100 mile bus journey. (R.A.F ATC Assistant Dixie Clerke refers to this on her tape). The Twinwood aircraft carried the Band equipment, baggage and instruments but a party of 9 musicians under Lt. Paul Morden remained in Bedford.

2.   The `White Cliffs' were not at Dover but at Beachy Head. The track from there to Dieppe en route to Paris is 90 miles - at 150 mph, 35 minutes as confirmed by Don Haynes himself.

3.   His claim that no planes had flown out of Bovingdon for the past week was incorrect. Records from SHAEF and Maxwell AFB confirm that the continental shuttle flights to Paris continued until 15.00 Friday December 15 1944; on Thursday 14 December four C-47s left Bovingdon en route Paris, two for Orly and two for Villacoublay. Norton AFB Flight Safety Facility and the Cumulative Loss Listing confirm that no cross-Channel C-47 flights were lost during November or December 1944.

4.   Had his Norseman story been true, Lt. Haynes would have haunted Orly Operations and Air Traffic Control, monitoring the search for Morgan's Norseman and waiting for developments, since the first news would come through the ATC network. Instead he spent 2 days searching Paris for Glenn Miller and Baessell, until Tuesday evening December 19.

5.   In the LOC version, Haynes did not contact General Barker until 18.00 hours on Tuesday evening, but in MINUS ONE he reports immediately on Monday afternoon ! The change was essential, to show that he wasted no time in reporting the loss of the Norseman - besides giving General Barker two full days to work out a plan of action - or inaction. Then he introduces this strange story of the `missing single-engined plane' but never claims specifically that it was Morgan's aircraft. Further, the sighting was passed to SHAEF during the weekend - and Haynes clearly knew Morgan was down by Saturday afternoon.

6.   Haynes' narrative of the telephone conversations is highly suspect. First, Major May would have his own office and telephone, not a desk and extension line in Barker's office. Second, Haynes neatly reinforces the `Honington' scenario by having Barker ask where Morgan obtained clearance. He was wrong here, too - Morgan's flight from Abbotts Ripton was cleared by telephone with Bovingdon on December 15.

7.   Haynes relates that Goodrich said the temperature at Twinwood Farm was 34 degrees - something the seriously-ill General would not know. And in MINUS ONE for Friday December 15 he relates that he himself got out of the car at Twinwood Tower and read the thermometer - and it registered 34F. !

8.   Morgan was not Goodrich's personal pilot. The General had an obsolescent B-17 bomber for his own use, and Morgan never flew a B-17, as George Ferguson confirms.

9. Goodrich, even if he had been well and able, could not agree to institute a search - that was the job of the Search and Rescue Organisation, and he had no aircraft to use on such duties. No search was ever initiated for the aircraft, on SHAEF's instructions. The last thing they wanted was for the Norseman to be found - with only two bodies and neither of them Miller's.

10. Finally, Haynes neatly switches emphasis from the pseudo bad weather at Twin-wood Farm to the icing-up hazard en route, creating a scenario for the loss of the plane - and of Glenn Miller.

3.   Haynes and the Confirmatory Signals

This interchange of signals is crucial to the mystery. We had previously assumed either that SHAEF simply did not know what had happened, and were delaying all procedures until news came in, or they knew what had happened and were awaiting developments. But in hindsight, reason suggests the latter hypothesis - that Haynes, Barker and Major May knew what had happened to Miller *before* Haynes flew in on Monday morning - but for some reason were waiting for confirmation. If, as they feared, the worst had happened, some sort of cover story would be essential - and by sheer serendipity, the 8th Air Force Norseman went missing that weekend.

How we obtained confirmation of these events and conclusions was extraordinary. The Confirmatory Signal (Fig.10), issued and circulated by US National Archives for 44 years had always been accepted as genuine. It supported Haynes' story that General Barker had telephoned General Goodrich on Tuesday evening, asking 8th AFSC to check out Haynes' story and signal back confirmation that Miller was on the Norseman. Early's Signal to Barker was dated Wednesday December 20, from which it was generally assumed that 8th AFSC had only required an hour or two to check and confirm the situation.

But in 1992 we found a copy of the real Confirmatory Signal (Fig.24) forming part of the supporting documents dispatched with the Missing Report on December 28 1944. It indicates indisputably that the teleprinter inquiry from Barker actually *arrived* on Wednesday morning, December 20, *but Early did not respond until December 22nd !*

The Barker-Goodrich telephone call described by Haynes simply did not occur - Goodrich was terminally ill and was flown home to Maxwell AFB Alabama that very day (December 20) and died in early January. Colonel Early handled the investigation at 8th AFSC, as we shall see.

On Wednesday morning at Milton Ernest, Col. Early began checking on the Haynes story - and realised at once that something was very wrong. Twinwood Farm had been closed on December 15. Morgan had departed from Abbotts Ripton direct to France, with orders for Bordeaux via B-42 Beauvais with no stop at Paris to drop Miller. Early telephoned Capt. Cramer at Abbotts Ripton and told him to delay compilation of the MACR until further notice. The Colonel then dropped everything and flew to Paris with Col. Traistor, another 8th AFSC officer; they interviewed Haynes on Thursday December 21st before reporting to General Barker at SHAEF. If Haynes made a written statement at the time, it has never been revealed.

Whatever transpired at SHAEF, Col. Traistor telephoned Capt. Cramer at Abbotts Ripton and instructed him on the contents of the MACR : Cramer compiled the document on December 22, and we found confirmation of this in Cramer's covering letter of the same date attached to the Missing Report : `*Inclosed herewith ETO CAS Form 2 and Missing Aircrew Report per verbal request Lt.Col. Traistor, 21 December 1944'.*

The two officers returned to Milton Ernest. Next morning (December 22) Early sent the true Confirmatory Signal (Fig.24). The die was now cast : Barker and the others decided to go ahead with the Norseman story and a number of important events took place that day :

1) The Haynes statement was `officially' reported to General Davies (Fig.20) who compiled his letter to General Eisenhower, for enclosure with the Missing Report. But there were two serious problems facing Davis : first, Cramer's MACR was unsigned - and may even have carried a deposition by Cramer stating why. Davis probably got round this by annotating the MACR `COPY', and a month later it would be replaced by the forged MACR #10770. Second, and much more serious, was Miller's Form 66-2, a Service History including in Section 38 a Chronological History of Military Experience. That problem would have to be faced when compiling the Missing Report : meanwhile, Davis had managed to put on record for the first time the Norseman story - sending a copy to Eisenhower.

2) Barker released the Miller Casualty Report containing the Haynes story.

3) A radio Casualty Signal was sent to the War Department.

4) A telegram was sent to the next of kin Helen Miller in New Jersey.

5) Col.Dupuy in SHAEF Public Relations prepared a Press Release.

6) At the first Paris concert the previous night, Thursday December 21, Barker covered up Miller's disappearance via a simple announcement by Sgt.Ray McKinley : *"Major Miller is unable to be with us this evening."*

7) Barker cancelled the two subsequent concerts for puerile reasons - that Colonel Otto Skorzeny's English-speaking raiders might attack Band members in the black-out !

8) The `ORIGINAL' Missing Aircrew Report was compiled by Capt. Ralph. S. Cramer. What SHAEF could not have foreseen was his outright refusal to sign it. Further, his covering letter dated December 22 states the MACR was dated the same day - *and had been compiled before Miller's Casualty Report was issued !* And the phoney MACR #10770 was dated a day later, December 23, to cover this anomaly.

Here, in this simple letter, is certain proof that Lt.Col. Traistor telephoned Adjutant Ralph S. Cramer from Paris after interviewing Lt. Don Haynes on December 21 : Cramer is underlining the fact that he is acting only under duress (from Col. Traistor) - that his MACR had been prepared on December 21, and dated December 22, pre-dating the other information released by General Barker such as Miller's Casualty Report. This also tells us that the so-called `ORIGINAL' MACR N-19 found in the Miller Burial File was not only an `extract' from Cramer's genuine Report - it had been re-dated.

+　　+　　+

Summation

* Haynes' account of the December 15 flight was blatantly based upon his recollections of the November 8 flight.

* Haynes last saw Glenn Miller when Don and Johnny Morgan left the Milroy Club in London, to drive back to Bedford in thick fog on Wednesday December 13 1944.

* Glenn Miller stayed in the Club with Tony Bartley and party until it closed at 02.30 a.m. Thursday morning. He was last seen walking away alone into the fog towards his hotel at Marble Arch.

* On that Wednesday morning, Don had booked Miller onto a Bovingdon-Orly flight the next day, Thursday December 14. Then he took Glenn's bags round to the Air Terminal in Old Quebec Street, 24 hours before the flight as per regulations.

* Haynes did not have Glenn's orders changed as he claimed. This was a ploy to explain why Miller accepted a lift from Baessell.

* Back at Milton Ernest, Haynes spent Thursday supervising the Band packing up for the flight to Paris on Saturday December 16. He knew Baessell was flying out next day to Paris in Morgan's aircraft (the same plane they had used on the November 8 flight !) and the Colonel probably did offer Haynes a lift. But the Exec. Officer was scheduled to fly with the Band - yet from this small beginning, Haynes' Norseman story began to take shape.

* Don Haynes spent Thursday night at Milton Ernest, partly because he had a dental appointment next day, and partly because the atmosphere was much more convivial than the ARC Officers Club in town, which was always crowded. He had the Band staff car and may have driven Baessell to Abbotts Ripton, watched him take off - a real twist in the tale !

* Twinwood Farm, on that wintry Friday in December 1944, was closed to all flying, as confirmed by military documents at the Public Record Office, Kew.

* After two days delay, the Band flew out to Orly in 3 C47s, two from Twinwood Farm and the third from Bovingdon to collect part of the Band.

+   +   +

We now turn our attention to the unique collection of documents found in the Glenn Miller Burial and 201 Files.

+   +   +

5

THE DOCUMENTS IN THE MYSTERY

1.   The Siege of Washington

WHEN the late Sqn.Ldr. Jack Taylor approached me in late 1986 with the suggestion that an investigation of the Miller saga could prove fruitful, he had obtained copies of only three documents in five years of research :

1) Missing Aircrew Report #10770 (Figs.8,9).
2) The Miller Casualty Report dated 22 December 1944 (Fig.6)
3) The Confirmatory Signal dated December 20 1944 (Fig.10).

I was reluctant to embark on a factual book, after 10 fiction novels, but after talking with Jack I grasped the significance of the inconsistencies and anomalies in the mystery. Always a sucker for enigmas such as UFOs, the Loch Ness Monster, Bigfoot, the Yeti and the way Time worked, from that moment I was irretrievably hooked. We began by examining the documents.

At that time MACR #10770 was regarded as probably genuine but inconsistent. The signature was illegible and the typed personal details beneath obliterated, making identification of the compiler impossible. That problem alone preoccupied dozens of researchers for a quarter of a century or more. But we made a start : written inquiries produced more items : an amended Miller Casualty Report dated March 1948 (Fig.7), and the `Finding of Death' documents for Glenn Miller, John Morgan and Lt.Col. Baessell (Figs.25-27). A few months later we obtained copies of all three `Reports of Death'(Figs.5,28-29). We learned that no search was made for the aircraft, and no official investigation was initiated either in the UK or on the Continent, in 1944. Further the Miller Finding of Death document gave his destination as Bordeaux - with no reference to stops at Twinwood Farm or Paris.

In 1987 we became aware that a Burial File was opened for every deceased US serviceman, even if his body was never recovered. These files were in the custody of the Mortuary Affairs and Casualty Support Division in Alexandria Va., with access via the Washington National Personnel Records Center, and it was essential to obtain copies for Miller, Baessell and Morgan. The history of our efforts to obtain these Files is extraordinary, covering a period of almost two years during which, sadly, Jack Taylor passed away. So too did Herb Miller - but not before he gave me written authorisation to investigate his brother's disappearance (Fig.30) Some of the documents in the Burial Files were included in *MILLERGATE - THE REAL GLENN MILLER STORY*, and with the additional illustrations in this sequel form a complete record, not only of the papers found in the Burial and 201 Files but copies of those documents which had been abstracted, officially or otherwise, during the past four decades.

Our broad front of inquiry included not only personnel documents, reports and witness statements, but an active search for Morgan's missing UC-64A Norseman and the route he took on that fatal flight. The first step was to locate any accident report involving Norseman 44-70285, or indeed any Norseman lost in 1944. On May 8 1986 we wrote to the USAF Inspection and Safety Center at Norton AFB California and they replied :

> `We have searched our files. We have no record of a December 15 1944 Norseman mishap'.

This was remarkable - Norton AFB held records of all mishaps to USAAF and USAF aircraft going back to WW1 ! A UC-64A reported missing on a routine flight surely constituted a mishap ? We tried again, this time citing another Norseman mentioned in the MOD Air Historical Branch Report shown in Fig.31, #43-5367.

> `We have searched thoroughly through our records to identify the December 26 mishap. None of the mishaps reported during this period was reported as `missing'. Only if we can identify a mishap are we able to provide an engine number'.

Norton AFB normally records all cases of destroyed, damaged or missing aircraft - yet we were able to identify from the Cumulative Loss Listing *eight* additional UC-64A Norseman aircraft reported written off in December 1944. Further, we noted the requirement for an engine number : was this why Missing Aircrew Report #10770 stated the Norseman engine number was `unknown' - to prevent identification ?

Early in July 1986, after discovering the anomalies in the typescript which convinced us that Report #10770 was totally spurious, we wrote to National Archives enclosing the Ansell Report. On August 5 they replied :

> `We double-checked the MACR #10770 microfiche against the original copies in that file. The fiche is complete. We are unaware of any additional information pertaining to that Report.'

And again on September 19 1986 :

`Enclosed are copies of MACR #10770 as requested. You may examine the original at any time. As a matter of policy, we do not comment on the content of files.'

On July 25 1986 we wrote to the Military Field Branch, National Archives in Washington inquiring if a Burial File for Major Glenn Miller existed, requesting further information on MACR #10770, the flight plan if it existed, a list of personnel who were based at Abbotts Ripton in December 1944, and details of the Norseman engine number. The reply, remarkably, lacked any useful information :

`We contacted the Department of the Army, Casualty and Memorial Affairs Division, Alexandria Va. and inquired about the Burial File for Major Alton G. Miller. . . **They are unable to locate the File.** *We contacted Air Force History and inquired about documentation pertaining to the loss of this plane.* **They were unable to supply the information you requested.** *Additionally, they were* **unable to provide any information pertaining to the 35th Air Depot Group** *that may have been of value. Finally, we contacted Military Reference Branch of National Archives. Although they have several files relating to the loss of the Miller plane,* **none of these contain the engine number.'**

Totally negative in content and betraying a wary reluctance to give anything away, this letter provides clear evidence of a deliberate policy of non-cooperation and deliberate delay in certain Army-connected Government departments. Mortuary Affairs and Casualty Support Division were, in fact, custodians of all Burial Files relating to deceased personnel, but certain sensitive Burial files of specific interest such as those of Major Miller, John Morgan and Col. Baessell which were the subject of constant inquiries had been taken over by the Washington National Personnel Records Center, with the tacit approval of Mortuary Affairs and Casualty Support Division. Their statement that they were `unable to locate the file' was manifestly untrue and misleading, as later correspondence demonstrated. Further, they were at that time fully aware that there were serious discrepancies between the published MACR #10770 and the `ORIGINAL' MACR #N-19, copies of which were in all three Burial Files. The statement that Mortuary Affairs and Casualty Support Division were unable to locate the files was also totally untrue, as our next response from MACS Division proved.

On August 27 1986 we wrote to the Military Field Branch (custodians of Missing Aircrew Reports) to inform them that MACR #10770 was a fabricated and unviable document, enclosing a copy of the Ansell Report (Fig.32) and asked for an enlarged `first copy'. We were anxious to identify the compiler, but the signature was undecipherable and his printed identification below had been roughly obliterated. The enlarged copy duly arrived on September 18, but was of no help in identifying the signatory. Further, the Military Field Branch insisted that Report #10770 was `the sole, original and genuine article (this in itself is a contradictory and misleading statement, because later in the struggle they said that they were merely the custodians of the documents and not responsible for their contents !). There was no mention of any other Report on file for Norseman #44-70285 yet they must have been aware that the real MACR #N-19 was in the Burial Files !

However, the writer did confirm that any Burial Files would be in custody of the

Department of the Army, which pointed us towards Mortuary Affairs and Casualty Support Division, Alexandria. We wrote once more to that Department on September 19. We also received at that time a response to a previous letter to the Military Reference Branch of National Archives. Mr.Reese wrote on October 15 1986 listing some but not all of the available documents (presumably in the Miller Burial File) including MACR #10770, the Casualty Reports and Reports of Death (all of which we possessed already) and some minor papers. This letter confirmed that there was contact and cooperation between Government departments, in this case MRB and Washington NPRC. Most important, it revealed that National Archives, at least, knew of the location of the Burial Files and had supplied us with copies of some documents from the three Files.

In retrospect, we believe that Mr. Reese should have provided a copy of the `ORIGINAL' MACR #N-19 from the Burial Files. He may not have known of the existence of these Files, but that seems most improbable, because of the continuous flow of public requests for information received since 1945. So many that the Files had to be `kept on top of the cabinet at all times'! The `ORIGINAL' never appeared in the MACR Register, Report #10770 having been substituted for it on 22 January 1945 when #10770 was fabricated.

But we find it hard to believe that the head of Military Reference Branch, National Archives, Washington DC (who was constantly approached for information on Glenn Miller) had not gone down the road a mile or so to the Washington National Personnel Records Center and looked at the Miller Burial File.

We wrote to Memorial Affairs in Alexandria again in October, asking for details of the Miller Burial File, and they replied on November 6 1986 :

`We have made repeated attempts to retrieve the individual (Glenn Miller) deceased File from Washington NRC. Requests for his File have been ongoing for years. These attempts and our current attempts have met with negative results. This Agency is merely the custodian for individual deceased personnel files, which are stored at Washington NRC'.

On January 30 1987 National Archives wrote :

`We have forwarded to you copies of all material we have been able to locate relating to the loss of Major Glenn Miller. As stated. . . we will gladly make original copies of MACR #10770 available to you. . .'

`Original' copies indeed ! And at that time, we had no concept of the wealth of information in the Burial Files and Miller's 201 File in St.Louis - data available to National Archives, had they chosen to reveal it. But we had failed to spot that Report #10770 was much too neat, well-typed and laid out for a wartime document, compared to the `Original' #N-19 : it was an inexcusable omission and we felt somewhat humiliated !

Now we were faced with an impenetrable barrier of non-cooperation, and ordinary channels were no good to us. We knew the Burial Files existed and where they were kept, and we were anxious to see precisely why the American authorities, i.e. the Adjutant General and the Department of the Army, had seen fit to suppress them for more than 44 years. The most probable explanation was that they contained evidence which conflicted with the official (Haynes) account.

We suspected that the Burial Files were concealed deliberately as a matter of high-level policy, a conclusion later confirmed by the dogged and implacable resistance to our requests for access. There was a distinct impression of a systematic and intentional dispersal of available information. For example, the Miller Personal 201 File was kept in St. Louis, Missouri. His Burial File was in custody of Memorial Affairs and Casualty Support Division in Alexandria, but accessible only via the Washington NPRC, where its existence could be concealed judiciously. The spurious MACR #10770 was included in the MACR Register in the Military Reference Branch - but the `ORIGINAL' was suppressed in the Burial Files in NPRC Washington. Even worse, Page 1 was in the Miller Burial File, whilst the existence of Page 2 was officially denied ! We found Page 2 in the Morgan Burial File.

At that stage in 1987 we had not obtained a copy of the `ORIGINAL' but we were certain it existed, if only as a template from which to fabricate MACR #10770. We also knew that several documents were missing from Burial Files and other sources, including :

* The `original' MACR compiled by Capt. Cramer on instructions from Col. Traistor dated December 22 1944. This was replaced by the `ORIGINAL' `extract; MACR #N-19 found in the Burial Files.
* Page 2 of the `SAMPLE' MACR, which was never found.
* Morgan's Service Record Card from Abbotts Ripton.
* His Form 5 (Flight Times Record) for November and December 1944.
* His flight log book containing details of flights, destinations etc. A pilot's Log Book was a personal record and not an official document.
* Glenn Miller's orders for Paris showing an incorrect serial number.
* The Norseman #44-70285 service documents and engine number record.
* Local weather reports from the Meteorological Office at Abbotts Ripton.

In 1992 we added to this list the vital AAF AGO Form 66-2, Section 38, Chronological Record of Military Experience for all three men - Miller's had been abstracted from his 201 File copy of the Missing Report (Fig.40) whilst Morgan and Baessell's 201 Files were destroyed in the 1973 St.Louis fire at NPRC.

Some official documents were deliberately misleading, e.g. the letter from the Adjutant-General Department written by Colonel Donnell to Helen Miller in which he stated that Morgan was cleared direct to the Continent (Bordeaux) via Twinwood Farm, and omitted all references to a proposed Paris stop to drop off Glenn Miller. Finally, there were the letters from National Archives stating they had no information on Glenn Miller other than the Casualty Report, Report of Death and Finding of Death documents. All of which, of course, cast serious doubts upon the viability of the Haynes story.

Of course there *was* additional information in the Burial Files and in Miller's 201 File : they contained the key to the whole mystery, but as long as they remained suppressed, the US government could cling to the Haynes Norseman story backed up by the fabricated MACR #10770 and the 8th AFSC `confirming' signal to General Barker on Wednesday December 20 1944 ! No wonder they reacted negatively - clearly we had to demolish the walls of Jericho a brick at a time and we began with the MACR #10770 itself.

On October 16 1986 we wrote again to the Military Reference Branch stressing that the Archives should cease circulating a manifestly forged and unviable document, MACR #10770. They responded that, as mere custodians of documents, `*they were not responsible for their authenticity or viability, and could make no comment'* ! They could have passed on this information to the Washington National Personnel Records Center, but they did not. In fact, five years were to pass before NPRC Washington wrote :

> `Your letter and book contain many statements that indicate that the National Archives has failed to correctly answer your request. (For release of the Glenn Miller 201 File - Auth.) You feel that we should verify and crosscheck all documents for accuracy before we dispatch them. However, since we are merely the physical custodians, we only provide storage and reference service. We do not routinely check forms and documents for content or accuracy. Responsibility for the content of any document in Major Miller's Official Military Personnel File rests with the legal custodian/creator of the record - the Department of the Army.*
> `If you wish to discuss the authenticity of or correction to any document in Major Miller's record, you should contact Department of the Army, Center of Military History, 3rd and M Streets SE, Washington Navy Yard, Washington DC. In order to obtain the release of further documents or information you will need to contact USA ISC-P (ASQNS-OP-F) Room 1146, Hoffman Building, 2461 Eisenhower Avenue, Alexandria VA.'*

Quote : `This Center is only responsible for providing what is available in the record, not determining what should or should not be in the record.' Unquote. The inference is clear enough : vital data available elsewhere may not be included in the official record, and its existence may not be revealed to inquirers, because some higher-level authority or person has so decided ! We determined that the chain of command in such matters runs upwards through the Chief Archivist of the United States, via the Adjutant General's Department to the Pentagon, the Department of the Army, the Department of Defense, The Army General Counsel and the White House. Restrictions on release of official information could be imposed at any of these levels : until 1979 and the Freedom of Information Act, control was extremely tight. The senior generals at SHAEF, as representatives of the Army, initiated the cover-up, and the present-day Army/Air Force General Staff in the Department of Defense in the Pentagon must share ultimate responsibility.

We concluded that there might be some secret repository of documents unavailable to general access, despite the Freedom of Information Act, as in the Irangate affair when funds derived from illegal arms sales were diverted to subsidise the Contras in Latin America.

The responsible organisation controlling access to 201 Files was identified as the US Total Army Personnel Command, Personnel and Logistics, Alexandria Va. 22332-0405, in the person of Mary Anne Quintard, Freedom of Information and Privacy Officer, and the ultimate selection of documents to be released was the responsibility of Ruth R. Gasparene. We obtained eventually from that source a copy of Miller's 201 File.

But the battle was not yet won : the File we received initially was in effect a grotesque practical joke perpetrated by some person in the US Total Army Personnel Command. It comprised some 382 photocopied papers weighing 5 pounds, of which 120 were blurred unreadable copies, a further 108 were documents from the 1942-1944 period (in which we had expressed no interest). Another 50 pages were public inquiry letters about the fate of Glenn Miller, going back to 1945; to all inquirers NPRC St. Louis addressed their standard reply :

> `Major Miller and Lt.Col. Norman F.Baessell were passengers aboard a C-64 (Noorduyn) transport plane piloted by Flight

Officer John R.S.Morgan. The plane departed from Abbotts Ripton, England, for Bordeaux France, and was last sighted at 1:55 pm on 15 December 1944 at Twinwood Field, England.'

This short extract from the Haynes story (his name is not mentioned on any document in US records, or in the 201 File received on May 6 1992) - omits any reference to an intended landing in Paris to drop Miller. But the 201 File was years away in our own future, and in 1986 we had to contend with the unhelpful policies and attitudes of certain US Government and military departments. Every silver lining has a cloud . . .

2. The Walls Come Tumbling Down. . .

The first real proof of deliberate obstruction to research by the US Army and Government departments was in a courageous letter from John F. Manning of Memorial Affairs, who wrote on November 6 1986 :

> `*We have made repeated attempts to retrieve his individual deceased personnel file from the Washington National Personnel Records Center. Requests for his file have been ongoing for years. These attempts and our current attempts have met with negative results.*
> `*This Agency is merely the custodian of the individual deceased personnel files which are stored at the National Personnel Records Center. The files document individual deceased service members from date of death or missing status through final disposition or determination of non-recoverability. The data in the files was compiled by the various agencies who were involved in actions pertaining to the decedent. . .'*

No more doubts ! The great cover-up was not only fact but ongoing today ! Washington NPRC had deliberately refused to release a sensitive file to its legal custodians in Mortuary Affairs and Casualty Support Division ! They might argue that they were housing the Files to facilitate handling inquiries, but the reverse is true : Alexandria and other departments insisted first that the Files did not exist; second, that they may have been destroyed in the 1973 fire at St. Louis; third, they could not be located; fourth, they had been misfiled, and finally they were in temporary custody of Washington NPRC.

But now we could now see a chink of daylight : the Files existed, we knew where they were - but would Washington NPRC finally release them ?

In September 1986, totally frustrated by constant shunting from one department to another, we wrote to the Military Reference Branch and Washington NPRC, demanding access to all Glenn Miller and associated documents in existence, under the Freedom of Information Act, 1979 - including Burial Files, Casualty Reports, any flight orders issued to John Morgan and records of air movements between Bovingdon and Paris on December 15 1944.

Further, we wrote to NPRC St. Louis at the same time in 1986, quoting John Edwards' unproductive approach in 1973 after the Great Fire, asking for information on the status of any personal 201 Files or Burial Files for Major Miller, Colonel Baessell and Flight Officer John Morgan. The reply from St.Louis on December 15 1986 (the anniversary of Miller's disappearance) was far from reassuring :

`The records. . .are not in our files. If they were here on July 12 1973, they would have been in the area which suffered most damage in the fire on that date and may have been destroyed'.

We persisted, and in a later letter, NPRC St. Louis admitted that they held the Miller 201 file - but were unable to release details of his military service in Europe without permission of the next of kin, Steve and Jonnie. The Baessell and Morgan 201 Files had been destroyed in the fire. The three Burial Files were not, and never had been in St.Louis, which housed millions of personal 201 files. Sensitive Burial files such as that of Major Miller were in the custody of Alexandria but controlled by NPRC Washington - departments of the US archival system. We wrote yet again to NPRC Washington demanding the release of the Burial Files.

In 1992 St.Louis provided a small booklet on the July 12 1973 fire, the cause of which was never discovered. Service personnel 201 Files including the Miller 201 folder were in a vault on the 6th Floor, and the Army records 1912-1959 had suffered most damage. `Army' included `Army Air Force' until 1947, and we were unable to explain why Miller's File survived and those for Baessell and Morgan were lost. We toyed briefly with the idea that the fire was started deliberately to destroy these files - but that was too big a quantum leap !

We believed that once we had the Burial Files we were home free, but we did not allow for the stubbornness of the last-ditch opposition. A blunt response arrived from NPRC Washington on December 19 1986 :

`The records. . . are not in our files.'

Total frustration. . . Even our request for data under the Freedom of Information Act had been ignored. We held a final telephone conference to decide our next move. On December 22 I wrote to the President of the United States, Ronald Reagan.

Dear Mr. President-

Major Glenn Miller

I appreciate you have problems at present, but the subject matter of this letter is of great importance to millions of people world-wide, and I trust it will receive attention at a sufficiently high level of your Administration to ensure the release of vital information. I write at the request of, and with the approval of, Herb Miller, surviving brother of Major Alton Glenn Miller. I began serious research into the disappearance of Glenn Miller in 1986, as a result of which I have established :

1. The sole self-styled `witness' of Miller boarding a Norseman plane at R.A.F. Twinwood Farm on December 15 1944 was Lt. Don Haynes, AEF Band Executive Officer. His evidence has proven to be totally fabricated, and neither he, Glenn Miller nor the Norseman were at Twinwood Farm that day. In fact, the airfield was closed to all flying.

2. The enclosed Missing Aircrew Report includes no eyewitness report by Haynes, nor is he named as `last person to see the aircraft'. Expert evidence

proves the Report was forged, probably at Maxwell AFB in March 1946. The real original report was suppressed in the Washington Archives.

3. *The MACR route is Abbotts Ripton/ A-42 Villacoublay Paris/ Bordeaux. The records of the pilot John Morgan show the initial destination was B-42 (A-61) Beauvais-Tille in Northern France. `B-42' was altered to `A-42' to account for Miller's `presence' as a passenger on the plane. He was due to fly to Paris on a Band concert tour on December 14 1944.*

4. *I have traced a Dr. Pecora, one-time Captain, US Medical Corps who is reputed to have signed a death certificate or some other document for Major Miller in France. He confirms that he was based at Rheims Military Hospital during the critical period.*

5. *Miller's superior Lt.Col. David Niven, Director of Troop Broadcasting, was not in Paris to meet the Norseman on December 15 1944 : he was in Spa, Belgium, at 1st Army HQ.*

6. *All major reporting procedures were delayed 9 days by order of General Ray Barker, G-1, including MACR, Casualty Report, Notification of Next of Kin, Press Release etc.*

7. *Herb Miller related that he was with Mrs. Helen Miller in her New Jersey apartment on Saturday December 16 when she received a phone call from Europe. She was extremely upset but would not discuss the matter with anyone, until she received a call from Gen. `Hap' Arnold at SHAEF, Paris, on December 24. Thereafter she repeated the fictitious Don Haynes story.*

8. *Helen Miller returned to California late 1948. Early 1949, she and her mother bought a 6-grave burial lot in Mountain View Cemetery, Altadena - but her family had only 5 members : herself, her two adopted children and her parents. I have been unsuccessful in discovering for whom the sixth grave was intended, or whether it is occupied.*

9. *I have written numerous letters to various U.S Government departments in an effort to locate and obtain a copy of Major Miller's Burial File, without success : I have been shunted around from one department to another. Today I received the enclosed letter from Mortuary Affairs and Casualty Support Division, Alexandria, stating that they have been trying unsuccessfully for years to recover the file (of which they are custodians) from the Washington National Personnel Record Centre. NPRC advise me that `the records are not on our files', `are misplaced' or `mis-filed'.*

I can only assume that this suppression of information is official, even though it is in contravention of the Freedom of Information Act, 1979. I believe the File contains vital information on the true events of the time, and I write urgently to request you to intervene on my behalf to approve access to

the Burial Files of Major Miller, the pilot John Morgan and the alleged
`other passenger' Lt.Col. Norman F. Baessell. I stand by ready to fly to
Washington at a moment's notice.

+   +   +

On December 23 1986 we wrote to the Military Field Branch (Mr. Boylan) enclosing a copy of the November 6 Alexandria letter. We said it was clear that a calculated cover-up operation was in train to deny us access to the Burial Files. If something was not done immediately about the other information we had requested, we would fly to Washington for a personal confrontation.

So the year 1986 ended in total impasse and no little frustration : we now knew for certain that the Burial Files existed, and where they were physically stored, but we had found it impossible to break down the bureaucratic barrier at all levels of US Government Archives. In the New Year we reopened hostilities with a frontal attack on January 2 1987. In a furious letter to the Records Center, Washington we asked three specific questions :

> *(a) Do you hold the Files as Alexandria says ?*
> *(b) Under the Freedom of Information Act, will you mail us copies ?*
> *(c) What is their present security classification ?*

Two long weeks passed without a reply. It was perfectly clear that some drastic action was now unavoidable : the only way we would reach the Files was in a Watergate-style burglary. I made a telephone call to Washington.

"National Archives ?"
"Yes, sir. How may we help you ?"
"This is Mr. Wright, calling from England. Can you give me the name of the top man in the Archives ?"
"Uh. . . you mean the Acting Archivist of the United States himself, sir ?"
"That's the chap."
"That would be Doctor Frank W. Burke, sir."
"Okay. Put me through to him."
A long silence. Then -
"You mean right now, sir ? He's. . . uh, he is not available right now. It might be best to speak to a Departmental Head. What is the nature of your inquiry ?"
"Major Glenn Miller," I said shortly.
"Major. . . Right, sir ! Putting you through to Mr. Chalou."
Waiting, I switched on my tape recorder. This should be on record.
"Mr. Wright ? This is George Chalou. How can I help you ?"
"I am a professional author and I'm having a great deal of trouble obtaining access to the Glenn Miller Burial File."
Another lengthy pause.
"Have you written us, sir ?"
"Frequently. Repetitively. Fruitlessly. You want more ?"
Mr. Chalou coughed delicately. *"I get the picture, sir."*
"Good. Here's the position. I learned of the existence of the Burial Files from Alexan-

112

dria, traced them to National Personnel Records Center in Washington. The last we heard, they had misplaced them. Seems they borrowed the Files from Alexandria - and they refuse to give them back."

"Right," Mr.Chalou said firmly. *"And there's no way they will get them back either ! That File has been under lock and key for years - and that's how it's going to stay !"*

I stared at the telephone, astounded. Here was the first direct confirmation of a deliberate official policy to suppress the Miller Files !

"In that case," I said slowly, *"we have a problem. I have reason to believe the File may contain vital evidence that Miller was not aboard the missing Norseman, and probably a death certificate of some kind. I've written to you people repeatedly and all we got was the run-around. Now, I want to see that File and I'll come to Washington if necessary."*

Mr. Chalou hesitated. *"Uh - that won't do any good. Even if we had the File..."*

"No ?" I said nastily. *"Well, I think you should know, Mr. Chalou, that I wrote to President Reagan a week ago with the full story, asking him to intervene."*

"YOU DIDN'T !"

"Oh, yes I did. So next time your phone rings - guess who ?"

A third long silence.

"Okay, Mr. Wright. Give me an address and phone number. I'll get right back to you."

"When ?"

"Uh - within fourteen days."

"Fine," I said. *"I'm flying over to Pasadena soon to check something out. I can call in on you if necessary."*

"Well," Mr. Chalou said cautiously, *"let's see what we can come up with."*

"Thank you very much," I said - and meant every word. I switched off the recorder.

Nothing of note happened for a week. Then on January 2 1987, Mr. Reese wrote from the Military Reference Branch :

`*This is a follow-up to your conversation with Mr. George Chalou of this office. The information on the Major Alton G. Miller Burial File was included in Mr. Boylan's letter.* (True : it was the minor documents, which we already had on file). `*Also enclosed, a copy of our reply to your `Freedom of Information' letter dated September 18'* (which contained nothing of real value). `*Over the years we have received numerous inquiries concerning the fate of Major Glenn Miller. With the exception of the documents we have listed in our replies, we have not located any other documentation in our Files.'*

This was a serious and important statement about the Burial Files. Mr. Reese was saying, in effect, that the only documents existing in his files were the minor examples he had sent. All of them, as we confirmed later, were copied from the originals in the Burial Files held by NPRC Washington nearby - with which Mr. Reese was almost certainly familiar. . . `*We have had numerous inquiries...over the years.'* Yet when the Burial File did eventually arrive, it contained no less than 36 items, some of paramount importance in the context of the cover-up operation ! Further, we had no real assurance that it was a complete package. . . The Reese letter was *prima facie* evidence of a cover-up at highest level, and we could not accept it under any circumstances. So on January 16 1987 we wrote to Mr.

Reese in desperation, asking him to check once more. Two weeks later a mind-boggling reply arrived from the National Archives :

> `The Director of the National Records Center had a staff member conduct an extensive search for the Miller Burial File. He was able to inform Memorial Affairs that the File had been located. When you visit, we will make available to you for examination the original MACR. We are unable to hire experts to examine the document as you requested.'

No mention of releasing the File : were they hoping against hope that I would not be able to make the trip to Washington ? The MACR at this stage was a secondary issue - we knew beyond doubt that #10770 was a fake. And if the File had been `misplaced', how had they managed to copy the minor documents we had been sent, from a File so frequently used it was to be `kept on top of the storage cabinet at all times' ? Significantly, according to Alexandria, they had been trying for years to recover the File from NPRC, who first refused, then said it had been mis-filed and then that they'd mislaid it. *Was it not remarkable that, within ten days of our last-ditch telephone call, it was `found' ?*

Equally disturbing, they were still representing MACR #10770 as the real and only `original' (presumably because it was the only one on the Register) - yet they must have known about the true `ORIGINAL' MACR #N-19 in the Burial File ! Clearly there was a deliberate official policy to conceal details of all sensitive files held, especially the Burial Files. On February 12 1987, a plaintive letter arrived from Mortuary Affairs and Casualty Support Division in Alexandria to qualify their November 6 1986 `bombshell' letter. They had not meant that `*NPRC were holding onto the File against MACS Division's will - only that NPRC had been unable to locate it. . .' *A copy of the File, they said, was enclosed.

Well, it was much too late to close that stable door - and needless to say, nothing was enclosed with the letter - certainly no Burial File ! At that stage, we were very depressed : things were looking very black. A week later we wrote to the US Attorney General demanding an investigation into the mystery of the sixth grave in the Miller Burial Lot in Altadena. It elicited the reply that `*there was insufficient evidence on which to act . . .* This was entirely predictable - this was a military, rather than a civil matter. At the same time we wrote a long letter to the Chief Archivist Frank W. Burke asking him to intervene on our behalf to have the Burial Files released. He was probably upset by our dealings with George Chalou, for we received no reply. But things were moving : on March 12 1987 came a frantic letter from Mr. John Manning at Memorial Affairs, Alexandria Va. to the effect that *they had mailed us a complete copy of the Miller File on February 5 1987.*

Great ! But where was it ? This was baffling. We had received their February 5 letter, saying the File was enclosed - *in an air mail envelope 9 inches by 4.* We had a premonition they were going to claim that the File had slipped out of the envelope flap en route... Nothing else happened, and on March 15 1987, we held a final conference; the project was closed down. We had done everything possible, but it was not enough. In the end, the system had beaten us.

+ + +

On March 19 a large envelope arrived, containing 36 items which, a covering letter assured us, comprised the entire Burial File of Major Glenn Miller. It had been sent (as Mr.

Manning said) six weeks earlier on February 4 1987.

By surface mail. . .

+ + +

3. Missing Aircrew Report #10770 (Figs.8,9)

■ The Evidence of Fabrication

When Report #10770 entered general circulation in 1948, it was believed to be the genuine original document and was universally accepted as such, despite the unease about its many inconsistencies. We were the first to note the typeface anomalies (Fig.33) and commissioned a New Scotland Yard typewriter expert Michael Ansell to examine the document and prepare a report on its authenticity (Fig.32). His assessment, that the Report had been typed on two quite different machines on different occasions, and was prepared for `pilot only', the passenger names being added subsequently, confirmed all our suspicions. We learned much later from a letter in Miller's 201 File signed by a Major Morrow that #10770 was probably fabricated on January 22 1945, as indicated by the spurious `date-time' stamp on Page 2, following the arrival in Washington of the valueless unsigned ORIGINAL MACR #N-19. The 5-week `delay' was necessary, to give time for the preparation of the document.

Before the Burial Files were released, Washington National Archives disregarded our warning that #10770 was a forgery, and to this day insist that it was `*the sole, genuine and original document'* and further, that *no other Report existed.* But the evidence was overwhelming : the real question was this : when and where had it been substituted for the real MACR, and by whom ? Some other version had been used as a template - without doubt that compiled by the so-far unidentified Abbotts Ripton officer on December 23 1944. But where was that original ? Who was the compiler with the undecipherable name and obliterated typed identification ?

Some questions were answered when we obtained the Burial Files. We found the real `ORIGINAL' MACR (#N-19) produced at Abbotts Ripton on 23 December 1944 - but it was unsigned ! But at this juncture in 1986,  we were uneasy and pessimistic, and thought that the genuine document must been destroyed after the facsimile had been made. Reason suggested that the wartime `original' must have contained sensitive information, perhaps a statement by Don Haynes or a deposition by the anonymous compiler.

Despite its errors, inconsistencies and anomalies Report #10770 had been signed, apparently, by someone in authority, even if his signature *was* illegible and his typed personal details had been carefully obliterated, to conceal his identity. We only obtained the name of Captain Ralph S. Cramer when the Burial File was released in 1987. But what forced the US Army Adjutant-General's Department to forge an MACR on 22 January 1945 ? How had the persons responsible persuaded the unknown compiler to countersign the forgery - or was the signature itself was forged ? Was he brought back home from Abbotts Ripton to sign the Report ? Why would he do so, after refusing to sign the `ORIGINAL' ?

The first clue to the forgery appeared in the `Passenger' section of the Report, in which the names of Miller and Baessell were typed much more heavily and solidly than the rest of the document - this is not discernible in the copy reproduced in MILLERGATE, but can be seen clearly in Fig. 8 in this book. The second clue came when we enlarged the document (Fig.33) several times and saw that a capital `B' in `Bordeaux' was slightly depressed, whereas the `B' in `Baessell' was not. Secondly, the figure `2' in `A-42' was twisted slightly clockwise, whereas that in Glenn Miller's serial number was not. Thirdly, in addition to the heavier typing, misalignments in the `occupants' list suggested that the names of Col. Baessell and Major Miller had been inserted at a different time to that of John Morgan.

Further, we noted that a capital `B' in `Bradunas' in the Declassification Certificate exhibited a characteristic depression similar that in `Bordeaux' but not in such pronounced fashion, from which we concluded that one of the machines used to type the MACR in January 1945 had also been used to complete the Declassification Certificate in March 1946 ! Now, this same Lt. Col. Bradunas, who signed the Certificate, was not on the staff at the newly set-up Maxwell AFB Historical Research Branch - he was a senior officer in the Adjutant General's Casualty Branch. A year earlier, on 12 February 1945, he was a major and Chief of the Notification Branch at Personal Affairs Division, Assistant Chief of Air Staff, Personnel - reason suggests that he had more than a minor part in fabricating Report #10770 in January 1945. On 12 February he wrote to Helen Miller :

> `Additional information has been received indicating that Major Miller was a passenger on a C-46 transport plane (Was this a misprint for C-64 - or had Miller been lost in a C-46 Curtis Commando transport ? Auth.) which departed on a mission to Bordeaux France on 15 December 1944. The report reveals that your husband's plane was last seen to leave its base at about 1.55pm and the time, place, and circumstances relative to its loss are presently unknown in this headquarters. Please be assured that a continuing search by land, sea and air is being made to discover the whereabouts of our missing personnel. Any additional information will be sent to you immediately by the Adjutant General or this headquarters.

This letter is a curious mixture of truth and outright lies. Bradunas studiously avoids any reference to Twinwood Farm or a projected stop at Paris - but he is certainly *au fait* with the MACRs in existence at the time. He quotes the MACR take-off time (13.55) according to the Haynes story as amended by Major May at SHAEF, but states the Norseman `left its base' at that time. Untrue - Morgan left Abbotts Ripton at 13.25 hours. Most important, Bradunas wrote that the circumstances `are presently unknown' - which was a lie. Temporarily, at least, the full Haynes story was being kept under wraps. Quite possibly the forged MACR #10770 had not yet been completed. Finally, Major Bradunas' reassuring words about a continuing land, sea and air search are pure hokum, as we have seen. There was no search, no investigation.

■ Compilation Date - December 23 1944

Instructions at the top of the MACR pro forma required that the Report should be compiled and dispatched within 48 hours of a crew member being *officially* reported missing - and the vital word is `official'. But we encounter an anomaly here : Miller's Casualty

Report was dated December 22 1944, and those for Baessell and Morgan on January 5. So legitimately, the MACR could be delayed until January 7, 23 days after the Norseman was lost ! A date stamp on Page 2 purports to say that it arrived in Washington on January 22 1945, 40 days after the incident - suggesting that it had been sent by sea mail. Yet this was a document concerning a missing VIP, which had already been the subject of an urgent Radio Casualty Signal between SHAEF MAIN and the War Department. (Fig.56). The `ORIGINAL' MACR £N-19 in the File bears no such stamp, but this is not surprising - it is certainly not the Report compiled by Captain Cramer, but a supposed `extract' from it. Further, we were to learn that Cramer, under duress, actually compiled and dated his report on December 22 - *before* General Barker at SHAEF had released Miller's Casualty Report. The `original' MACR's lack of signature precipitated the need for a facsimile version. Glenn Miller was officially reported as a casualty on Friday December 22 but the Confirmatory Signal from Milton Ernest (Fig.10) was not released to the public for some time. General Davis notified General Eisenhower `officially' the same day the Casualty Report was released and we believe these timings were significant and planned.

■ The Anonymous Compiler

The task of researchers world-wide would have been simplified if the compiler of the ORIGINAL MACR £N-19 and the owner of the forged signature on Report £10770 had been identified, traced and interviewed post-war. Enormous numbers of man-hours were expended on trying to decipher the scrawled signature, and computer enhancement was used to reconstruct the obliterated type-written identification beneath.

In our view, once we knew £10770 was a forgery, these details had been deliberately blurred on all National Archives copies issued, to conceal the identity of the compiler - including a copy issued to John Edwards in 1973. But it came as a considerable surprise to find that whilst Cramer's identity was clearly legible in the `ORIGINAL' MACR £N-19, it was unsigned ! It is logical to assume, however, that his real `original' compiled at Abbotts Ripton had also been unsigned - otherwise it would have been circulated freely and there would have been no need of a forged facsimile. It is also possible, we thought, that it had been suppressed because Cramer had included comments or information about the lack of an eyewitness statement, the failure to identify Lt. Haynes, and the use of `unknown' to describe information which was freely available, such as engine number and weather conditions.

We learned too late that the compiler, Captain Ralph S. Cramer, had died in the Seventies. Further (as far as we could ascertain) he had never been identified by any researcher or interrogated by any Government department. This was desperately unfortunate : he had been central to the mystery. Whoever erased his identification details had achieved his aim in delaying the inevitable for 44 years.

This was most extraordinary. *Why,* we pondered, *had Cramer not signed the `ORIGINAL' in 1944, but agreed to sign the fabricated version in 1945 ?* Or had he ? We obtained copies of several documents bearing his signature, routine papers from 35 ADRS at Abbotts Ripton, and we performed an experiment using black carbon paper and a sharp hard pencil. We were able to produce excellent facsimile signatures. Perhaps Cramer was hurriedly recalled to Alexandria, presented with Report £10770 and asked to sign it. The signature, therefore could be genuine - but to make absolutely certain, his personal details under it were obliterated.

To bring all these facts into perspective, it is necessary to retrace our steps back to SHAEF on Friday December 22, 1944. General Ray Barker had authorised the issue of Miller's Casualty Report, conferred with General Davis and agreed the text of the latter's letter to General Eisenhower (Fig.20). A Radio Casualty Signal (Fig.56) was on its way to the War Department, a telegram (Fig.57) to Mrs. Miller in New Jersey. Colonel Traistor had already telephoned 35 Air Depot Repair Squadron at 2 SAD, Abbotts Ripton and instructed Adjutant Captain Cramer to complete the MACR as soon as possible. Major Miller, he explained, would be officially reported missing as from December 22.

It all fits - and now we comprehend the terrible personal dilemma facing Adjutant Capt. Ralph S. Cramer at Abbotts Ripton. As a serving USAAF officer pledged to do his duty and obey the commands of his superiors, he could do either but not both. He knew already a great deal about the case; he was probably the first man at Abbotts Ripton to learn on Saturday December 16 that the Norseman was down and had started his own local inquiry. But on Monday Major May phoned him from Paris to hold fire on the MACR - apparently Major Glenn Miller had been on board, after being picked up with Col. Baessell at Twinwood Farm the previous Friday. The announcement was being delayed - and so was Cramer's MACR.

Two days later, on Wednesday morning, Col. Early over at 8th AFSC HQ at Milton Ernest, phoned Cramer at Abbotts Ripton, and began asking questions. He didn't like the answers he got from Cramer - Twinwood Farm had been closed on December 15, Morgan had been cleared direct from Abbotts Ripton to B-42 Beauvais and Bordeaux - he hadn't gone anywhere near Twinwood, or Paris for that matter. Early, greatly disturbed, hung up and flew over to Paris next day, Thursday December 21, with Lt.Col. Traistor from 8th AFSC. They interviewed Haynes and then reported to General Barker. We do not know precisely what happened at that time, but immediately afterwards Col. Traistor telephoned Cramer from Paris, telling him to compile the MACR to show Miller as a passenger and Morgan's route from Abbotts Ripton - Paris - Bordeaux. There was to be no eyewitness statement, Lt. Haynes was not to be identified and the take-off time was to be shown as 13.55 hours. He must exclude the Norseman engine number and local weather conditions, and there would be no search. A copy of the MACR must be sent to SHAEF as soon as possible. The aircraft documents, Morgan's flight plan, Service Record Card (Fig.36), Forms 5 and Flight Log Book were to be impounded.

But Capt. Cramer already knew that :

1.   Morgan had been cleared via telephone direct to B-42 Beauvais (evidence, his Record Card, orders from HQ 2 SAD Wattisham and the Col. Donnell letter to Helen Miller).

2.   His initial destination was B-42 (A-61) Beauvais, final destination Bordeaux (evidence his flight orders and Service Record Card)

3.   He had departed Abbotts Ripton at 13.25 (Fig.49)

4.   He had not landed at Twinwood Farm (evidence PRO records, R.A.F. witnesses and the anomalies in Haynes' story).

5.   If Baessell came on board, it was at Abbotts Ripton and not Twinwood Farm.

6.   Twinwood had been closed to all flying on December 15 1944 (evidence PRO record)

7.   The weather that day was fair, unlike that described by Lt. Haynes (Figs.21,22).

In short, Cramer had been ordered to compile (and sign) an incorrect, incomplete and misleading report concerning a VIP of the day - and reason suggested there was going to be a lot of flak, hassle and publicity before this thing was over. Captain Cramer's career, in fact, was on the line, and we believe that he took the only course open to him. He would complete their damned Report - exactly as he had been told - *but no way he was going to sign it* ! No one, we suggest, can blame the man.

So in his capacity as Adjutant, he had the MACR #N-19 typed out and duplicated in several copies, all unsigned. One was dispatched to Washington direct by air (there were aircraft leaving for America every day) and the others went to the usual locations on the Distribution List - 8th AFSC, 8th Air Force at High Wycombe, SHAEF REAR at Bushey Park, attention of the AG Department, Norton AFB in America and SHAEF MAIN at Versailles for the attention of General Ray Barker. In the last-named copy he took great care to stress that he had compiled the Report under duress from Lt.Col. Traistor.

There must have been absolute consternation in all these offices when the unsigned MACR arrived. Worse - we believe Cramer may have attached a deposition outlining his reasons for refusing to sign the document. He had to cover himself against the investigation he knew would follow - any investigatory Board would discover the facts, learn that the Haynes story was false, that General Barker and Major May almost certainly knew it, but went along with it.

We deeply regretted that Captain Cramer never received the recognition he deserved - he was a very brave man to defy authority at top level.

■   Route Details in MACR #10770.

Morgan's flight path from Abbotts Ripton to the English Channel has always involved intense controversy, and we were the first investigators to identify the route correctly. The MACR details are extremely confusing, but bear no relation whatsoever to the true route. The Report states `Course Bordeaux Via A-42' - but `A-42' is not qualified as `Villacoublay' by name, as are `Place of Departure' (Abbotts Ripton) and `Twinwood'. The word `Course' is misleading : it means `a compass course steered from the departure airfield to first destination' - in Morgan's case, about 150° from Abbotts Ripton to Dymchurch. We obtained a contemporary MACR for a P51 Mustang of 355 Fighter Group, 8th Fighter Command dated 15 December 1944; the aircraft developed a coolant leak north of Munster, Germany. The course at the time was due west, given as `270°'. The course for another P51 lost on the same day 60 miles east of Clacton on Sea was `100° OUT, 306° IN'.

Reason suggests that the true course in degrees was deliberately omitted from both the `ORIGINAL' and #10770 MACRs, firstly because it was essential to conceal Morgan's direct route from Abbotts Ripton to Dymchurch (i.e. a short sea crossing). Secondly, by omitting the course altogether, the lack of a search was justifiable. Until we obtained the Burial Files in 1989, we could confirm neither easterly nor westerly routes around London. Had the MACR course had been given as `150°' (east of London) it would have destroyed the Fred Shaw story of the Lancaster `bombing' entirely, but this was a relatively modern development. The `course' was omitted because it would jeopardise the Haynes story.

Further, `A-42' appears in both `Course' and `Intended Destination' sections, to stress that Morgan intended to drop Glenn Miller at Paris. In fact, only two entries in the whole Report support the Haynes story : `A-42' and the word `Twinwood'. Pilot George Ferguson and Col. Baessell invariably landed at Paris Orly, convenient for the city, whilst passengers for Versailles used Villacoublay. Miller, travelling over ahead of the Band, would not report immediately to SHAEF - their first concert was scheduled for December 21, affording Glenn almost a week of leisure. If he left Bovingdon on Thursday December 14, on the flight Haynes had booked, he would go into Paris Orly. Of course, Haynes insisted throughout that Morgan was bound for Orly (pure assumption because Morgan had *always* gone there) and obviously, Haynes had never seen an MACR or Morgan's Service Record Card (Fig.36). He never changed his mind as to Morgan's route and destination, and the similarity of `A-42' Villacoublay and `B-42' Beauvais was at once coincidental and attractive to those at SHAEF who prepared the cover-up story and the MACR compilation.

So who decided to enter `A-42 Villacoublay' in the MACR ?

Certainly not Haynes - his story demanded a stopover at Paris to drop Glenn, and Orly it was. Not Cramer himself, who knew the status of Twinwood Farm on December 15 1944 and had seen Morgan's orders, flight plan and Service Record Card - none of which included a stop either at Twinwood or Paris. Lt.Cols. Early and Traistor, it will be recalled, had flown to Paris on December 21 and interrogated Lt. Haynes, before seeing General Ray Barker at SHAEF. Traistor discussed the issue with Major May, who had already phoned Cramer to determine Morgan's take-off time. They decided to show Miller's destination as Villacoublay (A-42). Immediately afterwards, as the Missing Report shows, Traistor phoned Cramer at Abbotts Ripton and issued instructions.

Interestingly, Beauvais, a jointly-used base, had the American code A-61 as well as the British `B-42'.

■ Engine Number

If the remains of the fabric-covered Norseman were ever discovered, the canvas and painted airframe number 44-70285 would have rotted away. The sole remaining means of identification would be the plane's serial airframe number stamped on an aluminium plate riveted to the structure on the left side of the nose just ahead of the door, and the engine number stamped on a metal plate on the front crankcase at 5 o'clock, looking at the front of the engine. That would survive as long as the engine itself, and we were assured by the manufacturers Pratt & Whitney that they could identify the aircraft in which an engine was installed, given the engine number.

Aircraft engine numbers were recorded in several of the documents maintained for every aircraft, including the servicing schedule, repair and modification logs and the aircraft serviceability acceptance certificate Form 1 signed by the pilot. When Norseman #44-70285 was transferred to Abbotts Ripton from Wattisham in September 1944, flown in by Lt. Jean Pace and handed over to Johnny Morgan, all its documents went with it and were held in the Technical Control office in the same block in which Capt. Cramer's office was located.

So why was the engine number shown as `unknown' ? There are but two possible explanations : one, that Ralph Cramer was instructed to omit it, and two, that the documents were unavailable. When an aircraft was reported missing, the usual procedure was to impound the documents locally, against a possible inquiry to determine negligence where applicable. Once the aircraft was confirmed as lost, the documents were dispatched to Norton AFB in California, after it had been included in the US Air Force Cumulative Loss Listing. For some reason Norseman #44-70285 was not so included until 1947 - in which case the documents must have remained at Abbotts Ripton, and the engine number *was* available. The inference is unmistakable - the omission was deliberate.

Now, as a serving Air Force officer, Captain Ralph S. Cramer could not refuse to compile the MACR, or to omit certain other information if so ordered. He developed his own solution to that problem as we have seen, but there are two disturbing side-issues in regard to that engine number.

First, we found in the Burial Files a Press cutting and a Memo from CINFO (PR Division) shown in Fig.37, relating to the discovery of a Norseman on the sea bed off the French coast in 1973. A check on the engine number had confirmed that the aircraft was #44-70285. No other information was available. Despite in-depth investigation, and particularly in renewed discussions with John Edwards in Wimborne (who had carried out his Channel search for the Norseman in 1973) we could find no evidence to support the Press Report. Edwards told us positively that he had not discovered the engine number.

Second, in 1987 we were collaborating with TVS television in Southampton on an exploratory dive to a Norseman aircraft which had been located in 1980 by ex-RN captain Clive Ward, master of his own marine survey vessel. The intention was to obtain the engine number plate and check the number against available records. Accordingly we telephoned every possible US source to trace the engine number, including the Historical Center at Maxwell AFB in Alabama. There, we spoke to a Mr. Rodd about our plans for a dive and our need to find the engine number. He said cheerfully that we were too late with our dive - `*because someone had already been down to the wreck and removed the brass number plate, which was now in the National Archives* !'

We were flabbergasted, but naturally telephoned the Archives in Washington at once, speaking to a lady called Elaine Everley. After we repeated Mr. Rodd's story, she refuted it flatly. There were no artifacts in National Archives, she said firmly. Only documents. But she agreed to speak to Mr. Rodd and call us back. When she did so it was to report that Rodd had confessed the story wasn't true, that he'd told it `*just for a laugh'*. But some weeks later we learned that the engine number plates were in fact made of brass. *How did Mr. Rodd know that ?*

+   +   +

Initially, we took Rodd's statement and the clipping at face value, but with the discovery of the latter in the Burial File, it seemed to us that it had been sent to Washington from the Maxwell AFB Historical Center and inserted in the sensitive Glenn Miller File - but why ? Rodd, clearly, had seen the cutting and in good faith told us about it. Why, therefore, had Elaine Everley told us it was done `just for a laugh' and omitted all reference to the cutting ? It was extremely tempting to assume that the US Government knew the Norseman had been located and identified, but there was no concrete evidence to that effect. Yet the suspicions remained, and we were to encounter anomalies like this throughout the investigation.

■ Details of Occupants

The Ansell Report on MACR #10770 (Fig.32) indicates that the MACR was compiled originally for `pilot only' and passenger names added retrospectively. But the MACR was a forgery, compiled on two separate machines on several different occasions, so the conclusion was not surprising. The `ORIGINAL' MACR #N-19 was not the `original' at all, but an extract from the MACR compiled by Capt. Cramer at Abbotts Ripton on December 21 and dispatched to various addresses, including SHAEF Versailles, on December 22. That `original', which has never been located, was replaced in the Miller 201 File by the fabricated MACR #10770.

What, precisely, had Cramer inserted in the `Occupants' section of his `original' ? There are several possibilities :

1) Morgan may have been alone, but this is improbable, because his orders were to `ferry personnel' to Beauvais and/or Bordeaux. The pilot was the only casualty listed in the 35 ADRS History Sheet for December 1944, but he may have carried passengers from other bases who came to Abbotts Ripton to board the aircraft.

2) There is extensive evidence that Baessell was not a passenger. He is not listed among the `Missing' at the USAAF Military Cemetery at Maddingley, Cambridge; he is not listed on the Casualty Lists for the Second Air Division, 1943-1945, which included the 8th Air Force (cf Maxwell AFB letter, 29 March 1993). The `Glenn Miller History Sheet' issued by NPRC St.Louis *circa* 1973 states that only Morgan and Miller were in the lost Norseman. Baessell's dental data were requested from the AG Department in 1950 by the Provost Marshal Division. The Veterans Administration in New York held a Pensions Application Folder for Baessell, indicating that he drew a pension post-War. That folder has been suppressed by Federal Records Center, Suitland, Md. Baessell's Casualty Report (1948) shows the cause of death as `incident to disappearance of aeroplane'.

3) We have shown beyond reasonable doubt that Miller was not a passenger.

We believe, in fact, that Cramer's `original' may have shown Miller and Baessell as passengers, but included a footnote that the information had been included `at the request of Lt.Col.Traistor on December 21 1944'. This was reiterated in Cramer's covering letter in the Missing Report (Fig.40). Such an addendum, on a deliberately-unsigned document, would effectively destroy its integrity and viability, and make it impossible to release generally.

Finally, we believed we had located corroboratory evidence that Miller and Baessell were not aboard the Norseman, from the MACR Register page provided by Lt. Christopher M. Cwynar at Maxwell AFB Historical research Center : he sent me MACR copies for two P51 Mustangs lost on December 15 1944, plus the relevant page in the MACR Register (an item we had requested repeatedly from National Archives Washington). It included the entry for MACR #10770 -

Number	Crash Location	Air Force	Group	a/c Type	Ser.Number	Date Lost	Crew
10770	France	8th	15	UC-64A	44-70285	15-12-44	1

It turned out that, intentionally or otherwise, all previous copies of the page circulated to the public by Maxwell AFB had been `clipped off' in copying to delete the right-hand column, `total number of occupants'. The total `3', of course, was derived from MACR #10770 itself.

■ Miller's Destination `Bordeaux' ?

Miller's Finding of Death document, issued January 1946, and several others including letters from Col. Donnell and Major Bradunas, AG Department, indicated Bordeaux as his only destination, and this disturbed Helen Miller so much that she began the correspond-ence with the AG in Washington which forced the declassification and distribution of MACR #10770 in March that year.

The final solution of the mystery has been delayed (but not made impossible) by the abstraction from Miller's 201 File of his AAF AGO Form 66-2, Section 38, Chronological Record of Military Experience for June - December 1944, which contains his movements in the last few weeks of his life. It will also explain why so many documents state he was bound for Bordeaux.

Yet his orders for Paris do not mention Bordeaux, and we cannot dismiss the possibili-ty that he was in fact bound for Bordeaux and the United States - suggesting that the orders, like several other vital documents, may have been forged. And since no cross-Channel flights were lost from Bovingdon in December 1944, we are faced again with Joan Heath's account - of Miller flying home for Christmas, never to return. This may account for the `Bordeaux Crash' letter found in the Burial Files - when Miller failed to return, SHAEF (post-war known as US Forces European Theater) learned of the air sighting of a wrecked plane in thick woods near Bordeaux and ordered a search by a local US Army Graves Regis-tration Company. (Fig.39). Apparently nothing was found - or the result was suppressed because it would expose the Norseman story circulated by SHAEF as false.

■ Search and Investigation (MACR Para.16)

Morgan's failure to transmit a Mayday call and Position Report made a physical search for the Norseman problematical. Southern England in 1944 was a very crowded locality and reports of a land crash would have emerged quickly. Five days too late, SHAEF re-ceived a Royal Observer Corps report of a Norseman heading out to sea from Dymchurch, confirmed during a broadcast by the author from Radio Bedford by the female ROC member who had recorded the sighting, at a time consistent with a 13.25 departure from Abbotts Ripton on a direct flight to Dymchurch. General Barker and Don Haynes received the report at SHAEF on Wednesday morning December 20, too late to organise a sea search, whilst eliminating all possibility of a crash on land, and Haynes resolutely failed to identify that aircraft as Morgan's in his diaries.

Air Traffic Control emergency procedures ensured that an aircraft was classified as `overdue' 1 hour after ETA, and `Missing' 2 hours after ETA. Morgan should have arrived at Beauvais around 16.00 hours; carrying fuel for about 8 hours it would have been exhaust-ed by 21.00 hours on Friday evening. Beauvais ATC Tower would have phoned Abbotts Ripton soon after 17.00 hours to inform 2 SAD their Norseman as overdue : they would come through again at 18.00 to say he was now officially `missing'. No immediate action would be taken at that time to organise a search - Morgan could have been lost and made a precautionary landing at some other field in France or Belgium, or even in open countryside. The ATC organisation would do nothing until his fuel-out time at 21.00 hours had elapsed; meanwhile they contacted every possible airfield at which he might have landed.

The situation was complicated by the eruption of the German Ardennes offensive at 2 a.m. next morning - telephone lines would be given military priority - but ATC would establish no later than Saturday noon that the Norseman was down, confirmed by the Dymchurch sighting. With no sighting inbound over the French coast, a ditching was virtually certain. Survival time in the English Channel in December was measurable in minutes, not hours or days. Conceivably, Morgan may have crossed the French coast unseen, crashing in some remote area - but if, as Haynes claimed, Glenn Miller was on board, why did SHAEF not organise an extensive search along the route between Cap Gris Nez and Paris ?

The simple answer is that Miller was not on board, and the loss of a small liaison aircraft coinciding with the outbreak of a major offensive was given very low priority.

At that point we began to consider seriously the possibility that SHAEF had not wanted the Norseman to be found at all, and especially *after* release of the Haynes story - it would generate many difficult problems. There was also an element of *laisser faire* about such missions as Baessell's : George Ferguson relates that he and the Colonel would vanish for days at a time on the Continent, with the pilot servicing the plane himself - Ferguson claims with some truth that all he needed was a dime to release the cowling Zeüss fasteners. Sometimes they took along a mechanic to refuel and service the aircraft, but this was not the case with Morgan on his fatal flight.

Researcher John Edwards received in 1973 a letter from a F/Sgt Fox, the skipper of an R.A.F. search and rescue launch based at Ramsgate, who described a 2-day search of the eastern Channel for Miller's aircraft, but the facts say otherwise. Morgan's aircraft was not officially listed as missing for 5 days, and a search of all available wartime records failed to reveal any ASR search for the aircraft between December 16 and 31.

We know that Haynes was questioned unofficially by Colonels Early and Traistor on December 21, possibly making a written statement which may have been attached to the Form 66-2 accompanying the Missing Report sent to the War Department on 28 December 1944, but contrary to some reports there was no 8th AF inquiry into the Norseman loss. We received a letter from John J. Slonaker of the Historical Reference Branch, Washington dated November 8 1985 :

`Believe me - if we ever find a record of the 8th Air Force inquiry into the disappearance (of Glenn Miller) we shall notify all interested researchers, put the Xerox machine on stand-by, swing wide the doors and stand aside !'*

There is a serious inconsistency here : Major Miller was not 8th Air Force - his parent unit was HQ Squadron, Special Services Division, SHAEF. Any 8th AF inquiry, therefore, would be into the loss of the aircraft itself, but because of high daily losses it was not feasible to convene Boards of Inquiry for every missing 8th AF aircraft - unless there was some extraordinary reason. This might include the presence of a VIP on board, but the lack of any inquiry would confirm that Miller was not a passenger.

Similarly, all three Records of Death documents confirm that no investigation took place in 1944, but this referred to the occupants, not the aircraft. Yet there is evidence to suggest that in addition to Haynes' interrogation by the 8th AFSC officers, there was some form of official investigation into Miller's disappearance by the Provost Marshal Division in Paris. In 1988 we obtained from a member of the Glenn Miller Society a copy of a letter signed `*Peter'*. We dismissed it initially as a hoax, but there is an odd air of authenticity about it. The name of the addressee had been removed to protect his identity, and the letter was signed simply `Peter' with no surname. American writer Dale Titler knows the writer's identity. The text was as follows :

> `*Responding to your letter dated February 10 1984, be advised that I was a Criminal Investigation Division Agent assigned to the Glenn Miller case. After rather extensive investigation, we could find no evidence that, indeed, Miller and his plane was lost in the English Channel on a flight to France. We could uncover no criminal or illegal evidence which would indicate other than the kind of tragedy reported. We explored the possibilities of foul play or some distortions in the life of Glenn Miller. Of course the investigation was suddenly halted because of VE Day and the haste to return home. What did and has bothered me greatly was our inability and that of professional researchers to find any wreckage of the plane or the bodies. This one single matter makes one question the entire incident. But again, we could find no one who was concealing or otherwise thwarting the investigation.*
>
> `*It is, in my opinion, unreasonable to assume that both the plane and the bodies could not have been recovered or at least that this kind of accident could have occurred. Indeed, this has all the elements of a mystery, yet I must admit that I could find no contrary evidence. But deep down in my heart I have never accepted the finding as a plane lost in the Channel...'*

The writer was clearly intelligent and well-educated, and if the letter is genuine, it confirms that an investigation into the disappearance of Major Miller was initiated in 1944 and lasted until VE-Day, May 8th 1945 - no matter what the official USFET report stated. (Fig.38). We were concerned that this writer had not come forward earlier, particularly in the Seventies when Miller Mystery Fever was at its height - at that time John Edwards actually flew over the assumed route of the Norseman with TV presenter Angela Rippon ! Quite possibly, `Peter' had read Mr. George T. Simon's book *GLENN MILLER AND HIS ORCHESTRA (Bigbee Promotions 1973)* - but why had he not contacted the author ?

Suppose, we thought, that this was an exercise in disinformation initiated by the Department of the Army, Intelligence Division, with a vested interest in suppressing the truth of the matter ? Several researchers had been verbally `warned off' and the author's telephone was bugged for 6 months in 1987. Read in that context, the letter takes on a different image. If we accept the three Report of Death documents and the USFET Signal which stated that no investigation took place, why was this letter produced and circulated ? Most of the content is negative in effect, but one sentence drew our attention - `*We could find no one who was concealing or otherwise thwarting the investigation'.*

Now, this was very strange. The concept of a cover-up had not emerged in 1944-1945 at all. It was not until MACR #10770 was declassified and released in March 1948 that any suspicions arose. *Why,* we asked ourselves, *had a US Army CID agent assigned in December 1944 to investigate the disappearance of Glenn Miller considered the possibility of a cover-up initiated at the time of the incident ?* The idea was untenable. But if such a letter was circulated deliberately to foster the idea that a cover-up had been suspected, investigated *and eliminated* at that time, the benefits to its originators were manifest, serving to deflect any suspicions on the part of researchers. Readers must reach their own conclusions, as did we.

Our reasoning was as follows : SHAEF delayed all reporting procedures for 9 days, from December 14 - 23, either because they did not know what had happened to Miller, or because they did know and were awaiting developments. If the former was true, the Army CID may have been ordered to search and investigate - *confirming that SHAEF knew Miller had reached Paris* ! In which case the inquiry should have been abandoned after the Norseman story was released on December 24 - but according to `Peter' it continued until VE Day in May 1945. The inference is that SHAEF still did not know the truth and ordered the covert inquiry to continue. But was `Peter' based in Paris - or Washington ?

Even SHAEF would not take the risk of ordering an inquiry - then stating in the Records of Death that none had been initiated. Had an inquiry taken place, many people would have been questioned - and it would only take one, post-war, to open Pandora's Box.

■ Eyewitness Statements

The absence of any statement in MACR #10770 by Don Haynes baffled researchers for many years. Further, since he was in Paris when Capt. Cramer compiled his `original' MACR on December 21 1944, it seems certain it contained no such statement and did not identify Haynes as `person with last knowledge of the aircraft'. Indeed, it was these omissions which did more than anything else to destroy the credibility of his story and the MACR itself, and Haynes' own story. But in retrospect, it is obvious that both entries had to be excluded. Captain Cramer's first intimation that Miller may have been on board the Norseman was on Wednesday December 20 when Col. Early received the SHAEF teleprinter signal (Fig.24) and called Cramer about the Norseman. Next day, Thursday December 21, Traistor telephoned Cramer from Paris (see the Missing Report) and told him what to include and exclude from his MACR. Specifically, no mention of Lt. Haynes !

The dilemma shared by Early and SHAEF was this : if they included Haynes' name, it would make him vulnerable to interrogation. It would also inevitably migrate to many other documents. But omission of his name also meant excluding an eyewitness statement and they were reduced to two choices : either an anonymous resume of Haynes' Norseman story - i.e `An Off. of AEF Band witnessed the take-off' as included in Miller's Casualty Report (Fig.6) or no eyewitness statement at all, and this was probably the lesser of two evils. I believe very strongly that SHAEF at the time were not too concerned about the MACR's inconsistencies and omissions - they could not foresee that the Miller Mystery would endure for half a century and more, until it was finally solved. They really believed that the dust would soon settle, Miller would be forgotten and the mystery would die a natural death.

Just how wrong can one be ? They all made errors of judgment and fact - Haynes, General Barker, May, General Davies, even Eisenhower himself. Others knew the truth and remained silent - Cols. Early and Traistor, Lt.Col. David Niven (who judiciously divorced himself from the mess by keeping out of Paris and omitting Miller's name from all his post-war books). Most of all, certain Band members who formed the small group selected to play for Ike's celebration party on Saturday December 16 1944 at SHAEF. From a purely analytical viewpoint, the cover-up was ill-advised, ill-prepared, poorly enforced and extremely flimsy - yet it kept experienced investigators at bay for more than four decades. This says much for Army discipline and loyalty to one's friends.

4)   The Helen Miller/AG Correspondence

■ **The War Department Telegram** (Fig.57)

Following the release of Miller's 201 File in May 1992, we were able to fill in some details of the period following his disappearance, and the sequence is extremely interesting. Going back to SHAEF in 1944, General Barker had authorised on December 22 the telegram to Helen Miller. Such messages during wartime were on pre-printed forms, and the only information it contained was that `Your husband Alton G. Miller has been reported missing in flight'* (`action' had been deleted and `flight' inserted). Thereafter Helen received a number of letters from high-ranking officers in Paris and Washington.

■ **The Barney Giles Letter**

Lt.Gen. Barney Giles, Deputy Commander Army Air Forces and Chief of Air Staff wrote to Helen on December 23 1944, having been alerted by General Eisenhower the previous day. The letter, containing no factual evidence, is largely a eulogy of the missing band leader : there is only one disturbing statement - `Every effort is being made to locate Major Miller'.

Strange - if Haynes' story was true, Glenn and the others were drowned in the Channel and no search had being made at all. But if, as we believe, Glenn had arrived in Paris on Thursday December 14 and thereafter vanished without trace, it may have been true that SHAEF simply had no idea what had happened to him.

■ **The Major Bradunas Letter** (Fig.59)

It seems incredible, but after Glenn vanished, Helen Miller was given no further details for more than 6 weeks until Major Bradunas wrote to her on 12 February 12 1945, as Chief, Notification Branch, Personal Affairs Division in the Washington AG Department. This same officer, promoted to Lt.Col., would turn up a year later at Maxwell AFB to sign the Declassification Certificate on the forged MACR #10770. His letter reads :

`Dear Mrs. Miller -

I am writing you with reference to your husband Major Alton Glenn Miller, who was reported missing in the European area since 15 December 1944.
Additional information has been received indicating that Major Miller was a passenger on a C-46 (transport plane) nicknamed `Norseman' which departed from England on a mission to Bordeaux, France, on 15 December 1944. The report reveals that your husband's plane was last seen to leave its base at about 1.55 p.m. and the time, place and circumstances relative to its loss are presently unknown in this headquarters.
Please be assured that a continuing search by land, sea and air is being made to discover the whereabouts of our missing personnel. Any additional information received will be sent immediately to you by the Adjutant General or this headquar-

ters.

E.A.BRADUNAS
Major, Air Corps,
Chief, Notification Branch
Personal Affairs Division.

This letter is a masterpiece of deception. The `C-46' may have been a misprint - see Col. Donnell's letter to Mrs. Miller (Fig.58). This was the first information Helen Miller had received since Glenn vanished two months previously - and it was totally flawed. Bradunas knew about the Haynes story and had seen the ORIGINAL Missing Aircrew Report (from which he got the take-off time of 1.55 p.m.) - but fails to mention the stop at Twinwood Farm or a projected stop at Paris. Instead, he gives Glenn's destination as Bordeaux ! This hardly seems possible - but how could he tell Helen that according to Haynes, Morgan's destination was Orly, that according to the MACR it was Villacoublay, whilst Morgan's orders stated Beauvais ? Bradunas states that the C-64 was last seen `leaving its base' (Twinwood Farm ?) at 1.55 p.m. - whereas in fact it departed from Abbotts Ripton at 13.25. Bradunas does not tell Helen that Morgan, despite Haynes' story, started out from Morgan;s home field Abbotts Ripton.

Worst of all, Bradunas leads Helen Miller to believe that a major search by land, sea and air was under way to find Glenn - yet he was perfectly aware (as other documentation confirms) that no search was ordered, that no investigation took place, that Haynes' name never appeared in any official report and no official announcement of his `story' was ever issued.

We found this to be the most shocking example of deception in the whole case, and we were not surprised to find that Major, later Lt.Col. Bradunas, was involved in the declassification of the forged MACR #10770 at Maxwell AFB.

■ The General Witsell Letters

A letter received by Helen Miller dated 8 October 1945 came from Major General Edward F. Witsell, Acting Adjutant General. It explained carefully why it was necessary, 12 months after a person was held in missing status, to issue a Finding of Death document, after the War Department had given careful consideration to all the evidence placed before it, including witnesses - yet Haynes had not been called to give evidence. But there is one curious little passage :

> `*Occasionally relatives and friends of missing persons receive communications containing pertinent and reliable information which has not been reported officially to the War Department. If you have received any such communications, it will be greatly appreciated if you will forward copies . . . which will be returned if you so desire.'*

This addendum is very ambiguous : the Adjutant General's Department was genuinely interested in any leads or clues, either because they were anxious to prosecute the search to the bitter end - *or they wanted to know if any of the rumours approached the truth, in any degree.* The reader must judge for himself.

Major General Witsell wrote a second time to Helen Miller on 16 December 1945, Glenn's presumed date of death and the day on which the Finding of Death documents were issued. His letter begins :

> `Dear Mrs.Miller :
>
> Since your husband, Major Alton G. Miller, 0505273, Air Corps, was reported missing 15 December 1944, the War Department has entertained the hope that he survived and that information would be revealed dispelling the uncertainty surrounding his absence. However, as in many cases, the conditions of warfare deny us such information. The record concerning your husband shows that he was a passenger aboard a C-64 (Noorduyn) transport aircraft which failed to arrive at its destination Bordeaux, France. The aircraft was last sighted at 1355 hours, 15 December 1944, as it departed Twinwood Field, England. No other facts are known concerning the disappearance of his plane.'

Again, the insistence on Bordeaux as Miller's destination - and no reference to a stop at Paris ! The letter states that a Finding of Death was to be issued, but the reference to `conditions of warfare' is interesting. The war had now been over for 7 months; Lt. Haynes and the Band had returned home for demobilisation and were available for questioning. The restrictions of wartime Official Secrets Acts were no longer in force, and it was incorrect to say that `no other facts are known'. The letter, like all others, quotes the Haynes story but this is not surprising : from the early days of the incident three documents had ensured its perpetuation : Miller's Casualty Report, the spurious Confirmatory Signal from 8th AFSC to General Barker and the forged Missing Aircrew Report #10770. The thousands of officials and officers who later quoted the story were in no way involved in the conspiracy : they were merely quoting from the record, and it is true that Barker and the others were far-seeing in their plans.

Witsell's third letter and fourth letters in March 1948 (he was now Adjutant General of the Army, having been promoted) were addressed to Glenn's mother Mattie Lou Miller and we shall review them presently. Meanwhile, let us return to December 1944, after Helen received notification that Glenn was missing.

■ The General J.A. Ulio Letter.

This letter, the first from SHAEF to Helen Miller after she received the telegram dated 23 December 1944, is from the Adjutant General himself, Major General J.A. Ulio :

> *December 28 1944*
>
> `Dear Mrs.Miller :
>
> This letter is to confirm my recent telegram in which you were regretfully informed that your husband, Major Alton G.Miller, 0505273, Air Corps, has been reported missing in

G.Miller, 0505273, Air Corps, has been reported missing in flight between England and Paris since 15 December 1944.

I know that added distress is caused by failure to receive more information or details. Therefore, I wish to assure you that at any time additional information is received, it will be transmitted to you without delay, and, if in the meantime no additional information is received I will again communicate with you at the expiration of three months. Also, it is the policy of the Commanding General of the Army Air Forces upon receipt of the `Missing Aircrew Report' to convey to you any details that might be contained in that Report.

The term "missing" is used only to indicate that the whereabouts or status of an individual is not immediately known. It is not intended to convey the impression that the case is closed. I wish to emphasise that every effort is exerted continuously to clear up the status of our personnel. Under war conditions this is a difficult task as you must readily realise. Experience has shown that many persons reported missing are subsequently reported as returned to duty or being hospitalised for injuries.

In order to relieve financial worry on the part of the dependents of military personnel being carried in a missing status, Congress enacted legislation which continues the pay, allowances and allotments of such persons until their status is definitely established. Permit me to extend to you my heartfelt sympathy during this period of uncertainty.

This letter fails totally to add any further information to the contents of the telegram (Fig.57) which simply states that Miller was `*missing in flight.* Written only 2 weeks after Miller vanished, the letter infers that as soon as the MACR was received, the information therein would be passed on to Helen Miller - but at Abbotts Ripton, Ralph C.Cramer had refused to sign the ORIGINAL issued on December 23 : the AG, beyond doubt, had received a copy by 28 December but could not quote from an apparently worthless document. But this letter does refer to Paris as Miller's supposed destination !

There was a long hiatus until December 26 1945 when Helen received a letter from the Washington Personal Affairs Section AG Department, offering assistance in relation to claims for pay, gratuities, insurance and the like : Helen replied somewhat curtly that she needed no assistance from the Army. Two days later on December 28 she received a letter of sympathy from Hap Arnold, Commanding General, Army Air Forces, triggered by the issue of the Finding of Death documents. (Figs.25-27). It says nothing about his disappearance, whilst saying much about Glenn's qualities and accomplishments in the Air Force.

At the turn of the year, there had been a flood of rumours, theories, scenarios : this from the New York Mirror, February 26 1945 - "In New York" by Walter Winchell : `. . . *returned officers say Glenn Miller's plane was shot down by our own ack-ackers. . .'.* In the New York Daily News for December 22 1945, Ed Sullivan wrote in his "Little Old New

York" column : `. . .Mrs. Helen Miller got a very sympathetic `presumed to be dead' wire from the Air Forces - but can't understand the hocus-pocus about the plane being en route to Bordeaux when she knows it was bound for Paris. . .'

Ed Sullivan again, December 13 1945 - an extraordinary piece of `reporting' : `Don Haynes and other pals of Major Glenn Miller cushioning Helen Miller against the War Department letter which goes out one year after a soldier has been reported missing in action. . . It was on December 15 1944 that Major Miller took off from the RAF base in England, Twinwood Farms, for the flight to Paris to set up the Olympia Theatre concerts in Paris. . . His Band was to follow four days later . . . He and a Washington DC colonel, and the personal pilot of Gen. Goodrich took off in a single-motored C-64 Norseman which lacked de-icing equipment, though freezing winds swept the airport. . . Paris had not been told the plane was en route, so three days elapsed before Don Haynes, arriving in Paris got the Air Forces' searching parties in motion. . . Helen Miller and the two adopted children still believe that Glenn will turn up. . .'

There can be few more distorted versions of the truth - yet in some strange way Ed Sullivan had been told most of the Haynes story - perhaps Haynes appeared on the Sullivan radio show at least once. But where did Ed get the idea that the Band was to follow Glenn over 4 days later ? Because in fact, that is precisely what happened : Miller flew over on Thursday, the Band the following Monday after being delayed. But if the Band had travelled on Saturday December 16 as planned, `four days earlier' would date Glenn's flight as December 12 - significantly, the date his orders were cut !

Strikingly, Sullivan covers Haynes for the two wasted days searching Paris for Miller : `Paris had not been notified the plane was coming' - that was absolutely correct, because it was never bound for Paris !

And one more fascinating clip, from "Broadway" by Danton Walker in the New York Daily News, December 20 1945 : `Glenn Miller up to now described as only missing, will be officially proclaimed dead next month and the inside story of his death as it's being told is one of the most lurid incidents of the war. . .'

5.   The SHAEF Radio Signal E 77699. (Fig.56)

General Davis suggested to General Eisenhower on December 22 (Fig.20) that a Radio Signal should be sent to the War Department, but it was May 1992 before we obtained a copy. Signed by Eisenhower, numbered E 77699 and dated December 22, it was sent immediately on receipt of General Davis' letter. It quotes verbatim Glenn Miller's Casualty Report (Fig.6) released that same day, but omits any details of his mission. Once again, Lt. Haynes is not named (there is no official message, document or report bearing his name anywhere in the US records) and there is an interesting link with the USFET exchange of messages during the run-up to the declassification of MACR £10770 on 26 March 1946.

On 4 March, USFET in Paris signalled to the AG Department, Washington, referring to this same radio Signal E 77699 which, they said, stated that Miller's mission was to take part in a Christmas Day Broadcast - which was only part of his task. USFET (previously SHAEF) had received a copy of the forged MACR #10770.

Significantly, the USFET message revealed that a Confirmatory Signal was attached to the Missing Aircrew Report - presumably the genuine article (Fig.24) sent by Early to SHAEF on Friday December 22nd, triggering all the extraordinary events of that day listed below. The forged Signal (Fig.10) was prepared and circulated by the AG Department in

Washington after the War.

Interestingly, the USFET message dated 4 March 1946 states that the Norseman left at 13.55 hours from Twinwood Field with Major Miller as a passenger *and then adds in a different type face* `and one other passenger' !

After Don Haynes was interviewed on December 21 in Paris by Colonels Early and Traistor from 8th AFSC, several important developments occurred on the following day :

(a) General Davis wrote `officially' to General Eisenhower.
(b) The Radio Signal was sent to the War Department.
(c) Miller's Casualty Report was released.
(d) Capt. Cramer was instructed to prepare his MACR by Col.Traistor from Paris.
(e) A telegram was sent to Helen Miller in New Jersey.
(f) The Press Release was scheduled for Christmas Eve at 18.00 hours.
(g) Work began at SHAEF on compiling the Missing Report.

6. The Missing Report (Fig.40)

In May 1992 NPRC St.Louis provided a copy from Miller's 201 File, dated 28 December 1944 with several attached documents. Providing some remarkable evidence, it differs totally from a Missing Aircrew Report such as #10770 in which `missing' occupants are listed. Missing Reports were used for personnel missing or missing in action *other than those covered by Missing Aircrew Report.* The Report should have enclosed AAF Form 66-2, Record of Service which included in Section 38 a `Chronological Record of Military Experience' which proved to be the most vital document in the entire mystery.

Attached to the Missing Report was a covering letter from SHAEF confirming that a Form 66-2 was enclosed - but the Form itself was missing and has never been located. It is perfectly obvious why this document had gone astray - it recorded Miller's movements and duties from the time he arrived in England in June 1944 to the last day of his life - whenever that was. Personal Records were updated regularly by the Adjutant of their unit, copies being sent to the War Department for the Personnel Records Division and eventually for the officer's 201 File. Note how Morgan's Record Card (Fig.36) was updated posthumously.

The Section 38, we are certain, would confirm that Miller travelled by shuttle aircraft to Paris Orly on Thursday December 14 (and not aboard Morgan's Norseman the following day !). It would confirm he reported to SHAEF and stayed there that weekend, flying out from Buc Field with or without official permission - and it might even include an explanation of his non-return to Europe. This document, which contradicted the Haynes story and its confirmation by the SHAEF generals, was potentially explosive - and had to be suppressed. The Pentagon denies it was ever in the file : NPRC St.Louis confirmed that it was, but that access was denied by the Miller family.

7. The Finding of Death Documents (Figs.25-27)

Under American law, in the event of a person disappearing without trace in circumstances which indicate a substantial possibility of death, a period of a year and a day must elapse before the missing person is deemed for all legal purposes to be dead. Whilst Major Miller's Casualty Report was dated December 22 1944 and those for Morgan and Baessell January 5 1945, all three were officially deemed dead on December 16 1945. No legal death certificate can be provided, nor can a will be probated and estates bequeathed in the case of missing soldiers, but the Finding of Death document has the legal standing of a death certificate, except that in the case of insurance claims an additional signed certificate must be provided by the Veterans Organisation.

Confusion arose initially from two different versions of the Miller FOD document - the first was the standard Form 0353 Report released and circulated by National Archives for many years (Fig.25), showing Miller as `missing' and the words `in action' having been deleted. The aircraft destination, one again, is `Bordeaux' and there is no reference to Twinwood Farm, Orly, Villacoublay or Beauvais. Helen Miller received a copy. Remarkably, the document is undated and was probably issued towards the end of December 1945.

When finally we obtained the Miller 201 File from St.Louis, it included the FOD documents (on Form 0353-3) circulated to the several insurance companies involved in Miller's loss, and in all these documents Miller was shown as *missing in action'. This prompted us to question the terms of his insurance policies, without producing any positive results. Undoubtedly these documents, plus the Casualty Report containing the Haynes story, triggered Helen Miller's letters to the AG Department querying the destination, and led ultimately to the release of the false MACR #10770 a few months later. Indeed, her disbelief in the Haynes story was the driving force behind her search.

8.   The USFET Messages

It is reasonable to assume that USFET Headquarters in Paris, by January 1946, had been provided with a copy of the forged MACR #10770, but we found it remarkable that USAFE and USFET, responding to the AG's urgent inquiry, did not supply much more information. Obviously they had not seen fit to interview certain important witnesses, including Haynes (who could have been flown in from California), General Barker, Major May, Colonels Early and Traistor, Air Traffic and Operations Staff at Alconbury and Twinwood Farm etc. etc. The sequence of signals and messages between Washington, USFET and USAFE which began in late December 1945 and continued until February 1946 is of considerable importance in the case.

At that time two conflicting versions of the events on December 15 1944 existed : First, the story Haynes related verbally (but never in writing), which had migrated via many official documents into military legend and archives. Never issued publicly in written form, it was officially endorsed, supported and endlessly repeated by top echelon personnel at SHAEF, the War Department, the AG Department and National Archives to the next of kin and the general public alike. To support it post-war, the Department of Defense issued a meagre supply of documents `corroborating' the story - Casualty Reports, the Finding and Reports and Findings of Death documents, the genuine and spurious Confirmatory Reports from 8th AFSC and specifically, the false MACR #10770 fabricated in January 1945 and declassified on 26 March 1946.

Against this were the blatant anomalies in Report #10770, certain Morgan documents in general circulation including his Record Card and Forms 5, the abstraction and suppression of many documents, the failure of the US Government to issue any official statement, and the official policy of suppression and misinformation in National Archives and military establishments.

But why had the release of this forged Report become inevitable by 26 March 1946 ? The answer involved not only Helen Miller's pressure on the AG Department but the lack of signature on the `ORIGINAL' MACR #N-19 found in the Burial File. Perhaps too, the existence in the Files of Cramer's real `original' MACR dated December 22 1944.

As such, #N-19 was only an extract, a worthless and unviable document, suppressed in the Burial Files solely to prevent identification of the mysterious compiler of MACR #10770. The events which forced the release of #10770 began in late December 1945.

Helen noted two anomalies in the Finding of Death documents (Fig.25) which cited Glenn's destination as Bordeaux - but Haynes had said the Norseman was bound for Paris Orly. Further, there was no reference to a landing at Twinwood Farm or Paris, and she had noted in Glenn's orders that he was to proceed to SHAEF, Versailles. Secondly, it showed Glenn as `Missing in flight' - but the several insurance company versions found in the Miller 201 File stated he was `Missing in Action'. At that time Helen (who had rejected the Haynes story out of hand according to Herb Miller) became very concerned. She had been wrote in mid-January to Lt.Col. E.H. Korman of the AG Department asking for answers to her questions. That officer referred her inquiry to Col.Donnell of the AG Department on January 23, and a series of messages crossed the Atlantic between Washington and Paris.

AGO MUNITIONS BLDG 23 JAN 1946 40270

COMMANDING GENERAL EUROPEAN THEATER REAR PARIS FRANCE

FURTHER INVESTIGATION CIRCUMSTANCES SURROUNDING DISAPPEARANCE AIRCRAFT UC DASH SIX FOUR ABLE NO FOUR FOUR DASH SEVEN ZERO TWO EIGHT FIVE OF THREE FIVE ADG ON WHICH MAJ ALTON GLENN MILLER WAS A PASSENGER ONE FIVE DEC FOUR FOUR IS BEING MADE IN THIS OFFICE CITE SPXPC DASH S REQUEST DETAILED INFORMATION OF EXTENT AND RESULT OF SEARCH CMA WEATHER CONDITIONS OVER PLANNED ROUTE CMA WHETHER PLANE WAS EQUIPPED WITH TWO WAY RADIO AND DEICING EQUIPMENT AND THE SERIAL NUMBER OF ENGINE PD URAD EASY SEVEN SEVEN SIX NINE NINE DATED TWO TWO DEC FOUR FOUR STATES MILLER WAS MISSING BETWEEN ENGLAND AND PARIS WHILE MISSING AIRCREW REPORT SHOWS DESTINATION OF PLANE AS BORDEAUX REQUEST VERIFICATION OF PLANES DESTINATION ALSO ANY PROPOSED EARLIER STOPS ENROUTE AND MILLERS PLANNED ULTIMATE DESTINATION WITH PLANNED STOPS ENROUTE

`CMA' means `comma' and `PD' is `period' (full stop'). The `Message URAD' (`your radio signal') E 77699 (Fig.56) was that signed by Eisenhower and sent to the War Department on December 22 1944. The comment about the MACR content seems at odds with the evidence : both MACRs cite Bordeaux, but the anomaly arose from General Davis's letter to Eisenhower (Fig.20). He omits all mention of Bordeaux whilst including stops at Twinwood and Paris. We tried to establish why this was so - and the answer is blindingly obvious. On December 21 1944, only SHAEF had Haynes' version of the Norseman story - *and Haynes did not know Morgan was bound for Bordeaux until Cols. Early and Traistor arrived from England.* This proved conclusively that Haynes could not have met Morgan at Twinwood Farm - and in this one simple error the Haynes story is exposed as fraudulent ! Headquarters in Paris replied :

AG 704/31 JANUARY 46

PARIS WB 1907 REURAD DTD 23 JAN 46, SPXPC-S DETAILED INFO REQUESTED IN URAD REQUIRES FURTHER INVESTIGATION ACTION WILL BE EXPEDITED AND INTERIM REPORTS SUBMITTED

And a follow-up message :

WAR DEPARTMENT 2 FEBRUARY 46
MILLER ALTON GLENN 0505273 ROURAD DATED 23 JAN 46 AND OURAD WB 1907 :
CASE PROGRESSING. REPORT WILL BE FORWARDED UPON RECEIPT

And again -

WAR DEPARTMENT
WB 2895 SIGNED McNARNEY 7 FEBRUARY 46
MILLER ALTON GLENN 0505273 REURAD DTD 23 JAN 46 CITING SPXPC-S AND OUR SUBSEQUENT REPLY WB2277 LATEST. CASE PROGRESSING. REPORT SHOULD BE FORTHCOMING SHORTLY.

Clearly the AG department was becoming concerned - and this suggests that only a few people at the very top were privy to the truth. A further message arrived in Washington from Western Base Section Paris :

WAR DEPARTMENT
WB 3491 SIGNED McNARNEY
MILLER ALTON GLENN 0505273 REURAD DATED 23 JAN 46 CITING SPXPC-S 23 JAN 46 AND OUR SUBSEQUENT REPLY WB 2895 LATEST DESIRED INFO NOT RECEIVED TO DATE. IMMEDIATELY ON RECEIPT YOUR OFFICE WILL BE NOTIFIED

Why were the USFET investigations taking so long ? It seems reasonable to suggest that they were preoccupied with the anomalies in the case - no matter where they looked, they could find nothing to support the Haynes story in the MACR - and a great deal to refute it. And the final message to the War Department (below and Fig.38) exposes their inability to relate the Missing Aircrew Report to the Haynes story. Logically, the next essential step was to interrogate Haynes, but USFET does not recommend this : nor did the War Department or AG Department, despite Haynes being a civilian and available. Clearly, USFET could not quote him - his story of Station 595 Honington, Morgan's destination as Orly and numerous other statements conflicted with the MACR.

The message sent to USFET by USAFE on February 2 1946 was not original - it was a `certified true copy' made by none other than Major Walter B. Morrow, whom we have already met - who was in charge of Isolated Burials, Europe. A year later he would provide `evidence' for the Non-Recoverability Board in Paris - the only written evidence to support the fact that Colonel Baessell boarded the Norseman at Twinwood Farm - and that information came directly from the unpublished Haynes statement ! Like Lt.Col.Bradunas, Morrow appears to be one of the inner circle of officers actively engaged in the conspiracy.

USFET did not signal Washington until February 2 1946, a striking hiatus if one considers the urgency of previous signals. No doubt USFET were reluctant to send such a negative document to the War Department, attention AG Department - and releasing a copy of the USFET message to Helen Miller would hardly be productive. It reads :

EXTENSIVE SEARCH OF ALL RECORDS AVAILABLE TO THIS HEADQUARTERS FAILS TO REVEAL INFORMATION DESIRED. MISSING AIRCREW REPORT CONCERNING AIRCRAFT ON WHICH MAJOR MILLER WAS A PASSENGER DOES NOT GIVE ANY INFORMATION AS TO WEATHER CONDITIONS AT TIME OF TAKE-OFF OR ON PLANNED ROUTE, TYPE OF RADIO EQUIPMENT, OR WHETHER OR NOT AIRCRAFT WAS EQUIPPED WITH DE-ICING EQUIPMENT. MISSING AIRCREW REPORT STATES AIRCRAFT WAS ENROUTE TO BORDEAUX VIA A-42 (VILLA-COUBLAY).

Thus in February 1946, to satisfy Helen Miller, there was only one way out - the forged MACR #10770 lodged in Miller's Burial File in Washington would have to be released. But first it would have to be declassified - and Lt.Col. Bradunas was the man for the job. Why he had to do it at Maxwell AFB assisted by another AG Department officer Captain Muench is unclear - but they could hardly interfere with official documents at the Washington National Personnel Records Center itself.

9. The Colonel Donnell Letter (Fig.58)

Dated 6 February, this stated that `further investigation' had taken place - quoting the USFET Signal dated February 2. The `official records' to which he referred were extracts from MACR #10770 about departing Twinwood at 13.55 hours, bound for Bordeaux `via Twinwood Farm' - *but he made no reference to a proposed stop at Paris to drop Glenn Miller*. This pacified Helen Miller, at least temporarily, but everyone actively involved in the deception knew this state of affairs could not be prolonged indefinitely. In all probability the Adjutant General George F. Herbert called a conference of senior officers to discuss the problems generated by the USFET signal - but precisely who was involved ?

The Haynes story was featured in three documents : Miller's Casualty Report, the MACR #10770 in Miller's Burial File and the Confirmatory Signal in his 201 File attached to the Missing Report. (The MACR and Signal were proven forgeries). The `ORIGINAL' MACR #N-19 was a useless and unsigned extract from another document which could not be released. Haynes had not been interrogated officially, nor was he named in any report or document. Those who may have considered interrogation wisely decided against it. When he told Helen Miller the same story on returning home, she disbelieved it *in toto*. But she would have to be told *something*, shown some kind of official report to back up Haynes' account.

MACR #10770 had been prepared precisely for this kind of situation - once it had been declassified, and Lt.Col.Bradunas could do the job. We know nothing of his co-signer Capt. P.M.Muench, Air Corps - but it is a safe guess he was on the AG staff in Washington DC. There can be no further room for doubt - everything fits in. And now we can look at the source of the information passed to Col.Donnell. First, when preparing his letter to Helen Miller on February 6 1946, he was familiar with the inconsistencies and anomalies in the official account - but he knew a great deal about the case already.

The Donnell letter raises many questions. Why did it omit the one fact for which

Helen Miller sought confirmation - that her husband was to be dropped by the Norseman in Paris ? Why omit Villacoublay (specified by the MACR) ? Haynes was claiming in radio interviews (and later in his diaries) that Morgan was bound for Paris Orly ! Helen could not be shown Morgan's Operation Orders for a ferrying mission Abbotts Ripton - B-42 Beauvais - Bordeaux. Donnell played for time, omitting a Paris destination (which would undoubtedly increase Helen's demand for proof) but advised the Adjutant General that proof of some kind must be forthcoming - and quickly. Thus the release of MACR #10770 was forced on the AG department.

There were two outright lies in the Donnell letter :

`*The airplane. . .on which Major Miller was a passenger departed Twinwood Field at 13.55 hours 15 December 1944. The plane was unreported after take-off and failed to arrive at its destination. . .'*

Twinwood, in fact, was closed to all flying that day. Further, Morgan *was* reported after take-off, crossing the English coast outbound at Dymchurch, and that sighting was known to General Barker by Tuesday December 19 1944. And when the Acting AG Frank Herbert was talking to Los Angeles radio compere Jimmy Fidler in 1945, he revealed that Morgan was in radio contact with the ground 10 minutes after take off. Donnell's reference to a C-46 (Curtis Commando twin-engined transport similar to the C-47 Douglas Dakota) may have been a misprint, or if the Joan Heath story is true, Major Miller may have boarded such an aircraft to fly home for Christmas. But Donnell goes on to clarify one point which effectively destroys any doubt about Morgan's route :

`*The pilot. . . had clearance from Abbotts Ripton Field, under operation orders for Bordeaux, France, via Twinwood Field.'*

In recommending that Helen Miller should be `provided' with proof of the facts, Donnell knew that eventually a Board of Non-Recoverability would have to be convened after the issue of the Finding of Death document - and they too would require proof that Miller was a Norseman passenger. That Board, in fact, was not convened until March 1947, and its findings are assessed later in this chapter. So the Missing Aircrew Report would kill two birds with one stone . . .

Donnell had to be super-cautious about releasing information to satisfy the widow of a world-famous VIP who had vanished in mysterious circumstances. She was still living in the Tenafly, New Jersey apartment, perhaps in the hope that this would be where Glenn would come for her, if he ever returned, and she was following assiduously each and every rumour about Glenn's fate. Donnell wrote :

`**Further investigation by this Headquarters, and a search of the records, do not reveal any substantiation of the various occurrences embraced in your letters.'**

Nothing about an unsigned MACR, the USFET message omission of Twinwood Farm. Only that Glenn was missing `*en route to Bordeaux'* ! Nothing about Morgan's real departure field and destination, or any initial investigation. He goes on :

`The official records indicate the C-64 Eighth Air Force Service Command airplane, 44-70285 on which Major Miller was a passenger departed Twinwood Field at 13.55 hours (1.55 pm) 15 December 1944. The plane was unreported after take-off and failed to arrive at its destination, consequently the aircraft, passengers and pilot were reported and have since been carried in a missing status, presumed drowned.'

Quite deliberately, Donnell fails to identify the `destination' by name, whilst quoting Twinwood as the `departure airfield'. The reason for this omission becomes clear later in the letter.

`The matter of proper clearances by the pilot appears clarified by the fact that he had clearance from Abbotts Ripton Field, under operations orders for Bordeaux, France, via Twinwood Field. The plane was not a passenger-type aircraft conforming to a fixed schedule, and it is not apparent that the procedure followed by the pilot varied from that normally followed in the combat zone. As stated in your letter, the missing aircraft was not one of the ATC planes on which Major Miller was booked as a passenger, but a service plane, on which it is presumed that he became a passenger upon the invitation of Lt. Col. Baessell, also carried missing and presumed drowned.'

Donnell lies again : Morgan's procedure differed radically from standard - he was cleared by Bovingdon on the telephone, instead of landing there for Customs and flight planning. This paragraph was confusing to Helen. The telegram from SHAEF said that Glenn was bound for Paris - but there is no reference to Paris here ! Why would he be flying to Bordeaux, when his duty lay in Paris and the planned concert programme ? Further, the Norseman was far from the `combat zone' - the front line ran through the Ardennes far to the east of the Channel crossing routes. Donnell only `presumes' that Miller went on the flight `upon the invitation of Lt.Col. Baessell' - there is an implicit element of doubt we found intriguing.

Why did Donnell conceal so much information ? Well, it was not his responsibility to determine the content - he was merely the clerk. The crucial decisions were taken at higher level, i.e. the Adjutant General and the Department of the Army in Washington. Once initiated, the cover-up had to continue into the foreseeable future, and at this point, we believe, the top brass made a tragic error of judgment. They were unaware of, or under-estimated, the world-wide appreciation of the music of Glenn Miller : these old men really believed that once the war was over and the armies disbanded, the Glenn Miller mystery would fade into oblivion and all would be well.

So SHAEF, the AG Division in Paris and Washington, and the War Department were caught in their own trap : to support the deception, they had to condone subsequent actions and policies, starting with the fabrication of a spurious MACR #10770, forging the Confirmatory Signal, suppressing a vital Service Record document and shielding Haynes and other witnesses from interrogation. They authorised the abstraction of documents from files and even suppression of the files themselves. Strict control was imposed on the release of any information on the Glenn Miller case, including a moratorium on official statements from Lt. Haynes or any archival departments on the authenticity of various documents. Specifically, no information was to be released from the Burial Files or Miller's 201 File - even the existence of such Files was not to be admitted except under extreme pressure. They had a tiger by the tail and could not, dared not let go. And when the current generation of custodians of the truth sensed our determination to solve the mystery, they could only continue the ongoing cover-up and hope for the best - apart from passing the buck to the next echelon above. But as President Truman said - `The buck stops here'.

Unfortunately for the AG department in 1945, Helen Miller reacted strongly, and the sequence of events took on an aura of inevitability. Yielding to her demands, the AG initiated the February 1946 investigation in Europe - but told her little of the truth. Six weeks later, the forged MACR #10770 was declassified and released, but was not filed in the Register of Missing Aircrew Reports in Washington until the Norseman was included in the Cumulative Loss Listing in June 1947.

It was - and still is - circulated as the `*sole, original and genuine'* article by National Archives. . . but the Archives disclaim all responsibility for the contents, and refuse to have the document examined by typewriter experts.

Quod erat demonstrandum. . .

10. The `ORIGINAL' MACR #N-19 (Figs.34,35).

▓ General Format

Remarkably, #N-19 is not a true `original' document but an edited incomplete extract from an original we were never able to locate. However, we do know quite a lot about the `original' compiled by Ralph S. Cramer at Abbotts Ripton (see Pp. 115-134 incl.). Cramer compiled it under duress, following Col. Traistor's phone call from Paris on December 21 - and it was dated December 22, a day earlier than the forged MACR #10770. The reason it was not dated the 23nd was that Miller's Casualty Report had only been issued on the 22nd, i.e. the official notification that he was missing.

We would have given a great deal for a sight of that historic document - but it held too many secrets, let too many cats out of the bag. And in its way, MACR #N-19 was as blatant a forgery as #10770. For example, Page 1 is much shorter, compared with #10770, since the top heading with addressee, classification note and compilation instructions had been removed. So too had all material below Line 10 of the `occupants' section, the number of which (11) had been deleted and applied to an entirely new `REMARKS' section - presumably to fill the empty space ! A second `REMARKS' section appears on Page 2.

All this indicated, in our view, concealment of some information, possibly Cramer's deposition or a Haynes statement, and in this unsigned unviable state #N-19 could not be inserted in the Register of MACRs in National Archives. What remained after such drastic surgery ? Little by way of hard evidence, save for the intriguing lack of signature. It can be argued that the real Report (from which #N-19 was an extract) *may* have been signed - but such a valid document would have been retained on file and circulated ! Unless, of course, the impish Capt. Cramer had scrawled his truth-revealing graffiti all over it !

Strangely, on receipt of the Miller Burial File in March 1987, Page 2 of MACR #N-19 was missing, as was the section referring to `*person with last knowledge of aircraft*'. If Haynes had made a statement, it might be on the missing Page 2 ! We wrote in haste to the Military Reference Branch for the missing page, but to our disappointment, they replied that `*The reverse of Page 1 is blank and there is no Page 2*'.

End of story... It is difficult to describe our feelings at that time. To have come so far, only to be halted at the final hurdle... But, encouraged by our success in obtaining Miller's Burial File, we demanded and received those for Morgan and Baessell - and surprise, surprise ! The missing Page 2 was in Morgan's File - by accident or design, we could not tell. It was unsigned, there was no `date-stamp' and Capt. Cramer's identification was clear and legible.

This was a major victory and we began to assess the #N-19 Report in depth, for what it was worth. There are several obvious anomalies such as the irregular paragraph numbering compared with Report #10770, in which paras. 6, 7 and 8 (in #10770) have been contracted to 6 and 7 (in Report #N-19). Also, we noted again the new `REMARKS' paragraph seen on Page 1 (#N-19) and found a second `REMARKS' section on Page 2 ! This repetition is clearly out of context with the usual format of a military document.

■ The `Occupants' Entry

This was very interesting : there was no misalignment here, as seen in the fabricated MACR #10770, in which the occupants are classified as `Missing' followed by a so-far unexplained `,AC', but in #N-19, the typed annotation `MIA' (Missing in Action) has been amended and `PDD' inserted (We could find no official translation but assumed that it meant `Presumed Dead by Drowning'). But this alteration is mystifying : first, `MIA' had not been deleted. Second, it was only on the copy in the Miller File. Was a hand-written amendment `PDD' legal ? Let us not underestimate the importance of this point : on the one hand we have an officially-forged document showing three occupants as `missing'. On the other, we have a document which was suppressed officially for 44 years, which shows the occupants as `Missing in Action' - with a hand-written qualification `PDD'. And this made us think very hard. Why had the AG Department gone to the trouble of amending an obviously-forged document ? Remember, the `original' was an official report being compiled in the field, dealing with missing airmen, and the Unit Adjutant Cramer would be extremely careful to avoid confusion when the news was passed to next of kin by the AG department.

Had Morgan really been shot down by German aircraft over the Channel ? Why else would Captain Cramer insert `MIA' ? Or is this copied direct from the real `original' ? Further, where and when was the `PDD' added ? In Washington ? Even more mysterious, in front of each name on the occupant list is a `(c)' - almost certainly written by the same hand that penned `PDD'. What does it mean ? One explanation is that it means `correction' by the addition of `PDD'.

Even more mystifying, there was a copy of #N-19 in each of the Burial Files, an original and two carbon copies - but only the copy in Miller's Burial File is annotated as described. This mystery of `MIA' in the #N-19 MACR, echoed in the Miller Finding of Death documents issued to insurers, is intriguing : in Morgan's File is an amended Report of Death dated November 6 1952 :

`*Corrected `Battle Casualty' to `Non-Battle Casualty'. Previously shown as a Battle Casualty. Correction made per showing of the official records*'.

11. The Report of Death Documents (Figs.5,28,29).

The `official record' referred to above was Morgan's 1948 Report of Death. Miller's Report of Death (Fig.5) had been in circulation for a number of years and we located those for Flight Officer Morgan and Colonel Baessell in their Burial Files. We noted that all three were produced over a three-day period - Morgan's on 23 March, Miller's on 24 March and Baessell's on the 25th. But whilst the Cause of Death for Major Miller and John Morgan was `Airplane crash', that for Baessell was stated as `Incident to disappearance of airplane'. This infers that Miller and Morgan crashed in the same aircraft, but that Baessell's case was in some way different. Also, in `type of casualty' Miller and Baessell are listed as `Non-Battle', whilst John Morgan was a `Battle Casualty' ! This may have generated rumours that the Norseman had been shot down by German fighters - or even a British Spitfire.

In fact, it was a typing error corrected in an Amended Casualty Report for Morgan on November 6 1952 (Fig.61). One wonders why a document, of great value and importance to the next of kin, was not properly checked before release. The ROD document was a pre-printed pro forma incorporating the signature of the Adjutant General, and all three signatures are identical. This also applied to the Finding of Death documents, rubber-stamped for George F. Herbert, Assistant Chief of the Casualty Branch, who was involved in the Jimmy Fidler affair.

Lastly, we noted the annotation showing that no investigation had taken place into the death of each individual.

12. The Non-Recoverability Board Documents

■ The Major Morrow Letter

The post-war documentation process required that the remains of the missing men should be deemed `non-recoverable', and accordingly a Non-Recoverability Board of Inquiry (NRBI) was convened on May 9 1947 (Fig.43). An ostensibly-routine letter from HQ American Graves Registration Command, ETO Area, APO 58 US Army to the NRBI, signed by a Major Walter B. Morrow, is of considerable interest to us, because it is *the only official document to state that Lt.Col. Norman F. Baessell was picked up at Twinwood Farm* by Flight Officer John Morgan.

At this time (1947) the spurious MACR #10770 had been compiled but remained classified, unavailable to the general public, and both the `original' MACR compiled by Capt. Cramer on December 21 1944 and the `ORIGINAL' extract unsigned Report #N-19 developed from it were suppressed in the Burial Files. Major Morrow's information on Baessell, therefore, addressed to the Non-Recoverability Board convened in the Astoria Hotel, Paris on 7 October 1947 (Fig.44) could have originated only from the Adjutant General in Washington - who was, in effect, `feeding' the Norseman story to the Board members.

The Major Morrow letter reads :

```
            SUBJECT : Non-recoverable Remains

TO :       Non-Recoverable Board AGRC
```

141

1. It is recommended that the Board take action on the following case :

NAMES : MORGAN, JOHN R.S.   F/O   T-190776
BAESSELL, NORMAN F.   Lt.Col.   0-905387
MILLER, ALTON G.   Major   0-505273
ORGANISATION : 35th ADGP Repair Sq. Det. 2nd Strategic Air Depot 8th AF

PLACE OF DEATH : Unknown (Probably English Channel)

DATE OF DEATH : 15 December 1944
SYNOPSIS OF CASE : The three men mentioned above were aboard an Eighth Air Force Command airplane (C-64) which departed England en route to Paris, France. The pilot, F/O Morgan, took off from Abbotts Ripton, England and stopped at Twinwood Farms, where he picked up the other two men as passengers. The a/c was never seen again and, to this date, no word has ever been received concerning the plane or its passengers. In view of the fact that all territory crossed in the flight of this a/c was in Allied hands and no information has been forthcoming from Allied sources, it can only be assumed that the a/c went down somewhere in the water and that the three men concerned will not be recovered.
Reference is made to 2nd Indorsement from 2046 GRS Co. dated 21 June 1946, to Classified Message from USFET and letter to Mrs. Miller dated 6 February 1946.

2. Every effort has been made to correlate this case with records in this Headquarters, pertaining to unknown deceased interred in U.S. Military Cemeteries and reported isolated burials. The results are negative.

3. It is recommended that the remains, based upon the above information and research, be now declared non-recoverable.
WALTER B. MORROW
MAJOR Infantry
Chief, Isolated Burials.

Paragraph 1 refers to three documents stored at that time in the Burial Files in Washington - the `Bordeaux Crash Letter', the USFET message and Col. Donnell's misleading letter to Helen Miller. It follows that these papers must have been made available to the NRBI in Paris, presumably by photographed copies sent to SHAEF, now known as USFET (United States Forces, European Theatre) where the Haynes' story would be on record in Special Services Files. There is no mention of any MACR, but reason suggests the Board were given Report #10770. The whole affair was handled extremely well by the AGO department in Washington.

We considered it very significant that the letter, the USFET message to which it refers, and the Board Findings (Fig.44) make no reference to Lt. Haynes driving Miller and Baessell to Twinwood Farm, or that Haynes was the sole witness who saw Morgan land and depart, on a large and heavily-populated airfield (which was closed to all flying and where, according to three surviving witnesses, no Norseman aircraft landed on December 15 1944). The Findings refer to `evidence placed before it' but there is no reference to any witness being questioned. Further, it omits completely the Royal Observer Corps sighting over Dymchurch at 14.40 hours on December 15 1944, quoting instead the last sighting as 13.55 at Twinwood Farm.

The reason is plain - all these (and physical questioning of Haynes, Col. Early, Col. Traistor and Major May) would destroy the credibility of the Haynes story. As we have shown, the Board were given Missing Aircrew Report #10770 and were referred to the USFET message which merely lists the deficiencies in the MACR. Obviously the Board could not be told that the suppressed #N-19 was unsigned, and could not be shown to them.

■ The Non-Recoverability Board Findings

The Board convened on October 9 1947 in the Astoria Hotel in Paris but did not issue their Findings until November 8 - an unusually-long session, in view of the paucity of real evidence : so long that it suggests the officers involved were having a hard time reaching an agreement on their findings, as follows :

```
HEADQUARTERS - AMERICAN GRAVES REGISTRATION COMMAND
EUROPEAN THEATER                        APO 58  U.S ARMY

Proceedings of a Board of Officers appointed in accordance
with letter File AGAO.S 293.9 27 Mar 47 D-M, War Dept, TAGO
9 Apr 47. The Board met pursuant to Par.2, SO No.69, Head-
quarters, American Graves Registration Command, 9 May 47, at
the Astoria Hotel, Paris, France on 7 Oct 1947. The purpose
of the Board was to determine recoverability/identity of
certain casualties now under consideration by this Command.
    The Board reviewed reports of investigation, statements
of witnesses and other papers contained in the files of
American Graves Registration Command, ETA, pertaining to the
case of the following named casualty/casualties, the remains
of which have not yet been recovered. Case files and other
data are attached.
CASE No.  NAME                  ASN               GRADE
     8
          MORGAN, JOHN R.S.     T-190776          F/O
          BAESSELL, NORMAN F.   0-905387          Lt.Col.
          MILLER, ALTON G.      0-505273          Major

FINDINGS : The Board having carefully considered the evi-
dence before it, finds that the remains of said casualty/
```

casualties may be considered as non-recoverable and recommends that no further action may be taken to recover these remains.

JOHN H. EVANS, Col.INF.	WM D. MANN, Lt.Col. JAGD
JAMES F. METCALF, QMC	GEORGE E. CILLEY, Maj. FA/
GEO E. SPRINGER, Maj.,FA	GEORGE E.WOODS, Maj. CE

Department of the Army, OQMG Washington DC
8 November 1947

GEO.A.HORKAN
Brigadier General QMC

■ The AG Memorandum

These Findings, together with case files and other data, were sent to the AGO in Washington, and stored in the Burial Files of Miller, Morgan and Baessell. Four months later on 11 March 1948, preparations were put in hand to release certain documents to the general public including the next of kin, Helen Miller. These included the forged MACR #10770, amended Casualty Reports for Miller and Morgan (but not for Baessell) dated 19 March 1948, and Reports of Death for all three men dated 23-25 March 1948. This activity was triggered by the following memorandum, which also establishes beyond doubt Morgan's departure time from Abbotts Ripton :

AG 704 (11 Mar 48)   WIN/mrh/1B735/9048
                                                11 March
1948

MEMORANDUM TO : Officer in Charge, Casualty Section,
                Personnel Actions Branch, AGO

SUBJECT :   Report of Death
1. The following named officers of the Air Corps were reported missing, non-battle, in flight from England to Paris, France on 15 December 1944, by Casualty Branch Message Numbers 006037 and 358007.

Baessell, Norman F.	Lt.Col.	0905387
Miller, Alton Glenn	Major	0505273
Morgan, John R.S.	F/O	T190776

Flight Officer Morgan, only, was in a flying pay status.

2. Under the provisions of Section 5, Public Law 490, as amended, a Finding of Death was made in the case of the above named men (Sh&5 No. 4902) showing the presumed date of death as 15 December 1945.

3. Missing Aircrew Report #10770, dated 23 December 1944, reveals that subject persons constituted the crew and passengers aboard a UC-64A (Noorduyn transport plane), Aircraft Number 44-70285, nicknamed Norseman, which departed Abbotts Ripton, England, for Bordeaux, France via A-42. The aircraft was last sighted at 13.55 hours on 15 December 1944 at Twinwood Field, England.

4. The Casualty Section File of Major Miller shows that Flight Officer Morgan took off from Abbotts Ripton at 13.25 hours on 15 December 1944 for Twinwood, with operation orders for A-42, Bordeaux. He departed Twinwood Field at 13.55 hours on 15 December 1944, after having picked up two passengers, Lt.Col. Baessell and Major Miller, for Bordeaux, France via A-42 (Villacoublay, France, on the outskirts of Paris, France). General weather conditions over the English Channel on 15 December 1944, obtained by telephone from Foreant Weather Division, Assistant Chief of Air Staff, were intermittent rains, stratus clouds, ceiling 1,000-2,000 feet, southerly wind of 2 miles per hour, warm front.

5. The Quartermaster General, Washington, D.C., forwarded to this office a copy of a letter to the Commanding General, American Graves Registration Command, European Area, dated 18 December 1947, "Subject : Non-Recoverability of Remains, reference the Findings of a Board of Officers, Case No. 8, convened at this Headquarters on 7 October 1947." The Findings of the Board are as follows :

AG 704 (11 March 1948).
"Findings : The Board having carefully considered the evidence before it, finds the remains of said casualty/casualties may be considered as non-recoverable and recommends that no further action be taken to recover these remains."

Attached to the Proceedings is a recommendation from the Chief, Isolated Burials, American Graves Registration Command, European Theater Area to the Non-Recoverability Board, AGRC, Subject : Non-Recoverable Remains which is quoted in pertinent part as follows :

  1. Place of Death: Unknown. (Probably English Channel)

Date of Death: 15 December 1944.

Synopsis of Case: The three men mentioned above were aboard an Eighth Air Force Command airplane (C-64), which departed England enroute to Paris, France. The pilot, F/O Morgan, took off from Abbotts Ripton, England, and stopped at Twinwood Farms, where he picked up the other two men as passengers. The a/c was never seen again and, to this date, no word has ever been received concerning the plane or its passengers. In view of the fact that all territory crossed in the flight of this a/c was in Allied hands and no information has been forthcoming from Allied sources, it can only be assumed that the a/c went down somewhere in the water and that the three men concerned will not be recovered.

2. Every effort has been made to correlate this case with records in this Headquarters, pertaining to unknown deceased interred in US military cemeteries and reported Isolated Burials. The results are negative.

3. It is recommended that the remains, based upon the above information and research, be declared non-recoverable.

6. The plane was last seen at 1355 hours on 15 December 1944, when it departed Twinwood Field, England, flying on a course to Paris, France. The general weather conditions over the English Channel on 15 December 1944 were "intermittent rains, stratus clouds, ceiling 1,000-2,000 feet, southerly wind of 2 miles per hour, warm front. Exhaustive research in the European Theater of Operations, examination of the AG Files of the subject personnel and records at the Historical office, Army Air Forces, do not reveal any information relative to them or the plane after leaving Twinwood Field. The captured German records were searched with negative results. Considering also the fact that the course of the flight of the plane to Paris, France was in Allied hands, and no information has been received from that source, the only reasonable conclusion is that the plane crashed into the sea and carried the men in it to their deaths.

7. It is recommended, therefore, that pursuant to the provisions of Section 9, Missing Persons Act, the foregoing information be accepted as an official report of death, and that a casualty report be initiated stating that the men in paragraph 1, above, died, (non-battle, 15 December 1944,

when their plane crashed somewhere in the English Channel while on a flight from Twinwood Field, England to Paris, France and that Flight Officer Morgan, only, was in a flying pay status at the time of their death. Subject persons were in pay and duty status at the time of death, which was not the result of their own misconduct. The sytemat will be processed in accordance with Paragraph 2b, Bulletin 36, 1945. The casualty report and official report of death will include the following statement :

Finding of Death has been issued previously under Section 5, Public Law 490, 7 March 1942, as amended, showing the presumed date of death as 15 December 1945.
This "Report of Death" based on information received since that date, is issued in accordance with Section 9 of said Act and its effect on prior payments and settlements is as provided in Section 9.

WALTER B. HALLS   CONCURRED
Investigator   SANFORD COFFIN
                                                Captain AGD
                                     OIC Status Review and
                                        Determination Unit

Approved. Recommended action will be taken.

BY ORDER OF THE SECRETARY OF THE ARMY

                                              EARLE E. EWING
                                            Lt.Colonel, AGD
                                      OIC, Casualty Section
                               Personnel Actions Branch AGO

   This Memorandum raises some fascinating questions. First it refers to witnesses - but the Board Findings do not. Further, a representative from the Judge Advocate General's Department is present - a branch of the Adjutant General's organisation. It omits all references to Haynes or any statement made by him, the sole and vital witness to the Norseman departure. It quotes directly from MACR £10770, a forged and fraudulent document and quotes the Haynes story without citing his name.
   Certain other documents should have been available to the Board in Paris from the vital 201 Files at St. Louis, and the Burial Files in Washington. Some of these documents could have been sent by air transport, or by teleprinter, provided the AG Department had been selective in their choice - but there was precious little else they could send. Care had to be taken to ensure that nothing which might invalidate the Haynes story would be revealed to the Board's scrutiny.
Specifically :

147

(a) The St. Louis Miller History Sheet, based on Miller's 201 File which states specifically that only two men were aboard the aircraft.

(b) Morgan's Form 5 (Record of Flights) which place him at Abbotts Ripton on December 15 1944, not at Honington or Heston. (Removed from File).

(c) Morgan's Service Record Card which gives his first destination as B-42 Beauvais and his final destination as Bordeaux - with no landing at Paris. (Removed from File).

(d) The unsigned 'ORIGINAL' MACR #N-19 in the Burial File. (Could not be released).

(e) Col. Donnell's AG Department letter to Helen Miller specifying Glenn's French destination as Bordeaux with no reference to a Paris stop-over. (Deliberate omission).

(f) Miller's orders for Paris with incorrect serial number. (Removed from File).

(g) The Chronological Record of Military Experience in each man's 201 File which would reveal their movements in the last days of their lives.

Remarkably, the Findings refer to *investigations'* and `*Statements of Witnesses'* - but who were they ? We failed to locate the record of the Inquiry in the Archives of the American War Graves Administration files. Don Haynes is not named as witness in any official Burial File, 201 File, or in any official statement, document, letter, flight order, report, Press Release, memorandum, signal or radio message so far located in our investigation. Further, the Norseman story has not been featured in any official statement from any source we located, until it was used as the theme of the 1953 movie `*The Glenn Miller Story'* from Universal Studios, with June Allyson and James Stewart. And this was six years after the Non-Recoverability Board met in Paris in 1947.

Predictably, the movie made no mention of Haynes' part in the mystery at all, quoted an incorrect serial number for Miller and named the other Norseman passenger as `Colonel Burrell' - but it was essentially the Haynes `Norseman story' all over again. So from where did Universal Studios get their information ?

In 1988 the Library of Congress wrote to us :

> `*In 1954, as part of the publicity accompanying the first showing of the film The Glenn Miller Story, the Library was given a small amount of material relating to Glenn Miller. This was supposed to be the first instalment of a gift that would eventually include all of Glenn Miller's papers. In fact, no further material ever came. The material we received had been assembled by Universal International for the purposes of their film, and was given us by them, rather than by the Miller estate.*
> `*Amongst this material was a carbon of a typed transcript of Don Haynes' diary. This transcript was made by the studio for the purposes of the writers of the screenplay of the film. This is our "Don Haynes" diary : we do not have an original manuscript. I suspect that the original diary was returned to Haynes when the studio typist had finished making the transcript.'*

The letter has curious undertones. It omits the name of the donor of the material, but we know Haynes had given Helen Miller a copy of his original manuscript, and she presented it to Universal-International. But why was the promised additional material never delivered ? We can only assume that it contained confidential items, or information which contradicted the Norseman story.

Let us be quite clear about this matter of the NR Board. If the members had done their job efficiently, had the complete Burial and 201 Files flown over from America, called in every possible witness from Milton Ernest, Abbotts Ripton, Twinwood Farm, SHAEF and especially Haynes himself, they would have been forced to abandon the whole process. How could they certify the remains of Glenn Miller as `non-recoverable' because he was lost in the Norseman, when it was obvious that he had not been aboard the aircraft at all ? The huge inconsistencies and anomalies between Haynes' story and most of the official documentation reeked of fraud and deception. So who were the `witnesses' not called by the Board whose testimony would have demolished for ever the Haynes account, in addition to Haynes himself ?

First and foremost, Captain Ralph S. Cramer. Second, Colonels Early and Traistor from Milton Ernest who had interviewed Haynes in Paris on December 21. Third, General Barker and his ADC, Major May. All five officers were fully aware that the Norseman story was fabricated - May, it will be recalled, had gone to great trouble to ensure the MACR contained a viable Twinwood take-off time, and Morgan's destination as A-42 Villacoublay, not B-42 Beauvais. Fourth, Operations and Air Traffic Control staff at Alconbury, Twinwood Farm, Bovingdon. Fifth, staff officers at Milton Ernest, the Provost Marshal Division, ground Abbotts Ripton groundcrew, Captain Love (Adjutant, 2 SAD, Abbotts Ripton) and finally, members of the AEF Band itself. The list is lengthy and comprehensive.

In fact, the NR Board was a creature of the Adjutant General Department, which even had one of its officers on the Board, and the members saw only the evidence the AG Department thought necessary to achieve a satisfactory result. It all fits in very neatly - the NR Board was `fixed', beyond any shadow of doubt, by the AG Department in Washington. So we were not entirely happy and began searching the records for details of the NR Board investigations. The Army, we were informed, conducted a search of DCII records involving the A-Z Unit, 333 Cards, Clue Index and all available files on Alton G. Miller/ Alton Glenn Miller/ Glenn Miller, to determine the existence of Army Intelligence investigative records responsive to our request. That search, it was claimed, revealed no Army Intelligence Investigative File pertaining to the above references on Glenn Miller.

But this was quite untrue, in several respects. We know that Haynes was interviewed by Early and Traistor, and possibly made a written statement for inclusion with the Form 66-2 sent with the Missing Report (Fig.40) to the War Department in Washington. There was the investigation by USFET in 1946, the report on Page 125 by the Army CID agent `Peter' and the Non-Recoverability Board Inquiry itself. All these investigative procedures were ignored or suppressed by the Department of the Army in its report to us, and we considered it to be an exercise in disinformation. The AG Department and the Department of the Army did not want anyone digging too deeply into the story and ensured that only the right information (from their point of view) was released. They provided all the information given by Major Morrow to the NR Board in Paris in October 1947, and I regard their Findings and Memorandum as the most damning evidence of a cover-up.

All the information was there for the Board to uncover - and clearly the result was a total whitewash to get SHAEF and the AG Department off the hook.

13. The `Bordeaux Crash' Letter (Fig.39)

This extraordinary document, which is mentioned in other documents in the mystery, appears to be an interim report on a search carried out in the Bordeaux area for a crashed aircraft near which bodies had been seen. From the date (June 21 1946, only weeks after the compilation of MACR #10770) we concluded that it resulted from the USFET/USAFE inquiry earlier that year.

The letter, signed by a Lt. Brinkmann of 3046 Graves Registration Company based near Limoges, was addressed to the Commanding Officer, 551 QM Group at APO 809, in Europe. It is an isolated document with no prior or follow-up correspondence, which has been carefully preserved for more than 40 years. Now, if nothing had been found as a result of the search, there was no reason to retain the letter - but if some important evidence had been discovered, it rightfully belonged in the Files. In which case, it was extremely likely that other associated documents had been removed.

It seems clear that the wrecked aircraft had been seen from the air, with bodies nearby - had someone on the ground discovered it, a search party could have been led to the spot. Whether this was a random discovery or the result of a planned search, we do not know - some 18 months had elapsed since Miller vanished. The area, heavily-forested in those days, may have complicated the task of finding the crash site. But the letter, stored in the Glenn Miller Burial File, clearly established a connection between him and the crashed plane. The Graves Registration Company, in fact, had been advised that the remains they sought could be those of the Norseman occupants.

The Bordeaux Search Letter is mentioned in the Findings of the NR Board in 1947 :

`Reference is made to the 2nd Indorsement from 2046 GRS Co dated 21 June 1946, to Classified Message from USFET and letter to Mrs. MILLER date February 6 1947'.

The `2046' is probably a misprint for `3046' Graves Registration Company, and the second reference is to the USFET message to the AG Department dated 2 February 1946. But what are the implications of the Search Letter ? If we ignore for the moment the Joan Heath evidence and go back in time to December 1944, we recall that General Barker and other SHAEF officers suspended all reporting procedures for 9 days. Barker either believed that Miller had arrived in France and vanished, or was aware that something had happened to him and was awaiting developments. The delay was necessary, not so much in the hope that Glenn Miller might turn up, but in case the Norseman *did* turn up ! The real nightmare that haunted SHAEF was this : suppose Miller returned *after* SHAEF released the Norseman story ? Or suppose the wreckage of the Norseman was found - containing only two bodies, neither of which was Miller ? Suppose Morgan and Baessell had ditched and been picked up by some neutral ship, to be landed in Sweden, Spain or Portugal without Glenn Miller ?

Certain steps could be taken. A search must be ruled out *because it might find the Norseman* - the last thing SHAEF wanted. Don Haynes could be sworn to silence, and the Confirmatory Signal, which supported his story, had been `suitably adjusted'. It could, of course, be discreetly destroyed if Glenn Miller returned. True, the Adjutant at Abbotts Ripton, Capt. Cramer, was refusing to sign a Missing Aircrew Report but it could be suppressed, something could be worked out. A fabric-covered Norseman later recovered could only be identified by the engine number (quietly removed from all records in 1944). If incriminating or contradictory documents were in any AG Department File, they could be removed, `lost', `misplaced' - or the File itself suppressed. Most of all, SHAEF earnestly believed, the thing would be a Seven Day Wonder which would fade into oblivion as time passed : the boat would stop rocking and all would be well.

They hoped. . .

+   +   +

But what of the Bordeaux crash itself ? There were several eventualities in December 1944 : the Norseman might never be found, or if found, might not be identified. If it *was* located at some future time and only two bodies were found, the news could be suppressed. Lastly, if bodies *were found* after a long time, it might not be possible to identify them - and here we refer again to another intriguing part of the jig-saw puzzle.

In a Burial File letter dated October 6 1950, the Identification Branch in the Quartermaster Corps wrote to the Pentagon Liaison Section, Memorial Division, as follows :

`BAESSELL, Norman F. Lt.Col. AAF Serial Number O 905 387*

Information Required : All available dental information on above decedent.

A second document furnished the information :

`FOR CAPT RENNER QM LN 1D684 PENT URMSG 36 11 OCT ON NORMAN F BAESSELL 0905387 WD AGO FORM 63 DATED 16 APRIL 42 - TEETH MISSING*
R 6 7 8 14 L 6 7 13 14 15 16 NO FORMS 79 FOUND

The only possible requirement for dental details of a deceased person is to facilitate identification. It is possible, even probable, that Baessell's body had been found, for there must have been supporting evidence, perhaps his wallet or papers - to justify requesting that information. Had the C-64 been found, some four years after the aircraft disappeared ? Decomposition would make identification difficult. In the absence of any firm proof, we assumed that the 1946 Bordeaux area search had been unproductive, but an aircraft or bodies may have been found in 1950.

Remarkably, the Bordeaux Crash Letter was found in Lt.Col. Baessell's File but not in those for John Morgan and Major Miller. But what were the implications of the letter ? Again we are faced with various options. If one of two bodies found in a crashed aircraft was identified as Baessell's, the other must be Morgan's - but no sign of Glenn Miller. There would be an urgent need for the AG Department to suppress the news. Otherwise we can imagine the banner headlines :

<h2 style="text-align:center">GLENN MILLER AIRCRAFT FOUND !
BAND LEADER NOT ON BOARD !
MYSTERY DEEPENS !</h2>

Or, if there were three bodies, the headlines would scream :

GLENN MILLER FOUND !
PLANE CRASHED NEAR BORDEAUX !

Since there was no request for Miller's dental chart, we can be certain that his body had not been found. More than that - someone knew he had not been a passenger in the lost Norseman ! We should be quite clear on this point. Either way, the news could not be released. The absence of Miller's body would explode the Haynes myth once and for all - with disastrous consequences after the false story circulated by SHAEF. Conversely, if Miller's body was found near Bordeaux, the world would ask what he was doing there, when he was supposedly heading for Paris !

Certainly, something or someone was found - and the news was suppressed. If the aircraft had not been the Norseman, or the body was not that of Baessell, there was no reason to retain the Search Letter on file. But the inclusion of Bordeaux in the MACRs and the Letter opened up fresh speculation about Morgan's route, as we saw on Page 119. Briefly :

1.   Miller's destination is cited as Bordeaux in many documents.

2.   Morgan may have landed at Beauvais, dropped Glenn Miller and flown on to Bordeaux with Baessell. But there are serious problems here : the Colonel, if he was on board, obtained clearance direct from Abbotts Ripton to Beauvais, enabling Morgan to fly the shortest route east of London and thereby avoid landing at Bovingdon for clearance - and a Customs check. Further, their take-off time of 13.25 hours from Abbotts Ripton barely allowed them time to reach Beauvais in daylight. It is most unlikely that they would have taken off again at once in darkness from Beauvais to fly on for a further two hours to Bordeaux. The airfield at Bordeaux - or more correctly, Base Y-37 Bordeaux-Merignac - became operational on 6 December 1944 and remained so until 17 July 1945. A medium bomber squadron was based there from December 6, following a visit by Sqn.Ldr Tony Bartley and Lt. Pulitzer, who flew in with a Dakota to discuss what the French needed in terms of equipment to set up an R.A.F staging post. We surmised that Col.Baessell may have gone to Bordeaux to set up an 8th Air Force staging post using the southern route via the Azores.
The Norseman had plenty of fuel for such a flight - its range was 1150 miles in still air - but a night landing on a strange airfield was risky. Morgan may have attempted it, and could have crashed into thick woods during a night approach and landing.

3.   Alternatively, Morgan may have flown direct to Bordeaux from Abbotts Ripton. He had sufficient fuel - but his Operation Orders suggest otherwise, and the flight involved a very long (100 mile) sea crossing from Brighton to the Normandy coast.

But the Joan Heath evidence introduces a new dimension : she related that on Sunday December 17 she saw Glenn Miller leave Buc Airfield, a mile from Versailles, in a UC-78 Cessna Bobcat aircraft. He said he was going `Stateside' for a few days over Christmas, and a day or two later General Eisenhower told Joan that he was afraid Miller might never return. We reasoned that the UC-78, a small twin-motor plane, was taking Miller to some airfield where he could board a transAtlantic flight - and Bordeaux appears to be a prime candidate. Big transports could refuel there before leaving for the Azores and America, using the southern route to avoid the bad winter weather over Greenland and Labrador.

Assuming that Miller made the flight without permission, and that the Bobcat crashed in wooded country near Bordeaux, reason suggests that SHAEF and General Barker may have known about the trip - and were waiting for news of a search in the Bordeaux area. When nothing was found and the Christmas Day broadcast was imminent, the need for a cover story was ever more pressing - in effect, Miller was AWOL - and in wartime that spells desertion. So the Norseman story was created and released, and this remained one possible explanation of Miller's disappearance, until we obtained confirmation from the 112th Liaison Squadron History and the Cumulative Loss Listing that no Bobcats were lost during December 1944.

14. The Special Services Letters

We discovered two letters in the Burial Files containing very strong evidence that Major Miller flew to Paris Orly on Thursday December 14 via a Dakota shuttle flight. The sequence is somewhat convoluted and involved, but is undoubtedly viable. Until Paris was liberated in August 1944, SHAEF MAIN was based at Bushey Park near London; the Director of Troop Broadcasting was Colonel Ed Kirby and the Associate Director was Lt. Col. David Niven, Rifle Brigade, seconded to SHAEF Special Services. SHAEF MAIN duly moved to Versailles and Bushey Park became SHAEF REAR. In October 1944, Ed Kirby went home and David Niven became Director of Troop Broadcasting in Paris; he was replaced at Bushey Park by Major Johnny Hayes as Associate Director. Hayes' superior at SHAEF MAIN was Lt.Col. Robert W. Furber in Special Services, G-1 Division (commanded, as we know, by General Ray Barker himself).

Now, Niven - as we have seen - was Glenn Miller's immediate superior. About halfway through our investigation we had located a 1968 taped interview by a Mr. Woods, a BBC engineer who was attached to the AEF Band in 1944. We were concentrating on Glenn's flight from R.A.F. Bovingdon to Paris on Thursday December 14 1944, which had been booked the previous day by Don Haynes. Researcher John Edwards played for us a taped interview by a BBC engineer Teddy Gower, in which the latter stated that he had flown to Paris with Miller in a shuttle Dakota from Bovingdon just before the Norseman incident occurred. He had occupied the seat immediately behind Miller and the flight had landed safely at Orly. That was the last time Gower saw Glenn; the engineer died several years ago.

But Mr. Woods had a strange tale to tell. In November 1944 he was sent by the BBC to Paris to survey and improve the land line to London so that Band concerts in Paris could be relayed and re-broadcast from a London transmitter. He described flying to Paris with Miller early in November, meeting him at Bovingdon, and returned with him on November 18. Glenn had said : `Why don't we travel over together next time ?' and Woods agreed. He remembered going to Bovingdon several times, only for the flight to be cancelled because of weather. But finally he and Major Miller were given seats on Flight 2 of the day. Woods arrived at Bovingdon just as Flight 1 was taking off. To his dismay, he found that his main baggage (containing a large quantity of black market goods destined for friends in France) had been sent by error on Flight 1 ! Customs, naturally, were very curious and detained Woods, who eventually caught Flight 3. Glenn Miller, he said, flew out on Flight 2 - and when Woods arrived at Orly after a hazardous flight in atrocious weather, he learned that Flight 2 had ditched in the Channel after icing up. There were no survivors.

It was obvious, Woods maintained stoutly, that Glenn could not have gone down in the Norseman - he had drowned in the Channel early in November ! Woods, uncertain of the date of his flight, thought it might have been November 26 - but on that day, Glenn Miller conducted his Band in a concert at the Granada Theatre in Bedford ! Logically, it could not have been Mr. Woods with Miller on the December 14 flight - but could we prove it was Teddy Gower ? And thereby confirm Miller's flight on that day ?

From letters in the Burial File, it was clear that Woods, who was not attached full-time to the Band as an engineer, was replaced during November by Teddy Gower (who was). And this timing is critical. We have seen that on November 8 Glenn had accepted a lift in Morgan's Norseman from Twinwood Farm to Bovingdon, where he boarded a Paris shuttle. The aircraft was received by Mr. Alex Sleap who was photographed beside it, and later he saw Miller board a Paris flight. The Norseman, with Morgan, Baessell and Haynes on board, went on to Orly, and now we know Woods accompanied Miller on that flight.

We now turn to George W. Ferguson, one-time pilot of Baessell in the ill-fated Norseman. Describing *what he believed to be* the December 15 1944 flight he said :

> `In September 1944, I was detached from Wattisham to Brussels Everes with one of the C-64 Norseman aircraft, and in late October or early November, Baessell flew into Brussels with General Goodrich in Morgan's aircraft. The Colonel, who used to say I was `the best pilot in the world', told me that Glenn Miller was going to Paris soon to entertain the troops and he wanted me to fly Miller and himself over `a week early to show him the town." I was to fly my Norseman over to Twinwood Farm, pick up Baessell and Glenn Miller and take them to Paris. I said okay but I had to get permission from my Commander, who was a bit ticklish about deals like that.
> But on the day, permission was refused and Baessell called me from Milton Ernest to check I had clearance, and was furious when I told him my Commander had said no. "Get the hell back up there," he yelled, "and try it again ! Call me back here at The Castle !" But when I called him back at Milton Ernest, I found that he and Miller had already taken off. I asked who was the pilot and when they said John Morgan, I said "Oh, my God."'

With Ferguson no longer available, Baessell had to use John Morgan as pilot. Ferguson, holding the views he did about Morgan's flying abilities, was dismayed - *and he always believed that these events occurred on the December 15 flight*. Indeed, his account seemed to support the Haynes story ! But that was impossible because the AEF Band tour was approved at the November 15 conference chaired by David Niven - *and Baessell could not have known about that two weeks previously* !

The truth is that Ferguson, like Dixie Clerke and others, confused the November 8 flight (which happened precisely as he described) with the December 15 flight which never took place. The whole of Haynes' account of the December flight was based on the November 8 mission. There was ample supporting evidence in the Haynes diary, and we have reconstructed the events of November 8 in Pp.48 *et seq*.

Let us be quite specific as to the implications. If we are correct, the engineer who flew to Paris on November 8 with Glenn that day was Mr. Woods (who returned on November

18 with Miller), and not Teddy Gower. The latter's flight, sitting behind Glenn, must therefore have been on some later date *after November 8* !

Two matters had to be resolved : confirming the Norseman landing at Bovingdon and Sleap's sighting of Miller boarding a Paris flight, and checking Miller's movements *after* November 8 for any alternative date he may have travelled, other than December 14. The solution to the first query lay in the photograph itself : a light coating of snow lay on the ground, and we checked very carefully the Meteorological Archives in Reading for Bovingdon. We learned that whilst it had not snowed there on December 14 or 15 - *there had been light falls on November 7 and 8* !

Major Glenn Miller made no UK public appearances between November 7 and 18 1944 because he was in Paris for the conference. Haynes was there too, returning on November 17 in Gen. Goodrich's B-17. We accounted for every day of Miller's time between November 18 and the Milroy Club party - and Thursday December 14 was the only date on which he could have flown from Bovingdon. Moreover, this was the date on which Haynes had booked Glenn a flight, and his orders covered a flight to Paris *on or about* December 14 1944.

All that remained was to prove that Mr. Woods had disappeared from the scene *after* he flew home on November 18, and *before* Teddy Gower was attached to the AEF Band as sound engineer for the Paris tour.

We began by checking out the Woods story of an iced-up C-47 lost in the English Channel, and the Cumulative Loss Listing contains no record of any such loss on a cross-Channel flight from Bovingdon to Paris in November or December 1944. We now come to the critical part of this chain of evidence. Teddy Gower testified that he flew to Paris Orly seated behind Glenn Miller on some date just before the Norseman was reported lost. That is to say, *after November 18 but before December 15.* Could we confirm this ?

The Special Services letters in the Burial File contain the times at which the two BBC engineers were attached to the AEF Band. Here is the first letter :

SUPREME HEADQUARTERS
ALLIED EXPEDITIONARY FORCES (REAR)
G-1 Division
Directorate of Troop Broadcasting Services
APO 413

JSR/mh
21 November 1944

Lt.Col. R.W.Thurber
G-1 Division, SHAEF APO 757 (Main)
    Dear Bob,
    Thanks for your letter of 18 November and the document on fraternization. I had not realised it was "Secret" when we asked for it and I suspect we will have to hold up on using any portion of it until the classification is lifted.
    We got the dope on frequencies and they are in the works. We also told Bridgman to stick to the assigned frequency for 7th Army but whether or not you are referring to a cable from him after we instructed him to remain on 1477, I don't know. You are quite right about the 7th Army transmitter

being a bit coy about joining the net and I am not sure it would not be an awfully good idea for you, or someone in your office, to drop in and let them know it is still an Allied war !

Here's the situation on Mr. Woods. As you know, after our request of some weeks ago, the GPO and SHAEF Signals finally came across with the possibility of a landline from Paris into London. The line was not very good itself until tests had been made on it. The Army, believe it or not, does not have the equipment to test these lines and it appears that BBC has the only stuff which can do the job. Since we were very much concerned in seeing whether or not the line would work, we asked Bishop if he could send the equipment over to run tests on the lines, along with an engineer. Woods was the result and you may be interested to know the tests were quite good and I think we may get something out of the line if we can now work out with SHAEF PRD some system to get the line for AEFP whenever we need it. I am sorry the orders were just one way but I must confess the G-1 office here seems strangely reluctant to write two-way orders on first request. They invariably write them one-way and get the reservation, and it always takes five times as long to send them back to get a two-way job and it seems easier, most of the time, to get one-way orders and have you work on getting the people back to UK. We are going to make every attempt in the future to get two-way orders issued, however, and I hope you will be spared any embarrassment in this regard. The next arrival you can expect is Mr. Boor, Chief Engineer of AFN who will start work on installing some relay transmitters, but he, I think, has got two-way orders except for the necessary plane reservation to return when he has finished his job.

I am getting off a signal to Niven about the 1kw transmitters he has found in a dump. I am asking him to check whether or not they are voice transmitters with proper frequency possibilities. If they are, they would be a good bet for relays on the American side since a 1kw is obviously better than some of the 50 watt jobs which the Americans are getting ready to place around. I think the best thing is for the Americans to go ahead and put their 50-watters in and then if Niven can come thru with a bigger job we can always substitute.

I had a long session with Miller and Gorham a few minutes ago and I am afraid Miller has sold the General on his going over. Everybody keeps making remarks on how his going over must not interfere with the AEFP schedule, but it appears to me that what with the additional engineer, recording gear,

156

remote equipment and availability of recording facilities, it is not going to be as simple as some people seem to think. . .

Cordially

JOHN S. HAYES
Major, QMC,
Associate Director
Troop Broadcasting Services

This November 21 letter confirms that Woods was called in solely to check out the cross-Channel GPO lines, returning to Bovingdon on November 18. Lt. Col. David Niven was deeply involved in preparatory work, searching equipment dumps for the right kind of transmitter for the Band tour which had been approved on November 15 and in regard to which, Major Hayes of the British QM Corps, comments wryly, Miller had sold the General (Barker) on the idea.

The second letter contains vital clues. First, with effect from November 21 Gower had not as yet joined the AEF Band in Paris - but he would do so soon, travelling by military aircraft like Mr. Woods. At this time, on Thursday 26 November Glenn Miller appeared on stage at the Granada Theatre Bedford. On Wednesday 29 November and Wednesday December 6 he compéred with a lady named Ilse a `Music for the Wehrmacht' programme (mentioned in the Frank Wappatt tape). Glenn appeared in England for the last time on Tuesday December 12 at the Queensberry All-Services Club in London (the programme is shown in Figs. 65 (a) and (b) by kind permission of Mr. Derek Kilburn) and his orders for Paris were cut the same day.

On Wednesday December 13 Glenn Miller spent the evening at the Milroy Club, Stratton Street, Mayfair, in the company of Sqn.Ldr. Tony Bartley, Lt. Tony Pulitzer USAAF, Don Haynes, Johnny Morgan and Marjorie Kingsley, the resident singer at the Club. So his movements between November 18 and December 12 were fully documented.

Here is the second Special Services letter dated November 24 :

SUPREME HEADQUARTERS
ALLIED EXPEDITIONARY FORCE (REAR)
Directorate of Troop Broadcasting Services
APO 413

JSH/mh
24 November 1944

Lt.Col.R.W. Furber,
G-1 Division, SHAEF APO 757 (Main)
    Dear Bob,
As you know, the Miller organization is coming over to Paris on December 16, and will stay approximately 6 weeks. One of the things our good boss (**David Niven**) got himself mixed up in was requesting the BBC to send along one of its civilian engineers - by name Mr. E. Gower. Mr. Gower's job will be to pick up any broadcasts by Miller that he can manage in France while he is over there. (You know of course that his regular AEFP schedule is being maintained in his absence by

pre-recordings which are being made now and, as a result of which we will have 6 weeks' material stored up before Miller leaves for France). We have had to get Gower over on one of those civilian deals similar to Hayes and Woods, but this time the situation will be a little different because Miller wants Gower to live right along with them and to travel around in battle dress. Therefore I'm taking the liberty of telling Gower to look you up when he gets on the Continent so that you can fix up with him all the necessary permissions he needs to live with the Band in Paris, as well as billeting and other accommodations.

Frankly, between you and me I'm getting a little bored with acting as a Cook's Agency for all these civilians who must come over to see the war, but we're rather caught on this one because it's one of the General's commitments. . .

Cordially,

JOHN S. HAYES Major, QMC
Associate Director
Troop Broadcasting Services

So Teddy Gower was resident engineer with the AEF Band from the end of November, did not travel with the Band from Twinwood Farm and undoubtedly boarded the shuttle with Major Miller on December 14 1944. There are some loose ends - since Gower and Glenn would be working closely together, we would expect them to sit together, but if, as we believe, a small group of Band musicians went along to play at Ike's promotion party on December 16, one of them would probably sit with Glenn. Further, sound engineer Ted Gower would be needed at the party to set up the amplification system.

We rest our case.

15. The Confirmatory Signals (Figs.10,24)

We have dealt at length with these Signals on P.100, demonstrating that the document circulated for almost half a century by US Archives and the AG Department was re-drafted and altered to support Haynes' story of the mythical Barker-Goodrich telephone conversation on Tuesday December 19 1944. It was dated December 20, giving the impression that 8th AFSC at Milton Ernest had required only a few hours to confirm that Miller was aboard the Norseman. In fact, the genuine SHAEF inquiry was by teleprinter on Wednesday morning, Cols. Early and Traistor flew to Paris next day to talk to Haynes, after which Traistor phoned Capt.Cramer at Abbotts Ripton, telling him what to include in his MACR. Early returned to Milton Ernest on Friday December 22 and sent the genuine `Confirmatory' Signal to Barker that day, triggering off the whole reporting procedure culminating in the Press Release on December 24 1944.

The genuine Signal was found in the Miller 201 File in 1992, and a remarkable insight into US Army security procedures is seen in the document. It is on a standard Priority/ Confidential signal form which states :

This is extraordinary ! Any document the Army or AG Department wished to conceal or suppress could be re-typed in paraphrased versions - the content of the message could be changed, important facts deleted or excluded. The forged version begins with the word `copy' (which it wasn't). The words `SUBJ. MISSING AIRPLANE' follow (not found on the `Original') and `HQ V111 AFSC'. The following text : `AAF Sta 506, APO 636' is not in the `Original' which reads simply `From : HQ EIGHTH AFSC'. The forged document shows the Signal routing - `Thru : Eighth AF, AAF Station 101, APO 634' (R.A.F. Med-menham) - but the `Original' does not. This piece of creative reporting was produced by Major Albert G. Buelow - of the Adjutant General's Department. . . the organisation which was the *bête noire* of the entire mystery.

The `Original' arrived at SHAEF via coded teleprinter at 11.30 hours on 22 December 1944. Teleprinter transmission time is measurable in minutes; it was sent around 11.20 am and reached General Barker quickly, as a Priority message.

The inference is clear : the Haynes-Barker-Goodrich telephone conversation was wholly imaginary. Instead, Barker clarified the details of the Norseman story to be released and sent the interrogatory signal to 8th AFSC on Wednesday morning, December 20. The Norseman story could not be `cooked up' at a moment's notice - Barker had to consult with his senior colleagues - Gen. Davis at the AG's Department, Gen. Strong at G-2, and even perhaps General Eisenhower himself. It was imperative to prevent any search for the Norseman - its discovery with only two bodies would be fatal to the project. Most important, in case Miller never returned, it was essential to write something into the record, confirming the Haynes story, to justify Barker's actions in suspending all reporting action whilst `waiting for news'.

The forged Signal was essential, because the genuine document contradicted the Haynes story. But at this point, more and more people apparently were becoming involved, and the larger the number, the less viable our case. So who was involved in the conspiracy, and who was not ?

In Paris, certainly General Eisenhower, who took no active part himself. General Barker, Major May, Haynes, General Davis and perhaps Col. Dupuy in PR Division. At Milton Ernest, only Cols. Early and Traistor. There seems no doubt that, if Joan Heath's story is true, General Eisenhower was informed in the later stages before the Press Release. In any case - he insisted on `breakfast reports' on the main news each morning.

There was only one loose end - Captain Cramer at Abbotts Ripton. The bottom line was this : Haynes would never talk. Barker could guarantee Early and Traistor total protection. The background of the incident could be carefully suppressed, allowed to fade into history. Cramer had to be persuaded to include the right information in the MACR - and that might be difficult. Whatever happened to Miller was serious enough to warrant Barker putting his career on line - could all the others do less ? Early had come to know and respect Miller; no one else at Milton Ernest need be implicated. The full story would never come out. On Saturday December 23 Gen. Goodrich was evacuated on a hospital plane to Maxwell AFB Alabama, where he died soon afterwards. Until a successor was appointed, Col. Early was in charge at Milton Ernest - and remarkably we have never been able to trace even one officer from 8th AFSC who was willing to talk. The evidence of the valet Stilwell was vague and uncertain.

16. Morgan's Service Record Card (Fig.36).

Several vital documents were not located in Morgan's 201 or Burial Files : his Service Record Card, his Form 5 (Record of Flight Times) and his flight log book with details of all flights up to his death on December 15 1944. An anonymous donor in Alexandria Va. (perhaps an employee in National Archives) sent us a copy of the Card and Forms 5 for November and December 1944. Both documents contain evidence which flatly contradicts both the MACR #10770 and the Haynes story. Jean Pace, a contemporary pilot of the ill-fated Norseman, believes the Card is authentic and typical of the card index systems used in the US Army Air Force, each unit maintaining a Service Record Index of all personnel. On an airman being reassigned, details from the Card were transferred to the 201 Personal File which followed the individual to his next unit : on his retirement or death the File was sent to the National Personnel Records Centers at St.Louis Mo. or Washington.

Captain Cramer, therefore, was familiar with Morgan's service details. In the wake of the 15 December mission he would update the Card and complete the pilot's 201 File. But Cramer was horrified by the route and destination details on the Card, extracted from the pilot's flight plan : they conflicted sharply with the data he was required to incorporate in the Missing Aircrew Report.

Flight Officer John Morgan filled a variety of roles at Abbotts Ripton, including Assistant Engineer, Assistant Flight Line and Test Officer. The Card records the November 8 flight to Paris (during which he dropped Glenn Miller at R.A.F. Bovingdon before proceeding to Paris Orly) and his return on 18 November 1944.

On the fatal last mission on December 15 he is assigned from duty (routine) to Temporary Duty Bordeaux France via B-42, for the purpose of ferrying personnel as per Operation Order #5, Hq 2nd Strategic Air Depot (Abbotts Ripton). The flight was authorised by the Operations Officer - but we see here the first hint that this document too may have been fabricated. B-42 was Beauvais-Tille, 40 miles north of Paris, a joint British-American base, for which the American code was A-61. Why, then, does Morgan's Card refer to B-42 ? Because of its resemblance to A-42 - Villacoublay ? Was the Card another example of disinformation similar to the mysterious Provost Marshal report on `Peter's' investigation ?

Perhaps we are making too much of this point. But Beauvais accommodated two medium bomber squadrons of the 9th Air Force, not the 8th - so why was Morgan going there ? We have to accept the Card as genuine, but note that Morgan is posted `missing (non-Battle) on ferrying flight over English Channel en route to B-42, 15 December 1944'. Significantly, perhaps, there is no mention of any stop at Twinwood Farm. Morgan is later dropped from rolls of organisation (35 ADRS), whilst the card was up-dated after his death.

17. The SHAEF PR Memo and Press Release

Let us go back in time once more, on this occasion to Christmas Eve 1944 in Paris, where the streets were covered in snow and slush, and rail depots were crowded with reinforcements for the Ardennes battles. In the Information Room in Public Relations Division that morning, a Captain Wade received a memo from a Captain Cosgrove regarding the imminent Press Release on the loss of Major Glenn Miller. The previous day Cosgrove himself had been briefed by his Commanding officer Colonel Dupuy, Chief of PR Division, who in turn had received careful and detailed instructions from the SHAEF AG, General Davis, following General Davis's letter to General Eisenhower on December 22. (Fig.20).

On that day, Gen. Barker received the Confirmatory Signal from 8th AFSC (Fig. 24) : with the Norseman loss firmly on record, Barker issued the Miller Casualty Report (Fig.6), authorised the telegram to Helen Miller and prepared the radio signal to the War Department. The Paris AG General Davis wrote to Eisenhower referring to the impending Christmas Day broadcast to America, suggesting that the Press Release should be officially delayed for two more days, until 18.00A (19.00 Paris Local Time) before being released by SHAEF. The BBC would repeat the announcement 30 seconds later.

There is another logical explanation for the delay in issuing the Press Release : SHAEF wanted to give Glenn Miller as much time as possible to turn up, and the news was released on December 24, only a few hours before the scheduled broadcast to America.

Both Memo and Release (Figs.18,19) contain strange anomalies. Why did Col. Dupuy only want `a factual announcement that Miller was missing' ? Why did he insist on having the Memo itself returned to him ? Did Colonel Dupuy know something of the truth ? He would consult with the top brass on the best way to release the news - and would have asked the Director of Troop Broadcasting (who had arranged the concert schedule) for his advice. But Lt. Col. David Niven was absent from Paris from Friday December 15 until the New Year, ostensibly on a visit to old friends at 1st Army HQ, Spa, Belgium.

Dupuy, we believe, was a member of the small circle at SHAEF who were privy to the truth, but we were perplexed by his instructions that `he did not have to see the Release beforehand'. Heading the SHAEF PR Division, dealing with an announcement which would send reverberations around the world about a VIP of the day, he would surely be anxious to ensure that not one word or letter was out of place !

Yet he trusted compilation of the Release to a junior officer, Capt. Cosgrove, who apparently formulated the Release himself. We could see only two explanations : first, that Col. Dupuy was too overloaded with routine work connected with the battles in the Ardennes to attend to the Release himself - or he had taken out insurance against becoming embroiled in the aftermath which would follow the mysterious disappearance of a VIP of the day. There might even be an inquiry, or a CID investigation - but Col. Dupuy could always claim he did not see the Press Release before the deadline !

But why insist on the return of the Memo ? Because it was the only link between Dupuy and the Press Release - and here we have the strange instance of a routine Memo (normally an ephemeral document destroyed very quickly) being stored in a secret Burial File in Washington for 48 years. Obviously, the document was important - but why ? It only confirmed our original conclusion - that contrary to the National Archives' promise, we had not been provided with *every* document in the Burial Files.

18. The Miller Insurance Documents

Major Miller carried extensive insurance, according to correspondence found in the first release of 201 File documents in May 1992. The insurers included :

Ætna Insurance Company, Hartford, Connecticut
New York Life Insurance Company, Madison Ave. New York
Equitable Life Assurance Society, New York

Provident Mutual Life Insurance Company, Philadelphia
Connecticut Mutual Life Insurance Company, Hartford, Conn.

In each case a Finding of Death document similar to Fig.25 was issued by the Adjutant General Department, with one remarkable feature : Miller is shown as `missing in action' ! But this is no ordinary error, a missed deletion : the items are checked off to ensure the information is correct. The document, in fact, is a routine pre-printed Form 0353-3 used for personnel `missing in action', the words `in action' being deleted if inapplicable. Logically, the person issuing the FOD would correct the `in action' to `in flight' to correspond with the telegram sent to Helen Miller - unless Miller was really `Missing in Action'. See the HQ 8th Fighter Command Letter below. (Figs. 66,67).

We do not know the terms of insurance. The insurers may have settled a `Missing in Action' claim, but not an `accident' claim. Two of the companies were still active in New York, but neither had preserved records going back to 1944. We looked very carefully at the Finding of Death document issued to Ætna Life Insurance in March 1948 which described the cause of Miller's death as `Airplane Crash' - if Glenn had been aboard the Norseman when it ditched off Le Touquet on 15 December 1945, he may well have drowned, or died from exposure, but no one knew for sure. `Airplane Crash', on the other hand, infers that the crash site was found and the cause of death was `multiple injuries caused by aircraft crash'. The statement, in a way, is self-contradictory : it states place of death as `in the European Area' - but many official AG documents had specified `English Channel', whilst the MACR Register entry states `France' ! We decided it was not impossible that Miller could have been killed in a straightforward aircraft crash on the ground, and we reserved judgment on both the `Bordeaux Crash' and the letter from HQ 8th Fighter Command, which is discussed below.

19. The 8th Fighter Command Inquiry (Figs.66-67)

The following letter was found in the Miller 201 File in June 1992 :

HEADQUARTERS III FIGHTER COMMAND
Office of the Commanding General   Sep 17 1945

SUBJECT : Request for Dental Records
TO : Adjutant General, Washington DC
(Thru : Commanding General, Army Air Forces, Washington DC)

1. Request that any dental records concerning the following named officer be forwarded to this headquarters for comparison with dental records completed in the remains of an unidentified individual :

Major Alton G. Miller 0-505273

2. It is to be noted that subject officer was not on flying status, thus a Dental Identification Record was not completed. However, this officer was known to have been a member of

an aircrew of this command listed as MIA 15 December 1944.

For the Commanding General   BURDETTE W.ERIKSON
                                              Major,   AGD

A reply was sent some days later :

HQ, Army Air Forces, Washington 25, DC 28 September 1945
To : Commanding General, VIII Fighter Command, APO 634

The records on file in this headquarters concerning Major
Alton G. Miller, 0-505273 contain no Dental Identification
Record or other dental data useful for identification pur-
poses.
For the Commanding General   GEORGE R. KENNEBECK

What were we to make of this ? Our immediate reaction was that this correspondence might be related to the frequent `Missing in Action' references in Glenn's Finding of Death documents and also in the `ORIGINAL' MACR #N-19 in Miller's Burial File. Secondly, the originator was VIII Fighter Command, located in Germany after the war but which would be based in Britain until May 1945. Two points were relevant : if Miller had indeed `gone along for the ride' to see the air war, it would have to be in a 2-seater fighter aircraft, but the only possibility was the twin-engined P-38 Lightning which had a compartment behind the pilot's cockpit normally used for extra ammunition or freight stowage. No Lightnings were cited in Missing Aircrew Reports in December 1944.

Another alternative might be the A-24 Invader twin-engined fighter-bomber with a crew of three. The Missing Aircrew Report Register for December 15 shows that in all, 11 aircraft were listed as missing as follows :

No.	Area	A/c Type	Serial Number	Total Occupants
11484	Germany	B-26F	43-30275	3
12188	S.Pacific	P-47D	43-70275	1
11962	S.Pacific	P-47D	44-26551	1
11502	Germany	P-47D	42-49177	1
11008	Holland	P-47D	44-20471	1
10770	France	UC-64A	44-70285	3
10684	Germany	B-24H	42-51142	11
10676	Austria	B-24J	42-51346	11
14085	S.Atlantic	A-26	00-2424	3
11310	Germany	P-51D	44-15014	1
11069	Channel	P-51D	44-15557	1

Surprisingly, the Register entry for MACR #10770 identifies the area involved as `France' and not the English Channel - leading to still further consideration of the `Bordeaux Search letter' in the Burial Files. More to the point, there is the entry under Report #14085 for an A-26 Invader twin-engined fighter/bomber developed from the Douglas

Boston. The A-26 had an unusual background : commissioned in 1942, it did not enter battle service in Europe until the end of 1944, because of defects. Further, the aircraft specified in Report #14085 shows no date of manufacture and a four-figure serial number - and this is unprecedented. Lastly, it was lost over the South Atlantic. What was an experimental fighter-bomber doing in that area on 15 December 1944 ? We sent for an MACR copy and found that it was on a mission from South America, Miller was not listed in the 3 casualties and it had no connection with the mystery.

So this could not have been the 8th Fighter Command aircraft in which an Alton Glenn Miller had been reported as Missing in Action. In consequence we became very uneasy about the 8th Fighter Command letter - on 15 December the USAAF lost four P-47 Thunderbolts and two P-51D Mustangs. Miller could not have been a passenger in any of these aircraft.

We were left with the uneasy suspicion that the 8th Fighter Command letter was yet another example of disinformation intended to keep researchers busy exploring arid cul-de-sacs ending in a wall of frustration.

20. Glenn Miller's Orders for Paris (Fig.4)

In *MILLERGATE* we inadvertently quoted the travel date on the Orders as `on or about December 16', due to imperfections in the photocopy we obtained. The date should read `December 14'. Having said that, several anomalies are apparent in the Orders : first, assuming they were genuine (and this is by no means certain) they had been abstracted from the Glenn Miller Burial File or 201 File before we obtained a copy. Second, Glenn's Serial Number was incorrect. The Orders conflict sharply with Don Haynes' account of a last-minute change in plans :

1)   The Orders were flexible, instructing Miller to travel `on or about December 14' by military aircraft to SHAEF in Paris. There was no need to alter them.

2)   They were specifically for Miller, not for the Band, issued in 8 copies on Tuesday 12 December 1944, allowing 2 days for printing and distribution. The copies were as follows : Major Miller 4, G-1 at SHAEF REAR, Bushey Park 1, Air Transport Command 1, Transport Officer HQ Command Rear (Glenn's parent command) 1, and `AGM' 1 (presumably some connection with the Adjutant General's Office).

3)   No orders have ever been found for Lt.Haynes or the Band itself, and this version of Major Miller's instructions is the only one in existence.

■ The Incorrect Serial Number.

We were the first researchers to note that Miller's true Serial Number 0-505273 had been replaced by what appeared to be 0-606273, but we attributed this to a simple typing error on the part of the typist at SHAEF REAR, Bushey Park, London.

However, it was quite possible that the combination of `Major Alton G. Miller' and an incorrect serial number might result in his being unidentified, if he was unable to identify himself. We recalled the letter to John Edwards in 1973 from a Second World War veteran who was supposedly in the same Columbus Ohio hospital as Miller when the band-leader succumbed to head injuries. (But if Miller could not identify himself, how could the veteran do so ?)

Further, we had speculated that Miller may have been involved in a jeep accident in the Ardennes driving back to Paris and evacuated to Rheims hospital where Capt. Pecora was based, and then repatriated to Columbus, Ohio, where he died in late December 1944. There was corroboratory evidence in the letter from the New Jersey State Registrar (Fig.11), accepting that this was repudiated later as a `typing error'. We also have Herb Miller's evidence that Glenn never wore dog-tags because of an endemic body skin infection. He could only have been hospitalised unidentified *provided he had been unable to identify himself* - meaning severe head injuries. And finally the name of Capt. Pecora, USMC had been associated with a `Glenn Miller death certificate' or some similar document for more than 20 years.

The incorrect serial number, therefore, could hardly be ignored completely. Did the 8th Fighter Command letter refer to another Major Alton Glenn Miller who was, in fact, a fighter pilot lost in action on December 15 1944 ? There may have been, by incredible coincidence, another Major Alton Glenn Miller, serial number 0-606273, who had been a fighter pilot in the 8th Fighter Command and who was carried as Missing in Action from December 15 1944. But the name Miller does not appear in any MACR dated December 15 1944, other than UC-64A #70285.

■ The Issue Date.

The AEF Band tour in Paris was authorised provided that the AEF Band pre-recorded 6 weeks of broadcast programmes to ensure continuity. The job was completed on December 10 and the tour was finally approved. The last UK concert was at the Queensberry Club Tuesday December 12 (Figs.65). They were scheduled to fly out on Saturday December 16, and since Miller's orders enabled him to proceed earlier (`*on or about December 14*') Haynes would normally accompany the Band to Paris. He had visited Paris two weeks previously to complete transport and accommodation arrangements in the Hotel des Olympiades in Montmartre, returning on December 2 1944, and had no reason to change the orders for that requirement.

■ The Change in Orders.

Haynes describes a late-night conversation with Glenn walking back to the Mount Royal Hotel after a celebratory dinner in Kettners Restaurant given by the Marquis, after the December 12 Queensberry Club show. Haynes related that he was detailed to go over before the Band (which Miller would accompany himself) to arrange transport and accommodation. But Glenn, he said, changed his mind and said that *he* would go over early instead ! So Haynes said he changed Miller's orders next day (Wednesday December 13) and booked him on a Thursday flight out of Bovingdon. Major Miller, he said, had a `social engagement' in Paris and did not want to disappoint his hosts.

But Glenn's orders are dated December 12 (that very same day !) and next day, Wednesday December 13, Haynes made the Thursday flight reservation to Paris Orly from R.A.F. Bovingdon ! His story of changed orders is wholly fictitious : once again, he was using detail from a previous incident (his visit to Paris on December 1 to arrange transport and accommodation) to embroider his account of the December 15 flight.

21. The MOD Air Historical Branch Report (Fig.31)

The information in the Report was received from USAF Historical Research Center, Maxwell AFB Alabama *circa* 1972-3. The Report is associated with the late Henry Whiston, a Canadian who spent much time in the UK probing the Miller Mystery. Morgan's Norseman was not officially included in the Cumulative Loss Listing until 1947. UC-64A #44-70285, the report stated, was sometimes confused with #43-5367, reported missing on December 26 from Grove Field. Henry obtained a list of 8 C-64s listed as `written off' (but not `missing') in December 1944, as follows :

43-5313	**302 Transport Wing, lost from Grove AFB**	**16 December 1944**
43-36329	**2nd Air Base Depot reported destroyed**	**28 December**
43-35340	**302 Transport Wing**	**10 December**
43-39366	**In transit on Allocation**	**18 December**
43-35394	**10 Air Depot Group**	**19 December**
44-70244	**5 Strategic Air Depot**	**28 December**
44-70280	**4 Mobile Repair/Recovery Squadron**	**19 December**
44-70348	**2nd Air Depot Group**	**6 December**

We traced the history of each aircraft with difficulty and accounted satisfactorily for all except two : #43-5213, operated by 302 Transport Wing, 1st Air Transport Group, which was recorded as written off on Saturday December 16 1944, and #43-5367 (not in the list above but cited in the MOD Report). Further, we know from historical records that one Norseman was serviced and repaired at Grove during December 1944, which belonged to no unit at the base.

■ Norseman #43-5367

There was a serious discrepancy in this case. The MOD Report stated it was `lost' on December 26 1944, 11 days after Morgan went down. So why should it be confused with #44-70285 ? `Lost' could mean many things but #43-5367 was not on the list of 8 UC64As known to be destroyed in December 1944. It appears in the Cumulative Loss Listing *but it was not the subject of a Missing Aircrew Report.* Why was it mentioned at all in the MOD Report at all ? We checked with Maxwell AFB but they could offer no explanation.

At this stage we realised that the MOD AHB Report was far from being the simple information sheet we had taken for granted. It was worth a closer examination and we began identifying the units based at Grove Field near Wantage in December 1944. We obtained 5367's service record from America, as had Henry Whiston, the well-known Canadian researcher. He wrote to Maxwell AFB in 1973 :

`In November 1977, you very kindly provided me with the Individual Aircraft Report Cards for UC-64A Norseman bearing serial numbers 43-5367 and 44-70285, the first being the only C-64A on the CLL up to and including May 31 1945, by the USAAF in the ETO, the latter being the plane bearing Miller et al. In view of my subsequent researching that unearthed the fact that there were at least an additional eight UC-64A lost during the same period, a check of what those IARCs contain would be of some interest. With that in mind would you

please be so kind as to forward me the IARCs of : (here Whiston lists the missing Norseman aircraft).

`*Some time ago I received a letter from two former members of the 1st Transport Gp (Prov) to whom 43-5367 was assigned. One member was an Exec. officer named Frank A. Kelly who stated that a more correct identification would be the 314th Transport Squadron, 31st Transport Group, 9th Air Force - they were stationed at Grove Field (Station 519) at the time. Although their C-64 43-5367 was reported MIA (Missing in Action) on Tuesday December 26, he nevertheless erroneously held onto the belief that their aircraft was the one carrying Miller !*

`*Although the Card for 43-5367 indicates that the aircraft became MIA on 26 December 1944, and is listed as such in the CLL for aircraft missing up to and including 31 May 45, no Missing Aircrew Report was ever filed for 43-5367. This aircraft was assigned to HQ 1st Transport Group, 9th Air Force Service Command according to the CLL when it was reported MIA. However, the history of the HQ 1st Transport Group does not mention any aircraft losses in December 44 - at this time it was using a variety of aircraft including C-64s.*

`*MACR #10770 clearly links Major Miller and C-64 serial number 44-70285 together - yet the Aircraft Card for 44-70285 contains no entry between 28 July 1944 and 29 January 1947 - and no notation of the aircraft being MIA. The entries of 29 January 1947 and 1 May 1974 appear to be `catch-up' or write-off entries for book-keeping purposes.'*

This is an illuminating letter. The record shows that #43-5367 was completed in February 1944, flown to Fort Dix on February 24, then to Newark Field, New Jersey on March 31 and delivered to the UK on April 1 1944. It was then assigned to 1st Transport Group in France, which included 326 Ferry Squadron based at A-81 Creil, France. Some elements of the Group including #43-5637 were deployed at A-40 Chartres (326 Ferry Sqdn. `A' Detachment) and A-42 Villacoublay (326 Sqdn. `B' Detachment). Their C-64s ferried back delivery crews taking bombers and fighters to forward units in the combat zones.

Interestingly, on December 16 1944, a special operation was mounted from A-81 Creil and A-82 Verdun, France, to cover the Ardennes offensive. They also used A-93 at Liege and A-97 at Sandweiler. Since #43-5367 was positively listed as `Missing in Action' it may have been lost in the Ardennes area in the closing stages of the offensive on December 26. This also provides a clue as to why there was no Missing Aircrew Report : if the aircraft was shot down but the crew were rescued, there would be no `missing aircrew', no entry in the MACR Register but a record in the CLL.

■ Norseman #43-5613

The 43rd and 45th Air Depot Repair Squadrons at Grove performed the same function as 35 ADRS at Abbotts Ripton (Alconbury), but neither unit had a UC-64A Norseman on strength or had reported one `missing', particularly on December 26 as stated in the MOD Report. The 302 Transport Wing (part of the 31st Transport Group, 9th Air Force) based at Grove incorporated :

(a) The 314th Air Transport Squadron with 13 C-47 aircraft; six additional aircraft which were attached in December returned to their own bases without losses, Norseman or otherwise. No UC-64A was on strength.

(b) 313th Transport Squadron, based at Grove Field from December 7 1944 with 12 C-47 aircraft, which also reported no losses and no UC-64A Norseman on strength.

Why is this lost aircraft incident important ? A Norseman had been reported as destroyed by bombs jettisoned from returning Lancaster bombers on 15 December 1944, by navigator Fred Shaw. He believed this to be Morgan's aircraft, but we have shown conclusively that Morgan took the east-of-London route through the inactive AA Diver Gun Box to Dymchurch and the Channel. Shaw was mistaken - but if he saw an aircraft destroyed, it would not become the subject of a Missing Aircrew Report but an 'incident' involving 'writing-off' an aircraft, normally filed by the Air Force Safety and Inspection Center at Norton AFB, California.

We eliminated #43-5367 from our inquiries, and turned to #43-5313, reported lost from Grove Field on December 16 1944. It was operated by 1st Air Transport Group and it too was on detachment at that time to Chartres, France. Since no C-64s were operated by Grove squadrons, *it followed that #43-5313 was the visiting aircraft serviced there in December 1944*. Further, it was not the subject of a Missing Aircrew Report, and appears on the Cumulative Loss Listing, indicating that its eventual fate was known and recorded, and the crew accounted for.

■ The Bombed Norseman

This scenario, which received considerable publicity in the late Eighties, was carefully analysed in MILLERGATE - THE REAL GLENN MILLER STORY. Briefly, Lancaster navigator Fred Shaw and crew, with his pilot Flt.Lt. Victor Gregory, took part in a daylight raid by 134 R.A.F. Lancaster bombers from East Anglia on December 15 1944, against a rail-head target at Siegen, near Cologne. Their take-off was delayed until after noon by the same morning fog that delayed Morgan at Abbotts Ripton, and they took off around midday. Their course was southerly at 2,000 feet, passing through the de-activated Thames Estuary Gun Box (Fig.23) about 12.30, to Tunbridge Wells and Beachy Head. There, the bombers began to climb through cloud towards Amiens, reaching 20,000 feet before turning east for Siegen.

The plan called for an escort of USAAF P-51D Mustangs but they were unable to get airborne : the weather was deteriorating in East Anglia and the mission was aborted. The Lancasters turned back, retracing their route to Amiens and turning for Beachy Head - but most of them carried the dreaded 'cookies' - 4,000 pound thin-skinned block-busters which could explode during a heavy landing. The standing instructions were to dump all large bombs in a 20-mile diameter Channel Jettison Area in mid-Channel due south of Eastbourne. Further, the minimum jettison height, to avoid blast damage, was 6,000 feet.

As his own aircraft dumped the bombs, Fred Shaw was standing beside the pear-shaped clear Perspex observation panel and was able to look straight down at the sea below, watching the bombs explode on impact. He related on tape that he saw a silver-grey Norseman skimming the water at low level and surrounded by bomb bursts : the aircraft was engulfed in a violent explosion and disappeared. Shaw said that the bomb-aimer Pritchard suddenly shouted 'There's a kite down there !', and shortly afterwards the rear gunner Harry

Fellows said the same thing.

Curiously, no one else in the bomber force saw the incident and Shaw did not speak of it until the Eighties. Moreover, by that time Pritchard and Fellows were dead. Further, the crew never reported the incident on return to base. We probed the evidence in depth and learned several facts which cast doubts upon Shaw's narrative :

* The Lancasters dumped their bombs at 6,000 feet above a solid overcast (confirmed by weather observations). There may have been some small gaps in the cloud, and the identification of a small grey aircraft at a distance of a mile in poor visibility was questionable to say the least.

* Other crew members contacted, including the pilot Flt.Lt. Gregory, had seen nothing and Shaw did not make a formal report on returning to base, as he was obliged to do by regulations. Shaw, they said, made no comment at the time, which struck us as remarkable.

* Actual weather reports in the Channel at the time (Figs.21,22) confirm there was total cloud-cover at 800 feet, with layers of stratus rising to 15,000 feet. There may have been small breaks in the overcast but at 6,000 feet, one would be lucky to see an aircraft flying at sea level. Other crews on the raid reported that they dropped their bombs blind on `G-Fixes', H2S radar pin-pointing or on dead-reckoning navigation.

* Eight other UC-64A aircraft were reported destroyed or written off in the ETO on 15 December 1944 - but only #44-70285 appeared in the MACR Register. None were lost in the Channel area and all were crash write-offs, and their locations were known at Norton AFB, California. Of particular interest to us was #43-5613, reported destroyed on December 16 1944.

* A careful study of flight times showed that, assuming Morgan departed Twinwood Farm at 13.55, overflew Bovingdon en route to Beachy Head and managed to get 40 miles off course to enter the Jettison Area, there was still an irreconcilable time-gap of 1 hour between the time the last of the Lancasters passed through the Area and Morgan entered it. In fact, they were all back at base before he could reach the Area. We noted too that there was no confusion between `military time' and British Summer Time - all aircraft used the same time base, otherwise Air Traffic Control would have been a shambles.

* From evidence in the Burial Files and from other sources already described in this book, John Morgan was cleared direct to B-42 Beauvais and flew east of London through the de-activated `Diver' Gun Box. He was reported crossing out to sea at low level at Dymchurch and that sighting was reported to General Barker at SHAEF. From Dymchurch, unable to cross inland at Cap Gris Nez because of low cloud, Morgan flew south a few miles offshore until he ditched 6 miles west of Le Touquet. That route lay 60 miles east of the Channel Jettison Area.

The Fred Shaw Tape was recorded in South Africa by Mr. Alan Ross of the Glenn Miller Society in Britain, and whilst not wishing to cast doubts on his integrity, it is a fact that the GMS cherish to this day the Norseman story, featuring Miller as an innocent victim of circumstances forced into a suicide trip against his will.

Taking an unbiased view, the reader must weigh the value of this evidence, an unsupported and uncorroborated statement of a single witness, regarding an incident which occurred more than 40 years previously. Shaw and his crew *may* have seen an aircraft through 6,000 feet of cloud skimming the Channel waves - but it could not have been Morgan. He took a route far to the east over the Thames Estuary, Kent and Dymchurch en route to Cap Gris Nez.

In our estimation, Shaw may have seen *something* - but what, when and where are moot points. One possibility was that he had confused his dates. Moreover, at the time of the bombing (around one p.m.) UC-64A #44-70285 was on the ground at Abbotts Ripton waiting for weather clearance.

Now, the Lancasters crews were anxious to return home before bad weather closed in on their bases. They jettisoned bombs from 6,000 feet through the overcast on DR or GEE fixes, and I doubt if any penetrated as far as the centre of the jettison area located in mid-Channel due south of Eastbourne. They would probably jettison somewhere on the eastern edge of the 20 mile diameter circle, and this is important and relevant to what follows. But as yet we had no clues as to the route taken by #43-5313 after leaving Grove Field to return to Chartres on December 16 1944.

However, I received in January 1993 a letter from George E. Buckley of Milford, Connecticut, in which he stated that on December 11 1944 a group of glider pilots commanded by Capt. David Kull picked up seven L-1 artillery-spotter aircraft from R.A.F. Burtonwood, England, with orders to deliver the aircraft to Chartres, France. The first leg was to a base near Hemel Hempstead, north of London, where they spent the night. Next day they went on to their base at Aldermaston near Oxford, stopping for breakfast before flying on to a strip near Bexhill, on the south coast.

At that point bad weather grounded the formation for several days, and the L-1 pilots were uncertain of the date they left Bexhill - Capt. Kull believed it was on December 15 that they prepared to leave for Chartres, but we have documentary evidence to show it was Saturday December 16. That morning they noticed a single-engined plane identified by several of the pilots as a UC-64A Norseman standing on the flight line - it had not been there the day before, and it is safe to assume it came in that morning. Kull was ordered to follow the Norseman, which presumably had better navigational equipment than the spotter planes and was also bound for Chartres. The seven L-1s took off after lunch (the precise time is not known) and in fact there was quite a procession of aircraft in the convoy : L-1 pilot Irwin Morales stated that the Norseman in turn was following a British amphibian (almost certainly a Walrus) and they crossed the coast at Dieppe.

While the L-1s were over the Channel at approximately 300 feet, they were almost swamped by a series of explosions from bombs jettisoned by aircraft above cloud. One L-1 pilot saw the Lancasters through a small break, a formation of 134 aircraft dispatched to Siegen near Cologne. The planned raid was aborted on Friday December 5 when the group reached Amiens and they turned back, dumped excess bombs in the Channel and flew home to East Anglia. On this particular day, the L-1 formation emerged from the welter of foam and spray, they noticed that the Norseman was no longer with them. They reached the French coast without further mishap but one L-1 developed an oil leak and landed at Rouen for repairs, proceeding to Chartres next day. The loss of the Norseman was duly reported and it was not the subject of a Missing Aircrew Report, since its fate was known.

It is noteworthy that the L-1 formation's route from Bexhill to Dieppe takes them close to the eastern boundary of the Bomb Jettison Area. The documentary proof is in the form of an Aircraft Delivery Receipt dated December 16 signed by Captain David Kull. (Fig.81).

So where did the confusion arise ? The solution is simple : the Siegen raid was laid on again the following day, December 16 - using the same aircraft and route. Most of the Lancasters identified and bombed the target, but a number did not - and they jettisoned their loads into the Channel. Some of these bombs exploded near the formation of L-1s, the Walrus and the Norseman - and UC-64A #43-5313 was destroyed. The incident was reported and went on file at Norton AFB Safety and Inspection Center as `written off'. It did not form the subject of a Missing Aircrew Report on December 16 and appears on the Cumulative Loss Listing.

This evidence provides a full and confirmed explanation of Fred Shaw's sighting, reinforcing the case for Morgan's route via Abbotts Ripton/Dymchurch/Beauvais.

22. Glenn Miller's Personal Effects.

When an American airman was killed or posted missing in England, his personal effects were shipped to Effects Quartermaster, STOUS, Warehouse Division, US Forces Liverpool. But where *were* Glenn Miller's effects on December 15 1944 ? And what happened to them ? On March 21 1946, Mr. T.A. Corcoran of Wm. M. Mortimer & Company, insurance loss adjusters, wrote from 111 John Street New York to the Army Effects Bureau, Kansas City Quartermasters Depot :

Gentlemen :

This office represents the Equitable Fire & Marine Insurance Company who are in receipt of a claim from the estate
of Major Alton G. Miller, Army Air Corps. This claim is made
under a personal effects insurance policy issued by the
company.
Would you please advise what personal effects, if any, were
returned to his widow.

Very truly yours,
WILLIAM M. MORTIMER COMPANY
T.A.CORCORAN.

On March 28 1946, Kansas City replied :

`This acknowledges your letter of March 21 1946, regarding
personal effects belonging to Major Alton G. Miller. To date
the Army Effects Bureau has not received any property be
longing to Major Miller.   WM.H.GARNHARDT
1st Lt.   QMC Assistant

The fate of Miller's personal effects has preoccupied researchers for many years. The AEF Band's future movements after Paris had never been clearly defined, but there were no publicised plans for a return to the UK. Six weeks from December 21 (first concert) brings us to February 10 1945 and the frontiers of war were moving westwards all the time towards Berlin. The Band played concerts in Paris in the Olympia and Marignan Theatres, the Palais de Glace, the 40th General Hospital, the Grand Hotel AAF Club, the Rainbow Corner ARC Club and at many hospitals.

From April 25 they spent 12 days in Nice, returning May 6 to Villacoublay in three C-47s. On to Regensburg on June 13 to entertain at nearby bases, and then Schweinfurt and Bad Neustadt on July 9. After their last show in Germany at Bad Kissingen they flew to Venlo in Holland on July 15, then back to Paris. A week later they took the train to Le Havre and sailed for home on August 5 1945.

The initial 6-week tour was extended for the duration. Surviving members confirm they had taken all their personal effects with them, and so, we must presume, did Glenn Miller. The Baessell and Morgan Burial Files contain much correspondence on personal effects - but for Miller - nothing. He lived in rooms at the Mount Royal Hotel at Marble Arch. In Bedford he slept at the ARC Officers Club in town. He used Milton Ernest Officers Club occasionally for meals and recreation, but never stayed overnight. Accommodation was always inadequate, reserved for visiting officers from other 8th Air Force bases; the Billeting Officer could not reserve a special room for Major Miller, on the off-chance he might visit.

So Glenn Miller kept no personal effects at Milton Ernest, other than perhaps a towel and spare shaving gear in the Club locker room. The valet at Milton Ernest Hall, Alan Stilwell, related that on the day after Glenn vanished (Saturday December 16) several Provost Marshal officers came and removed all Miller's kit after sealing it up in boxes. But we feel certain that all his effects (other than instruments, music, arrangements etc kept with the Band equipment) were at the Mount Royal Hotel. The probable explanation is that Lts Don Haynes and Paul Morden may have collected some items at Milton Ernest before leaving for Bovingdon and Paris. Alan Stilwell, as the tape reveals, was old and infirm, and constantly interrupted very loudly by Mrs. Stilwell, who did not seem to understand what was going on. Further, it was not until Wednesday December 20 that Col.Early received the teleprinter inquiry from General Barker at SHAEF, suggesting that Miller was missing. Early would have informed Barker of the removal of Miller's effects by the Security men.

If the PM officers arrived Saturday morning after the Norseman vanished, to remove Miller's kit, we might speculate, based on the Metcalfe report, that Miller had been arrested on Thursday 14 or Friday 15 December for some criminal offence that would warrant seizure of effects by the Army Provost Marshal. If there is substance in the rumour that Major Miller was court-martialled in New York for black market activities, the Stilwell tape may take on a new significance. But what real evidence is there ?

US Army Records at Falls Church, Va. hold no court martial records for Miller or Baessell. Haynes said Glenn took a single D-Bag on the fictitious December 15 flight. On November 8, Major Miller took a single bag to Paris for the conference on November 15 . Joan Heath said he carried a single bag and a PX container of Christmas presents when he flew home from Buc Field. His orders for Paris limited baggage to 65 pounds - not enough for all his effects, so Lt. Haynes either took Glenn's effects back to Bedford on Wednesday December 13, after the party at the Milroy Club, with the intention of shipping them over with the Band equipment, or left them in the Mount Royal Hotel. This seems most probable, since the tour was initially for 6 weeks, after which they were to return to the UK.

Haynes mentions shipping from Twinwood Farm only a trombone, some music etc, details of which are on record at the Wright-Paterson Museum Glenn Miller Exhibit - not a word about clothing, valuable personal items etc. One suggestion is that, if Haynes shipped Miller's effects to Paris with the Band and on arrival realised that Glenn was not coming back, he may have quietly disposed of the effects in Paris, but we could visualise no reason for doing this.

But anomalies remain. If Miller's main effects were left in the Mount Royal Hotel, as may have been the case, they would have been returned to his wife. Haynes had booked him on an Orly flight on Thursday December 14 1944, probably with just a single D-Bag. The standard baggage-handling procedures for air travel to the Continent from Bovingdon were simple : a traveller would check in at the Air Transit Booking Center in the Langham Hotel, downstairs from Miller's London office, and be allocated a booking on a specific day plus a flight number. He would board an Air Force bus at the Air Terminal, Old Quebec Street near Marble Arch, carrying his single permitted item of baggage weighing 65 pounds, thence to Bovingdon, where he would be given a seat number. The order over the Tannoy to board the plane would simply announce : `Flight Three for Paris Orly boarding now'.

The bags would be taken out and loaded : entering the aircraft, the passenger would find his seat and depart - without having his name broadcast at all in the Terminal. In that context, it would have been surprising if Miller had been recognised amongst the many officers waiting for a flight. The baggage may have been checked by Customs before loading, on the alert for any cases suspected of smuggling, and this brings us to the connection with the `court-martial' scenario. Briefly : Miller was a friend of Col. Baessell, a known black market operator. He had spent time in Paris with Baessell in November, `seeing the town' if not actually painting it red. Despite his huge earnings in peacetime, Glenn had been living on the $85 a week major's pay, whilst financing the development of his property in California. We could find no evidence that Miller was in serious financial straits, and even if he was totally innocent, the Customs may have found it hard to resist a peek into his bags at Bovingdon. With what result, we can only speculate. . .

In our view, Miller took only a single mandatory bag on the Paris shuttle on Thursday December 14. His remaining effects were left in the Mount Royal Hotel. What happened to them at that time is anyone's guess.

SUMMATION OF DOCUMENTARY EVIDENCE

1. Initially we located only three documents - Miller's Casualty Report, MACR #10770 and the Confirmatory Signal (which we believed mistakenly to be original). We did not know the Burial Files existed, and John Edwards told us in 1986 that Miller's 201 File had been destroyed in the 1973 fire in St.Louis Records Centre.

2. Herb Miller gave us a written mandate to investigate on his behalf the disappearance of his brother Glenn. This was declared null and void by NPRC St.Louis.

3. Norton AFB consistently denied having any record of any Norseman mishaps.

4. When we learned of the existence of the Burial Files, we asked Alexandria for copies - and they advised us the Files could not be located. This was not so : they were the custodians but the Files were held by the National Personnel Records Center Washington DC.

5. The US Air Force Historical Branch said they could provide no information of value.

6. The Military Reference Branch, National Archives, said that no File contained the Norseman engine number.

7. We advised the Military Field Branch, National Archives, that Report #10770 was a forgery : they replied that it was the `sole, original and genuine document'. The Branch said they were only custodians, not responsible for the content of documents.

8. Military Reference Branch denied all knowledge of Burial Files - but sent us copies of documents contained in the files. . . They also sent us copies of the false MACR #10770 - but none of the genuine `ORIGINAL' MACR #N-19.

9. Important documents were widely distributed in different files, branches and establishments, and at least three important items were abstracted from the Burial Files : Miller's orders for Paris, Morgan's Service Record Card and his Forms 5 (Flight Times Record). Two other important records `vanished' : the December 1944 History Sheet for 35 ADRS at Abbotts Ripton (Morgan's unit) and the AEF Band History for the period July 1944 to December 1944. All other monthly summaries are available.

10. On November 6 1986 Memorial Affairs and Casualty Support Division, Alexandria Va. finally admitted the existence of the Burial Files, said they'd been loaned to the National Personnel Records Center in Washington - who refused to give them back.

11. On December 15 1986, St.Louis Records Center told us that Miller's 201 File was not there and probably destroyed in the 1973 fire. At other times, inquiring about the Burial Files, various Washington departments advised us that the Burial Files were lost, misfiled, misplaced, could not be found.

12. On December 22 1986 we wrote to President Reagan asking for help.

13. We wrote to NPRC Washington on Jan 2 1987, asking specifically if they held the three Burial Files. We received no reply.

14. On January 16 1987 we telephoned George Chalou in National Archives.

15. On January 30, National Archives said the Burial Files had been `found', offered to let us look at them but made no effort to send copies.

16. We asked the Attorney General to intervene. Response : `Not enough evidence'.

17. On March 12 1987 National Archives wrote to say that Burial File copies were on the way ! Nothing was received.

18. March 15 - the Miller Burial File arrived, containing 36 items.

19. With the Ansell Report we proved MACR #10770 was forged including signature, and

the compiler's identity obliterated deliberately.

20.   We found the `ORIGINAL' MACR #N-19 in the Burial Files, with Captain Cramer's full identification - but unsigned. It was an `extract' from a genuine original Report.

21.   Burial File documents confirmed the Morgan route east of London to Dymchurch, and that Glenn Miller flew from Bovingdon to Paris on Thursday December 14 1944.

22.   The `Missing Report' infers that Miller was not the victim of an aircraft accident. The Report covering letter revealed that Craner's original MACR was dated December 22 1944, and was compiled on the orders of Col.Traistor, 8th AFSC. from Paris.

23.   The covert unrecorded December 1944 investigation in Paris was confirmed.

24.   The Non-recoverability Board Findings in 1947 were `fixed' by the AG Department.

25.   The film *THE GLENN MILLER STORY* was based on the spurious Haynes diary.

26.   We located FOD and other documents showing Miller as `Missing in Action'.

27.   The Report of Death documents state no investigation took place in 1944.

28.   Substantial evidence confirms the high-level SHAEF cover-up.

29.   The Special Services letters and Haynes' own evidence confirm that Miller went to Bovingdon on Thursday December 14 1944 to to catch a Paris flight. But there is no sound evidence to show that he was arrested at Bovingdon.

30.   The AG Department (Col.Donnell) deliberately withheld vital information from Helen Miller. The letter stated that Morgan was cleared direct to Bordeaux with a stop at Twinwood but none in Paris.

31.   None of Glenn Miller's personal effects were ever recovered.

32.   The Bordeaux Search Letter and the request for dental details of Col.Baessell suggest that he, or his remains, may have been found but the discovery kept secret. The correspondence from the Veterans Organisation also suggests strongly that Baessell survived the War and drew a pension.

33.   Glenn Miller's orders included an incorrect serial number which, since he never wore dog tags, could have resulted in mis-identification. The orders were not changed at the last moment, as Haynes suggested.

34.   The MOD Air Historical Branch Report includes misleading information on Norseman #43-5367 supplied by Maxwell AFB circa 1973.

35.   In 1971 the Provost Marshal Division asked the AG Department if Miller's fingerprints

were on file. The AG answered `No' - but the prints *were* available.

36. In 1950 USAFE Paris signalled Washington for Baessell's dental details and they were supplied as requested, presumably to facilitate identification of a body. They were on file at that time - but were presumably destroyed in the 1973 fire at NPRC St.Louis. There was a corresponding request for Glenn Miller's dental data in the letter from 8th Fighter Command (Fig.66) in September 1945, but there was no connection with the Baessell request. Strangely, the inquiry revealed that no dental records are available for Glenn Miller. We found none in his 201 File but we were denied access to his Medical File by the U.S Army Surgeon-General quoting the Freedom of Information and Privacy Acts, 1974.

37. The final proof of Miller's fate is in his 201 File, Service Record Section 38, from June 18 - December 31 1944, in the Form 66-2 sent to the Washington AG Department from Paris. NPRC had previously admitted that this record was on file, but access was denied by the Miller family. Later, after the Army General Counsel in 1993 denied it existed, NPRC St.Louis retracted that statement. The Service Record from 1942-1944 had been released, setting a precedent. Further, the Form 66-2 was the only document of the 8 attached to the Missing Report which is missing, and it was either :

(a) abstracted from the Report *before* the latter was sent to the Miller 201 File in NPRC St.Louis and is in the possession of the AG Department, or :

(b) was and still is in the 201 File but is being deliberately suppressed on orders from top level in the Pentagon.

The prior admission by NPRC St.Louis, subsequently withdrawn, confirms the culpability of the US Army, specifically the Adjutant General Department supported by the Army General Counsel himself. We remain convinced that the Form 66.2 and Miller's Chronological Record of Military Service from June - December 1944 is still in existence but is being deliberately suppressed.

+ + +

6 February 1946

Mrs. Glenn MILLER
Cotswold Apartments
TENAFLY, NEW JERSEY

Dear Mrs. MILLER:

Your recent letters to Lt. Col. E.H. Koreman, AGD, were referred to this Headquarters on 23 January 1946, in keeping with the policy of obtaining all available data connected with missing persons.

Further investigation by this Headquarters, and a search of the records, do not reveal any substantiation of the various occurrences embraced in your letters.

The official records indicate the C-64 Eighth Air Force Service Command airplane, No. 44-70285, on which Major MILLER was a passenger, departed Twinwood Field at 13.55 hours (1:55 P.M.), 15 December 1944. The plane was unreported after take-off and failed to arrive at its destination, consequently the aircraft, passengers and pilot were reported and have since been carried in a missing status, presumed deceased.

It has been established that the aircraft was a C-64 model, and it is believed any reference to a C-46 model was due to a clerical error which resulted in transposition of figures.

Major MILLER has never been reported as a prisoner-of-war, nor has information from sources, other than your letter, indicating his presence in different localities, been reported to this Headquarters.

The matter of proper clearances by the pilot appears clarified by the fact that he had clearance from Abbotts Ripton Field, under operations orders for Bordeaux, France, via Twinwood Field. The plane was not a passenger-type aircraft conforming to a fixed schedule, and it is not apparent that the procedure followed by the pilot varied from that normally followed in the combat zone. As stated in your letter, the missing aircraft was not one of the ATC planes on which Major MILLER was booked as a passenger, but a service plane, on which it is presumed he became a passenger upon the invitation of Lt. Col. Baessell, also carried missing and presumed deceased.

It is regretted that no additional information is available, and that further investigation failed to substantiate as fact the reports included in your letters. You may be assured that the Theater Commander and his staff have the fullest realisation of the mental and physical strain you are undergoing and no effort or individual will be spared in bringing to light any reports that can be substantiated as fact by further investigation of Major MILLER's or any other missing case, in this theater. All such cases are kept open under constant survey and any additional information will be furnished you immediately upon availability.

Sincerely,

J.N. DONNELL
Colonel, AGD
Asst. Adjutant General

Fig. 58

Letter - Col. Donnell to Helen Miller

AAF 201 - (10770) Miller, Alton Glenn
0505273

12 February 1945

Mrs. Helen D. Miller
Byrne Lane
Tenafly, New Jersey

Dear Mrs. Miller:

I am writing you with reference to your husband, Major Alton Glenn Miller, who was reported missing in the European Area since 15 December 1944.

Additional information has been received indicating that Major Miller was a passenger on a C-46 (transport plane) nicknamed "Horseman" which departed from England on a mission to Bordeaux, France on 15 December, 1944. The report reveals that your husband's plane was last seen to leave its base at about 1:55 p.m., and the time, place, and circumstances relative to its loss are presently unknown in this headquarters.

Please be assured that a continuing search by land, sea, and air is being made to discover the whereabouts of our missing personnel. Any additional information received will be sent immediately to you by The Adjutant General or this headquarters.

Very sincerely,

K. A. BRADUNAS
Major, Air Corps
Chief, Notification Branch
Personal Affairs Division
Assistant Chief of Air Staff, Personnel

Fig. 59

Letter - Major Bradunas to Helen Miller

WAR DEPARTMENT
THE ADJUTANT GENERAL'S OFFICE
WASHINGTON 25, D. C.

351600

NON—BATTLE CASUALTY REPORT

NAME	SERIAL NUMBER	GRADE	ARM OR SERVICE	REPORTING THEATRE
MORGAN JOHN R. S.	T 130 776	F/O	AC	ETO

PLACE OF CASUALTY	DATE OF CASUALTY DAY	MONTH	YEAR	FLYING OR JUMPING STAT	TYPE OF CASUALTY	SHIPMENT NUMBER
ENGLAND	16	DEC	44		MNG	006037-14-0-1X

NAME AND ADDRESS OF EMERGENCY ADDRESSEE

THE INDIVIDUAL NAMED ABOVE DESIGNATED THE FOLLOWING PERSON AS THE ONE TO BE NOTIFIED IN CASE OF EMERGENCY, AND THE OFFICIAL TELE-GRAPHIC AND LETTER NOTIFICATIONS WILL BE SENT TO THIS PERSON. THE RELATIONSHIP, IF ANY, IS SHOWN BELOW. IT SHOULD BE NOTED THAT THIS PERSON IS NOT NECESSARILY THE NEXT-OF-KIN OR RELATIVE DESIGNATED TO BE PAID SIX MONTHS' PAY GRATUITY IN CASE OF DEATH

MR.-MRS.-MISS—FIRST NAME—MIDDLE INITIAL—LAST NAME	RELATIONSHIP	DATE NOTIFIED
MRS. W. MORGAN	MOTHER	9 JANUARY 1945

NO. AND NAME OF STREET-CITY-STATE		
11715 MEMORIAL AVENUE	DETROIT	MICHIGAN

REMARKS: AG 704 (2 Jan 45) [ ] CORRECTED COPY   LMB

ETO Ship 002. F/O took off from Abbotts Ripton having cleared for Twinwood and having operation orders for A-42, Bordeaux, left Twinwood in C-64 #285, and has not been heard from since.

ACTION BY PROCESSING AND VERIFICATION SECTION: REPORT VERIFIED _____ FORM 43 _____ AG 201 REQ. _____

CASUALTY BRANCH FILE ATTACHED _____ OR CHARGED TO _____ DATE _____

PREVIOUSLY REPORTED   NO _____ YES _____ (AS INDICATED BELOW):

FILE NO.	MESSAGE NO.	TYPE	DATE AND AREA	E. A. NOTIFIED

FORWARDED TO →

SPEC. IDEN.	TELEGRAM	WOUNDED	LETTER	CORRES.	S. R. A. D.	CERTIF.	M. & M.	NON-DEL.

REPORT NOT VERIFIED _____ NO FORM 43 _____ NO CAS BR FILE _____ CHECKED BY _____ REVIEWED BY _____

THIS SPACE FOR USE OF MACHINE RECORDS BRANCH, A.G.O.

ACCT. AREA	CASUALTY STATUS	ORIGINAL CAS. DATE DAY	MO	YR	MESSAGE NO.	LATEST CAS. DATE DAY	MO	YR	REFERENCE AREA	ENEM PCS.	RESIDENCE STATE		COUNTY	COMP	RACE
34 35	36 37 38	39	40	41	42 43 44 45	46	47	48 49	50 51	52	53 54	55	56	57 58	59

DISTRIBUTION "A" [ ] COPIES

(ALL TYPES OF CASUALTIES PERTAINING TO MILITARY PERSONNEL. EXCEPT WOUNDED.)
COPIES FURNISHED: SEE CASUALTY BRANCH MEMORANDUM NO. 48, 1944.

DISTRIBUTION "B" [ ] COPIES

(ALL WOUNDED MILITARY PERSONNEL AND ALL TYPES OF CASUALTIES PERTAINING TO CIVILIANS WHO ARE W. D. EMPLOYEES. EMPLOYEES OF W. D. CONTRACTORS AND OTHERS SUBJECT TO MILITARY LAW.)
COPIES FURNISHED: SEE CASUALTY BRANCH MEMORANDUM NO. 48, 1944.

W.D., A.G.O. FORM NO. 0365
16 JUNE 1944

Fig.60

Casualty Report - Flight Officer John R.S. Morgan

DEPARTMENT OF THE ARMY
~~WAR DEPARTMENT~~
THE ADJUTANT GENERAL'S OFFICE
WASHINGTON 25, D. C.

NON—BATTLE CASUALTY REPORT

AG 201	NAME	GRADE		DATE CAS. REPORT RECEIVED
	MORGAN JOHN R S	F/O		
	ASN T190776	SON		

NAME AND ADRESS OF E. A.	MRS W MORGAN 11716 MEMORIAL AVENUE DETROIT MICHIGAN		DATE ~~TELEGRAM~~ SENT 19 Mar 48

THE INDIVIDUAL NAMED BELOW DESIGNATED THE ABOVE PERSON AS THE ONE TO BE NOTIFIED IN CASE OF EMERGENCY, AND THE OFFICIAL TELE-GRAPHIC AND LETTER NOTIFICATIONS WILL BE SENT TO THIS PERSON. THE RELATIONSHIP, IF ANY, IS SHOWN BELOW. IT SHOULD BE NOTED THAT THIS PERSON IS NOT NECESSARILY THE NEXT-OF-KIN OR RELATIVE DESIGNATED TO BE PAID SIX MONTHS' PAY GRATUITY IN CASE OF DEATH.

THE SECRETARY OF ~~WAR~~/HAS ASKED ME TO EXPRESS HIS DEEP REGRET THAT YOUR **SON**

GRADE	NAME	SERIAL NUMBER	ARM OR SERVICE	REPORTING THEATRE	F OR J STATUS	SHIPMENT NUMBER
F/O	MORGAN, JOHN R.S.	T 190776	AC		K	072019- U-3X

TYPE OF CASUALTY	PLACE OF CASUALTY	DATE OF CASUALTY			CASUALTY CODE
		DAY	MONTH	YEAR	
DIED	IN ENGLISH CHANNEL	15	DEC	44	

REMARKS:
AG 704 /11 MAR 48/   ☐ CORRECTED COPY   REPORT OF DEATH ISSUED 23 MAR 48 ekm

MEMO S.R. AND D. UNIT. APPROVED BY OIC. CAS. SEC. PA. BR. DIED WHEN PLANE CRASHED SOMEWHERE IN THE ENGLISH CHANNEL WHILE ON MISSION FROM TWINWOOD FLD, ENGLAND TO PARIS, FRANCE. IN PAY AND DUTY STATUS AT TIME OF DEATH, NOT RESULT OF OWN MISC. FINDING DEATH ISSUED PREVIOUSLY UNDER SEC.5, PUBLIC LAW 490, 7 MAR. 42, AS AMENDED, SHOWING PRESUMED DATE DEATH 16 DEC. 45. RPT DEATH, BASED ON INFO REC'D SINCE THAT DATE, IS ISSUED IN ACCORDANCE WITH SEC.9 OF SAID ACT, AND ITS EFFECT ON PRIOR PAYMENTS AND SETTLEMENTS AS PROVIDED IN SEC.9.
          Home Add: Detroit, Wayne Co., Michigan.
PROCESS IN ACCORDANCE WITH PAR. 2B, OPER. BUL. 35, 1945.

ACTION BY COMPOSITE SECTION: REPORT VERIFIED___ ___FORM 43___ ___AG 201 REQ.___

CASUALTY BRANCH FILE ATTACHED___ ___OR CHARGED TO___ ___DATE___

PREVIOUSLY REPORTED   NO___   YES___   (AS INDICATED BELOW):

FILE NO.	MESSAGE NO.	TYPE	DATE AND AREA	E. A. NOTIFIED
Public Law 490		DED	16 DEC 15 ETO	16 DEC 45

FORWARDED TO →

	SPEC. IDEN.	C. & P.	TELEGRAM	LETTER	CERTIF.	F. REL.	CORRES.	REPAT.	B. R. & D	NON-OFL
				✓						

REPORT NOT VERIFIED___ NO FORM 43___ NO CAS. BR. FILE___ CHECKED BY ___ REVIEWED BY ___

DISTRIBUTION "A" ☐   29 COPIES   DISTRIBUTION "B" ☐ 31 COPIES

WD AGO FORM 0365
1 MAY 1945   EDITION OF 1 JAN 1945 MAY BE USED.

Fig. 61

Amended Casualty Report - Flight Officer John R.S. Morgan

JOHN ROBERT STUART MORGAN

FAMILY TREE

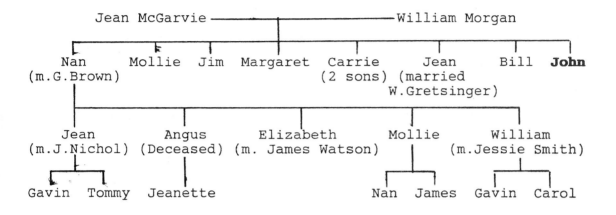

Fig.62

Morgan Family Tree

Clf. ....
X̲c̲ 6 036 049
N̲ 12 859 933

DETERMINATION OF LIABILITY AND CERTIFICATION
BY THE COMMITTEE ON EXTRA HAZARDS OF SERVICE
NATIONAL SERVICE LIFE INSURANCE

Name of
insured ....John R. S. Morgan........

Date of
death .....12/15/44.........

Entered active
service ....

Active service
terminated ....

Date of application
for insurance ....

Face value
of policy, $..10,000..

Plan
5 LPT.........

Effective Date
6/1/43...........

Age at Issue
21........

Changed to $............

Premiums
paid to ....

Date of total
disability ....

Due date of first premium
covered by waiver ....

Date for application for
premium waiver ......:..........

Does total disability
continue? ....

If not, date terminated

Disease or injury causing disability or death and statement of facts:

**Missing when aircraft failed to arrive at its destination in France.
Officially declared dead. On transport mission.**

(IF ADDITIONAL SPACE IS REQUIRED USE REVERSE OF FORM)

On the basis of the evidence recited above, it is the decision of this committee that the disease or injury resulting in the above-numbered claim is traceable to the performance of duty in the military or naval service and that said disease o injury is traceable to the extra hazards of such service. Accordingly, by virtue of the authority conferred upon the Administrator of Veterans' Affairs it is authorized and directed that transfer be made pursuant to the provisions of Section 60 of the National Service Life Insurance Act of 1940 from the National Service Life Insurance Appropriation to the Nation Service Life Insurance Fund of

☒ an amount which, when added to the reserve of the policy will equal the then value of such benefits under abov policy.

☐ an amount sufficient to cover the premiums on the policy for the period while the payment of premiums by the insure is waived by reason of the total disability of the insured.

FOR THE ADMINISTRATOR OF VETERANS' AFFAIRS:

IL/ejp

COMMITTEE ON EXTRA HAZARDS OF SERVICE

Member.

H. N.

Member.

Date ....MAR 1 2 1948.........

vice

Chairman.

I CERTIFY that in accordance with Section 607 of the National Service Life Insurance Act of 1940 the calculations the above-numbered claim are as follows:

.... Monthly premiums of $................................. $...............................

From .... to ....

Commuted value of policy.. $...............................

Reserve.............. .... $...............................

Amount to be transferred.. $...............................

Date ....

Insurance Accounts Section, Finance Servi

U. S. GOVERNMENT PRINTING OFFICE   16—39483-1

Fig.63

Life Insurance - Flight Officer John R.S. Morgan

London Casino, Old Compton Street, W. 1

Telephone : GERrard 6877

PROGRAMME

Week commencing MONDAY, DECEMBER 11th, 1944

"What with the high quality of its goods and services, its encouragement to thrift, its tendency to equalisation between man and man, what, above all, with the good fellowship it promotes between consumer, producer and distributor, the Co-operative Movement seems to me to have established a good title to be regarded as an advanced version of the Socialist society in which we all believe."

C. E. M. JOAD.

N.B.—Nine million Co-operators in Great Britain own the 200 factories and warehouses that manufacture C.W.S. goods.

Fig.64

Queensbury Club Concert Programme December 12 1944 - Page 1

Monday, December 11th

"YOU'VE HAD IT," REVUE GIVEN BY 540 COAST REGIMENT by permission of LT./COL. J. H. W. RICHARDS, O.B.E., R.A.. with MAJORS MALLINSON and BOARDMAN, GNRS. WATSON, MORRIS, McCLEAN, CPL. DAVIES and L/BDR. BIRD

Produced by GNR. WATSON

DANCING TO HAL KENT'S BAND

Tuesday, December 12th

THE AMERICAN BAND OF THE A.E.F.

conducted by

MAJOR GLENN MILLER

Executive Officer Lt. Don W. Haynes
Programme Director W.O. Paul Dudley.

Piano	S/Sgt. Mel Powell	French Horns Cpl. Addison Collins, Jnr.
	Cpl. Jack Rusin	Violins
Drums	T/Sgt. Ray McKinley	S/Sgt. George Ockner
	Cpl. Frank Ippolito	S/Sgt. Harry Katzman
Guitar	Sgt. Carmen Mastren	Col. Ernest Kardos
Bass	S/Sgt. Trigger Alpert	Cpl. Eugene Bergen
	Cpl. Joe Shulman	S/Sgt. Carl Swanson
Trumpets	M/Sgt. Zeke Zarchy	Cpl. Milton Edelson
	Sgt. Bob Nichols	Sgt. Dave Herman
	Sgt. Whitey Thomas	Cpl. Phil Cogliano
	Sgt. Bernie Priven	Cpl. Joseph Kowalewski
Trombones	Sgt. Jimmy Priddy	Sgt. Dave Schwartz
	Cpl. John Halliburton	Cpl. Henry Brynan
	Cpl. Larry Hall	Cpl. Earl Cornwell
	P.F.C. Nat Peck	P.F.C. Fred Ostrovsky
Vocalist	Sgt. Johnnie Desmond	Cpl. Morris Bialkin
Crew Chiefs	Sgt. Steve Steck	Cpl. Bob Ripley
	Cpl. Eugene Steck	Cpl. Stanley Harris
	Cpl. Arthur Malvin	Cpl. Emanuel Wishnow
	Cpl. Murray Kane	Cpl. Dave Sackson
	Cpl. Lynn Allison	Cpl. Nate Kaproff
Saxophones	S/Sgt. Hank Freeman	Cpl. Richard Motolinski
	Sgt. Michael Hucko	Arrangers T/Sgt. Jerry Gray
	Sgt. Vince Carbone	M/Sgt. Norm Layden
	Sgt. Jack Ferrier	S/Sgt. Ralph Wilkinson
	Cpl. Fred Guerra	S/Sgt. Jimmy Jackson
	Cpl. Mann Thaler	

Production T/Sgt. George Voutsas and Sgt. Harry Hartwick
Stage Manager Sgt. Julius Zifferblatt
Announcer Cpl. Paul Dubov
Assistant Executive Officers T/Sgt. Jack Sanderson and Cpl. Tom Cochran

DANCING TO HAL KENT'S BAND

Thursday, December 14th

DANCING TO TOMMY KEMP'S BAND

Friday, December 15th

CARNIVAL NIGHT — SAM DONAHUE'S U.S. NAVY BAND

DANCING TO TOMMY KEMP'S BAND

Saturday, December 16th

GERALDO AND HIS ORCHESTRA with LEN CAMBER, SALLY DOUGLAS, PAT FROST and CELIA LIPTON

DANCING TO NED WHITEBREAD'S BAND

Sunday, December 17th

R.A.F. SKYROCKET'S ORCHESTRA with URIEL PORTER, MORTON FRAZER, TALBOT O'FARRELL, ELSIE CARLISLE, PATRICIA MORNE, A.T.S. GIRL PIPERS

M.C. : PATRICIA MEDINA

(The British Film Star)

Important Notice to Members

It has been brought to the Club Management's notice that some members are still allowing their Cards to be used by non members.

It is hoped that members will co-operate with us by showing their Identity Cards when asked in order that we may stamp out this unfair method of depriving a member of a seat by the misuse of a Membership Card.

Fig.65

Queensberry Club Concert Programme December 12 1944 - Page 2

HEADQUARTERS VIII FIGHTER COMMAND
Office of the Commanding General
APO 634

SEP 17 1945

SUBJECT: Request for Dental Records.

TO   : Adjutant General, Washington, D.C.
         (Thru: Commanding General, Army Air Forces, Washington, D.C.)

1. Request that any dental records concerning the following named officer be forwarded to this headquarters for comparison with dental records completed on the remains of an unidentified individual:

Major Alton G. Miller, O-505273

2. It is to be noted that subject officer was not on flying status, thus a Dental Identification Record was not completed. However, this officer was known to have been a member of an aircrew of this command listed as MIA 15 December 1944.

FOR THE COMMANDING GENERAL.

BURDETTE W. ERICKSON,
A.G.D.
Major,
Asst. Adjutant General.

Fig.66

Inquiry Letter - 8th Fighter Command

1st Ind. AFTAS-14

Headquarters, Army Air Forces, Washington 25, D.C. 28 September 1945

To: Commanding General, VIII Fighter Command, APO 634 c/o Postmaster, New York, N.Y.

The records on file in this headquarters concerning Major Alton G. Miller, O-505273 contain no Dental Identification Record or other Dental data useful for identification purposes.

FOR THE COMMANDING GENERAL:

GEORGE R. KENNEBECK
Colonel, Dental Corps
Deputy for Dental Service
Office of The Air Surgeon

Fig.67

Reply to 8th Fighter Command Letter

AIRMAIL

WAR DEPARTMENT

17 FEB 1947

QMCQR 293
Baessell, Norman F., Lt.Col.
A.S.N 0 905 387

SUBJECT: Additional Information that may lead to the Recovery and Identification of Remains Not Yet Accounted For.

To   Commanding Officer
          American Graves Registration Command
          European Theater Area
          APO 887, c/o Postmaster
          New York, New York

          1. Reference is made to WD, OQMS Letter, File and sub-
ject as above, dated 25 November 1946, for which there is no
record of receipt of a reply in this office.

          2. It is requested that every effort be made by your
command to locate or identify remains of this individual and the
results of your investigation, whether positive or negative, be
returned to this office by indorsement on the above referred to
letter within 20 days of receipt of this communication.

          FOR THE QUARTERMASTER GENERAL

                              MARTIN G. RILEY
                              Major, QMS
                              Memorial Division

                    AIRMAIL

Fig.68

File 293 Letter - Search for Baessell

NON

—BATTLE CASUALTY REPORT

RC 10 JAN 45

NAME	SERIAL NUMBER	GRADE	ARM OR SERVICE	REPORTING THEATRE
BAESSELL NORMAN F	O 905 387	LT COL	AC	ETO

PLACE OF CASUALTY	DATE OF CASUALTY			FLYING OR JUMPING STAT	TYPE OF CASUALTY	SHIPMENT NUMBER
	DAY	MONTH	YEAR			
ENGLAND	15	DEC	44		MNG	006037-1-C-1X

NAME AND ADDRESS OF EMERGENCY ADDRESSEE

THE INDIVIDUAL NAMED ABOVE DESIGNATED THE FOLLOWING PERSON AS THE ONE TO BE NOTIFIED IN CASE OF EMERGENCY, AND THE OFFICIAL TELE-GRAPHIC AND LETTER NOTIFICATIONS WILL BE SENT TO THIS PERSON. THE RELATIONSHIP, IF ANY, IS SHOWN BELOW. IT SHOULD BE NOTED THAT THIS PERSON IS NOT NECESSARILY THE NEXT-OF-KIN OR RELATIVE DESIGNATED TO BE PAID SIX MONTHS' PAY GRATUITY IN CASE OF DEATH

MR.-MRS.-MISS—FIRST NAME—MIDDLE INITIAL—LAST NAME	RELATIONSHIP	DATE NOTIFIED
MRS AMANDA L BAESSELL	WIFE	8 JAN 45 bhl
NO. AND NAME OF STREET-CITY-STATE		
615 K STREET NORTHWEST WASHINGTON D C		

REMARKS.

AG 704 (2 JAN 45)   ☐ CORRECTED COPY

ETO Ship #002.   Airplane No 44-70285 departed Twinwood Field for France, plane missing and unreported since departure. Passenger.

ACTION BY PROCESSING AND VERIFICATION SECTION:	REPORT VERIFIED	FORM 43	AG 201 REQ.

CASUALTY BRANCH FILE ATTACHED_____OR CHARGED TO _____DATE_____

PREVIOUSLY REPORTED   NO._____YES_____AS INDICATED BELOW.

FILE NO.	MESSAGE NO.	TYPE	DATE AND AREA	E. A. NOTIFIED

FORWARDED TO →	SPEC. IDEN.	TELEGRAM	WOUNDED	LETTER	CORRES.	S R A D.	CERTIF.	M. & M.	NON-DEL.

REPORT NOT VERIFIED____NO FORM 43____NO CAS. BR. FILE____CHECKED BY_____REVIEWED BY_____

THIS SPACE FOR USE OF MACHINE RECORDS BRANCH, A.G.O.

ACCT. AREA	CASUALTY STATUS	ORIGINAL CAS. DATE			MESSAGE NO	LATEST CAS. DATE			REFERENCE AREA	CREW POS.	RESIDENCE		COMP	RACE
		DAY	MO	YR		DAY	MO	YR			STATE	COUNTY		
34	35	36	37	38	39 40 41	42 43	44	45	46 47	48 49	50 51	52 53 54	55 56	57 58	59

DISTRIBUTION "A" ☐ _____ COPIES

(ALL TYPES OF CASUALTIES PERTAINING TO MILITARY PERSONNEL, EXCEPT WOUNDED.)
COPIES FURNISHED SEE CASUALTY BRANCH MEMORANDUM NO 48, 1944.

DISTRIBUTION "B" ☐ _____ COPIES

(ALL WOUNDED MILITARY PERSONNEL AND ALL TYPES OF CASUALTIES PERTAINING TO CIVILIANS WHO ARE W. D. EMPLOYEES, EMPLOYEES OF W. D. CONTRACTORS AND OTHERS SUBJECT TO MILITARY LAW.)
COPIES FURNISHED SEE CASUALTY BRANCH MEMORANDUM NO 48, 1944.

W.D., A.G.O. FORM NO. 0365
16 JUNE 1944

Fig.69

Col.Baessell - Non-Battle Casualty Report

No.	Area	AF	Gp	Type	SN.	Date	Crew	Total
10398	BURMA	10	3CC	C-47A	42-93379	14.12.44	3	6
10377	IN.OCEAN	20	40	B-29A	42-93831		11	11
10982	GERMANY	9	370	P-38J	42-67940		1	1
10775	ITALY	12	47	A-20K	44- 570		4	4
10378	BURMA	20	40	B-29	42-24457		11	12
10376	BURMA	20	40	B-29	42-24574		11	11
10401	BURMA	20	40	B-29	42-24626		11	12
11484	GERMANY	9	386	B-26F	42-96275	15.12.44	6	6
12180	SWPAC	5	35	P-47D	42-27860		1	1
11962	SWPAC	5	35	P-47D	42-28531		1	1
11502	GERMANY	9	373	P-47D	42-29177		1	1
11006	HOLLAND	9	373	P-47D	44-20471		1	1
10770	**FRANCE**	**8**	**35**	**C-64A**	**44-70285**		**1**	**3**
10584	GERMANY	15	376	B-24H	42-53142		11	11
10676	AUSTRIA	15	461	B-24B	42-51346		11	11
10485	S. ATL	3	33	B-24J	00- 2424		3	3
11310	GERMANY	8	355	P-51D	44-15044		1	1
11069	CHANNEL	8	364	P-51D	44-15557		1	1
14388	CHINA	14	2	C-46A	42-96713	16.12.44	4	4
11259	FRANCE	8	95	B-17G	42-97232		9	9
10789	ITALY	12	86	P-47D	42-27082	1	1	
10956	BURMA	10	80	P-47D	42-27507		1	1
10751	GERMANY	9	358	P-47D	44-10469		1	1
10491	CKSLOVA	15	456	B-24J	44-40876		11	11
10783	GERMANY	15	465	B-24J	42-51631		10	10
10610	GERMANY	15	456	B-24H	41-28964		9	9
10611	GERMANY	15	456	B-24H	41-29549		11	11
10673	GERMANY	15	31	P-51H	42-24890		1	1
11194	PHILIS	13	347	P-51B	43-28575		1	1
10661	FRANCE	12	324	P-47D	42-26852		1	1
10498	ITALY	15	465	B-24J	42-51879		10	10
10494	ITALY	15	461	B-24J	42-51922		11	11
10603	ITALY	15	465	B-24H	42-52564		10	10
10496	ITALY	15	464	B-24J	42-78671	17.12.44	10	10
10701	CKSLVA	15	461	B-24J	42-95304		10	10
10989	BELGIUM	9	405	P-47D	42-27323		1	1
10788	ITALY	12	86	P-47D	42-27938		1	1
11676	GERMANY	9	324	P-47D	42-28571		1	1
10984	GERMANY	9	365	P-47D	42-28634		1	1
10980	GERMANY	9	365	P-47D	42-28645		1	1
11008	GERMANY	9	48	P-47D	42-28800		1	1

Fig.70

Extract from MACR Register

(S-11-6-45)
RTB:BT:dt
September 5, 1945

In Reply Refer To: __351509__

Mrs. Amanda L. Baessell
~~615 K Street, NW~~ *724 So. St. Asaph St. apt. 313-13*
Washington, D. C. *Alexandria. Va.*

Dear Mrs. Baessell:

    The Army Effects Bureau is forwarding to you the following personal property, recently received here, belonging to your husband, Lieutenant Colonel Norman F. Baessell:

            1 package and contents

    My action in transmitting the property does not, of itself, vest title in you. The items are forwarded in order that you may act as gratuitous bailee in caring for them pending the return of the owner, who has been reported missing in action. In the event he later is reported a casualty, and I sincerely hope he never is, it will be necessary that the property be turned over to the person or persons legally entitled to receive it.

    When delivery has been made, I shall appreciate your acknowledging receipt by signing one copy of this letter in the space provided below, and returning it to this Bureau. For your convenience, there is inclosed an addressed envelope which needs no postage.

    I regret the circumstances prompting this letter, and wish to express my hope for the safe return of your husband.

Yours very truly,

F. L. KOOB
1st Lt., QMC
Officer-in-Charge
SJ Branch

1 Incl--
    Envelope

Fig.71

Personal Effects - Lt.Col. Norman F. Baessell - Letter #1

ARMY SERVICE FORCES
KANSAS CITY QUARTERMASTER DEPOT
ARMY EFFECTS BUREAU
601 Hardesty Avenue
Kansas City 1, Missouri

(S-12-1-45)
RTB:BT:bm
September 26, 1945

In Reply Refer To: ___351509___

Mrs. Amanda L. Baessell
~~615 K Street, Northwest~~   *724 - So. St. Asaph St,*
Washington, D. C.   *Alexandria, Va.*

Dear Mrs. Baessell:

The Army Effects Bureau has received and is forwarding to you the following additional property of your husband, Lieutenant Colonel Norman F. Baessell:

1 carton and contents

As previously indicated, my action in forwarding such effects does not, of itself, vest title in you. The property is transmitted in order that you may safely keep it on behalf of the owner, pending change in his status.

When delivery has been made, I will appreciate your acknowledging receipt by signing one copy of this letter in the space provided below, and returning it to this Bureau.

For your convenience, there is inclosed an addressed envelope which needs no postage.

Yours very truly,

P. L. Koob

P. L. KOOB
1st Lt., QMC
Officer-in-Charge
SJ Branch

Incl--
Envelope

Fig. 72

Baessell Personal Effects Letter #2

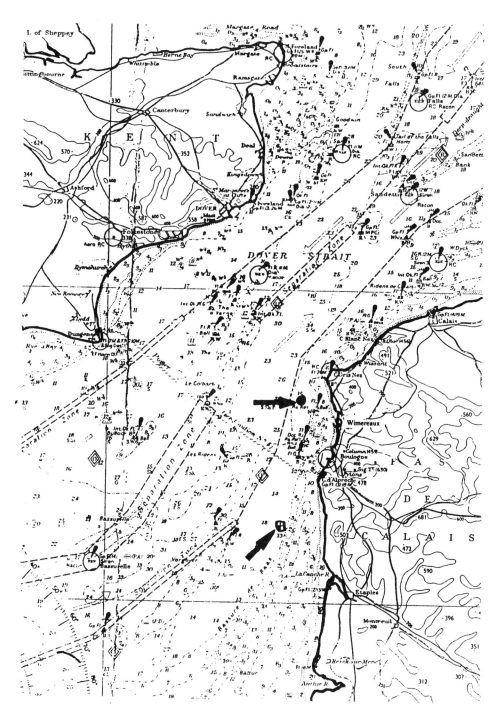

Position of the John Edwards Aircraft ●

Position of Clive Ward Aircraft ⊞

Fig.73

Sunken Aircraft in English Channel

Fig.74

Side-Scan Sonar Image - John Edwards

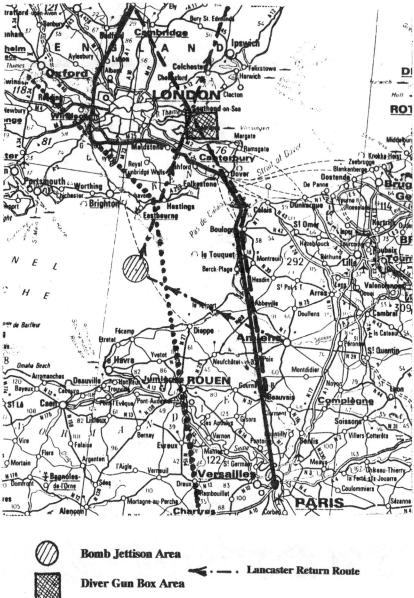

⬤ **Bomb Jettison Area**

◼ **Diver Gun Box Area**

◀ — · — · **Lancaster Return Route**

— — — Morgan Route December 15 1944 - Abbotts Ripton - Dymchurch - Cap Gris Nez - Beauvais

━━━━━ Standard Norseman Route via Twinwood Farm - Bovingdon - Maidstone - Ashford - Hythe - Ca[Gris Nez - Paris

⬤⬤⬤⬤⬤⬤⬤ Norseman 43-5613 Route December 16 1944 - Grove Field - Bexhill - Chartres

Fig.75

Cross-Channel Routes

GLENN MILLER 'WAS MURDERED'

by FRANK DURHAM

Glenn Miller: New facts

A MAN who has spent more than £7,000 and devoted 12 years to solving the mystery of American bandleader Glenn Miller's death has come up with a startling new theory.

Thirty - five - year - old John Edwards says that Miller was not aboard the plane in which most people believe he died when it crashed into the Channel.

He claims he has evidence that the bandleader was murdered in Paris three days AFTER the plane plunged into the sea.

Mr. Edwards believes that Miller, who was a bit of a lad with the ladies, died of a fractured skull somewhere in the city's red light district of Pigalle.

Cover-up

And he suggests that the fact that the Norseman plane he was supposed to have been aboard crashed was seized on by the authorities and became a convenient cover-up for Miller's death.

Among the evidence that Mr. Edwards has collected to support the theory that Miller was not aboard the fatal flight in 1944 is the eye-witness account of a man who says he saw Miller board a Dakota plane at RAF Bovingdon, Herts, the day of the crash.

This, claims Mr. Edwards, is the plane that Miller actually flew to France in.

The original journey began when the ill-fated Norseman aircraft

Continued on Page 21

Continued from Page 1

took off from Twinwoods airfield, near Bedford.

According to Mr. Edwards's research the Norseman later landed at Bovingdon where Miller left the plane before it took off again for Paris.

Then Miller joined the Dakota and made the cross-Channel trip.

The new facts came to light because Mr. Edwards actually set out to disprove earlier suggestions that Miller was not aboard the Norseman when it crashed.

"Now I have to admit that I was probably wrong. It looks as if it is true that he was *not* on the plane."

Now Mr. Edwards wants to put an end to speculation by raising the crashed plane from the sea bed.

He believes he has found the spot where the plane plunged into the sea and hopes to raise the £15,000 needed to salvage the wreck.

"I have the military numbers of all three men who took off in the plane —Miller's is one of them. Their metal identity tags should still be intact. "But the way the evidence is piling up I don't expect to find Glenn's body in that aircraft," said Mr. Edwards.

Did he die in Paris?

Mr. Edwards backs his theory of an official cover-up of the real circumstances of Miller's death with the fact that there was never a proper official inquiry.

The "missing aircrew report" of the incident is vague, says Mr. Edwards.

"Even the weather conditions were listed as unknown. But more than 30 years later I have been able to discover the most detailed meteorological reports for the day in question."

Mr. Edwards added: "I have met with difficulty when trying to solve the mystery. Records have been reported burned and other information — such as the missing aircrew report— is unaccountably vague.

"A firm which had shown interest in backing my project to raise the aircraft from the Channel was advised not to do so by the Glenn Miller estate."

Why does he believe that Glenn Miller was murdered?

Mr. Edwards, a former RAF officer and now a sales export manager, says: "Pieces of information that I have collected over the years have all suddenly fallen into place.

"I have evidence that an American military doctor in Paris signed Glenn Miller's death certificate.

"And retired U.S. Air Force Lieutenant-Colonel Thomas F. Corrigan, recalls that a member of the Provost Marshal's police office in Paris had told him of Miller's murder.

"I now have in my possession a list, which includes the name of the provost officer who dealt with the case, together with other names of the Provost Marshal's staff. All can confirm this account.

"I also have the name of a man who played in the band with Miller, who states that it was common knowledge that those close to him knew very well he was murdered in Paris."

A Norseman aircraft similar to the one involved in the mystery

Fig.76

Reveille Article

NEW CLUE IN GLENN MYSTERY

By ANDREW GOLDEN

THE brother of war-time star Glenn Miller has backed up a claim that the legendary band leader did **NOT** die in an air-crash.

"My own theory for years was that he never even left England, but died somewhere of cancer," said Herb Miller, 66.

It has always been believed that Miller was on a plane that crashed into the Channel en route to Paris in 1944.

But two weeks ago top British diver Clive Ward claimed exclusively in the Sunday Mirror that he had located Miller's plane . . . and no one was on board when it sank.

Herb, of Dulwich, South London, said: "I have never believed the story that my brother died in the plane crash. I would love to know the truth."

He dismissed Mr. Ward's claim that Glenn died of a heart attack in a Paris brothel.

"He just wouldn't have needed to visit such a place," he said.

Herb, who has a band

Herb—theory

playing Glenn Miller music, said it would help if the plane could be raised from the sea bed.

"Then we can check the serial number and know for sure if it was the plane that Glenn was supposed to have been in," he said.

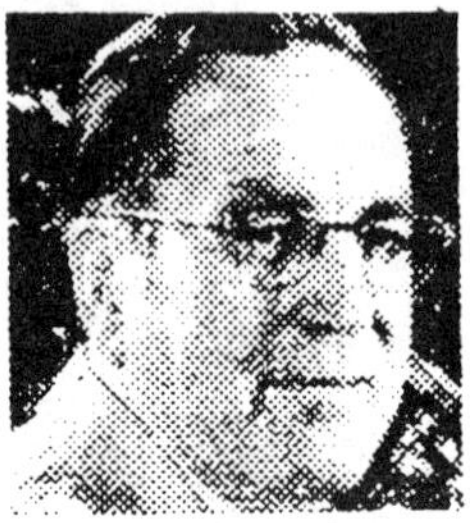

Fig.77

Press Cutting - Herb Miller

AGPC-G 201 Miller, Alton G.   21 January 1946
(21 Jan 46) 0505273

Mr. George Eyerman
████████████████████
████████████████

Hollywood, California

Dear Mr. Eyerman:

        Mr. Jimmie Fidler has advised me that you have information con-
cerning Major Alton Glenn Miller, who was reported as missing in
flight on 15 December 1944 and who subsequently was officially recorded as dead under the provisions of Public Law 490, 77th Congress, as
amended.

        I will be grateful if you will furnish me the same information
you gave to Mr. Fidler regarding Major Miller. This office is interested in securing data having a bearing on the status of all personnel
whose exact status is unknown and all leads are thoroughly investigated in an effort to obtain complete information. I can assure you
that the fact that you have furnished information to Mr. Fidler will
in no way reflect upon you, nor will it result in your being caused
any unpleasantness.

        I am inclosing for your convenience a franked self-addressed
envelope and will appreciate your replying as expeditiously as possible.

                            Sincerely yours,

                            EDWARD F. WITSELL
                            Major General
                            Acting The Adjutant General of the Army

1 Inclosure

   Copy furnished: Return to Captain Newmark 4641
        Casualty File   Smith 4641
                             Casualty Branch
                             21 January 1946

                            Fig.78

            Letter from US Adjutant General to George Eyerman

Captain P. M. Newmark   30 January 1946
The Adjutant General
War Department
Washington 25, D. C.

Dear Sir:

        In reply to your letter of January 21st. regarding
Major Alton Glenn Miller I wish to inform you the following is
all I know about Major Miller.

        While in Verdun France at the time of Major Miller's
accident the Stars and Stripes had the incident in there paper,
at wich time there was nothing mentioned about what kind of air
craft, who the pilot was, or if anyone else was lost. This lack
of information immediately started all kinds of rumors among the
soldiers, so said information that I gave Mr. Fidler was only
inquiry on my part.

        This has evidently been a misinterpretation, and I am
very sorry I cannot give you any specific information on this case.

                                    Sincerely yours,

                                    /s/ George R. Eyerman
                                    GEORGE R. EYERMAN

Certified True Copy of
letter on file in War Department

JOHN T. BURNS
Lt. Col., AGD
Adjutant General

Fig.79

George Eyerman Reply to Capt. P.M. Newmark, AG Department

Fig.80

Major Glenn Miller (left) and Major Sidney Smith

AIRCRAFT DELIVERY RECEIPT   •   SPECIAL INSTRUCTIONS

Capt. David J. Kull   12-16-44   _L/C_
FROM PILOT   DATE   AIRCRAFT TYPE

41-18957   590-   ~~FERR.~~ FLIGHT TEST
AIRCRAFT NO,   STATION AND UNIT

Pfc McKinney A-40   12-12-44   BURTONWOOD
SIGNATURE OF RECIPIENT   DATE   PLACE

DESTINATION _____
                        STATION AND UNIT

                MY FLYING TIME WAS _____ 7 _____ HRS. _ 05 _ MIN.

_____ FERRYING SQUADRON
        OPERATIONS OFFICER

                SIGNATURE OF PILOT _David J. Kull Capt AC_

326 FS FORM
NO. 327   1 ST COPY RETURNED TO FERRYING SQUADRON OPERATIONS

                        Reproduced by 902 w ENG. A.F. HQ CO IX ENGINEER COMMAND

Fig. 81

L-1 Aircraft Delivery Receipt December 16 1944

INQUIRY TO FIELD

Sus 30 Sep 46

NAME

Miller, Alton Glenn (Major) AC

ARMY SERIAL NUMBER

0505273

SOURCE OF INQUIRY

Ltr from Major Miller's attorney: Mr. David Mackay, 506 Madison Avenue, N.y. N. Y.

REASON FOR INQUIRY

Desires investigation be made re item appearing in newspaper indicating that part of the plane in which Major Miller was travelling was found on one of the Brittany beaches.

ORIGINAL INQUIRY HELD IN CORRESPONDENCE SECTION, ROOM NUMBER:

1E 541

ACTION TAKEN BY INVESTIGATION AND CORRESPONDENCE SECTION 30 August 1946

[ ] RADIOGRAM [ ] TELEGRAM [XXX] IMMEDIATE ACTION LETTER [ ] INDORSEMENT

MESSAGE CLASSIFICATION

SPXPC-G

SENT TO

CG, WESTERN BASE SECTION, ETO

INFORMATION REQUESTED (*Describe fully. MUST BE PARAPHRASED IF OUTGOING COMMUNICATION WAS CLASSIFIED "SECRET," "CONFIDENTIAL," "RESTRCITED."*)

Request information on which to base reply to following quote newspaper article submitted by the attorney of Major Millers estate:

..."A salvage crew cleaning up the Brittany beaches has reportedly discoverd the tail of an airplane which has been identified, by its numbers as the one the late Maj. Glenn Miller was aboard when he disappeared Dec. 14, 1944 on a flight from England to France".......

Routine radio sent COMGEN WBS in reply to Mess. #271001, 30 Sep 46. [illegible] sent Mr. Mackay for addit inf [illegible]. Reply recd from Mr. Mackay [illegible] radio sent COMGENWBS [illegible] furnishing facts as stated by Mr. Mackay. [illegible]

Fig.82

The Brittany Beach Report

6

THEORIES AND SCENARIOS

1. The Wilder Fringes

Information relevant to such an enigma as Glenn Miller's disappearance may originate in three or more areas : eyewitness accounts, documentary evidence and rumour. As we have seen, all three are dubious at the best of times : worse, they pass on by word of mouth into the realm of `fact' until their sheer frequency of repetition stuns the listener into belief. Don Haynes made no written statement except in his diaries, in which we can place no reliance whatsoever : he left no official account of the events he said occurred on December 15 1944. As regards any statement he may have made on December 21 to Colonels Early and Traistor in the Hotel des Etats Unis in Paris, no copy has been found.

This did not deter Haynes from verbal statements over the years : we located a curious tape possibly recorded on the West Coast of America in 1958, in which Don Haynes relates the story once again to an interviewer named Andy :

ANDY : Another question often asked is when was the last time you, Don Haynes saw Glenn Miller ?

HAYNES : Andy, you know Glenn took - *(At this point there is a break in the sound of about seven seconds, indicating the tape had been carefully edited before release. We have been unable to find an unedited version and there is no clue to the full length of the deleted portion).* The tape continues :

ANDY : - it ?

HAYNES: Yes. I had been over to Paris four weeks previous to this date to make arrangements for billeting the Band, and for bus transportation, and the various places we were to play to check they had amplification systems and so forth. But three days before I was due to leave, and precede the Band by another couple of days, Glenn said that he thought that he would go on ahead, and that I would bring the Band over afterwards.

ANDY : And he never gave you any reason why he was - ? *(Haynes interrupts).*

HAYNES No. He was. . . Glenn gave the impression that he had a lot of things to do and a very short space of time and as if he didn't have enough time to all the things he had planned to do. And this was not unlike him - because he would make split-second decisions. Even back in civilian life he was one to make split-second decisions, and was seldom ever wrong. So I said, well, Glenn, I have orders cut to precede the Band to the Continent. And he said in his unmilitary jargon - "Well, uncut 'em and get some cut for me !" Which was done. But I do have a funny feeling that he went on a trip that I had arranged with Colonel Baessell and Flight Officer Morgan in my place, and I can't help but sort of feel that I'm sort of on a rain check, as it were. The last time I saw Glenn was when I drove he and Colonel Baessell to a Beaufighter base about three miles outside of Bedford, England. That's in the Midlands about 52 miles north of London. It was a cold rainy foggy afternoon which is typical of English weather - they have summer over there on a Wednesday afternoon during July. We waited for the plane which was coming to pick them up from another base, piloted by a wonderful guy, Flight Officer Morgan, with whom I had flown all over the European Theatre. We didn't think he would find the field, but finally he did with his instrument flying, and came down and landed on the runway and didn't even shut the motor off. I drove the staff car out to the runway and put Glenn and Colonel Baessell on the plane. That was the last time I saw him - a funny thing there that I might add was that as Glenn stepped on the stair to get into this C-64 Norseman - it was a single-engined plane - he gathered his trench-coat about him to ward off the chilling mist, and before closing the door of the ship, he glanced up at the horrible weather and said `Even the birds are grounded today !'

This is classic Haynes stuff. There is no mention of Glenn having an appointment in Paris - that explanation would emerge ten years later in Don's diaries. On this tape, he categorically denies, after questioning, that Glenn gave him any reason for his wish to travel ahead of the Band. But subsequently Haynes realised that his story of the December 15 flight was so outlandish that he would have to generate reasons for Glenn opting to fly in atrocious weather in a tiny plane with no navigational equipment and a non-commissioned pilot. Further, he had to explain how Morgan found Twinwood Farm and landed in heavy rain with a 200 foot cloud-base : the pilot, he said, had flown a full tour of bomber missions (quite untrue) and they had `flown all over the European Theatre together' - also untrue. In fact, Morgan had been assigned to Norseman flight duties in late September 1944 from Jean Pace, moving from Wattisham to Abbotts Ripton. He flew General Goodrich and Colonel Baessell into Brussels in late October, where Baessell began setting up his projected flight with George Ferguson to take Glenn Miller to Paris on November 8. In November Morgan made four trips to Orly with Baessell, including the November 8 flight when Haynes went along; they dropped Glenn Miller at Bovingdon before going on to Paris. On November 25 Haynes caught a Bovingdon shuttle to Paris to arrange Band accommodation, returning on a similar scheduled flight on December 2. Haynes had certainly not flown `all over the ETO with Haynes'.

By 1958, Haynes had been asked on numerous occasions how Morgan managed to get into Twinwood in such foul weather. In the 1958 tape he makes no mention of Morgan's `bomber missions' - but stresses he had exceptional instrument flying abilities. *Not so*, says George Ferguson who often flew with Morgan and said that he had poor instrument-flying ability. *Not so*, said we - Morgan had received extensive instrument flying training including a Beam Approach Training Course ! We smiled wryly, listening to Haynes' account of the `birds grounded' incident - in his diaries he records that incident as happening firstly, outside General Goodrich's house where Baessell called briefly; secondly, whilst the staff car waited outside the Control Tower for Morgan to arrive, and thirdly, on the runway immediately prior to take-off.

Haynes' personal loyalty for Glenn Miller was frequently marred by the extraordinary errors and inconsistencies in his story.

2.   Scenarios and Rumours.

We have collated an extraordinary number of `true' explanations for the disappearance of Glenn Miller, from the telephone calls and letters we received following the publication of MILLERGATE. Here is a short selection -

1.   Norseman Shot Down by German Fighters - common rumour.
2.   Killed by jettisoned Lancaster Bombs - the Fred Shaw Story.
3.   Murdered in Paris - The John Edwards Story.
4.   Died of Cancer in London - brother Herb Miller.
5.   Shot Dead by Baessell - common rumour.
6.   Shot in Hotel Georg Cinq - the Mr. Weaver Story.
7.   Lived in UK until his death in November 1989 - Desmond Carrington.
8.   Went AWOL from Paris and died en route to America - Joan Heath.
9.   Glenn Miller was a Super-Spy. . . The Halpenny Story.
10.   Joy-riding in USAAF fighter, was shot down - 8th Fighter Command Letter.
11.   The Pasadena Connection - died in an Ohio hospital in December 1944. Speculation based on John Edwards story of letter from WW2 veteran.
12.   Court-martialled in New York, sentenced to 10 years in a military prison - the Metcalfe Story.
13.   Knew too much, killed by Parisian black marketeers. Denis Cottam Story.
14.   Fatally injured in jeep accident in the Ardennes. Speculation, (Dr. Pecora).

15.   Mugged/killed by bomb in London December 14 1944 - Speculation.
16.   Lost when C-47 Paris shuttle ditched in Channel after icing-up. Mr. Woods.
17.   Died in Rhodesia in 1956 - the Halpenny Story.
18.   Disappeared in November 1944, impersonated by Major Sid Smith.

By disposing of these fanciful theories, we could reduce the problem to manageable size by taking areas of probability, in which certain events *could* have happened, of which we do have proof in varying degrees :

* Miller did not board his Paris plane, went AWOL and remained in England.
* He met disaster on Thursday morning December 14, walking back to his hotel.
* He reached Bovingdon but never caught his Paris flight. Possibly arrested.
* He caught the flight but on reaching Paris vanished without trace.
* He died as a result of foul play or accident in France.
* After playing at Ike's December 16 party, he went AWOL and was lost en route home.
* He reached home but for some reason failed to return.
* He was injured in France and flown home unidentified.
* He disappeared on some earlier date in November 1944.

The main thrust of our investigation was to eliminate as expeditiously as possible the more outrageous stories. We applied a simple criterion : was there any supporting documentary or eyewitness evidence ? The reader must judge for himself.

■ Shot Down by German Fighters, Taken POW

A search of German fighter squadron records post-war produced no reports of a passenger-type plane shot down over the Channel. Further, had Miller been captured, the Germans would have seen this as a great propaganda opportunity, capable of affecting Allied troop morale, and they would have announced it without delay. A written inquiry found in Miller's 201 File from the AG Department to the Prisoner of War Department in Washington asking for information brought a negative reply.

■ Killed by Jettisoned Lancaster Bombs

We have discussed this scenario at length on Page 168 *et seq*, proving conclusively in the process that Morgan's Norseman could not have been involved in any incident on Friday December 15 1944. The evidence confirming that he departed Abbotts Ripton at 13.25 hours and flew east of London to Dymchurch and a watery grave off Le Touquet is beyond question, as is the conclusion that Glenn Miller was not aboard the aircraft. We would not wish to deprive Fred Shaw of his moment in history - certainly he saw a Norseman engulfed by bombs in mid-Channel, but it was UC-64A #43-5613, not Morgan's #44-70285. Further, it was on the repeat Siegen raid on December 16 1944, not the aborted mission the day before - on that day the Channel was covered by a full overcast at 800 feet, and it would have been impossible to see from 6,000 feet an aircraft at sea level. On the other hand, the weather on December 16 was already breaking up, and the formation of L-1 aircraft following Norseman #43-5613 from Bexhill to Chartres were able to see the Lancaster formation through breaks in the cloud. Finally, the L-1 aircraft delivery receipt from Chartres confirms the incident date as December 16 1944.

Fred Shaw cannot be blamed for confusing the dates - this happened to many other witnesses including Dixie Clerke and George Ferguson. Nor can we criticise author Roy Nesbitt in his `Aeroplane' article for believing that Morgan had over-flown Bovingdon, west of London, en route to Beachy Head and the Channel Bomb Jettison Area - Roy was unaware of the evidence in the Miller Burial and 201 Files, and he did not know that the Diver Gun Box in the Thames Estuary set up to ambush V-1 flying bombs was inactive on Friday December 15 1944.

The `Lancaster Bombs' theory, in fact, enjoyed an ephemeral popularity for a year or so, but the factual evidence was always against it, in reference to flight times, routes, airspeeds, restricted areas and the like. The final proof of the L-1 aircraft delivery flight from Bexhill, and the actual observation of Norseman #43-5613 being destroyed by bombs was merely the icing on the cake.

■ Murdered in Paris

Rumours that Glenn Miller was murdered or killed in a street brawl in the Rue Pigalle red light district of Paris have circulated for many years - we traced correspondence dated as far back as 1969. During that period the name of Pecora was encountered frequently as a doctor who had signed a death certificate or similar document for Major Miller (Page 65). Miller was reported to have died from head injuries (Page 66). We identified other connections in the Denis Cottam Story (Page 64) - he was informed by a bordello madame that her war-time boyfriend, a Captain in the US Provost Marshal Division, had seen and identified Major Miller's body. He had been murdered by black marketeers because, she said, `he knew too much'.

All these accounts were based on the premise that Miller reached France safely - that he was not aboard the Norseman, and Cottam was told by the bar tender in Fred Payne's British Bar that Miller was in the bar the day he was supposedly lost in the Channel. Once we established that the band leader travelled to Paris on Thursday 14 December 1944, these stories could not be ignored. But in 1973 researcher John Edwards (Page 65) was featured in an article in the now-defunct newspaper *REVEILLE* (Fig.76). He claimed that Miller was murdered in the Pigalle district on Monday December 18, three days after the Norseman went down, after sustaining a fractured skull. He mentions the `American military doctor' but does not name him - he finally recalled the name when we interviewed him in 1987.

As previously noted, Edwards possessed the photograph of Mr.Alex Sleap (Fig.55) who related that he had met the Norseman at Bovingdon and later saw Miller board a Paris shuttle flight. We now know that this occurred on November 8 and since Edwards based his whole theory on the fact this occurred on December 15, his story became unviable. Three years elapsed before we confirmed Glenn's December 14 flight.

There is no sound first-hand evidence whatsoever for the `murder' scenario. The bordello queen's story of the Provost Marshal Captain is circumstantial, but if we accept Joan Heath's evidence, Miller was alive on the morning of Sunday December 17 1944 when she helped him board a UC-78 Bobcat at Buc Field for an alfresco trip `Stateside' to visit his family. Edwards in 1987 knew nothing of this.

But what concerned us was the multiplicity of rumours, each of which attracted researchers over the years and deflected them from the real mother-lode of information in official records. We became convinced that many, if not all, were deliberate attempts at disinformation organised at high level in the US Army and Archives departments - supported by a concentrated programme of `scare tactics' like threatening calls, quiet `words of advice' from `friendly Americans', bugged telephones, threats of legal action and the like. We suggest that all these scenarios be regarded primarily in that light : their sheer volume and inventiveness can hardly be simple coincidence.

■ Died of Cancer in England

The sole source of this scenario was the late Herb Miller, whom we interviewed in 1987 (Page 71). He was also interviewed by the *Daily Mirror* in 1985 (Fig.77) but prior to our encounter we had rejected the cancer theory, as described on Page 83. Herb admitted frankly that he had no evidence to substantiate his belief, and that it was based wholly upon his disbelief of the Haynes story : if Glenn was not aboard the Norseman, he must have stayed in England. However, by June 1992 we were engaged in a final battle with the US Army Surgeon-General, amongst others, for access to Glenn Miller's 201 File including the medical section : until that issue was resolved, we could not dismiss the cancer theory. See also the Herb Miller-Russell Harty interview on a later page.

■ Shot by Colonel Baessell

We failed to trace the origin or any written version of this rumour, but like all the rest, it has a curious connection with other (circumstantial) evidence which endows the story with a shred of viability. After discovering in 1992 that Col. Baessell probably survived the war and drew a pension, we considered the possibility that Morgan was the only occupant of Norseman #44-70285. Major Miller and Baessell may even have disappeared *together* - and this could place Baessell in the vicinity at the time of Miller's death. If as we suspect, the Colonel *was* deep into the black market and Miller was using his VIP status to cover smuggling activities, Baessell might have been at Bovingdon when Miller was arrested and he may have incriminated the Colonel. But this is gross speculation and there was not a shred of evidence to support this rumour.

There is, however, an extended scenario which deserves mention. George Eyerman, the central figure in the Jimmy Fidler affair which is discussed on a later page, had stated that he was at a Paris airport to meet Miller's plane, but when it landed, Miller was not on board ! It has been suggested, quite without foundation, that Baessell shot Miller en route and jettisoned the body overboard - as we have said, nothing surprises us in this intriguing mystery ! However, we did find it disconcerting that a senior member of the AG Department, Col. Frank Herbert (who later became Adjutant General himself) sent a Captain Newmark to Hollywood to `reason' with George Eyerman - as a result of which George withdrew his statement *in toto* in a letter to Col.Herbert.

Yet Eyerman told Jimmy Fidler during a Los Angeles radio broadcast that some of Miller's Band had preceded him, that they and others including Eyerman had been at a Paris airport to meet Miller's plane, that the plane landed safely but Miller was not on board ! We regarded this statement as very important, if only because of the several interpretations that could be placed upon it.

First, if Eyerman was referring to the Norseman, and Miller *was* aboard when it departed from England, we could not eliminate the possibility that he had either jumped overboard in mid-Channel - or had been pushed. It is well-known that he disliked flying : it is remotely feasible that, watching the sea flow underwing very close to the wheels, with the weather closing in, Glenn may have panicked and jumped. But this is pure speculation, with no corroborative evidence of any kind other than Eyerman's story.

Second, if George was referring to the shuttle flight from Bovingdon to Orly on Thursday December 14 1944, it is improbable that Miller could have leaped from a passenger aircraft which carried an air quartermaster attendant. But suppose Glenn had simply not boarded the Dakota ? We recalled the Metcalfe story of Miller being court martialled in New York for black market activities in Europe - of which we were unable to find any proof. But there was a slight loophole : if Miller *was* arrested at Bovingdon on Thursday December 14 1944, the shuttle flight would arrive in Paris without him (as Eyerman reported). Further, US Court Martial Records in Falls Church, Virginia, stated that whilst there were no court martial records involving Glenn Miller, any accused person might suffer a nervous breakdown and become unfit to plead - in which case there would be an entry in his 201 Medical File. And the US Surgeon-General had denied us access to Miller's File - citing the FOI and Privacy Acts.

Thus we could not totally eliminate the possibility that George Eyerman had been telling no more than the truth - before his cosy chat with Captain Newmark of the AG Department. Indeed, if Miller had not boarded the December 14 flight, the court martial theory was perhaps the most viable explanation we could find.

We did, however, discard the theory that Miller was shot by Col.Baessell.

■ Shot in Georg Cinq Hotel in Paris

In late 1991 a Mr.Weaver called from Winchester with a somewhat disjointed story. In 1957 he had served with the R.A.F. Police and was told by a colleague that Glenn Miller was shot in the Georg Cinq Hotel in Paris in December 1944 by an Englishman who later became Sales Manager of an oil refinery located near Manchester. Mr.Weaver could not be accurate about dates or names, but recalled that he was told Major Miller had died instantly.

We investigated this story as thoroughly as possible, to the extend of writing to the Police Department Archives in Paris for murder records of the period : we were informed that no incident was reported to the Gendarmerie or the Sûreté, probably because no civilian was involved. It was routine for the Allied Forces to conduct their own investigation - and we recalled at once the Denis Cottam story of the madame and her Provost Marshal boyfriend, and the persistent rumours about Miller being murdered in Paris. We remembered the mysterious Dr. Pecora who had reputedly issued a death certificate - and we began to extrapolate the meagre information we had into a major scenario - a `what if ?' exercise in speculation. Suppose, we pondered, the incident occurred in the course of a party at the hotel (which was much frequented by Allied top brass at the time) and some senior officers were either involved or present. What action would be taken ?

It is all supposition and conjecture - depending on precisely *who* was involved - and since almost all British personnel in Paris at the time were in uniform, we can assume that the culprit may have been a British officer of high rank. The thoughts of those present would certainly be focussed on the impact of the news when it was released - specifically on troop morale. Men were fighting and dying in the frozen battlefields of the Ardennes and would resent senior officers junketing in Paris at the same time. It was barely possible, we thought, that the killing might have been hushed up and all concerned sworn to secrecy : Miller could be interred in an `unidentified isolated burial' operation in which his name would not appear on any official lists. And fortuitously, the missing Norseman provided an ideal cover story. Finally, was this the `social engagement' to which Haynes refers ?

Now, far-fetched as it may seem, there are some strange nuances about this story which, we suspect, may be interwoven with Denis Cottam's story of the Paris madame with an Army Provost Captain boyfriend who supposedly identified Miller's body. In 1973, John Edwards learned that four Army Provost Marshals had been involved in an investigation of Miller's murder, and obtained four names and addresses, all of which - strangely - were in Albuquerque, New Mexico. But Randolph AFB near Albuquerque, in fact, was the home base and training school for Provost Marshals, and the four men were :

Major H.D.Black, 7405 Gerris Avenue South East Albuquerque, NM
Major Wm.R.Hanna, 211 North Madison, Albuquerque NM
Lt.Col. Lyman P.Davison, 8305 Cutler Avenue North East Albuquerque NM
Capt. Everett D.Skinner, 1823 North Madeira, Albuquerque NM

Further, the name of the madame's boyfriend was a Mr. Bill Witberger of the Provost Marshal Division, and Major Davison's second name was Peter - was he the `Peter' involved in the 1944 investigation (Page 125) ? We wrote many letters in search of these men without result : NPRC at St.Louis and the Washington Records Center were unable to trace them - but we learned later that this is SOP for all inquiries about retired Provost Marshal officers. Perhaps someone out there knows where we can find Captain William Witberger. . . ?

But if this incident really happened, at what time and date ? Ignoring for the moment Joan Heath's account (see below) and assuming Miller flew into Paris before the Band, we can place the incident between 14.00 hours December 14 (after Miller landed at Orly) and 14.00 hours December 18, when Haynes arrived in Paris and found Miller missing. Reason suggests that he contacted SHAEF at once, was told something serious had happened and to get out to see General Barker without delay. In the LOC diary, he does so on Tuesday, and in MINUS ONE, on Monday evening. And next day the Norseman story emerged. . .

Before we leave this matter of the Provost Marshal involvement, mention should be made of a record (Figs.47,48) of a telephone call, found in the Miller 201 File, dated April 1971 - just before Don Haynes died. It was from an officer named with an undecipherable name, Deputy Provost Marshal at Randolph AFB, to `Records Center' (presumably the St.Louis Overland complex) quoting Glenn Miller's name and serial number. The caller asked "Are fingerprints on file ?"

Beneath the request is written `*Congressional Interest - Negative Again'* and below, the answer provided by a Mrs.Hicks : *"No fingerprints on file"* and alongside `WW2 Classified Files 10 May 1956'. This document fired the imagination : who wanted Miller's fingerprints in 1971, around the time of Haynes' death ? Why were they required ? What was the `Congressional Interest' noted ? Was a Congressional Committee already investigating Miller's disappearance in 1971 ? Was it SOP to keep a record of officers' fingerprints ? More important, why was the Provost Marshal Division in Albuquerque interested ?

Later we found a document in Miller's 201 File (Fig.48) which may be relevant. When he first joined the Army in 1942 Glenn was attached to the Army Specialist Corps, a non-military organisation apparently used to induct and train specialists in all fields before releasing them to the Regular Army. The ASC Department sent Miller's personal documents to the AG Department, and the covering letter listed the contents - including Glenn Miller's fingerprints.

So that, whilst the AG Department possessed Miller's fingerprints as far back as 1942, they denied having them in 1971 when the Provost Marshal requested them - almost certainly for purposes of identification. Why did the AG Department lie ? Well, had Miller been identified by the Provost Marshal Division, this would have destroyed totally the carefully-fabricated facade of deceit and concealment maintained over the years.

Was it mere coincidence that the PM inquiry was dated just before the death of Don Haynes in 1971 ? If so, it was but one of many such `coincidences'.

■ Lived in England until 1989

In 1990 the BBC broadcaster Desmond Carrington included a strange story in his programme :

> `An extraordinary happening recently : a bizarre notice appeared attached to a tree in the New Forest - a large substantial board which says - and I quote - "In memory of Alton Glenn Miller, born March 1 1904, died November 18 1989, having lived 45 peaceful and happy years in Great Britain. His last request - for his ashes to be scattered in the New Forest, and his music and his memory forgotten. His last words were `I never deserved my fame'. Goodbye, Glenn my dear - the story is ended'.

Our immediate reaction was to regard this as an elaborate hoax - or at best, part of the disinformation programme clearly being implemented by person or persons unknown. But some months later we received a call from a Mr.Hoare living in Winchester, to say that after leaving the R.A.F. he was friendly with an ex-R.A.F. sergeant, also de-mobbed, who had lived from 1945 to 1946 in the Dormer House in Calshot Road, Fawley, on Southampton Water. This was part of the old Drummond Estate, a long-established Hampshire family, and at the end of the war and subsequently, the Dormer House was leased to the R.A.F. flying boat base at Calshot for use as accommodation, although there were also civilian residents. The Administrative Officer at the time was Squadron Leader (later Air Commodore) Gaines, who died in 1983.

The sergeant told Mr. Hoare that during this period an American ex-officer wearing civilian clothes came regularly to meet a lady in one of the Dower House apartments, and the sergeant had no difficulty in recognising Glenn Miller - he was a great fan of the band leader and had seen his two films several times. Mr. Hoare investigated and learned that a Mrs. Drummond was living in the Dower House at the time : she was quite young and married to a Mr. Cyril Drummond, who was some 59 years her senior and failing in health. Mr. Drummond, in fact, died in 1945 and the American visited Mrs. Drummond quite regularly.

Mr. Hoare said it was probably sheer coincidence that the famous plastic surgeon Sir Archibald McIndoe lived at Fawley, only a mile or so from the Dower House. We began an in-depth probe of the links between the two stories, but after contacting all the crematoriums and Registrars of Births and Deaths in Hampshire, we found no record of the death of an 85-year old white male on November 28 1989. Had we done so, it would have been ironic, in that we had spent the four years before that date actively searching for a man who may have still been alive a few miles from Southampton ! It seemed possible that Glenn may have assumed a new name, or changed his own by Deed Poll, which made identification very difficult, but rather than abandon the matter entirely we marked the file `pending' and kept it open. Sure enough - when we encountered the `*Ghost Stations'* narrative by Bruce Halpenny, it contained the story told by Mrs. Betty Hockey. In March 1945, she attended a concert party at R.A.F. Beaulieu, only a mile or two from Fawley and Calshot. Major Miller arrived, accompanied by some other US officers, but other guests were discouraged from speaking to him.

Clearly, there is some evidence supporting the thesis that Miller remained in England - the Desmond Carrington story, Mr. Hoare's account of life at the Dormer House Calshot, and Mrs. Hockey's concert party at Beaulieu. Further, the Hoare and Hockey dates agree to some extent, i.e. early 1945 : the `farewell' notice-board in the New Forest, if genuine, suggested that Miller remained in England after his disappearance in 1944 for the next 45 years - and he vanished only 2 weeks before the first day of 1945 !

■ Joan Heath Story - Miller, AWOL from Paris, died en route USA.

We received an interesting letter from a Mr. Vic Porter of Teddington, Middlesex, relating the story told by a lady named Joan Heath. She was a WAAF MT driver assigned to Air Marshal Tedder at SHAEF MAIN Versailles, and whilst she is now 76 years old, she is very active and intelligent, with an excellent memory. Her statement reads :

`In December 1944 I was an LACW MT driver based at SHAEF Headquarters at Versailles, France, but it was probably December 17 when I was asked to drive Major Glenn Miller to an aerodrome near Paris. I was on late duty and I had, with several of my friends, gone to the general Mess to get a coffee. We had only just arrived when General Eisenhower and Major Glenn Miller came into the Mess also in search of coffee. Someone suggested we order something stronger and an impromptu party developed, which lasted until the early hours. A quartet of Glenn Miller's musicians was playing during this time. Most of the people were half-tipsy including some American aircrew. At about 2 or 3 a.m. the question of taking Major Miller to an aerodrome arose and General Eisenhower said : "Joan will take you to your aircraft".
`I was still on late duty and I had my car with me, so about 9 am. I drove Major Miller to Buc, together with his officer's valise and two PX boxes filled with Christmas presents. He said that he was going `Stateside' to see his family. At Buc Field he boarded a small aircraft - I recognised the crew who had been at the party. I am not sure what type of aircraft it was but it had twin engines and the tail rested on the ground. It was not a C-47 Dakota which I knew, having previously flown in the type. I have been shown a picture of a UC-78 "Bobcat" and it closely resembles the aircraft Miller boarded at Buc, which was a landing strip in open country about a mile from Versailles. On this occasion

186

the weather conditions were appalling, with snow still falling.

'I was able to hand Glenn Miller's valise and parcels up to him – Glenn stood on the steps of the aircraft, wished me a Happy Christmas and gave me a farewell kiss. After he entered the aircraft he turned to his right and sat down. I could see him in a window as the aircraft taxied away.

'Some days later I drove General Eisenhower in my car and I asked him if he had heard from Major Miller. He replied that he had not and added, I thought a little sadly, that "maybe he would never hear". The news, he said, was being kept quiet because Major Miller had gone without permission.

This account is remarkable for a number of reasons :

1) If true, it is the first positive evidence that Eisenhower knew what had happened to Miller - yet in a taped interview after the war he made no reference to the incident.

2) Whilst Joan was uncertain as to dates, it is a fact that on Saturday December 16 1944, there was a big party at SHAEF in honour of Eisenhower's promotion to General of the Army, held in a large communal dining room in the SHAEF complex, a compound which was surrounded by barbed wire fences with strict security. Both male and female Army officers used the dining room which was adjacent to the Officers Mess.

3) This could well have been the 'social engagement' mentioned by Don Haynes.

4) During a U.S. West Coast radio programme in 1946, the compére Jimmy Fidler stated that it was common knowledge that some of the musicians 'went over to Paris ahead of the Band'. Moreover, the general consensus amongst researchers is that some Band members knew part or all of the truth but were sworn to secrecy. Certainly, after the Queensberry Club show on December 12 the Band had no further engagements until their first Paris concert on December 21 1944.

5) Teddy Gower, the BBC engineer attached to the AEF Band from November 24 1944, flew with Miller to Orly on December 14 1944, travelling in the seat behind the band leader. We had always speculated why he was aboard, because reason suggests he would travel with the main band party on December 16. But his services would be needed at Eisenhower's party, to set up microphones and amplification equipment.

6) Buc Field, Code Y-4, became operational on 28 August 1944 immediately Paris was liberated, according to Research Division, USAF Historical Research Center, Maxwell AFB Alabama. It was used almost exclusively for air movements of *prominente* such as Winston Churchill and Mrs. Churchill. Maxwell AFB confirmed that the resident unit was 112th Liaison Squadron, using UC-78 Cessna Bobcat aircraft which fitted Joan Heath's description exactly and which she identified from a photograph. The 112th was permanently attached to HQ Squadron, SHAEF MAIN and assigned to ferrying/transport duty servicing VIPs and top brass from SHAEF.

7) The UC-78 was not capable of transAtlantic flights : the inference is that it was transporting Miller to some other base where he could board a larger aircraft such as a Douglas DC-4 (C-54). We were able to confirm that no Bobcat aircraft or west-bound transAtlantic passenger aeroplane had been lost in December 1944. There was no Missing Aircrew Report for a UC-78 in December. We also considered the possibility that a crashed Bobcat may have been the subject of the `Bordeaux Crash Letter'(Page 150).

8) Joan also recalls hearing an American pilot at SHAEF saying he had collided with an unseen aircraft on the day she saw Miller take off. Vic Porter recalls hearing a radio programme post-war in which one of Miller's superior officers said that if he hadn't attended that party `he would be alive today;

9) In Piers Brendon's book *IKE* (Secker & Warburg, 1987) we find :

> `When Ike had reason to celebrate, no one entered into the festive spirit more eagerly. Certainly it seemed that he had every reason to do so on Saturday December 16 1944, when indeed the whole SHAEF Headquarters was en fête. For the Supreme Commander had just been nominated for promotion to a newly-created rank, General of the Army.
> That day too, Mickey McKeogh got married to a WAC sergeant (in the beautiful but freezing chapel at Versailles) and Ike attended the wedding, drank champagne at the reception and kissed the bride. . .'

10) The Denis Cottam evidence suggests that Miller was in Fred Payne's British bar in Montmartre on Friday December 15 1944, at the time the Norseman went down. If true, Miller could have attended Ike's party the following evening.

11) Joan Heath said she had seen Col. David Niven at SHAEF several times, but he was not at the party. This tallies with his account of visiting Spa on Friday December 15.

Joan was not absolutely certain of the date but Haynes and the Band arrived at Paris Orly on Monday December 18, by which time Glenn had gone. The Norseman story was under consideration as early as Monday evening when Haynes reported to General Barker, inferring that SHAEF already knew Miller had flown out the day before. Ramstein AFB in Germany confirmed that Buc, code number Y-4, housed the 112th Liaison Squadron from September 1944 to June 1945. In Lord Tedder's book *WITHOUT PREJUDICE* (Cassell, 1966) he wrote that he (and Joan Heath, presumably) was at SHAEF on December 16 when the German offensive began, then at Verdun on December 19 with Generals Eisenhower, Dever, Bradley and Patton. He was back at SHAEF from December 21 - 31, just before he left for London and Moscow. Joan Heath is not mentioned in the book.

If Joan's story is true (and we believe the corroboratory evidence is very convincing) Eisenhower was deeply implicated. From his conversation with Joan he knew of Miller's flight home, and that she had driven Glenn to Buc Field. Almost certainly, it was his decision to keep the news secret.

■ **Glenn Miller - Superspy**

We located an interesting broadcast taped on North-East Radio by presenter Frank Wappatt. He had been interested in the fate of Glenn Miller for seven years, and his account contains some strange statements :

"At two o'clock on 15th December 1944, after a 2-day delay waiting better flying conditions, we are told that Miller concluded he could wait no longer, and the plane took off in bad weather from a small airfield near Bedford. The aircraft, a C-64 Norseman, was never to arrive in France."

According to various sources, Morgan took off at 13.25 from Abbotts Ripton (AG Memorandum), 13.45 from Twinwood Farm (Haynes diary) or 13.55 (MACR #10770). Miller was not delayed : his booked flight on 14 December 1944 was the earliest he could leave after the final Queensberry Club concert. The 2-day delay applied to the AEF Band Flight, from Saturday December 16 to Monday December 18. And the story of bad weather existed only for Don Haynes - aircraft were leaving Bovingdon as late as 15.00 hours on Friday December 15.

But later in the tape, Frank refers to a British band-leader Ray Shields, relating a story some may find hard to believe. Shields claimed that he had had a vision of an arm wearing an American officer's uniform, which he believed to be that of Glenn Miller who was trying to contact him. He approached a British medium Carmen Rogers, who passed on instructions via a seance to Shields, purporting to come from Glenn Miller. The band-leader followed the instructions and said he learned that no search was ever made for the aircraft. (That fact has been common knowledge via the MACR for more than 40 years !) Further, Shields claimed that Glenn Miller's effects had been taken away from Milton Ernest Hall before his disappearance was made known to the public - but Miller kept no effects there and Shields quoted the Milton Ernest valet Stilwell. When saying goodbye to Glenn Miller the day he disappeared, Glenn had told Stilwell `he would see Stilwell either that afternoon or first thing next morning'.

I have a copy of that tape and can find no such reference. Shields went on to claim that he had seen documents issued by Supreme Headquarters at High Wycombe, Bucks (but SHAEF REAR was located at Bushey Park, Herts). These documents were the MACR, Miller's Casualty Report and Report of Death. The plane, he said, was on its way not to Paris but to Bordeaux.

Finally, Shields suggested that Glenn Miller was involved in some way with espionage - that he found that his broadcasts to the German troops were being tampered with, upon which Glenn refused to do another broadcast. It was, Shields insisted, `mind-bending - the early stages of Big Brother 1984' ! Further, all Miller's wartime recording discs had vanished from a storage facility in London. Wappatt confirmed that they were missing (they had probably been stolen by private collectors). Further, Shields said, Miller had taken a crash course in German to collaborate 100% with British and Allied Intelligence ! His broadcasts to German troops, of course, were mild propaganda - but no more than that, and Wappatt found no trace of such broadcasts having been tampered with or modified. There is no evidence of any kind to support claims that Miller had been involved in espionage.

■ Shot Down in USAAF Fighter Plane

This has been discussed at length on Page 162.

■ The Pasadena Connection

All investigative writers encounter problems in differentiating rumour from fact, real evidence against speculation, and we began our research in 1986 by drawing up clear terms of reference. Any information, theory or scenario unsupported by evidence would be treated as rumour. Second-hand or uncorroborated evidence would be treated as circumstantial until supporting evidence changed its status. But we reserved the right to speculate, given reasonable grounds and a degree of justification : on that basis we reviewed the David Niven connection (Page 59) in the light of evidence from other sources, as a preliminary to extending our researches into America, and the results are tabulated below for ease of reference :

1) According to Niven, he was in Spa, Belgium on December 15 1944, and could not have met the Norseman in Paris, had Miller been aboard.

2) Niven *was* in Paris on Thursday December 14 and could have met Miller at Orly.

3) David had a so-far unidentified companion on his trip to Spa.

4) His real purpose at Spa was to rescue Marlene Dietrich, who was evacuated west by jeep and was at Spa at the same time as Niven.

5) Reason suggests that both jeeps travelled back towards Paris together. Their route passed through Marche and Rheims.

6) Historically, the name of Dr.Pecora has always been associated with Miller and a possible death certificate. Pecora, still alive, confirms he served at the Rheims Military Hospital during the Battle of the Bulge. He treated many casualties but no one that he *identified* as Glenn Miller.

7) Marlene's various biographies describe an accident with an over-turned jeep, at which she stopped to give assistance.

8) Niven did not return to Paris and was absent throughout the critical period from 15 to 31 December 1944.

9) Despite an exhaustive check of all Allied cemeteries in Europe, no trace of Glenn Miller's grave was found.

10) As confirmed by Herb Miller, Glenn never wore dog tags because of an endemic skin infection. Further, his orders for Paris bore an incorrect serial number. If he received head injuries and could not identify himself, he may have been evacuated back to America - authorised by Dr. Pecora at Rheims Military Hospital.

11) In 1973, John Edwards received a letter from a World War 2 veteran who claimed to have been in the same hospital ward in Columbus, Ohio when the band leader died from head injuries.

12) In April 1987, we received a letter from the State Registrar in Trenton, New Jersey, that Glenn Miller had died in Ohio in December 1944, giving an inquiry address as the Division of Vital Statistics, Columbus, Ohio. That letter was later disclaimed as `a typing error' (Fig.11).

13) In January 1949, Helen Miller and her mother Anna purchased a 6-grave burial lot, number 2584, in Mountain View Cemetery, Altadena, California. The graves were in two groups - 4, 5 and 6, and 10, 11 and 12. There were only 5 members in her family : herself, her two parents and her two adopted children. Helen died in 1966 and was interred in Grave #5. Her parents Fred and Anna Burger were cremated and their ashes interred *between* graves 10 and 11, and 11 and 12 respectively. Thus, only one of the 6 graves is officially occupied and inevitably we asked ourselves for whom the 6th grave had been intended. We were refused permission to make an electronic scan of the Lot which would not have disturbed nor desecrated it in any way.

We know that Glenn Miller left England on December 14 and was not a passenger on the Norseman. Unless he had been murdered or suffered an accident and the body had been concealed, only two alternatives remained - either he had been severely injured and repatriated to America, or he had flown home clandestinely and never returned. The Joan Heath account supports the latter thesis very strongly, but unless we obtained Miller's 201 File (including the Medical Section) and the final Service Record with his last movements, his fate would remain a matter for speculation. But we believed sincerely that the evidence set out above more than justified extending our inquiries to America. The results are set out in MILLERGATE, but we are now able to add flesh to the skeleton facts available in 1987.

First, the existence of a massive cover-up was not only possible - we had incontrovertible evidence in the form of documents variously forged, suppressed, altered or actually abstracted from official files. Further evidence confirmed that Helen Miller had been denied vital information, and that the Miller family in California were exerting every effort to prevent us publishing MILLERGATE. Yet we could find no evidence of interference with any other author (scores of books and articles have been written about the disappearance of Major Miller, many containing gross errors and assumptions).

This phase occurred in 1986, at an early stage in our investigations, and we began by writing to the Pasadena Cemetery Association (representing Mountain View Cemetery in Altadena) to confirm Helen's dates of birth and death and details of family members interred in Lot 2584. This elicited the information set out above, revealing that 5 of the 6 graves were unoccupied, and we wrote in January 1987, this time revealing our interests and our authorisation from Herb Miller to investigate Glenn's death. We asked for a simple denial - that Glenn Miller was not interred in Lot 2584. The letter was headed `confidential'.

Now, at that point in time it would have been to our mutual advantage if the PCA had issued such a statement - we would then have abandoned the line of inquiry as unproductive. But for some reason PCA were not prepared to issue a denial - moreover, they had shown our `confidential' letter to Mr. Steve Miller himself ! Remarkably, Steve made no attempt to contact us : instead, he wrote a furious and accusing letter to Herb Miller in Dulwich, London, saying in effect : `*Get this guy off our backs !'*

In February 1987, lacking a response from Steve, I asked American researcher Royal Frey, a friend of the Miller family, to forward a letter to him. This read in part :

`My dear Steve -
*Royal Frey has kindly offered to forward this letter. He will have told you of the
considerable progress I have made towards solving the mystery of Glenn's
disappearance - I am a professional author, and at first sight my interest could
be seen as financial. This is far from true - I am comfortably placed, having 8
novels published.*
*`I was a wartime Spitfire and Hurricane pilot and spent 25 years in aviation. I
was an Air Traffic Controller and a trained aircraft accident investigator, which
seems adequate experience to undertake this investigation. Initially it became
increasingly clear to me that Glenn was an innocent victim of circumstances,
going along willy-nilly with a `press-on' macho colonel and an inexperienced
non-commissioned pilot.*
*`I believed I could show that Glenn had certainly not "leaned on" Baessell and
Morgan to make the flight, regardless of bad weather, but gradually I noted
many discrepancies : the weather was in no way like the "200 foot cloud-base
and pouring rain" described by Don Haynes. I learned that Bovingdon-Paris
shuttle flights continued until 15.00 on Friday December 15 1944 and it seems
certain Glenn was aboard one of them. Certain facts have now emerged :*

1) *Glenn made it safely to Paris.*

2) *He and several SHAEF officers dined out in Paris : there was an unfortunate
   accident in which Glenn sustained a fractured skull, dying early on Friday 15
   December 1944.* (Note : these speculations, derived from an interview with John
   Edwards, were erroneous but we did not know this at the time - Auth.)

3) *The death certificate signed by Captain David Pecora, US Medical Corps
   was seen many years ago by Lt.Col. Corrigan, USAF, and that some form of
   certificate was used by David Mackay to obtain probate for the will.* (Note :
   what Tom Corrigan saw, in fact, was the Report of Death documents : lawyer
   Mackay used the FOD document as a legal death certificate. Auth.)

4) *Herb (Miller) tells me Helen received a telephone call from Paris the day
   after Glenn went missing - contrary to reports that she was not notified until
   December 23 1944.*

*`We have suspicions, therefore (and at this time I stress they are only suspicions)
that Glenn was shipped home and cremated or interred in a grave in the Burger
family lot at Mountain View Cemetery, Altadena. The letters we have received
from the PCA fail to clarify the matter. In my last letter to them, I suggested that
if I was correct, all unnecessary publicity for the family could be avoided. Given
a signed affidavit that Glenn is in Mountain View, I would guarantee to keep the
location totally secret - my aim throughout has simply been to disprove the
various theories.*
*`I also offer continuing privacy for the family and I guarantee to omit all men-
tion of yourself and Jonnie, save as a purely historic reference. Let me repeat
that I am trying to produce this book in a way which will cause minimum incon-*

venience, disturbance and personal trauma to the family - an aim with which Herb agrees fully.

`*To demonstrate my sincerity, I am more than willing to send you a copy of the MSS before we go to press - we will amend any points you consider need attention.'*

Steve wrote to Herb Miller in very strong terms after receiving this letter : the latter's agent Jonathan Bailey rang me to say Herb was somewhat distressed but also angry - his reaction had been `What the hell have you got to hide ?'. We wrote at once to Steve as follows :

`*Dear Steve -*

`*I am extremely sorry that family friction has been caused by my investigations. I have tried always to protect the interests of the family because Glenn was and is one of my lifelong favourites. Please allow me to explain what has transpired.*

`*First, Herb was involved only in so far as he gave me an invaluable interview : I undertook to pass on to him everything I learned and this I have done.*

`*Second, the other assistance I received from him was a letter (of authorisation) to the PCA, introducing me as a serious researcher and asking them to provide all possible help.*

`*I do not wish to go again into the reasons which led me to believe that Glenn may be interred in the family Burial lot - but would ask you to put yourself in my position. I received three letters from the PCA, stating that Helen was interred in Grave 5, and her parents **between** Graves 10 and 11, 11 and 12. Finally I asked them for a straightforward `yes' or `no' to the question "Is Glenn Miller interred in Lot 2584 ?" I offered complete confidentiality, given a signed confirming affidavit. They have not thus far provided a denial.*

`*We have two ways of resolving this dilemma. First, that a plain denial is forthcoming from the PCA that our conclusions are mistaken. I will publish that denial willingly and in full. Second, if I am right, we should cooperate in deciding what shall be published, if anything. I undertake to follow your wishes to the letter.*

`*I trust this letter will show that I have only your best interests at heart.*

This letter (unanswered, as were all the rest) was a significant turning point in the inquiry. We had regarded the Pasadena Connection as just one more whacky scenario to be eliminated - as soon as the PCA and/or Steve Miller issued their official denial. But this was not forthcoming : it seemed that we had disturbed a hornet's nest ! More to the point, we were now convinced that Pasadena really had `something to hide' - and we asked a friend in LA, retired Flying Tigers engineer Bill McAllister, to investigate. His report was disturbing in the extreme :

`*In the case of the missing Corpse, I set off with my fellow-sleuths Murray Hamilton (well-known flyboy and oilman), Sterling Blakeman of the USAF 100th Bomber Group Association Historical Committee and a PR man from Green Hills Cemetery. From the last named, a comment that the wariness of admin staff at Mountain View during our visit was due to inditement and possible incarcera-*

tion of two members of staff for mortuary practices.

`*Helen is in Lot 2584 but no one will confirm who is also in the unmarked Lot with her. We identified the Lot with the help of groundskeepers, in lack of any help from the Cemetery Administration, who said later they had had many inquiries from English people.*

`*Finally, all my helpers here agree there is a bizarre strangeness about the Cemetery's attitude ! Good luck with the book - BILL.*

Our US attorney Clifford R.Anderson wrote to the Pasadena Cemetery Association.

`*Dear Mrs.King -*
I have been retained by author Wilbur Wright in connection with obtaining information as to the existence or non-existence of the burial of Mr.Glenn Miller. I understand you have refused to admit or deny that Mr.Miller is buried in your facility, on the grounds of privacy. Yet, in a letter of January 15 1987 you did set forth three people who are buried there : even the identity of the purchasers of the plot and the names of the three persons buried there.
I find this inconsistent. Mr.Wright is a legitimate author researching the life of one of the country's great heroes. I am at a loss to understand your position.
Yours very truly   *CLIFFORD J.ANDERSON*

At that point in time, we had been trying for almost a year (from December 2 1986) to obtain a simply confirmation from Mr. Steve Miller and/or the Pasadena Cemetery Association, that Glenn Miller was not buried in Lot 2584 in Mountain View Cemetery : Bill McAllister had been sent packing, Steve Miller had responded to none of our letters and had written instead to Herb Miller complaining bitterly. The situation, we felt, could have been resolved much earlier, and the delay had served only to deepen our suspicions that something was amiss.

On September 24 1987 we wrote direct to the PCA , pointing out that we had written to them several times asking for a simple denial, without result. We outlined our position, should we have to go to litigation, mentioning a large sum in loss of profits etc. and the resultant adverse publicity to the Miller family. All this, we said, could be avoided by the simple denial we sought but we would seek an injunction, if necessary, to probe the cemetery records. Back came a letter from a Mr.Brown at Mountain View Cemetery on 2 October 1987, which stated :

`*In our letter dated January 15 1987 we have given you all the information on interments on the East 1/2 Lot 2584 that we have. Examination of interment records does not reveal the name of Alton Glenn Miller or Glenn Miller.'*

We responded by listing the evidence in our possession : we suggested that it was quite possible that a body had been interred, possibly unofficially, early in 1949 and the event unrecorded and unknown to the present administration. Our reasoning was fairly clear at that time :

1)   The persistent refusal to deny or admit anything generated suspicion.

2) To speculate, if Glenn's remains had been located in 1948, the State Department and the Adjutant General's Department would not wish to have the news released - they had been circulating the Haynes story of the Norseman consistently whilst knowing it to be false.

3) Helen Miller would insist on re-interment in a suitable location near her home in California. But since Findings of Death and Reports of Death had already been released, no death certificate was available - which ruled out legal interment.

4) The obvious solution was a quiet but unofficial re-interment in Mountain View, where Helen had purchased a 6-grave Lot for her 5-member family. The US Government could arrange such things - and quite possibly it was done without the knowledge of the PCA or the Mountain View Cemetery management. For that reason we requested first, a denial statement signed before a notary public; second, access to Cemetery records and third, permission for an electronic scan of the Lot.

A Mr. Olafson responded to Anderson's opening broadside on behalf of the PCA on November 3 1987 :

> `Dear Cliff -
> With respect to Mr.Wright's letter, the interment records of the Association are quasi-public and may be inspected at any time during business hours. The other suggestions set forth in his letter are not acceptable to the Association. In this state the remains of a decedent cannot be interred anywhere without a permit from the appropriate state or country office, and without the appropriate records being maintained accurately describing the exact place of interment. Mr. Wright's inference that remains were interred without such a permit and without the appropriate records is a direct accusation that my client has violated the law, which is untrue and defamatory in nature. In view of the pending litigation involving a local mortuary and crematory, the publication of any untrue allegation that my client has violated any law relating to the interment or disposal of human remains could have very serious implications.'

Mr. Olafson wrote to us again on December 21 1987 :

> `The information you have received regarding the interments in the East 1/2 of Lot 2584 is the sum total of the information available. The Association has reviewed whatever records that may exist and copies of all public records have been made available to you.'

Some eight months passed without further progress, until the Miller family got into the war by engaging new attorneys, Laveley and Singer from Century City, Los Angeles. We had circulated friends and fellow-researchers with the idea of holding a seminar into the Glenn Miller mystery - a proposal to which the Millers reacted strenuously. The event was no more than a working lunch at a Midlands hotel with everyone covering his own expenses, but we received a broadside from Los Angeles : apparently, we had not sought permission from the Glenn Miller Trusts, Steve and Jonnie Miller. Moreover, it seemed we were violating applicable state statute and common law, federal and state laws prohibiting acts of `unfair competition', `false designation of origin' and `deceptive trade practices', to say nothing of `copyright infringement', `violation of state and federal securities laws', and/or violation of laws pertaining to solicitation of monies for purportable charitable or educational purposes'. . . We reached at once for the dictionary to look up `purportable', without success. Once the laughter subsided, we recognised the letter for what it was - a thinly disguised `frightener'. Further, we were admonished to immediately cease and desist using Glenn Miller's name for commercial purposes without prior written consent from Steve Miller, amongst others. (This remarkable statement ignored tacitly our several letters to Steve Miller which had gone unanswered !). The letter was couched in the usual tortuous legal phrases designed to scare off unwanted customers, and we replied promptly, defining our own rights :

> `Any writer can conduct research into such matters and must be free to benefit financially from his work. The dictionary defines `scenario' as `a summary of the plot of a play', i.e. a work of fiction. No scenario, per se, can be `false or fabricated'. However, if an author makes a definitive statement claiming certain facts are true, this is a different matter. He is not saying "This could have happened -" (pure speculation) but "This did happen" (statement of fact).
> Glenn Miller was a VIP in his own right : all such persons are liable to be written about, and it is ridiculous to suggest that no one can write about Miller without first obtaining permission.
> The whole situation could have been resolved at the outset by a simple denial by the PCA and Mr.Miller. We have leaned over backwards to assist, protect and insulate the Miller family from adverse publicity : for our pains we have been ignored, abused and threatened. It is difficult to see how we could establish a dialogue with Mr.Miller in such circumstances.
> We are advised that there is no legal requirement anywhere in the world to seek prior permission before conducting an investigation of this nature. There is a requirement to clear the use of material, but Mr. Miller has consistently refused my offer to provide a copy of the book MSS for his perusal and amendment where necessary.
> Even at this late stage we are prepared to send a MSS copy without prejudice and we await your further instructions.'

There was no immediate response and we wrote again to Laveley and Singer on 12 October 1988 advising that we were proceeding with the publication of MILLERGATE, and that we were prepared to meet Mr. Miller in Los Angeles if necessary. Our offer of a MSS copy was accepted on 21 October 1988 - and as a salutary warning they sent us a 30-page transcript of a case taken up by actor Clint Eastwood, to demonstrate what happened to `criminals' like us. The letter ended by defining their clients' rights against all manner of dreadful eventualities which seemed to us quite meaningless in the general context.

The MSS (at that time entitled `Search for a Legend') was dispatched on October 26 1988, with a note :

> `Our purpose in sending this MSS for your client's consideration is to strive for minimum publicity and inconvenience. He should mark clearly in red ink any

items he wants changing and return the MSS for amendment. A revised version will be provided by return. If that meets with his approval, we should be able to draw up a written release. We now have full copies of the Burial Files for Glenn, Morgan and Baessell : if your client has not already seen these files, we would be pleased to provide copies. We would suggest a period not exceeding 90 days as adequate for assessment of the MSS.'

We were extremely uneasy about the degree of interference exercised by the Miller family, which contrasted remarkably with the restrictions applied to numerous other authors - which was nil, no matter how outrageous and speculatory their material might be. We wrote to attorneys Laveley and Singer in Los Angeles quoting one book published in the UK which contained no less than 13 specific errors, and another published in 1980 with 4 major errors and numerous unjustified speculations. Why, we wondered, had we been singled out for such special attention ? Was it, perhaps, because we had got closer to the final solution than anyone else ? We asked the Miller attorneys what authorisations had been given, or alternatively, what legal action had been initiated against other authors, but predictably, there was no response.

On 6 December 1988 we wrote to them again, asking when we might expect acknowledgement of receipt of the MSS and replies to our various letters : again, there was no response and on January 14 1989 we sent a fax message :

'IN THE ABSENCE OF ANY RESPONSE TO OUR SEVERAL LETTERS REFERRING TO THE PROVISION OF A COPY OF THE MSS WE NOW INTERPRET YOUR FAILURE TO RESPOND AS A TACIT ADMISSION THAT YOUR CLIENT
(a) HAS NO OBJECTIONS TO THE PUBLICATION OF THE BOOK
(b) REQUIRES NO CHANGES IN THE CONTENT
WE DEEPLY REGRET THAT ALL OUR EFFORTS TO ACCOMMODATE YOUR CLIENT BY ALLOWING HIM FULL ACCESS TO THE MSS PLUS A PERIOD OF THREE MONTHS IN WHICH TO READ IT HAS BEEN IN VAIN.'

We saw this unwarranted delay as a `stalling' exercise intended to delay publication as long as possible : five days later Laveley and Singer replied that because of the holiday season and other circumstances, their clients had not yet had the opportunity to meet and discuss the `inaccuracies and fabrications' in the MSS. We were asked to `*discontinue our strategy of sending self-serving and posturing letters which attempt to assert legal positions based on erroneous assumptions and misinformation'*. There was no written warning that the boogey-man might get us if we didn't behave, but the inference was plain to see. Incensed, we replied on 25 January 1989 :

`Thank you for your letter. The following points are relevant :
1. *The sole part of the MSS relating to your clients is in Chapter 6, a total of 7 pages, #146-153.*
2. *To suggest that a 3-month period is insufficient to form an opinion is ridiculous : a discussion lasting half a day would be ample. We regard your attitude as simple delaying tactics, confirmed by a review of previous correspondence and your reluctance to respond.*

3. It is impossible to continue further if you insist on introducing an element of personal vilification which helps no one. The deadline of January 15 1989 has elapsed and this correspondence is now closed.'

Some 5 months elapsed, with no contact from Los Angeles. A brief note dated June 27 said that the Miller family were `finalising comments' and a reply would be sent within a few days. But it was not until August 29 1989 that we received a long and rambling letter from Los Angeles, in which the writer made the basic error of confusing legitimate speculation with statements of fact : throughout the MSS we had been scrupulous to differentiate between the two. There was comments about an `imagined scenario' (a scenario being an imaginary story outline by definition) concerning rumours which we had described as being in general circulation - the attorneys wanted us to identify the source of such rumours, which was manifestly impossible, when some stories were current in Britain, America, Canada and Australia at the same time.

A few simple corrections were requested - details of the house Glenn was building, not in Arcadia (as had been reported in several contemporary books) but in Duarte, with a Monrovia address. Helen Miller had died on June 2 1966, not June 6. The letter refuted our statement that we had had no response to our letters from Steve Miller - but the fact remains that between opening our inquiries in December 1986 and receiving our first letter from Laveley and Singer in July 1988, answering on behalf of Steve, we had written 3 times to him without response.

The required minor changes were made and later in 1988 we received the `all-clear' from Los Angeles to publish the book, now named MILLERGATE. But in retrospect, we were baffled by the extreme reactions displayed by the Millers and their attorneys - the correspondence confirmed that we had taken all possible steps to protect their privacy - yet we were accused of `unprofessional conduct' ! What were their motives ?

One further possibility exists, to explain why Helen Miller purchased an apparently-unnecessary 6th grave in Burial Lot 2584. It is this : perhaps she knew what had happened, that Glenn was alive but would not be coming home. But one day he would pass on, and Helen wanted his last resting place to be beside her own, in Mountain View Cemetery.

■ Court-Martialled in New York

In 1990 we received a letter from an ex-R.A.F. engineer Mr.Metcalfe :

`In late December 1945 I was detached to an American Air Force base at Foggia, Italy, where I read a news item concerning Major Miller, either in the "Stars and Stripes" newspaper or some official bulletin. It said that a Major Alton Glenn Miller had been court-martialled in New York in December 1944 for black market activities in the ETO. He was sentenced to 10 years in a military prison.'

We wrote to the Historical Branch at Ramstein AFB in Germany, which held wartime copies of the Mediterranean issue of `Stars and Stripes', the US forces newspaper, but no issue between November 1944 and March 1945 carried such a story. On January 15 1991 we wrote to the US Army Court of Military Review, Falls Church VA. asking for information of any court martial involving Miller and/or Baessell. They replied March 18 1991 :

`In response to your inquiry, we have searched the court martial indices and do not find a court martial conviction in either of these names. Further, cases in which the accused is tried in absentia are permanent court martial records. This office also retains records of proceedings in cases which result in acquittal. The records also include court-martials held in the ETO as well as other jurisdictions world-wide.'`*

This seemed fairly straightforward - until we thought of cases in which an accused had been arrested and indicted, but for medical reasons had been found unable to plead. We telephoned Falls Church on 0101-703-7561758 and spoke to a Mary Dennis. She advised us that there would be no permanent court martial record in that event, but there would be an entry in the accused's 201 personal file, Medical Section.

There was one remaining aspect which occupied our attention : *If there was substance in the Metcalfe Story, why was the court martial held in New York ?* We recalled that Helen Miller had remained in New Jersey for almost three years before joining her family in California - we had assumed that she believed that this was the first place Glenn would seek her if he ever returned. But further inquiries showed that all military courts martial for the Eastern Seaboard States in America were held at the military prison on Ryker's Island in the East River of New York. That was as far as facts could take us - we might speculate that Miller had been arrested at R.A.F. Bovingdon, as a known associate of Colonel Baessell, on Thursday December 14 1944 - and had been flown back home for trial. Further, because of the intense strain to which he had been subjected for six months, we further speculated that he may have had a nervous breakdown and had been flown south to a hospital near Columbus Ohio - with which we have already established connections. But it was only speculation at the best of times - there was no substantive evidence and we abandoned that line of inquiry as inconclusive.

■ Mugged or Killed by Bombs in London

The last time Glenn Miller was seen alive was at 02.30 hours outside the Milroy Club in Stratton Street, Mayfair, London on Thursday December 14 1944. He said good-night to the remaining members of his party, R.A.F. pilot Tony Bartley and USAAF Lt.Pulitzer, and walked off into the fog heading north for the Mount Royal Hotel at Marble Arch. From that moment we can evolve a number of possible scenarios in which Glenn caught the Bovingdon bus later that morning about 09.30, reached Bovingdon Terminal and was either arrested, or caught a shuttle flight to Paris. There is much evidence to suggest that he arrived safely in Paris, but we looked closely at another possibility - that he may have been mugged and killed during his lonely walk to the hotel. (It is a historical fact that one could walk unmolested through British cities in the black-out during the war). But we checked the New Scotland Yard Archives and confirmed that there was no such incident reported.

A second possibility was that Miller was killed by a flying bomb, but again, the Imperial War Museum confirmed that no V1s or V2s were launched at London that night. Since Miller, as far as we can ascertain, did leave England, the viable theories are reduced to the two already mentioned - arrest, or a safe flight to Paris where Glenn Miller vanished without trace. But we should not disregard entirely the George Eyerman story, in which he described waiting in Paris for Miller's aircraft - which arrived as expected but with no trace of the band leader on board.

Of all rumours to reach print in the past 45 years, that produced by Bruce Barrymore Halpenny (©*GHOST STATIONS, Casdec Ltd, 1986*) is the most extraordinary. His account, summarised and reproduced by kind permission of the author, begins :

`From the evidence, Miller was a spy and his music was the means for sending coded messages *(presumably to the Resistance - but who was he spying for ?)*. The OSS were using him and by December 15 1944 he was getting snappy and restless. Nothing to do with the flight to Paris, because he never took off in the Norseman. Lt. Don Haynes was said to have been at Twinwood Farm but post-war many people began to doubt Haynes' story. Here are the facts :
The C-64 Norseman came in as planned and took off, according to Haynes, at 13.55 hours *(Wrong - Haynes quoted 13.45 as departure time from Twinwood)*. Haynes drove Miller and Baessell to the field - *(the narrative now follows closely the Haynes diaries)* - and the weather was very bad (sic). Morgan was `a very experienced pilot with 32 missions on B-24s, a good pilot'. Halpenny's description of the boarding, take-off and disappearance of the plane is pure Haynes fantasy. But here we come to the startling part of the Halpenny version :
`As the Norseman taxied round for take-off, Miller and Baessell got out, using a secret tunnel leading from Twinwood Farm to Thurleigh Field (2 miles away). There, they were spirited away to an unknown destination. Morgan after take-off flew to nearby R.A.F. Podington which was `the furthest American airfield west of Twinwood' (meaning Morgan would not have to fly over any US base which might identify him. But what of Burtonwood on Merseyside ?).
`At Podington the Norseman was destroyed by being broken up and buried in a recent bomb crater. There was no search for the aircraft - because it never left for Paris. Here, Halpenny quotes the evidence of an ex-WAAF `Muriel Dixon' (married name Dixie Clerke) and also of John Edwards (whose information was at times far from reliable). But, Halpenny continues, Major Miller had to be got rid of `to save an international scandal' *(which is not defined or described)*. The task fell to Colonel Baessell `*who was Executive Officer and General Goodrich's personal pilot'* ! He was neither, of course. Halpenny's account opens with the letter from Mrs. Betty Hockey. She claimed that she attended a concert party at Beaulieu, Hampshire, in March 1945 and Major Miller arrived with some other officers. He was on his way to Beaulieu Airfield, and no one approached him.
So what was the truth, according to Bruce Halpenny ? He was contacted by a Wing Commander Stidolph who told him that he met Morgan in Rhodesia - the pilot had been joined by Baessell in 1950 : Miller was also there, but wanted to move to Singapore. Morgan had told Stidolph that the `Hoover Boys' (FBI) were `in on it' and many people had been warned off. *(The FBI handled internal American affairs - overseas commitments were the responsibility of the OSS until the CIA was created in 1947)*. Miller, Stidolph said, had been ill for some time with cancer and wished to visit a doctor in Singapore, introduced by Baessell, who might help him. Glenn stayed in the East for some time and Morgan said he was feeling his old self again. But Glenn believed he was being watched, and the two returned to Rhodesia where Miller died in 1956.

Ex-R.A.F. Special Security man Bruce Halpenny Barrymore is the author of the 'Ghost Stations' series, serving during the Suez period and the nuclear testing programmes. We wrote at once to the Chief Registrar of Births and Deaths in Zimbabwe, to request a death certificate copy, but of course, none was forthcoming. It is difficult to assess fairly this hodge-podge of rumour, speculation and conjecture - it contains much of the fictitious Haynes story - yet accuses him of being the central figure in the 'cover-up'. There is no real confirmation of the second-hand evidence of the R.A.F. Wing Commander, the destruction of the Norseman at Podington, the visit of Miller to Singapore or his 'death' in 1956. Specifically, there is no reference to his motives which forced him into exile - and the 'spy' aspect has long since been exploded by analysis of his 'Music for the Wehrmacht' programmes.

But Mr.Halpenny's account appears to have connections with the recent discovery that Baessell survived the war and drew a pension, the 1950 request for his dental data (presumably for identification) and the 1970 Provost Marshal request for Miller's fingerprints.

*　　*　　*

The scenarios, theories and rumours we have described in this chapter by no means exhaust the vast head-waters of speculation - we have merely isolated some of the more ingenious, outrageous and often hilarious accounts about the disappearance of Major Glenn Miller. In our own investigations, we have tried scrupulously to exclude unjustified speculation and conjecture - there has been too much of that already. Rather, we have relied predominantly on documentary and eyewitness evidence, and only in such cases as the Pasadena Connection (which features an abundance of circumstantial evidence) have we ventured to construct a scenario which might fit the case. Part of the problem posed by the Miller Mystery is the almost embarrassing volume of evidence - many readers of MILLERGATE tell me thay had to read the book twice before the jigsaw pieces fell into place. But until we penetrated the Miller 201 Personal File, it would all remain conjecture.

■　Disappeared in November 1944 - Impersonated by Major Sid Smith

Startling as it may seem, this scenario (suggested by a one-time member of the Glenn Miller Society) has a weird flavour of reality and we could not fully abandon it. Major Miller, it will be recalled, flew to Paris on November 8, being dropped at Bovingdon by John Morgan to catch a shuttle flight to Orly. He attended the November 15 conference on the forthcoming Band tour, and according to George Simon and Geoffrey Butcher, he returned on November 18.

But when Joan Heath said her recollection of the date of the Eisenhower party was shaky (we identified it as Saturday December 16th) we examined her story once more, specifically the fact that it had been snowing heavily - she described a foot of snow on the runway. Inquiries at R.A.F. Meteorological Archives in Reading had already confirmed it did not snow at Bovingdon on December 15 - moreover, the actual weather reports (Figs.21,22) contained no references to snow - indeed, in the prevailing synoptic situation over Europe snow was improbable.

On the other hand, the records did confirm that light snow occurred at Bovingdon on November 7-8th, and French records show considerable snowfalls in Northern France in the latter half of November. Could it be possible, we wondered, that Miller had departed from

Buc Field at Versailles on November 18 - en route for America and a well-earned leave ? We began a close check on his movements and found some anomalies. First, he made only two public appearances at AEF Band performances between November 18 and December 15 1944. According to Geoffrey Butcher, on Sunday November 26 1944 Major Glenn Miller appeared on the stage at a `Carnival of Music' charity concert at the Granada Cinema, Bedford, and conducted four USAAF dance bands in the concert finale'.

As far as we can establish, he did not play an instrument at all, and it would not have been difficult to teach a `stand-in' the rudiments of conducting. His last appearance was at the Queensberry Club on Tuesday December 12 (Figs.65). Again, according to our best information, he did not play the trombone and spent most of the performance talking to various people.

If, as we may speculate, he vanished on November 18 from France, and for some reason the top brass wished to conceal the truth, who could they employ to impersonate Major Miller ? Look at Fig.80 : one officer is Glenn Miller, and the other is Major Sid Smith, Security Officer at 8th AFSC, Milton Ernest at the time Miller vanished. But which is which ? Was the resemblance sufficient to pass muster for Service audiences, few of whom had ever seen Miller ?

It could only be done with the cooperation of the AEF Band musicians - and the general consensus of opinion has always been that the Band `knew something' but refused to talk about it. Miller appeared only twice in public after November 18 - the `impersonation' scenario was pure speculation, but there are several curious correspondences.

■ Oddities and Enigmas - The Jimmy Fidler Story.

On 15 January 1946, a Major Batson working in the Radio Branch of the War department, Bureau of Public Relations in Washington, addressed a brief report to the Chief, Casualty Branch, Adjutant-General's Office, concerning a broadcast by a well-known West Coast radio compére, Jimmy Fidler :

1. Attached is a reconstruction of a report made during his regular broadcast last Sunday night by Jimmy Fidler.
2. This office recommends that the Casualty Branch contact Mr.Fidler and request the information he states is available, on the basis that the Army is always most anxious to obtain additional information about casualties and not as a challenge to the accuracy of his report.

The reconstruction is as follows :

On his regular broadcast 13 January 1946 at 21.46 - 22.00 EST, Jimmy Fidler stated essentially the following over the American Broadcasting System :

`*All of you remember the disappearance about a year ago of Major Glenn Miller over the English Channel His plane was reported missing and never accounted for. Well, I have received proof that the plane in which Glen Miller left England did land on the Continent - but Glenn was not among the passengers when it landed ! I have been in touch with an Army soldier who is prepared to document this report. I shall be glad to make this information available to the proper authorities.'*

The transcript of a telephone conversation between Colonel George F. Herbert, Chief, Casualty Branch, AGO (`H'), and Jimmy Fidler (`F') reads as follows :

F. I don't have any additional information. I don't believe you would call it additional information. We have a young soldier here related to a member of the motion picture industry who was stationed on the day this happened in the dispatching office at the airfield where Miller was supposed to land.

H. Yes, sir - ?

F. His story which I did not tell in full on the air, was that Miller's Band. . . members of his Band had preceded him . . .that several were present for the purpose of welcoming him on the day he was supposed to arrive.

H. Yes, sir -

F. And that on this day no plane which was supposed to come to that field failed to come to that field -

H. I see. Well now, Mr. Fidler -

F. And among these was the plane on which they had expected Miller would be. but he was not on the plane -

H. Yes. I wonder if it would be possible to get the name of the man who gave you the information so that we can query him and find out exactly what he knows because we, the War Department, are not in possession of any infor-mation that is later than 10 minutes after Major Miller and the plane in which he was riding took off -

F. Uh huh - I see -

H. They took off at 1.45 in the afternoon of the 16th December 1944 and they were reported in 10 minutes later. Then we don't have anything subsequent to that time. Now it's possible that this man might have some information that would warrant our going to the Field for additional information -

F. Well, that strikes me as possible too. It certainly was enough information and the fellow seems to know enough, or at least to be convincing enough, to warrant investigation.

H. Yes, sir !

F. How can I wire you his name and address, sir ?

H. Well, you can wire that to Colonel George F. Herbert - Chief of the Casualty Branch - Room 3058, Munition Building, Washington 25 -

F. Washington 25 - Yes, sir -

H. And if you have anything, or have stumbled onto anything that might be of value to the War Department, of course, next to his immediate family, we are the most interested -

F. That's right, of course -

H. Because we're trying to obtain information on every man who was initially reported missing in action, though subsequently we may have had to make a death finding under the Law on him.

F. Yes, I see. All right, Colonel Herbert. I will have this information in your hands by night letter today. It will be sent today.

Now, this is a remarkable conversation because :

1) This same Colonel Herbert subsequently signed the Findings of Death documents.

2) There may be confirmation here of Joan Heath's story of some Band members who flew over to Paris ahead of the main party. Perhaps they waited at the airport to welcome Miller on December 14 - but which airport ? Orly - (according to Haynes), Villacoublay (- re the MACR) or Beauvais (- Morgan's orders) ? First, we can eliminate Villacoublay - Major May's contribution to the MACR. Also, Beauvais - because Miller was not aboard the Norseman. It could only have been Orly, and we presume he was on an Orly shuttle from Bovingdon on Thursday December 14 to play at Ike's celebration party on Saturday.
   But according to George Eyerman, he was not aboard when it landed ! Why did Miller miss the plane ? We are back to the `arrest and court martial' scenario - and we can discount Mr.Woods' story that Glenn had caught a Paris flight which had iced up and gone down the Channel - records show that no shuttle was lost in December.
   Alternatively, the second scenario was that the small group of musicians were waiting at Orly on Friday December 15 for Morgan's Norseman - but Miller was not aboard ! This infers that the C-64 landed at Orly, and that Morgan and Baessell were the only occupants (contrary to the NPRC Miller History Sheet which cites Morgan and Miller as the only occupants !) and that opens up a real can of worms ! Miller was not on aboard at all - but possibly, to support the `missing Norseman story', Morgan and Baessell were `persuaded' to disappear quietly and permanently (echoes of Bruce Halpenny's Rhodesian epic !). Which brings us back to the Baessell Pension Folder .
   Did something happened during the flight ? Was Miller murdered and his body dumped, or did he jump overboard ? Conjecture again, of course and quite unjustified. Was there any substance in the `Shot by Baessell' story ? That would provide ample reason for his enforced emigration to Rhodesia.

3)   Herbert let slip something of paramount importance - he said that they took off on 16th December 1944 (not 15th) and that they were `reported in' ten minutes later. After that, no further contact. But this contradicts all other reports and statements - Haynes described the Norseman as disappearing into the overcast at 13.45 hours, with no subsequent contact. The Press Release states `No trace of (the aircraft) has been found since its take-off'. Miller's Casualty Report states `No trace of airplane can be found' - but no mention of radio contact 10 minutes after take off. Worse - Baessell's Casualty Report states `Plane missing and unreported after take off' ! The Confirmatory Signals state `Missing and unreported since departure Twinwood Field' ! This opens up possible confirmation of Joan Heath's story - was Col.Herbert referring to Miller's flight from Buc in the Cessna Bobcat ?

4)   Herbert quoted the Haynes take-off time of 13.45 - yet both the ORIGINAL #N-19 MACR and the forged MACR #10770 both stated 13.55. Further, he carefully avoids identifying `the field' at which Miller was supposed to arrive. The 13.45 time was first mentioned by Haynes, according to his diary, on reporting to General Barker but as we have seen, Major May decided that was too tight a schedule to accommodate Morgan's flight from Abbotts Ripton to Twinwood Farm. He changed it to 13.55 hours. From where did Herbert obtain the 13.45 take-off time ?

The next step in this strange saga was a letter dated 15 January 1946 from Jimmy Fidler to Colonel Herbert :

Dear Sir :
The name of the Army man who has been out of the service several months is Sgt. George Eyerman. You may write him in care of Miss Helen Clark of Holly-wood.(Washington had deleted the full address before releasing the documents from the Miller 201 File).
Certainly this will not reflect on Eyerman, and I have assured him of my backing in case of any serious consequences.
            Regards   *Jimmy Fidler*

Four days later on 21 January 1946 Colonel Herbert replied :

Dear Mr.Fidler -
Thank you for your letter of 15 January in which you furnished the name of former Sergeant George Eyerman, recently discharged from the service, who claims to have information regarding Major Alton Glenn Miller.
A communication has been forwarded to George Eyerman in an effort to secure all information he might possess regarding the status of Major Miller, whose presumed death has been officially recorded by the War Department. I can assure you that any information which may be obtained from Mr.Eyerman will in no way reflect on him nor will it result in his being caused any unpleasantness. Our sole purpose in communicating with him is to check thoroughly any data having a bearing on the status of Major Miller and such action is in accordance with our policy of doing everything humanly possible to obtain definite information in the cases of all personnel who have been carried as missing and for

whom it subsequently became necessary for the War Department to make death findings under the provisions of Public Law 490, 77th Congress, as amended. Your interest in this matter is fully appreciated.

GEORGE F.HERBERT Chief, Casualty Branch, AGD.

At this point, something remarkable occurred, about which the reader must draw his own conclusions. In order to emphasise the urgency of the situation, a letter was hastily written to George Eyerman in Hollywood that same day by Major General Edward F.Witsell, Acting Adjutant General, copy to a Captain P.M. Newmark of the Casualty Branch.

Dear Mr.Eyerman :

Mr.Jimmie Fidler has advised me that you have information concerning Major Alton Glenn Miller who was reported as missing in flight on 15 December 1944 and who subsequently was officially recorded as dead under the provisions of Public Law 490, 77th Congress, as amended.

I will be grateful if you will furnish me the same information you gave to Mr.Fidler regarding Major Miller. This office is interested in securing data having a bearing on the status of all personnel whose exact status is unknown and all leads are thoroughly investigated in an effort to obtain complete information. I can assure you that the fact that you have furnished information to Mr.Fidler will in no way reflect upon you, nor will it result in your being caused any unpleasantness.

I enclose for your convenience a franked self-addressed envelope and will appreciate your replying as expeditiously as possible. Sincerely yours

EDWARD F. WITSELL Major General
Acting Adjutant General of the Army

Why was the Adjutant General himself probing what appears to be just another rumour about Glenn Miller ? Why was Captain Newark brought in ? Why did Col. Herbert himself write to George Eyerman ? The sergeant's reply to Captain Newmark is staggering in its implications :

Dear Sir :

In reply to your letter of January 21st regarding Major Alton Glenn Miller I wish to inform you the following is all I know about Major Miller.

While in Verdun France at the time of Major Miller's accident the Stars and Stripes had the incident in their paper, at which time there was nothing mentioned about what kind of aircraft, who the pilot was or if anyone else was lost. This lack of information immediately started all kinds of rumors among the soldiers, so said information that I gave Mr.Fidler was only inquiry on my part. This has evidently been a misinterpretation and I am very sorry I cannot give you any specific information on this case.

Sincerely yours

George R.Eyerman.

Now, this is an astounding *volte face*. None of the items cited in Eyerman's denial letter - aircraft type, name of pilot and other casualties - were mentioned at all in his statement to Colonel Herbert. That statement concerned the movements of some Band members to Paris, their meeting a plane supposedly carrying Miller and their surprise when he was not on board. In fact, even to the unbiased eye, Eyerman's denial statement has all the hall-marks of a dictated message, and we believe he was interviewed personally by a member of the AG Department. He was persuaded to keep to himself what information he had, and to sign a statement (itself carefully couched in semi-legal format) designed to terminate the matter once and for all.

A copy of Eyerman's statement was sent to Jimmie Fidler in Hollywood, and the correspondence was stored in Miller's 201 File in St.Louis, Mo. Ironically, Col. Herbert himself disclosed far more information than George Eyerman, revealing for the first time that there was a brief communication with Morgan's aircraft (Norseman or Bobcat ?) 10 minutes after take off. There can be no doubt that this is vital to the investigation - why else would that information be suppressed for more than 45 years ? More to the point, what transpired during the radio contact ? In 10 minutes Morgan would have flown no more than 25 miles from Abbotts Ripton, using Alconbury Local Frequency : about that time he would change to an area frequency. One possibility is that he may have radioed Twinwood Farm, been advised that the airfield was closed and no passengers were waiting, and then pressed on towards France. And finally, why would the Adjutant General, at the heart of the Miller Mystery, cite the date of Miller's disappearance as December 16 1944 ?

Clearly, the AG gave the matter absolute priority, sent a man to talk to Eyerman and if possible shut him up. If Washington had not obliterated the Hollywood address, we might have located Eyerman and learned the whole story - and Washington justified this action under the Freedom of Information Act and Privacy Acts, on the grounds that disclosure would cause the Miller family distress and inconvenience. It was an act of cauterisation which sealed off permanently a potentially damaging leak.

■ The Thomas Simpson Connection

A copy of a strange telegram was included in Miller's 201 File. It was from the AG Department in Washington, dated 29 October 1945, addressed to H.A. 1st Class Thomas Simpson of the Hospital Staff, U.S. Naval Hospital, Norfolk, Virginia. Simpson, an ordinary seaman, had earlier telephoned the Adjutant General himself, General Witsell, on Sunday 25 October 1945 about Major Miller, and the AG replied :

REFERENCE YOUR TELEPHONE REQUEST SUNDAY 25 OCTOBER MAJOR ALTON GLENN MILLER 0505273 STILL CARRIED ON WAR DEPARTMENT RECORDS AS MISSING IN FLIGHT EUROPE 15 DECEMBER 1944'.

Why, we wondered, had a simple sailor based in a Navy hospital telephoned the Adjutant General direct about a missing band leader ? Had he been a personal friend ? Or had he turned up some information which made him doubt the publicised version of Miller's disappearance ? Clearly he had enough `pull' to telephone the top brass about Major Miller - but we may never know the full story. One can speculate on `H.A' (Hospital Artificer) Simpson's relationship with Glenn Miller - as far as we can determine he was never a member of the peacetime Glenn Miller Orchestra. But why was that telegram preserved in the Miller 201 File for almost half a century ?

■ The Brittany Beach Affair (Fig.82).

On 30 August 1946, the AG Department Casualty Branch in Washington sent the following signal to HQ USFET :

> `REFERENCE MAJOR ALTON GLENN MILLER ZERO FIVE ZERO FIVE TWO
> SEVEN THREE AC REPORTED MISSING IN FLIGHT BETWEEN ENGLAND
> AND PARIS FIFTEEN DECEMBER FORTY FOUR RADIO E SECTION SHAEF
> DTD TWENTY TWO DECEMBER FORTY FOUR AND CASE SUBSEQUENTLY
> REVIEWED PURSUANT PROVISIONS OF PUBLIC LAW FOUR NINETY
> SEVENTY SEVENTH CONGRESS AS AMENDED AND FINDINGS OF DEATH
> MADE DATE BEING SET AS SIXTEEN DECEMBER FORTY FIVE REQUEST
> INVESTIGATION ON WHICH TO BASE REPLY TO FOLLOWING QUOTED
> NEWSPAPER ARTICLE SUBMITTED BY THE ATTORNEY OF MAJOR MILL-
> ER'S ESTATE COLON QUOTE
> "A SALVAGE CREW CLEANING UP BRITTANY BEACHES HAS REPORTED
> DISCOVERING THE TAIL OF AN AIRPLANE WHICH HAS BEEN IDENTI-
> FIED BY ITS NUMBER AS THE ONE THE LATE MAJOR GLENN MILLER
> WAS ABOARD WHEN HE DISAPPEARED DECEMBER 14 1944 ON A FLIGHT
> FROM ENGLAND TO FRANCE. . ."
> IT IS REQUESTED THAT A REPLY BE SUBMITTED THIS OFFICE EARLI-
> EST PRACTICABLE DATE AND DIRECTED TO ATTENTION CAPTAIN P M
> NEWMARK ROOM ONE E FIVE FOUR ONE PENTAGON BLDG WASHINGTON DC
> WITSELL TAG DASH G.

The reoccurrence of the names Witsell and Newmark was noteworthy - the latter had been assigned to check out the George Eyerman story, as well as the Brittany Report, from which we concluded that he had been designated as a full-time operative on the case - yet his name had never previously been encountered ! Initially we regarded the discrepancy in the date (December 14) as an error - but we had earlier pondered on the Woods Story, in which `Miller's C-47 shuttle to Orly had iced up and crashed in the Channel'. It had been satisfactorily eliminated by checking official records : no cross-Channel flights were lost in November or December 1944.

Further we were disturbed by the lack of reference to type of aircraft, i.e, Norseman. This was clarified by the response from USFET on 22 November 1946 :

`To AG Washington ATN Capt. P.M.Newmark Rm. 1E541 Pentagon Bldg

1. An intensive investigation has been conducted in an effort to comply with basic communication. However no information has been received indicating that salvage crews recovered parts of the airplane in which Major Miller was a passenger. Neither is there a record of any parts of airplane #70285. All possible interested activities and the French authorities report no record of recovery of parts of the missing airplane.'

This apparently innocuous message is loaded with dynamite ! The writer is clearly referring to two entirely different aircraft : `the airplane in which Major Miller was a pas-senger' and `Airplane #70285'. And this is no simple error : the Adjutant General wrote to David Mackay on 12 December 1946 :

`I am referring to my previous correspondence in which you were advised of the investigation being made in the case of the late Major Alton Glenn Miller. A report has been received from the overseas commander regarding the intensive investigation made to uncover definite information bearing on the alleged recover of Major Miller's plane, as stated in a newspaper article referred to in your recent letters. The pertinent parts of the report are quoted for your information :
"No information indicating that salvage crews recovered parts of the airplane in which Major Miller was a passenger could be found. Neither is there a record of the recovery of any parts of airplane #44-70285. All possible interested activities and the French military authorities report no record of recovery of the parts of the missing airplane.*
All commercial news agencies in Paris, France were also contacted in an effort to trace origin of the news release. These agencies state that they have no knowledge of the release mentioned in basic communication.'
Sincerely yours   Edward F.Witsell Major General

The inference, we submit, is absolutely clear : a newspaper report was quoted to the Adjutant General by David Mackay; the AG caused extensive investigations to be made, providing opportunity to get on record the `unceasing efforts' of the AGO to solve the mystery. On October 1 1946, David Mackay wrote to the Adjutant General :

`Answering your inquiry of September 30, I regret I cannot tell you the name of the paper in which the article concerning the late Major Glenn Miller appeared. Major Miller's former manager clipped the article from a Chicago newspaper on or about July 16 1946 and sent it to me, but he does not recall the name of the paper in which it appeared. There was nothing in the article indicating the name of the agency issuing the report and I have no information on this point.*

Clearly, Haynes had surfaced again in summer 1946 to release yet another red herring. It should have been possible to identify the Chicago newspaper and check the source - but seemingly the AG ran into a dead end. The only reasonable explanation was that the rumour had been an AGO/Haynes exercise in disinformation designed to strengthen the Norseman story. But reference to two different aircraft was disquieting : no west-bound transAtlantic flight had been the subject of a MACR, and we had to consider the possibility of an identifiable crash incident, details of which would be on file at Norton AFB Safety and Inspection Center in California. But repeated requests to Norton resulted in the same res[ponse : `Only if we are provided with details of an aircraft number and date can we identify a mishap'. We could not rule out the possibility that Miller flew out of Bovingdon on Thursday December 14 bound for Bordeaux-Azores-Bermuda-New York and the aircraft came to grief en route. But this would be no reason for the enormous cover-up operation which followed. It seemed increasingly probable that Glenn flew out of Buc Field to Bordeaux where he caught an aircraft bound for the U.S.A. Since he had not arrived home in New Jersey, he may have met his fate shortly after arrival - and we are back to Columbus Ohio once again.

+   +   +

7

THE GREAT CONSPIRACY

1. The Extent of the Cover-Up

We found several official documents to be forged, whilst many others were missing. Further, there were many examples of blatant misinformation, deliberate omission of important details - and all were designed to perpetuate the fabricated Haynes account of Miller's disappearance.

■ Forgeries

* MACR #10770 was fabricated at Maxwell AFB in January 1945, using the unsigned #N-19 as a template, after one false start (the SAMPLE MACR).
* MACR #N-19 itself was a doctored extract from the original MACR, which was never found.
* The Confirmatory Signal date was altered to support Haynes' story of General Barker's contact with 8th AFSC, Milton Ernest. The real Signal, located in the Miller 201 File, disproves it.
* The Quartermaster General's correspondence with Mrs. Baessell was forged, including her signature and that of Lt.Koob, QM Division. Baessell's personal effects may never have been recovered.

■ Omissions

* Don Haynes' name, from all official documents and reports including Miller Casualty Report, Missing Aircrew Report, General Davis letter, etc. etc.

- Miller's destination Paris - from Col. Donnell letter to Helen Miller and the Finding of Death document.
- Morgan's destination Beauvais - from all MACRs.
- Capt.Cramer's Identity Details below MACR #10770 signature.
- Norseman Engine Number from MACRs.
- True Weather Data from MACRs.

Missing Documents

- Glenn Miller's Paris orders.
- Morgan's Flight Orders, Forms 5, flight logbook.
- Baessell's Orders for Bordeaux.
- 35 ADRS History, December 1944.
- AEF Band History - June - December 1944.
- Glenn Miller 201 File, Service History June - December 1944.
- Missing Report WD AGO Form 66-2.
- Haynes Written Statement to Cols. Early and Traistor.

Misinformation, Intentional or Otherwise.

- MACRs #10770, #N-19.
- Press Release.
- Film *THE GLENN MILLER STORY*
- George Simon book *GLENN MILLER AND HIS ORCHESTRA.*
- NPRC St. Louis History Sheet showing Morgan and Miller only Norseman occupants.
- NPRC St.Louis Letter 25 July 1991
- Col.Donnell letter to Helen Miller.
- Major Bradunas Letter to Helen Miller.
- Don Haynes' diaries.
- The Ferguson Tape.
- Gen. Davis Letter to Eisenhower.
- Glenn Miller Casualty Report.
- The Missing Report.
- The Confirmatory Signals.
- The New Jersey Registrar's letter.
- MOD AHB Report.
- National Archives Letter Aug 5 1986.
- All FOD Documents.
- All ROD Documents.
- Brittany Beach Report.
- George Eyerman Retraction Letter.
- Telegram to Helen Miller.
- AG Denial letter - Miller fingerprints on file.

Obstructionism, Intentional or Otherwise.

- National Archives rejection of Herb Miller Authorisation Letter.

- George Chalou Denial of Burial Files.
- PCA Refusal to issue denial of Miller interment in Mountain View Cemetery.

■ Denial of Information Availability

- Norton AFB - Norseman and other Mishaps.
- National Archives Letter July 1986.
- George Chalou Telephone Call.

■ Supply of Irrelevant Information

- Miller 201 File extracts, US Total Personnel Command, Alexandria.

2. New Evidence

In the winter of 1992-1993 we saw a steady influx of fresh information which required detailed evaluation. Much of it was extremely important in the context of the mystery, and we began to look again at the possible passengers aboard John Morgan's Norseman.

■ Lt.Col. Norman F. Baessell

Whilst we had always been convinced that Glenn Miller was not a passenger, we had automatically assumed that Col. Baessell was on board : moreover, since Morgan did not land at Twinwood Farm on Friday December 15, but cleared direct from Abbotts Ripton to Beauvais, we assumed that Baessell had boarded at Morgan's home field. Indeed, we had speculated that Don Haynes (who was at Milton Ernest that weekend and was using the AEF Band staff car) may have driven Baessell the 25 miles to Alconbury.

Further, at a very early stage in the investigation we had contacted the USAAF Cemetery at Maddingley, Cambridge, for confirmation that Miller, Morgan and Baessell were listed amongst the `missing'. The Cemetery staff checked and confirmed this on the telephone while we waited. Later in the investigation we spent some time looking at possible reasons for Baessell going to Bordeaux - but perhaps we made an error in assuming he was going there. John Morgan's Record Card shows his orders for ferrying `personnel' from Abbotts Ripton to B-42 Beauvais and/or Bordeaux. Possibly Baessell may have been going to Beauvais and Morgan was going to Bordeaux on some other task.

Additionally there was the enigma of the `Bordeaux Crash Letter' in the Miller Burial File : we could not reasonably eliminate the possibility that Morgan had been bound initially for Bordeaux and then Beauvais, even if his 13.25 take-off from Abbotts Ripton would bring him to Bordeaux after dark, following a long and hazardous flight of more than 100 miles across the Channel.

In October 1992 there was an extraordinary development - a letter from a Mr. Keith Jones of Canterbury, Kent :

> `Some years ago I went along to the American Military Cemetery at Maddingley and looked along the memorial to the missing. Whilst I could find the name of Major Miller and Flight Officer Morgan, the name of Lt.Col. Norman F. Baessell could not be found. Enquiries at the Memorial Office brought blank looks

and fewer answers - the strangest being "Oh, it's okay - it's just an oversight."

For the first time we began to re-think the Baessell angle - and to look for other evidence, because if Keith Jones was correct, we now faced a secondary mystery - what happened to the brave Colonel ? We looked again at the official notes on Miller's career issued in 1973 by the National Personnel Records Center in St. Louis, which state :

> `On December 15 1944 he left from Twinwood Field, England, for Bordeaux, France, aboard a UC64A Noorduyn-type aircraft (nicknamed "Norseman") number 44-70285. The pilot of the plane was Flight Officer John R.S. Morgan, T-190766 of the 35th Air Depot Group. The plane never reached its destination and the two men were reported missing as of the December 15 date.'*

There is no mention of Lt.Col. Baessell, nor of Paris Villacoublay as the destination. Yet the statement is remarkably detailed, containing a resume of Miller's career which proved to be extracted *in toto* from his 201 File held by NPRC in St. Louis. It hardly seems possible that this report circulated to the public would contain two such major errors !

In the 201 File we found another intriguing document - a request to the Adjutant General from the Provost Marshal Department in Randolph Field, New Mexico dated 1971, asking for any dental data on Col. Baessell. A responding letter from the AG enclosed the appropriate information - but we sensed a mystery here. Any official request for dental information on a deceased person infers a desire to identify the body of the deceased - but in this case the officer had not only died on December 15 1944 (27 years earlier) but had been officially lost at sea in a crashed aircraft ! Further, the date of the request coincided with the death of Lt. Don Haynes and the release of his spurious diaries.

We decided to check once more on the fate of Baessell's 201 File which, St Louis advised us had been destroyed in the 1973 fire. We had to accept this assurance, but at the same time we learned that items from the File had been provided to the Veteran's Administration - and this was very interesting. Basically, the VA organisation represents the interests of surviving service veterans in regard to welfare, documentation etc., whilst deceased veteran records are held at NPRC St. Louis (201 Files) or the Casualty and Memorial Affairs Division in Alexandria.

All these facts appeared to suggest that Baessell may have survived the war to draw a pension. In October 1992, with little hope of results we wrote to the VA Regional Office in North Capitol Street Washington, asking for information on Col. Baessell. Much to our astonishment they wrote back on October 8 to say that they had a `pension claims folder' but that it had been retired to a Federal Records Center. `*Unfortunately'*, they went on, `*the personnel at the Center are unable now to locate the folder.'* The VA would continue to search through the system but it might take some time.

They wrote again on October 27 to advise that the folder had been requested from the Federal Records Center at Suitland, Maryland, and was currently in transit to them. This told us that the file existed and had been found, and whilst waiting we telephoned the VA in Washington to ask if this `pension claim' related to Mrs. Baessell's `widow' pension, or to Baessell's own pension. We were told that, without making a specific check, VA pension records applied to pensions paid to surviving veterans. Widows pensions were handled by a separate department.

Four days later on September 1 a third letter arrived, confirming that the pension file was at Suitland, Maryland, and had been dispatched to the VA in Washington. We would receive a copy as soon as the file arrived. But the weeks passed without further contact, and in January 1993 we wrote direct to the Federal Records Center in Suitland asking for a copy of the Pension File. In response we received a harshly-worded response that such records were available only through the VA. We wrote at once to the latter on February 8 1993 :

`Department of Veterans Affairs
Regional Office
941 North Capitol Street NE
Washington DC 204231

Dear Mr. Fischl -

Pension File - Norman F. Baessell
Your Ref. 372/2721 XC Q6 0326 392

I refer to your several letters during the past 6 months, during which I have requested repeatedly a copy of the Pension File for the above deceased officer. Last week I received a letter from Federal Records at Suitland MD advising that they cannot provide file copies direct and that I must request copies through your regional office.
In view of the extensive lapse of time since I first requested this record copy, I am increasingly concerned that this may not be entirely due to administrative indigestion. As a professional author it is imperative that I obtain a copy of this file, which you promised me as far back as October 1992, without further delay. To that end, will you please telephone me collect on the above number at any time, to advise the reason for delay and when the documents may become available. Time, I should stress again, is of the essence.

Yours sincerely

WILBUR WRIGHT

There was no response to this letter. And in the back of our minds always was the disturbing forgeries of the Quartermaster's letters to Mrs. Amanda Baessell. Clearly we were being given the old familiar run-around : we also learned that this same Suitland location handled FBI Records. In March 1993 we sent this telegram :

DEPARTMENT OF VETERANS AFFAIRS 941 NORTH CAPITOL ST NE WASHINGTON DC

REQUEST URGENT RESPONSE TO REQUEST FOR PENSION DETAILS NORMAN F.BAESSELL REF. 372/272C XC 06 036 392 PROMISED OCTOBER 1992 WRIGHT SOUTHAMPTON UK

There was no reponse to this message, from which we concluded that Baessell's Pension File not only confirmed that he had survived the war, but that there was information in the File which could not be released. Lastly, while we had previously given no credence to

Bruce Halpenny's story that Baessell and Miller had lived in Rhodesia until the latter died in 1956, it now appeared possible that Baessell may have survived at least until 1950, when the PM division was seeking dental records.

But this new scenario generated enormous problems. If Baessell had not been on board the Norseman, what did happen to him ? Had he vanished voluntarily ? Had he drawn his pension in his own name - or under a false name - which is why Suitland would not release his File ? Another point : Baessell, according to George Ferguson, was a regular officer and entitled to a pension if he survived the war. Had he been quietly `persuaded' to disappear quietly, following an arrest for black market activities, and the facts concealed by showing him as a Norseman passenger ? Was there a secret deal here ? There were endless variations on the theme - and we would not solve this problem without access to the Pension File at Suitland, Maryland.

3.   The Joan Heath Story

This was outlined on P.186, but further research uncovered a vital chain of facts and events. Joan had identified a Cessna Bobcat UC-78 as the plane Glenn boarded that Sunday morning, and we established that the 112th Liaison Squadron USAAF was based at Buc Field, providing VIP transport, i.e. Bobcats. However, the aircraft was too small to make a transAtlantic flight : clearly it was giving Glenn a lift to some other base where he would pick up a pre-arranged ride home for Christmas. We were able to confirm that no UC-78 Bobcat was listed as missing or destroyed during December 1944 nor any west-bound transAtlantic flights - and this posed a monumental problem to us. We knew that Miller was not buried in any US war cemetery in Europe and that there were no reports of criminal action or bomb incidents on the night of December 14 1944, the last time he was seen alive (excluding Joan's story for the moment). We know that he departed for France that same day, was seen in Fred Payne's Bar in Paris on Friday December 15.

Accepting Joan's story, on Sunday morning December 17 1944 Major Glenn Miller was taken by the 112th Squadron Bobcat to some other base, from which he hitched a ride home to the U.S.A. The burden of proof was upon us to show what happened thereafter - which required a process of elimination. This began with the assumption that Miller did, in fact, reach the U.S.A - but for some reason failed to return to Europe.

At this point four possible explanations were recognised - illness, accident, suicide or unwillingness to return to the war zone. Personally, I do not believe he was capable of the last - he was a brave dedicated man, albeit under great pressure of work, health and perhaps some financial worries. In the summer of 1944 Glenn wrote to his brother Herb :

`I am totally emaciated, although I am eating enough. I have trouble breathing -
I think I am very ill.'

But I had several interviews with Herb before his sad demise, and whilst he said he believed Glenn may have died of cancer in England, and that the news may have been suppressed, he could give no explanation why the family had not been notified - and the false Norseman story concocted. Much earlier, in January 1983, Herb was interviewed on radio by Russell Harty. Here is an extract from the recording :

HARTY : Now, how do you think Glenn died ?

HERB : Well, he had done ninety programmes in 30 days and he was a shadow of himself. He was smoking cigarette after cigarette, from butt to butt . . . You know, I think he just had to go into hiding to die.

HARTY : Do you think he had cancer ?

HERB : I think he had cancer, yes.

HARTY : He was actually promoting cigarettes for Chesterfield - ?

HERB : Promoting his own death, you might say Yes.

After discussing Glenn's character briefly, they return to Glenn's health.

HARTY : What do you think he did ? Or went ?

HERB : I think he went to Milton Ernest. It was a sort of hospital for the brass there. And there I think he died.

This is very revealing : Herb, in fact, knew very little about the USAAF and Glenn's service career. Milton Ernest Hall, three miles out of Bedford, was the headquarters of 8th Air Force Service Command, which handled the supply, modification, repair and replacement of all 8th Air Force aircraft. The only medical facility there was the standard base sick quarters, for the use of all ranks who could be treated locally. Strangely, Herb closed the interview by saying : "I'll tell you what I'm gonna do - I'm gonna keep looking - and if I like what I find I'll tell you."

The inference is clear - Herb did not really believe his own conclusions about Glenn's death from cancer - and he had no evidence to support it. Moreover, six years later he admitted quite frankly to me on tape that he still had no clues - only that the Haynes story was totally false. It was on that basis that he provided me with written authorisation to investigate Glenn's disappearance. There is no firm evidence that Glenn died in England - but a number of facts suggest that he may have died in America :

1) A letter from a WW Two veteran to researcher John Edwards in 1973 stating that the writer had been in a hospital ward in Columbus, Ohio when Glenn Miller died in December 1944, possibly from head injuries.

2) The letter from the New Jersey State Registrar to me stating that Glenn died in December 1944 in Columbus, Ohio. (This was later repudiated as a `typing error' when I pointed out that we were dealing with the famous band leader).

3) The impenetrable wall of non-cooperation when we asked the Bureau of Statistics in Columbus for a copy of the death certificate. They did not deny there could be one on file - just made it impossible to obtain a copy. I offered to send the appropriate fee by air mail - but they said such information was available only to US

citizens who applied in writing. I had a friend in Fort Worth, Texas request a death certificate, sending the necessary fee - this was returned with a note to say that all death certificates must be collected in person. I rang pilot George Ferguson, who drove into Columbus and asked for a copy death certificate. He was told that `There were maybe a million deceased Millers on file and perhaps a thousand with the forenames Alton Glenn. It might take weeks or months to locate the certificate'. Yet when I telephoned them a few days later under a false name and asked if they could help me trace a World War 2 buddy who had died in America, they said "Sir, all our records are fully computerised - give us the details and we can get back to you within thirty minutes." I gave them Miller's details and my telephone number - and heard no more from Columbus, Ohio.

4) Herb Miller's account to me (on tape) that Helen Miller had received a phone call between Saturday December 16 and December 23 (when she got the telegram) which distressed her a great deal. Herb was there with her at the time and said she would not tell the family anything. Could this have been the news that he had died in a Columbus hospital ?

Yet there seemed to be no viable reason why the news of his death from illness should not have been released : he may have gone home without official permission but for such a VIP the rules would have been bent significantly to legalise the position retrospectively. We have to consider the possibility that he may have had a nervous breakdown and been confined to a suitable institution, or that because of the incorrect serial number and name `Alton G. Miller' on his Paris orders, he may not have been identified. Significantly, his orders are amongst the documents missing from his 201 File - but copies have been circulated for almost 50 years.

The same reasoning further applies to `death by accident', and if we accept that Miller would not have deliberately remained in America in wartime, we are left only with suicide - and that possibility must be addressed. We know he had been under tremendous strain from overwork; further, his income had decreased perceptibly since 1942 and the break-up of his famous orchestra. True, there were royalties from films and recordings, but these would diminish with time : further, Glenn had embarked on building his own home in California, at considerable expense. But the post-war episode involving attorney David Mackay and his forced repayment of some $750,000 to the Miller children seems to eliminate money worries as a reason for Glenn taking his own life.

However much we speculate, we know that the facts are contained in the Chronological Record of Military Experience which should be in Miller's 201 File in St. Louis Mo. - a document which, the Army Counsel General tells us, is not in the File. But this contradicts the statement by St. Louis earlier that it *was* in the File, but the Miller family denied access, quoting the FOI and Privacy Acts - something they would not do if there was nothing to hide. We have Dale Titler's statement, repeated from a conversation with Steve Miller, `*that* `*there was something in the File they did not want made publicised'*. There was Steve's friend, the late Royal Frey who stated that he had seen the whole 201 File `*and there was nothing in it but routine stuff'*. How did Frey obtain access, when all others were denied ? And was it possible that Frey had interviewed Don Haynes in 1969 and `forgotten to take along a tape recorder' and promptly forgot everything Haynes said ?

What reliance could we place upon the statement of the Army Counsel General that

`We have given you everything in the 201 File' on the one hand, and on the other `we are denying access to certain information under the FOI and Privacy Acts' ?   Lacking the final evidence on the AGO Form 66-2, we are certain of only one thing - that whatever happened to Glenn Miller was so terrible, or involved other important people, that it had to be suppressed at all costs.

■   The AGO Form 66-2

On May 1 1993 we decided that we would make no further progress via the Army Counsel General in locating this vital document which, we believe, holds the solution to the whole mystery. The Missing Report to which it was supposedly attached was sent from the Paris AG Department to the AG Casualty Branch in Washington, the habitat of such people as Col. Herbert and Capt. Newmark (of the Jimmy Fidler affair), Col.Donnell (who wrote a hugely misleading letter to Helen Miller) and Major Bradunas (who wrote an even worse example - and was implicated in the forgery of MACR #10770).

It was the duty of these officers to ensure that all personal documents relating to a serving USAAF officer arriving from overseas were eventually lodged safely in the person's 201 File. We had been previously assured by NPRC St.Louis that the Form 66-2 for the period June - December 1944 was on file but access was denied by the Miller family. Equally, we had been assured by the Army General Counsel that we had been given all available and releasable information in the 201 File. Further, that the Form 66-2 was not in the File.

Someone was telling a porky - but who ? To clarify the situation we wrote to Mr. Pellegrini at NPRC St.Louis, who replied on May 17 1993 :

`We have been unable to locate any Army or Air Force Regulation which specifically directed how to complete the Form 66-2, or what action to take when Item 38 (Chronological Record of Military Experience - Auth.) was filled with entries. An informal review of some records of Army Air Force officers indicated that when the space allowed for Item 38 was filled to capacity, a mimeograph copy of Item 38 was taped on top of that portion of the Form 66-2 to allow the chronological record to continue. We also noticed that the Item 38 sections were sometimes cut out of blank Forms 66-2 and taped on top of the corresponding portion of the form being used, in order to continue.'*

This information was extremely important and we wrote back at once :

`Dear Mr.Pellegrini -

Major Glenn Miller - Form 66-2, Item 38

Many thanks for your extremely valuable letter dated May 12 - I am impelled to write straight back to you as follows :

1)   You will appreciate that of all the official documents associated with the Miller mystery, this is undoubtedly the most important. USAAF Regulations required that Item 38 had to be updated following the demise of the person involved, before it was sent back to Washington from overseas - indeed, that was why it is mentioned as an inclosure to the Missing Report. Significantly, the Form 66-2 was the only document missing from the 8 enclosed with the Missing Report on December 18 1944, but there are several possibilities :

2) *(a) It may not have been enclosed with the Missing Report because, if it showed Miller's movements up to the date of his death, it contradicted the `Norseman' story related by Lt. Don Haynes. As such it may have been part of the conspiracy revealed by my researches.*

   (b) It may have been enclosed and sent to the AG Casualty Department in Washington, but was abstracted from the Missing Report before it was sent to NPRC St.Louis and Miller's 201 File. If so, this was the work of one or more of four officers : Col. Frank Herbert (later AG himself), Capt.Newmark, Major Bradunas and Col.Donnell.

   ✱ *Col.Herbert was implicated in the Jimmy Fidler affair (see 201 File) and made contact with ex-Sgt George Eyerman, who had important evidence about the Miller affair, described in Fidler's LA radio programme. But Herbert sent Capt.Newmark to talk to Eyerman, who subsequently retracted his entire story.*
   ✱ *Capt.Newmark was involved in the `Brittany Beach' affair in which a fictitious `report' from a newspaper was circulated by Lt.Haynes, to the effect that Miller's Norseman plane had been found.*
   ✱ *Major Bradunas wrote a totally misleading letter to Mrs.Miller in 1945 (see the 201 File) and was also implicated in the forgery of MACR #10770 at Maxwell AFB in January 1945.*
   ✱ *Col.Donnell wrote an equally misleading letter to Mrs.Miller in 1946.*

   (c) The Form 66-2 may have reached NPRC St.Louis but was subsequently removed from the 201 File. In that respect, I have a letter from NPRC stating unequivocally that the Item 38 History for period June - December 1944 was on file, but access was being denied by the Miller family, quoting the FOI and Privacy Acts. Further letters from NPRC and from the Army Counsel General contradict that statement, stating that I had been given all `releasable' information from the File.

3) *This is why I wrote to you some time ago asking if there was a `two-tier' system for 201 Files, enabling certain information to be restricted. I have examined the photocopy of Miller's Item 38 from 1942 - June 1944 in the light of your letter (enclosed) to determine if there was any indication of a continuation sheet being taped onto the sheet, but without result. Certainly, there seems to be ample room for additional items. In fact, I believe the Item 38 continuation sheet for period June - December 1944 was quite extensive, covering Miller's move to London, England and his move with the Band to Bedford. For the next 6 months he was based in London working at the Langham Hotel and living at the Mount Royal Hotel. During the summer he was called to SHAEF to see General Bedell Smith about taking over the*

USAAF Military band - which Miller declined. On November 8 1944 Miller and Haynes flew to Paris to attend a conference on the projected Paris tour held on November 15, returning on November 18. His last UK concert was on Wednesday December 13 in London, and evidence suggests he flew to Paris on a shuttle Dakota the next day. One surviving witness states Miller was in Fred Paynes' British bar in Paris on Friday December 15 (the day the Norseman was lost) and another states that Miller attended a party celebrating Eisenhower's promotion on Saturday December 16 and flew home for Christmas from Buc Field near Versailles on Sunday December 17. He did not return.

4) All this activity suggests a substantial Item 38 continuation sheet. Would you please carefully examine the original Item 38 document (enclosed) for any evidence that a continuation sheet was taped to it. Also, I am not quite clear if an officer's original 201 File followed him round from assignment to assignment, or was held in a central records department and updated by copy continuation sheets from his various units. Oddly, the typing on the enclosed sheet suggests that it was typed on one machine at a specific time. I am of the opinion that the Paris AG, or the Adjutant, HQ Squadron, Special Services Division SHAEF in Paris, prepared a fresh Item 38 sheet from June - December 1944, incorporating all movements and orders including his orders for Paris, to travel `on or about' December 12'. In that respect it is strange that those orders are missing from his Burial and 201 Files. If you have anything important to contribute please call me collect on the above number or write back airmail.'

■ Freedom of Information and Privacy Acts

On May 12 1993 we received an informative letter from Robert Gellman, Chief Counsel of the 103rd Congress of the United States, responding to our request for information on the definition of `citizen' in the FOI and Privacy Acts, under which the Army General Counsel and the Miller family were denying access to Miller's 201 File. Our interpretation of the Congress information booklet was that these Acts did not apply to dead persons. Mr. Gellman wrote :

`*The Sub-Committee does not normally provide legal advice to FOIA requesters. The law contains a variety of remedies for those who are dissatisfied with the way in which an FOIA request has been processed by a federal agency.*
The particular issue that you raise is not entirely free from doubt. There is case law that both supports and denies the proposition that dead people have privacy rights. The circumstances involved in any given case may have an effect on the decision to disclose or withhold. To make matters more complex, practices vary from agency to agency.
The proper response is for you to file an administrative appeal of the denial, failing which you will have to apply to federal district court.'

We had already tried an appeal in June 1992, and would certainly and predictably fail because the people to whom we appealed were those who had denied access in the first place ! But getting involved in court action, with the prospect of astronomical legal fees, was another matter altogether, and we postponed taking a decision until this book was published and a copy sent to the Miller family. We began looking for an attorney in Washington and meanwhile we awaited the results of our appeal.

3.   Reactions from America

On November 4 1992 we received an important letter from the Army General Counsel in the Pentagon :

`This responds to your appeal of June 22 1992 against denial of your FOIA request for a copy of the personal 201 File of Major Alton Glenn Miller. US Total Army Personnel Command partially denied your request on May 6 1992, but provided you with Major Miller's File except for the addresses of third parties. Upon review we have determined that this information must be withheld under the Privacy Act and Exemption 6 of the FOIA. Because of changes in our FOIA as interpreted by the Supreme Court, we must regrettably deny your appeal.'*

This was a remarkable decision. In the first place we had never requested any third party addresses. All we wanted was Miller's Service Record from June - December 1944. I wrote at once to the Army General Counsel on January 22 1993 :

`I am at a total loss in trying to understand what is going on in your Department. Your letter dated November 4 refers to certain `third party addresses', access to which has been denied. Please note that :

(a) I have never requested such names and addresses.
(b) I have never expressed any interest in such material.
(c) I have no intention of writing to any of these addresses.
(d) I cannot conceive why such public inquiries should be subject to secrecy.

I refer once more to the contents of my letter dated 3 November 1992 in which I state specifically that I seek only items of information from the 201 File related to Major Miller's disappearance - entries in his medical record (which you advise contains no helpful information) and most important, details of his movements, duties and assignments for the period June 14 to December 31 1944. I have been provided earlier with 201 File data showing Major Miller's Army history from 1942 to his departure for UK in June 1944. This is by way of a precedent and there can be no justification for a denial of similar information for the later period.'*

This elicited a curt response dated February 1 from a Garth K. Chandler, Assistant to the General Counsel :

`You reiterate in your letter that you are not seeking the names and addresses *deleted from Major Miller's 201 File. As I have stated in my recent letter to you, but what you apparently have difficulty in understanding, you have been provided everything from Major Miller's File except the names and addresses of third parties. There is nothing else to release to you.*

As I pointed out in my letter, if you disagree with this determination, you are free to seek judicial review on your own initiative and through the courts, not through this office.

We consider this matter closed.'

Perhaps so - but we thought otherwise. Our response was quick and to the point :

`*Dear Mr. Chandler -*

You may consider the matter closed but that is not the case. Your statement that I have been provided with everything from Major Miller's 201 File is demonstrably untrue : the item I have requested repeatedly, to the exclusion of all others, is his Service Record for the period June - December 1944. **I have already been advised by National Personnel Records Center St. Louis that this record is in the File, but that access was being denied by the Miller family.** *Further, a precedent was established by the release to me of his Service record from 1942 to June 1944 (as enclosed).*

I quote the letter from US Information Systems Command dated April 7. 1992 : "per response from NPRC St. Louis, all information deemed releasable without the consent of Major Miller's relatives has been released to you." '

There was no response to this or any more letters to the Pentagon. But previous correspondence gave another picture altogether. John L. Carver at St, Louis had written to me back in July 1991 to confirm that such items as Miller's past duty assignments had been suppressed under the Privacy Act of 1974 - yet this very information had been released to me by US Army Total Personnel Command for the period 1942 to June 1944 ! This was clearly an example of duplicity : NPRC had advised us that the Miller 201 File had survived the 1973 fire intact - and reason suggested that if the File contained the Service history from 1942 - June 1944, it also contained the history for the subsequent period up to December 1944, which had been enclosed with the Missing Report in December 1944. I wrote to Mr. Carver on 22 October 1991 pointing out that the `Military Experience Data Sheet' he had sent me terminated on June 13 - the day before Miller flew to England - and that he had stated no further data on this aspect could be released without the permission of the next of kin - tacitly confirming that there was further information of this nature in the File.

All of which served to reinforce our belief that the Service record contained the final evidence we sought - Major Miller's movements during the critical period from Thursday December 14 1944 to December 31 1944. Significantly, neither US Army Total Personnel Command nor the Army Counsel General had denied that the Service record was in the file - only a sweeping statement that everything available had been released - except information suppressed by the Miller family under the Privacy Act.

Now the battle lines were drawn, and our primary requirement was to establish the legal position in regard to the FOI and Privacy Acts. I wrote to NPRC St. Louis, US Army Total Personnel Command Alexandria and the Army General Counsel asking the same question :

`Is Miller's Service Record from June - December 1944 currently not in the 201 File, or is it in the File but access is denied by the Miller family, or is the File in some other location ?'

There was no response to either letter, but as a further precaution, we wrote to the Attorney General querying an earlier decision by NPRC St. Louis - that our research mandate given in writing by Herb Miller was unviable since he had subsequently died. Lastly, we wrote to the Attorney General for his views on two important points as follows :

(a) The FOIA stipulates that all information more than 30 years old should be released *except where such release constitutes a threat to national security'*. Clearly, Major Miller's fate almost 50 years ago did not qualify.

(b) The Privacy Act denies access to information which might, if released, prejudice or adversely affect the privacy of the relatives of a deceased person - but did that apply where such denial is used to conceal criminal activities ? To wit - the concealment of Major Miller's fate by General Eisenhower and other senior officers in December 1944.

The Attorney General promptly referred us back to the military authorities, said they could not advise us on the FOI and Privacy Acts - and how about hiring an attorney of our own ?

+   +   +

By March 1993 a climax was approaching : all sides were laying down battle lines, and it was very obvious that instructions had been issued to certain departments to terminate all further correspondence with us. We received no response to letters to the Pentagon - and NPRC St.Louis sent a final response to our inquiry about the existence of Miller's Service Record from June 18 - December 31 1944.

`*We have reviewed the entire record of Major Miller and we can report that :*

1) *There is no separate portion of Glenn Miller's records which has been withheld from you. The same record has been used to answer all your questions. There is no segregated portion of this record which we are not allowed to reach. In other words, there is only one record, not two.*

2) *Our review shows that you have received copies of all documents in the record which are date between June 1 and December 31 1944. Copies of these documents are again enclosed for your convenience.*

3) *There are no additional records on the WD AGO Form 66-2, AAF Officers Qualification Record and there are no other entries on the Form under Item 38, Chronological Records of Military Experience.*

Our review showed no other details of Major Miller's service for the period June 18 - December 31 1944, other than those already provided to you.'

But this letter opened a very slight crack in the defensive facade : we now knew that the vital Chronological Record of Military Experience we sought was part of the AGO Form 66-2, supposedly attached to the Missing Report in 1944. But had the vital June - December 1944 Record Sheet really been enclosed - or Miller's record from November 1942 - June 17 1944 ? Or had the closing entry sheet been extracted from the Form 66-2, not by anyone in the US Military Archives (who had no axe to grind) but by someone in authority at SHAEF in December 1944 (who had several axes in need of attention !) *before* the Missing Report was sent to St.Louis Records Center ?

The reactions of the Miller family to our researches provide a valuable clue. The Record Sheet *may* have contained the information referred to by Dale Titler - *`Something quite uncharacteristic of Glenn, which they did not want publicised.'* They had denied access quoting the FOI and Privacy Acts - but because a criminal conspiracy and cover-up had been involved, it was not impossible that their legal grounds might be uncertain.

That being so, the military authorities might not wish to test their case in court, preferring to `lose' the missing record. But what did it contain ? Paris Adjutant General Davis, via Special Services Division at SHAEF, Miller's parent unit, had access to and control of Miller's current personal file. His duty movements in December 1944 would be recorded up to the precise moment he was `officially' posted as missing - but what date would be cited ? Consider the following :

* Glenn Miller was last seen alive in England was at 02.30 hours on the morning of Thursday December 14 1944, outside the Milroy Club in Stratton Street, Mayfair, London, by Sqn.Ldr. Tony Bartley and Lt. Tony Pulitzer.

* From France we have the recorded evidence of Denis Cottam (admittedly second-hand) that the bartender in Fred Payne's Bar in Montmartre had served Glenn Miller on Friday December 15 1944, the same day the Norseman was posted `missing'.

* We could not place too much value on the purely circumstantial evidence of David Niven and the first-hand statement of Col. Hignett, that Niven had a so-far unidentified companion with him at Spa, Belgium.

* We have the Jimmy Fidler account from Miller's 201 File, suggesting that several of Miller's musicians preceded the main Band party to Paris by a few days .

* Most important, the first-hand eyewitness account of Joan Heath, describing Ike's promotion party and Miller's presence there.

Whilst striving to be as unbiased as possible, and avoiding unnecessary speculation, we believe that the generals, especially Davis, were forced to abstract the vital June - December 1944 record from the AGO Form 66-2 - for this reason. Right up to the time the Press Release was issued at 18.00 hours on December 24, SHAEF clung to the belief that *there was a possibility he might show up !* They had no confirmation that he was dead, seriously injured or detained anywhere - just that he had flown out of Buc Field on Sunday December 19 heading for home.

But once the `Norseman Story' had been released, *SHAEF were forced to go along with it - as we have seen.* His Chronological Record, routinely updated by the Adjutant, HQ Squadron, Special Services Division, SHAEF, recorded his movements up to Sunday December 17 - Miller may even have been taking a legal furlough. The record would expose the Norseman account as phoney - and it had been backed and confirmed by the top brass themselves. Gen. Davis took the only possible action - he attached the earlier part of Miller's record to the Missing Report, and suppressed the vital closing page.

So perhaps we have been doing the Army Counsel General an injustice. Perhaps the closing Record Sheet had never reached St.Louis. But the evidence cannot be denied - the Miller family have known the truth for a very long time - and fought to preserve its confidentiality. Who can blame them ?

In MILLERGATE we speculated why Helen Miller purchased a 6-grave burial lot in Mountain View Cemetery, Altadena, California in early 1949, when there were only 5 members in her family. We now accept that the number of graves may have been a function of the size of the lot purchased, but the basic anomalies still remain. Why did the Pasadena Cemetery Association refuse to deny for almost a year that Glenn Miller was interred in one of the `vacant' graves ? What triggered the Cemetery staff into physically ejecting Bill McAllister and his party of investigators (who described the staff's attitude as `bizarre') ? We can understand and appreciate the Miller family's refusal to permit an electronic scan of the burial lot to determine which of the 6 graves were occupied - even if such a scan would not have disturbed or defiled the area in any way whatsoever. Moreover one would reasonably assume that they would welcome such a scan if only, as Steve Miller put it, `to get this guy off our backs'.

And finally we cannot ignore the additional evidence set out in this book supporting the postulate that Glenn Miller flew home to America in December 1944 and did not return to Europe, and that Col. Baessell survived the war to draw a pension.

+   +   +

8.

FINAL SUMMATION

We have excluded, largely because of lack of space, many other equally-strange rumours and scenarios encountered during the last five decades, but taking the long view and the vast range of theories and speculations, it seemed to us far beyond the bounds of possibility that the stories had been `self-generated' by people seeking self-glorification in vicarious associations with the famous. Exceptions to the rule featured a degree of eye-witness or circumstantial evidence to support them - but we were left with the solid conviction that most of the stories were deliberate creations of official or unofficial US agencies, to divert researchers into arid and unproductive cul-de-sacs.

As such, they were as much a part of the Great Cover-Up as the many forged documents, the fictitious Haynes diaries and the threats, usually by telephone, to researchers who were possibly getting a little too close to the truth. One somewhat naive effort was the abortive but well-publicised attempt by the Miller family to purchase the remains of the Twinwood Farm Control Tower - a feeble gesture to perpetuate the myth of the Norseman and an innocent Glenn Miller flying off into the sunset to die a hero's death somewhere out in the Wide Blue Yonder.

The object of all these ploys was to consolidate the Haynes story - but generally the truth will out. Haynes himself is not named in any official document, report, letter, signal or file even remotely connected with the Miller mystery. He made no official written statement and is not mentioned in any MACR. There was evidence to suggest that whilst a small caucus of senior officers and officials knew the truth of the matter, they used every possible channel to disseminate the Haynes story, such that numerous minor officials and departments became part of the cover-up, quoting and re-quoting the Haynes story.

The question most frequently asked is "But why the cover-up ? What was it that was so terrible that it had to be concealed, disguised, suppressed and denied from Monday December 18 1944 until the present day ? It is doubtful if those at SHAEF ever learned the truth - but they were faced with an impossible situation involving a top rank VIP of the day. They knew that Miller had flown home for a few days after attending Ike's party on Saturday December 16. They delayed all reporting procedures until Christmas Eve in the hope that he would return, and finally, in the absence of any true explanation, a false (Norseman) story was created and propagated far and wide to the present day. In this context the conspiracy was not to protect the missing bandleader *but to shield the reputations of those involved in the conspiracy - among them a future President of the United States of America.*

I have no reason to make excuses for my apparent failure to crack the mystery : I now knew a great deal more than any other researcher, living or dead, and we have accumulated a vast store of new evidence. I am often asked my own personal opinion of Miller's fate - and here I must go along irrevocably with Joan Heath's account. At 76, she is still alert and active, with an excellent memory of her days at SHAEF driving Air Marshal Tedder. Her account of Ike's party is corroborated in his biographies, and she successfully identified the Cessna Bobcat. We confirmed that 112th Liaison Squadron at Buc Field used Bobcats exclusively to ferry around VIPs - including Winston Churchill and his wife. We know that no Bobcat or west-bound transAtlantic flight was lost in December 1944, from the 112th Squadron history and records at Maxwell AFB Historical Center. Joan has been interrogated a number of times and has never changed her story or the essential details.

I confess to being deeply disappointed in failing to make the final breakthrough : I had relied strongly on the continued existence of Miller's Service Record in his 201 File, but once I learned that it formed part of the AGO Form 66-2 sent to the AG in Washington by General Davis, one of the conspirators, I knew it was lost forever. The Miller family are the only people in possession of the full truth - and at this time I doubt that wild horses would drag it from them.

Yet perhaps a personal appeal might do so. An appeal on behalf of the many researchers who have spent half a century delving into the mystery, and especially on behalf of the millions of Glenn Miller fans world wide who deserve to know the truth at last. The strange disappearance o of Major Miller has become one of the major enigmas of the 20th century : after fifty years it is now history, and all the major characters in the play have gone.

What would I do, given the final secret ? I would like to see established a permanent Glenn Miller Museum in a location acceptable to the Miller family - a display in quiet and reserved format which would become a Mecca for all his loyal fans.

Whatever happened to Glenn, I feel that the time has now come to pierce the veil of secrecy once and for all. Because the mystery is not going to go away - I took over from Henry Whiston and John Flowers in the Sixties, John Edwards and Ken Perfect in the Seventies, Denis Cottam in the Eighties and Jack Taylor in the Nineties. There will be others after me, and in the end they will prevail.

Finally, I turn to the question of speculation in this book and in MILLERGATE. Speculation is, in effect, the construction of a possible scenario based upon whatever evidence is available, and the analysis/evaluation of that scenario in the light of the strength of such evidence. Evidence itself is an anomalous term - it may include facts, rumours, hearsay - the list is endless. But no researcher would eliminate even the most outlandish tale without checking it out as far as he can. Nevertheless, it is essential to differentiate between speculation and reasoned evaluation of evidence, and wherever possible I have labelled speculation accordingly.

There remains the important aspect of justification : at what point does a rumour or story merit investigation ? We considered this point very carefully when investigating the Pasadena story and Mountain View Cemetery - and began research only after long and serious consideration.

I hope the Miller family will agree to draw aside the veil - I think Glenn himself would approve mightily.

+   +   +

THE END

Wilbur Wright
Southampton 1993

INDEX